# Approaches to Social Inequality and Difference

Series Editors
Edvard Hviding
University of Bergen
Bergen, Norway

Synnøve Bendixsen
University of Bergen
Bergen, Norway

The book series contributes a wealth of new perspectives aiming to denaturalize ongoing social, economic and cultural trends such as the processes of 'crimigration' and racialization, fast-growing social-economic inequalities, depoliticization or technologization of policy, and simultaneously a politicization of difference. By treating naturalization simultaneously as a phenomenon in the world, and as a rudimentary analytical concept for further development and theoretical diversification, we identify a shared point of departure for all volumes in this series, in a search to analyze how difference is produced, governed and reconfigured in a rapidly changing world. By theorizing rich, globally comparative ethnographic materials on how racial/cultural/civilization differences are currently specified and naturalized, the series will throw new light on crucial links between differences, whether biologized and culturalized, and various forms of 'social inequality' that are produced in contemporary global social and political formations.

More information about this series at
http://www.palgrave.com/gp/series/14775

Peter Hervik
Editor

# Racialization, Racism, and Anti-Racism in the Nordic Countries

**palgrave**
macmillan

*Editor*
Peter Hervik
Department of Culture and Global Studies
Aalborg University
Aalborg, Denmark

Approaches to Social Inequality and Difference
ISBN 978-3-030-09040-1          ISBN 978-3-319-74630-2   (eBook)
https://doi.org/10.1007/978-3-319-74630-2

This Palgrave Macmillan imprint is published by the registered company Springer Nature Switzerland AG
The registered company address is: Gewerbestrasse 11, 6330 Cham, Switzerland

# CONTENTS

# NOTES ON CONTRIBUTORS

**Carolina S. Boe** is a postdoc at the University of Aalborg. She is part of the project "A Study of Experiences and Resistances to Racialization in Denmark (SERR)." Boe is trained as a social anthropologist at Aarhus University, Denmark, and as a sociologist at Université Paris 5 and Université Paris 7, France. Her research is on migration, the anthropology of confinement, prison systems in France and the USA, prison radicalization, and the relationship between racialization and radicalization.

**Mathias Danbolt** is Associate Professor of Art History at the University of Copenhagen, Denmark. Danbolt is working on a research project on the effects and affects of Danish colonialism within the field of art—a continuation of the postdoc project "Colorblind? Theorizing Race in Danish Contemporary Art and Performance."

**Mahitab Ezz El Din** has a PhD in Media and Communication Studies from Örebro University, Sweden. Her recent research focuses on media and conflict, identity constructions, peace journalism, and media and migration issues.

**Camilla Haavisto** is an Senior Lecturer in Communication at the Swedish School of Social Science, University of Helsinki. She is a media and communication scholar interested in minority claims-making, anti-racism, and the circulation of news between the Global South and the Global North. From the perspective of a politics of listening, she is mapping the field of civic anti-racism in Finland, focusing particularly on the communicative agency of actors in the field.

**Peter Hervik** is Associate Professor of Migration Studies at the Department of Culture and Global Studies, Aalborg University, Denmark. Hervik has conducted research among the Yucatec Maya of Mexico and on the representation in the news media of religious and ethnic minorities in Denmark. He is also the project leader of "A Study of Experiences and Resistances to Racialization in Denmark" (SERR). His research within this project deals with racialization in social media weblogs and Facebook comment threads.

**Karina Horsti** is Senior Lecturer in Cultural Policy and Academy of Finland Fellow at the University of Jyväskylä. In the field of transnational migration research, she has worked on cultural diversity policies, nationalist populism, and mediated representations of refugees and asylum seekers. Her research examines public remembering of forced migration and the commemoration of border-related death in Europe.

**Nasar Meer** is Professor of Race, Identity, and Citizenship in the School of Social and Political Sciences at the University of Edinburgh and Royal Society of Edinburgh Research Fellow. Among many other research topics, Meer works on the topic of race as a category of both social theory and public policy, the former as a means of understanding modernity and difference and the latter in terms of race quality and public policy.

**Lene Myong** is Professor of Gender Studies, University of Stavanger, Norway. Her research interests include transnational adoption, racial formation in Scandinavia, migration, and welfare state biopolitics. Her work has been published in journals such as *Cultural Studies*, *Sexualities*, and *GLQ*.

**Asta Smedegaard Nielsen** is a postdoctoral researcher, Aalborg University, Denmark. Her research is within the areas of media and migration, race and whiteness, gender studies, theories of affectivity, and media studies. She is part of the research project "Loving Attachment: Regulating Danish Love Migration (LOVA)."

**Kjetil Rødje** is a Senior Lecturer at the Department of Media and Communication, University of Oslo.

**Tuija Saresma** is a Docent/Adjunct Professor at the Research Centre for Contemporary Culture, Department of Art and Culture Research, University of Jyväskylä, Finland. Her research interests include affects, migration, intersectionality, racialization, and populist rhetoric as well as hate speech in social media. She studies the intersectional experiences of mobility and belonging and is the PI of a multidisciplinary research project Arts of Belonging.

**Christian Stokke** is Associate Professor of Social Anthropology at the Department of Culture, Religion, and Social Studies, Faculty of Humanities, Sports, and Educational Science, at the University College of Southeast Norway. He teaches multiculturalism, intercultural understanding, and religion. He publishes on multiculturalism, anti-racist education, intercultural communication, and religious education.

**Tess Sophie Skadegård Thorsen** is a doctoral researcher of media, race, and representation at the Department of Culture and Global Studies, at Aalborg University, Denmark. Thorsen is part of the project "A Study of Experiences and Resistance to Racialization in Denmark (SERR)." Her research is on the practices of representation of various minoritized groups in the production of Danish film.

**Sayaka Osanami Törngren** is a postdoc researcher at Malmo Institute for Studies of Migration, Diversity and Welfare at Malmo University. She is engaged in research on race, ethnicity, intermarriage, and mixed identities, color-blind racism and "interracial" relations in Sweden.

**Mantė Vertelytė** is a doctoral researcher in Migration Studies at the Centre for the Study of Migration and Diversity (CoMID), Department of Culture and Global Studies, at Aalborg University, Denmark. Vertelyte is part of the project "A Study of Experiences and Resistances to Racialization in Denmark" (SERR). Her research is on friendship relations across differences (class, "race," ethnicity, gender) and racialization practices among youth in Denmark.

# LIST OF FIGURES

# PART I

# Debating Racism and Racialization

# CHAPTER 1

# Racialization in the Nordic Countries: An Introduction

*Peter Hervik*

The authors of this book address the issues of racism and related phenomena in the Nordic countries and invest a comprehensive effort to dig deep into the cumulated academic experiences and the analytic approaches in order to come to grips with the discrimination, racialization, color racism,[1] Islamophobia, anti-racism, and inclusion and exclusion of especially so-called non-Western minorities in the Nordic countries. In a heavily mediatized society, they seek, in particular, to single out critical media events that are representative for how processes of racialization take place in an environment dominated by commercial interests, anti-migrant and anti-Muslim narratives and sentiments, and a surprising lack of research-based knowledge of racism and racialization. Or, these events are sought out to show "turns", "transformations", and furthering of inequalities along

[1] I use this term as a shorthand for the dominance of racism against people of color in research and everyday conversations, acknowledging that there are other broad categories and forms of racism, and that "race" and "color" legally are not identical.

P. Hervik (✉)
Department of Culture and Global Studies, Aalborg University, Aalborg, Denmark
e-mail: hervik@cgs.aau.dk

© The Author(s) 2019
P. Hervik (ed.), *Racialization, Racism, and Anti-Racism in the Nordic Countries*, Approaches to Social Inequality and Difference,
https://doi.org/10.1007/978-3-319-74630-2_1

racial lines through strong emotional and affective engagements in debates. Most generally, the volume asks to what extent racism in the Nordic countries has been overcome long ago, or are we witnessing new kinds and more subtle forms of racialized practices?

## NORDIC RACIALIZATION

Researchers in the Nordic countries agree that the discrimination of visibly different minorities has become subtler in the last 20 years, which continues to have serious consequences for many of these minorities as well as contributing to a more and more polarized society. In the Danish context, white Danes make approximately double the income of non-white Danes. Their employment rates are significantly lower, while many decide to stay outside the job market in low-income, private-sector jobs, with incomes far below the minimum wage. Non-Danish immigrants and Danes with ethnic minority backgrounds from other countries are poorly represented in higher institutions of learning as well as in leading positions. In addition, they are unequally divided in residential areas. The list goes on to account for representatives in school boards, residential bodies, and ownership of residential units. While there are certainly exceptions, the averaging gives a murky image of the situation; for people of color and of East European origin in Denmark, there is a patterned attempt both privately and officially to explain away any issue of discrimination. This is most notably in response to reports and research on mediated events, everyday conversations, and in in-depth interviews as well as a habitual whiteness that systematically denies minorities' experiences of discrimination.

Issues of racism have attracted researchers from anthropology, media studies, gender studies, and sociology, to examine critical media events that interrupt people's routine and monopolize the media platform (Hebb & Couldry, 2013). Sometimes these events are pseudo-events, sometimes they occur outside the media, but most often they become news as journalistic social constructions following the genre, jargon, and epistemology of news journalism. These particular events convey racializing points and embody unsaid forms of racialization. They are practices of communication often with hidden and subtle practices of racism and racialization built in—and increase—polarization of society and, as the term "critical" suggests, threaten to cause serious harm to people implicated in the event. Media players, whether authors, commentators, or sources, use ideas of "cultural incompatibility", unwanted presence, fixed identities, racial-cultural logic of belonging, anti-intellectualism, anti-feminism, and intense adverse criticism. These ideas again rest comfortably on morality as the basis for understanding "difference" in the 2000s, which creates an environment where violence, confrontation, austerity measures, and "zero-tolerance" are the chosen forms of expression as the possibility of dialogue has been surpassed. The dominance of moralism and news media's reliance on stories about conflict, drama, violence, and moral panic bring out tensions between legal frameworks, research-based findings, and moral arguments and common sense, populist reasoning that calls for changes in legal conventions and more direct forms of democracy sometimes also referred to as mob rule or street democracy.

The authors of this book are researchers concerned with what is happening in the Nordic countries. Most of them have finalized their dissertations on racism, racialization, and anti-racism within the last decade. Most of them are engaged in large research projects directly relevant to the book's topic. They are writing contributions to this book from within their own research expertise, half also with experiences as racialized minorities. None of the authors entertain fantasies about a shared Nordic cultural and political community but are well versed in intra- and inter-Nordic similarities and differences. Authors have sought to avoid the traps of methodological nationalism, which would risk reducing different case studies to expressions of historical-cultural differences or policy differences between the countries. The truth is that variations and diversity do not follow frozen national borders but are often regional as well as showing tremendous mutual borrowing and political distancing from events debated in other Nordic countries. This is, of course, not the same thing as saying that histories and country differences are not a factor to account for, but it is saying we should be careful not to reduce findings to be the outcome of national differences. There is a clear need of studies that goes beyond an Anglo-Saxon tradition, and beyond Eurocentrism (I will come back to further ahead), and in that regard chapters contribute to developing analyses of racism that is grounded in the Nordic countries with studies and theorizing that take place in these countries.

Much of the contemporary interests in racialization come via dialogue with a broad version of critical race theory, post-colonial and de-coloniality studies, general interest in colonial histories, and, perhaps more importantly, as academic responses to issues and phenomenon that go on in society. Some of these researchers derive their interest and anti-racism efforts from their own recurrent experiences of denial and sharing vicariously the experiences of others. Regardless if they experience discrimination themselves or from others, the fact is that minorities' experiences of racial discrimination increased drastically back in the 1990s, not least among Somalis in Denmark (Møller & Togeby, 1999).

Authors use a variety of means and methods to analyze the media events. Since all of the contributors have done substantial primary research in this area or are currently engaged in larger projects, they do not fall back on a single, mechanically executed method but invest more creatively and broadly in the analyses. They use ethnographic methods, discourse analysis of political discourse, and different forms of media analysis.

While authors of this book depart from grounded studies, whether face-to-face interactions, including in-depth interviewing, sustained social interaction, shorter interviews with authors of texts, commentators, or text analysis, they recognize how the media shapes racialized thinking; promotes moral panic, moral outrage; and spurs action and policies. They equally share the insight, a classic in traditional ethnographic interviews, that analytical terms should not be forced upon interviewees risking contamination of the material (Carsten, 1995).

Two decades ago Nordic researchers documented that since indigenous citizens had little social interaction in their everyday lives with people of immigrant background, but still held strong stereotypes and distorted views of refugees and migrants, they relied almost exclusively on the news and popular media for their knowledge and attitudes (Gaasholt & Togeby, 1995; Hervik, 1999a). Today, there is an "inescapable presence of media as a contemporary cultural force engaged with the mediation of hegemonic forms and resistance to them; the growth and transnational circulation of public culture; the creation of national and activists social imaginaries, ..." (Ginsburg, 2005, pp. 21–22). This volume is informed by the premise that most of what people generally know today about other migrants and refugees derive from this presence of social media, traditional news media, and popular media. First, the media amplifies racialization and extends it in space and time. Second, the media frames and re-frames racialization and thereby becomes a performative agent of racialization. Third, the media co-constructs racialization due to the inseparable institutions of media and politics (Hjarvard, Mortensen, & Eskjær, 2014) most clearly seen in political spin communication. This book therefore focuses primarily on the media and media analysis. We refer to other works for analyzing comparative intra-Nordic complexities of policy making that may work to reflect as well as amplify racialization in the Nordic countries (see, for instance, Brochmann & Hagelund, 2012; Hansen & Wæver, 2002).

All authors are fully aware that using terms such as racism carries the risk of enhancing or transforming forms of asymmetric relations phenomena that were not of racist content to begin with. Authors ask how news coverage and public media debates serve to promote the politics of fear, securitization of minorities, racialization of minorities, and the threat of incompatible difference. Moreover, authors set out to analyze the reactions to the content and circulation of anti-racist claims.

The authors also insist on the importance of larger forces in the structural conditions and circumstances within the grounded studies. The studies are contemporary media debates and authors seek answers within the "horizon of history" (Gadamer, 2003), yet they recognize how racial issues appear from the level where the brown child tells her mother, "I don't want to be brown anymore", to mega-narratives of clashes of civilizations. Authors know and agree that the micro-level analysis must be seen as integral to larger processes of change. They all do include the broader scope, albeit to varying degrees.

## GLOBAL POPULISM AND INEQUALITY

From the contemporary perspective on racial and national inequality, I would argue, however simplistically it may be, that there are at least five central integral forces that come out of the engine room to create and re-create this nexus of racialized inferiorization. The *first* force comes from experiences of existing inequality and the endeavor to overcome it or efforts of increasing it. This comprises everything from original dispossession of land and labor (Butler & Athanasiou, 2013; Harvey, 2003) to constructions of the precariat (Standing, 2014). Often overlooked by scholars, and certainly not a welcome fact in political circles, is that, at a deeper level, migration is predominantly caused by inequality, or the experience of inequality, in any of its many forms and with strong, often desperate, investment into overcoming it (Glick-Schiller, 2014). A *second* force can be approached as "white" privilege, where entitlement racism ("white is right") is one articulation of it; even if the white privilege dominates, there are other ones, hence the inverted commas. One of the most difficult issues with the term white is that it is often taken for its "face value" as actual skin color, while racism researchers insist it is a social construction or a metaphor for a privilege that comes with people who are predominantly white (see Meer, this volume). Yet, the terms brown and black are also racial categories and not "natural" categories. To illustrate, we could ask, if Italian explorer Christopher Columbus was white or brown? Did the perception of his "whiteness" or "brownness" change over time? And are Italians and Spanish people are predominantly white or brown today? Where? The implication of each answer explodes from 1492 (I shall return to that further ahead). The literature on racism is dominated with color racism, which leads to an almost exclusive focus on "white" privilege and, not yet, on other racialized privileging with "white" being one particular, and perhaps, generic expression of racial privilege. A *third* force lies within nationalism and the enforcement of the nation-state, and everything that comes with it. Nationalism is one "context" that gives racism meaning (Lentin, 2008) and is often regarded as an ultimate political weapon of recruitment onto which people are expected to be willing to forsake their families and die for the nation's protection whether within the borders or in faraway places. Nationalism comes with the imagination of homogeneity and therefore with a strong motivational force to decide who does not belong and should not have the same equal footing as the original indigenous population. The *fourth* central force that contributes to racialized inferiorization could have any number of headings, but the ideas of accumulation of capital, excessive capital, creed for wealth, the claims of rights coming with capital, as well as neo-liberalism's ideas and practices of free markets. In short, neo-liberalism and the idea of the unrestricted free market and belief that social problems will find "natural" solutions. A *fifth* force is the dynamics of identity formation and identity politics in the modern world. Who are you? And who are you not? Masterfully expressed in Dr. Kritzinger's story to General Heydrich in the documentary Conspiracy on the Wannsee Conference. The story went that a man failed to cry when his beloved mother died, whereas he cried inconsolably when his much-hated father died. The point is that identity formation had as its object the hatred of his father. When the object of hatred was gone, there was nothing left to give him an identity. This point echoes Carl Schmitt's idea that you don't know who you are until you know whom you hate; and it is reinvented by Samuel Huntington in the Clash of Civilization ideology but without mentioning Schmitt (Hervik, 2011).

All these "forces" are closely related and have long histories. Some would object that colonialism, legacies of imperialism and colonialism, and racism should be included as separate forces producing racialized inferiorization. And rightly so. However, regardless of how strong and important identifying legacies of colonialism and imperialism are, such identification in my view fails to analyze the efforts to uphold privilege and inequality beyond establishing (rightly so) that they are more generic than the overt expressions of colonialism. However, as in classic theories of power parlance, there must also be a theory that explains the production and reproduction of these legacies, since the legacies, like origins of word meanings, do not explain continuity by themselves. As for racism, researchers have again and again argued against single-axis explanations and pointed to how racism is integrated into other structures and forces, and that seeing racism as part of constructing incompatible difference, inequality, inferiorities and superiorities, nationalism, and more is important, which does not, in any way, undermine the importance of racism. Racism is simply a much more complicated and complex phenomenon that should not be reduced to one specific historic version or a single, isolable dimension. The recent turn to intersectionality is a reflection of this acknowledgment of racism's complex interrelationship with other forms of subordination.

The World Trade terror attack in 1993 did not provoke a war on terror that obviously did not happen until 2001. When the attack took place in 2001, deadly terror attacks had already taken place at embassies in Nairobi and Dar es Salaam and more, but with a new president, the "War on Terror" was adopted as a strategy. Denmark and Norway joined allied forces in 2003 and sent soldiers off to Iraq, and later Afghanistan. But the production of inequality, coloniality, nationalism, an enemy image of Islam, did not start with the attacks on 9/11, 2001. Those attacks were both a symptom, a separate contributor, and a pre-text for inferiorizing other "civilizations" or "culture" as seen in Samuel Huntington (1993, 1996) and Bernard Lewis' works (1990).

"The War on Terror" and new regimes of securitization and monitoring brought out a language of "radicalization", "Islamist terrorism", "foreign fighters", and so on. These discourses and practices of racialization, racialized integration, are issues that have brought Muslims to the forefront of negative public attention in the Euro-American world with one effect being that racialization is now directed at entire communities of people associated with Muslims, Islam, or "Muslim culture" that as "a whole way of life" becomes explanations for peoples' belief and social actions (Hervik, 2015; Kundnani, 2015). Thus, when politicians ask Muslims to apologize for certain terrorist attacks to members of the nation-states in which they reside, the premise is that there must be a hidden solidarity between the killers and presumed Muslims (Roy in Guenif-Souilamas et al., 2015).

Islamophobia is precisely the political claim that it is "Something particular about Muslims/or Arabs that makes them capable of carrying out such acts (9/11)" (Lentin, 2008, p. xv), which only makes sense if Muslims are regarded as a "race".

Until 2001, processes of racialization were present in the Nordic countries, but only Swedish scholars would use the term "racism" more consistently to capture what was going on (Keskinen & Andreassen, 2017). Anders and Berit Wigerfelt's study of everyday racism in Klippan, southern Sweden, used "racism" and connected it to the presence of radical right-wing groups (2001, 2014). In other Nordic countries, race and racism are still tabooed words, or dare one say, they are not used due to political correctness, particularly when talking about anti-Muslim or anti-Islamic racial slurs.

## The Nordic Scene

"The Nordic" welfare states and the Lutheran-Evangelical historical tradition and other shared features are pillars in a larger dialogue about "the Nordic", which is generally associated with positive identity (Hastrup, 1992). One of these associations is that "the Nordic" is a unit of cooperation and initiatives based on ideas of similarity and tradition, which according to Lene Hansen functions as an intermediate level between the national and the European. This association has come under serious challenge from a neo-nationalist upsurge in the post-1989 era (Hansen, 2002).

The traditional Nordic emphasis on social egalitarianism, as eloquently described and analyzed by Marianne Gullestad as "equality as sameness" and expressed in the Swedish metaphor for the local community and nation called "the folk home" or "the people's home" (folkhemmet) (Gullestad, 2006), has come under pressure in the racialized and culturalized reactions in the last decades due to refugees fleeing from war, atrocities, and increased focus on the extreme poverty around the world. Thus, in the last 20 years, the Nordic countries have become more intolerant toward newcomers and ethnic minorities, but with enduring claims of post-racial, color-blind ideology that somehow transcend the history of colonialism, eugenics, and xenophobic expressions that see reactions to people outside their "natural" settings as a "natural" if not instinctive response.

Nordic societies are committed through the human rights declaration to combat racial discrimination, such as Islamophobia. Yet, recent violent events in Paris and Copenhagen have contributed to new political efforts to avoid radicalization of ethnic minority youth through an intensification of anti-radicalization programs without also dealing with Islamophobia and related forms of racial discrimination (Hervik, 2017). Such an effort is both a response and a reproduction of the morality-based, increasing racialization of these and other groups that places them in vulnerable positions and as targets of recruitment. It is these ongoing processes and dynamics with which this volume is concerned.

After the mega events around 1989, European attention centered on the Balkan war in the first half of the 1990s. The Nordic countries received their share of refugees. Most of the refugees were Muslims, but at the time, however, negative sentiments and racializing remarks were not articulated as anti-Muslim racism, just like racism more generally was not used as a common articulation of negative, inferiorizing relations between the national "we" and the foreign newcomers. There was talk about perceived and actual hierarchies of refugees and migrants, but they were debated in terms of multiculturalism and "cultural differences" and not talked about in terms of "race", "racialization", or "anti-racism" (Hjarnø, 1995; Schierup, 1993).

For its part, Denmark became "white" in the late 1990s as media and voters shifted to parties advocating anti-immigrant policies, which made Danes more aware of their "whiteness" and acted upon it through their voting. By then, the dominant negative focus was on Somali refugees, who were not (yet) regarded as a problem for being Muslims, but their "incompatible" racialized and cultural difference were again and again singled out by politicians in the news media as a particular Somali problem (Fadel, Hervik, & Vestergaard, 1999). In this process, Somalis were considered so different that it was assumed they could never be integrated, which reminded Danes about the incompleteness of their white nation with these bodies in the midst. In this way, the Somalis and the Danes were racialized as part of the same categorization and reasoning.

What is true for the Nordic region is that the last 25 years have brought a very high number of heated debates about engagement in wars in the Balkans, Somalia, Iraq, Afghanistan, Syria, and more and the arrival of refugees, migrants, asylum seekers as well as the role of ethnic minority groups already in Nordic countries. A total of around 17,000 Bosnian war refugees came to Denmark, where the strategy became to avoid any concentrations of asylum seekers in one place. To reach this objective, refugees were distributed widely across the landscape and thereby attempting to minimize their influence on Danish culture. (For documentation of the early debates on the Bosnian refugees in the Nordic countries, see the three books from the comprehensive Scandinavian project Ålund, 1998; Berg, 1998; Schwartz, 1998.) This three-country project did not include conceptualization of refugee experiences of exclusion using terms like racialization or racialized integration or studies that used research-based insights to understanding the meeting of refugees of war with the Scandinavian policies or news media.

By the mid-1990s, the first explicit heated media debate about the controversial word "Negro" happened to take place in the midst of national debates on what to do about the country's Bosnian refugees (see Vertelytė and Hervik, this volume). The Danish debate about the term "Neger" (Negro) started a discussion, but it never came close in intensity as the debate did in Norway in 2002/2003—a debate that showed how the preoccupation with skin color and the rights of racializers to name it. By the early 2000s, the public sphere in Denmark was no longer a space for dialogue for an area for serious battling and confrontation following a core value of neo-conservatism (Hervik, 2008, 2011) and motivated by the discomfort of "whitened" population in the presence of more than a tiny number of immigrants. The debate and the emergence of strong ideas of cultural incompatibility began to fuel other early academic treatments of racism in Denmark (Hervik, 2002; Rasmussen, 2004; Røgilds, 2002; Wren, 2001). But when an exhibition in connection to the Danish slave trade was discussed critically, the racism terminology and post-colonialism had not entered into the analysis of these themes (see Olwig, 2003). By 2015, racism and racialization were still talked about as rotten eggs, but as Kjetil Rødje and Tess Skadegård Thorsen show, regardless of the meanings of racial signifiers and anti-anti-racism, racism has entered the public debates. This even if incongruence rules the so-called debate (this volume).

The rise of right-wing and radical right-wing parties in Europe started in smaller affluent European countries, and the Nordic ones were no exception (Gingrich, 2006). When four prominent members of the Progressive Party in Denmark broke out in 1995 to form the Danish People's Party, a new path opened up for the unfolding of neo-nationalism and populism (Hervik, 2011). Other parties joined them in a policy that eventually turned Denmark into a country with one of the most restrictive integration policies in Europe. The success for the Sweden Democrats to enter the parliament in Stockholm (Riksdagen) was with 5.7% of the votes and later peaking in the polls with 19% support (Statistics Sweden, 2016). Entering the parliament, other parties agreed not to cooperate with them at both the municipal and the national level (Lööw, 2009) in a series of initiatives to isolate the party. In Norway, the populist Progress Party was for the first time accepted into government as a partner of the Conservatives in 2013, with partial support from the center-right parties. The party received 16.3% of the votes in this election, while the opinion pool had them at one point above 30% of voters' support. In Finland, the rise of the populist anti-migrant and Eurosceptic environment coincided with the success of the Finns Party (*Perussuomalaiset*), established in 1995. The party has increased its popularity in each parliamentary election, gaining a major victory in 2011 by receiving 19.0% of the vote.

In the new Danish government of November 2001, Prime Minister Anders Fogh Rasmussen based his minority government on the votes of the Danish People's Party. Most significantly, he launched a fierce populist right platform directed at the "elite", the opposition, refugees, migrants, unemployed, welfare recipients, and Danes with migrant background, not least Muslims. Restrictive after restrictive measures targetting "non-Westerners" were passed by the parliament, in what is most correctly described as based on neo-nationalism and neo-racism combined with folkish criticism of the elite. From the start, Rasmussen launched the strategy of a "Cultural War of Values" based on ideals of American neo-conservative values and similar to the cultural war discourse subscribed to by Ronald Reagan (Hervik, 2014). The strategy was copied by the largest newspaper in 2004 and soon ended in the infamous Danish Muhammad cartoon affair. *Jyllands-Posten*'s leadership used their entitlement ideas to back up the initiative to ridicule, mock, and insult Muslims in Denmark, through the newspaper's very own drawing contest, where cartoonists were asked to draw the prophet Muhammad as they saw him resulting in a major media event.

The Danish Muhammad cartoon reverberated into all the Nordic countries and brought controversies with it. The Norwegian *Magazinet* publication of the cartoons on January 10, 2006, provoked foreign anger against Norway (see Stokke, this volume). In Sweden, artist Lars Vilk's roundabout dog provocations, depicting the Prophet Muhammad's face on the body of a dog, were particularly rousing. In 2007, local newspaper, Nerikes Allehanda in Örebro decided to publish one of Vilk's drawings together with the praising of freedom of speech, which sparked new controversy in Sweden and against Sweden (see Ezz El Din, this volume).

Six years later, on July 22, 2011, Norway witnessed a major terrorist attack by the radicalized, right-winger, Anders Breivik, who had been a member of the Progressive Party and whose ideas and ethos were shared by many right-wingers in the other Nordic countries, except of course for the violence (Boisen & Hervik, 2013; Eide, Kjølstad, & Naper, 2013). Supposedly, Breivik's urge to cultivate the deadly project that included the killings of young left-wingers began eight to nine years earlier (Bangstad, 2014), which is precisely during Norway's major and furious media debate about racial epithets. The "*Neger* debate" is well-researched by Marianne Gullestad (2006), who acknowledged her own optimism and perhaps naivety upon entering the debate "to assume that issues of race thinking, ethnicity and nationality could be discussed rationally at the present conjuncture" (2006, p. 11). She wrote this in 2005 while communicating the reactions to her first book in Norwegian (Gullestad, 2002) and explained how she "was met with firm and articulate resistance" (Gullestad, 2006, p. 11).

A flip side of the new anti-elite, anti-Muslim, anti-left-wing, and anti-feminist populism is anti-intellectualism. Premier Minister Anders Fogh Rasmussen's war of values strategy fiercely attacked intellectuals and the elite, in a classic the-elite-has-betrayed-you strategy, which follows an already noted decline of scholarly authority as perceptively captured by Marianne Gullestad (2006). This anti-intellectualism has continued and entered the academia itself as Lene Myong and Tobias Danbolt's analysis shows (this volume), where the public circulation of research-based knowledge of racism and racialization is undermined rather than read and understood. This criticism follows more broadly a tendency of the times to express ourselves publicly in whichever way one feels like (Essed, 2013). In Norway, the populist right has been attacking the "political correctness" of the cultural and intellectual elite for several decades, gradually pushing the boundaries of what is acceptable to say publicly about minorities. Gender populism in Finland holds a strong element of anti-intellectualism, which is part of a broader anti-elite argumentation. In her study, Tuija Saresma found that gender populists subscribe to the assumption that there are irreducible differences between women and men, femininity and masculinity. Any attempt by elites, or other, to even out "natural" differences must be fought back at any cost (Saresma, 2018).

### Scholarly Responses

The field of ethnicity and race research has been, and to a large extent still is, bifurcated with a clear division between a sociological focus on race and racism and an anthropological emphasis on cultural difference (Alexander, 2004). With a few exceptions, European anthropologists have not been at the forefront of theoretical developments on racism in Europe, particularly regarding theories interpreting "culture" as "a new concept of race" and leaving issues of rapidly growing culturally based and value-based inclusion and exclusion to be taken up by other disciplines such as cultural studies, sociology, and the interdisciplinary "IMER" studies (International Migration and Ethnic Relations) (Balibar, 1991; Barker, 1981; Goldberg, 2006; Gullestad, 2006; Hervik, 2004; Stolcke, 1995).

The emergence of neo-racism as a concept and category first took place in Denmark within the anthropological team research project, "Structuring Diversity"[2] (Hervik, 1999b; Jørgensen & Søderhamn, 1999), and followed soon by geographer, Karen Wren (2001) (see also Rasmussen, 2004), who argued that cultural racism was damaging because of its subtle and almost invisible character and the relative sexual equality "allows the demonization of other 'backward' cultures in their midst which are perceived to oppress their women" (2001, pp. 146–147). The team project was carried out when tabloid *Ekstra Bladet* launched an unprecedented three-month, anti-foreigner campaign and the Danish People's Party was established. As such, the conceptualization of neo-racism with neo-nationalism came out of the analysis of these events more so than through the emerging literature. One of the first sessions on contemporary racism in the meetings of the European Association of Social Anthropologists occurred in 2002, leading to a special issue of the Nordic journal *Ethnos* edited by Marianne Gullestad and myself (see Hervik, 2004). Later, this collaborative effort leads to a presidential session of the American Anthropological Association (AAA) in 2005 called "Initiating Trans-Atlantic Dialogues on Race and Cultures", where American experts were commenting on European, mostly Nordic, presentations. There were other more individualized attempts earlier to introduce neo-racism or related concepts into anthropology, such as Stolcke (1995), although she maintained that "cultural fundamentalism" was the proper category to use rather than neo-racism.

Outside of anthropology and sociology, Lene Myong and Rikke Andreassen stand out with pioneering work on racism and racialization in Denmark. Myong's contribution came through a comprehensive and much acclaimed thesis that built empirically on in-depth, qualitative

---

[2] As part of that project, I taught a course on racism to anthropology students at the University of Copenhagen in 1996, and by arbitrary circumstances, I also taught the first course on racism at the anthropology institute at the University of Oslo in 1999.

interviews with Korean adoptees in their late 20s and early 30s who had been transnationally and transracially adopted into white Danish families (Myong, 2009). Today, a group of transnational adoptees contributes to critical anti-racist activism. Rikke Andreassen's thesis is a substantial study of the Danish media coverage between 1971 and 2004 of visible minorities focusing on the closely related themes of nationality, gender sexuality, and race (2005). While the thesis laid out the groundwork for a Danish language book on the media coverage, it was Andreassen's study with Anne Folke Henningsen of human exhibitions in Tivoli and the Zoological Garden around 1900 that hit an Achilles heel of Danish self-understanding (Andreassen & Henningsen, 2011). The effort of Myong and Andreassen has contributed significantly in making scholarship on race-related issues known in Danish academia. Recently, more and more seminars and conferences are organized around racialization, and networks are created at some universities to facilitate talk about "race" and experiences of racism (see, for instance, Andreassen & Vitus, 2015).

Besides the research in Swedish racism by historian Anders Wigerfelt and ethnologist Berit Wigerfelt (Wigerfelt & Wigerfelt, 2001), and anthropologist Karin Norman's work on cultural racism and xeno-hostility (2004), racism studies in Sweden have been dominated by researchers outside of anthropology and sociology with their foci on post-colonialism, critical race theory, feminist theory, and more (Hübinette, 2013; Keskinen & Andreassen, 2017; Mulinari & Neergaard, 2017).

In Norway, anthropologist Marianne Gullestad was for many years the key voice of anthropology of racism, which included both studies in Norway and the colonial legacies of Norwegian missioners' photographic documentation in Cameroon (Gullestad, 2007). Much later, Sindre Bangstad's work on Islamophobia, and not least the eminent treatment of the Breivik case, brought him international acclaim (Bangstad, 2014).

One of Finland's key figures in racism and racialization research is Suvi Keskinen, who works within a post-colonial feminist perspective and critical studies on racialization and whiteness in the Nordic context. Her key contributions revolve around the different ways national identity relates to the welfare state in economic (and cultural) chauvinism that reveals a fortification against migrants and certain foreign influences. Her work also contributes significantly to the dismantling of the basics of power relations between the state and migrants, men and women, and between generations. *Complying with Colonialism* is a book that signals a paradox in the Nordic region (Keskinen, Tuori, Irni, & Mulinari, 2009). On the one hand, four of the Nordic countries, defined here as Sweden, Norway, Denmark, and Finland, tend to represent their historic positions as outside of the colonial project, nurturing a self-image as both humane and equal in gender terms. On the other hand, the Nordic people have tended to identify themselves with former colonial European regimes' idea of "the other", with its division between "the civilised" and "savages" (ibid.).

Departing from own experiences and vicarious experience of discrimination and relating these to social science approaches to dominant processes in society, a new generation of Nordic scholars with immigrant histories may signal that the academic research knowledge and methods of color racism can be adapted and developed to Islamophobia.

When working with the review of relevant Nordic studies of racism, racialization, and racism, the disciplinary and interdisciplinary backgrounds do play a role; even though I do not want to exaggerate them, they reveal some important differences. While anthropologists have traditionally produced analysis on the basis of sustained social interaction with those whom they study (in faraway places under difficult circumstances), tended to side with the minorities and the muted. In Denmark, Lene Myong was one of the first to document that Korean adoptees that lived racializing discrimination were silenced and rejected both in their white families and in society. She comes from a gender studies and critical adoption studies background using in-depth interviewing and thick description for her fine-grained analysis. European anthropologists have been reluctant to work on racism, while their American counterparts have been far more engaged, for instance, resulting in the highly praised, nationally traveling exhibition project "RACE—Are We So Different?" created by the AAA (Goodman, Moses, & Jones, 2012). In the USA, racism studies are divided in various disciplines but they are more firmly established, whereas Nordic research is more oriented toward post-colonialism and with less public resonance.

### Nordic Exceptionalism, Ethno-Centrism, and Coloniality

Historically, the "Nordic Race" has again and again been constructed at the top of the evolutionary hierarchy, first as a "race" and later through "culture", "welfare state", "equality", "gender equality", "tolerance", "generosity", and "happiness". The American Immigration Act of 1924, for example, includes a statement: "Our own data from the army tests indicate clearly the intellectual superiority of the Nordic race group" (Brigham 1923 cit. in Goodman et al., 2012, p. 34).

A large set of qualitative interviews in the late 1990s showed that Danes tended to see themselves as the best examples for human kind for its informality (Fadel, 1999), non-conformity, anti-fanaticism, and good sense of humor (Hervik, 1999a, 2002). According to Sayaka Osanami Törngren (this volume; see also Heinö, 2009), Swedes see themselves as democratic, liberal, equal, and tolerant individuals, while Anders Hellström and Tom Nilsson (2010) found that the Swedish Democrats subscribed to an image of themselves and the Swedish nation as "the good ones". Likewise, Norwegian self-understanding is that of people being neutral, good-intentioned, and "close-to-nature" to such an extent that the derogatory term "Negro", for instance, transforms into a neutral word, once it reaches the Norwegian border (Gullestad, 2006). Finland may be described as the ambiguous exception, even racialized exception. On the one hand, part of the Nordic community, but on the other, historically represented by the Swedes as belonging to a lower race (Rastas, 2012, p. 90). Finns have traditionally supported gender equality as central for national identity and self-understanding; many consider Finland (along with Iceland) as a model example of equality. However, the rise of the populist climate has also generated "masculinist" claims, according to which gender equality "has gone too far" (Saresma, 2012, p. 14). An emphasis on traditionalist and conservative values has caused a clash with the general liberalization of society: gender-neutral marriage and the right of homosexuals to adoption have recently roused heated debates between conservatives and liberals (Lähdesmäki & Saresma, 2014).

The Nordic countries seem to share a racial exceptionalism that tacitly denies colonialist engagement and "supported a narrative in which racism 'proper' is understood as something that primarily 'exists "far away", "in the past", or "on the extreme right wing", in a Nordic context'" (Danbolt, 2017, p. 108). While the positive self-image with the "region's unprecedented understanding of equality, tolerance and solidarity" (ibid.) serves as a strong branding device, the same brand is under attack and being replaced with a nationalist protection device serving to signal to potential refugees and migrants they should stay away from Denmark and also making life difficult for those already in the country.

The war of values strategy and entitlement racism got Denmark into serious trouble in its own country and around the world. The Muhammad Cartoon affair became a major media event whose coverage has revealed an incongruence between how people abroad see Denmark and Danish self-understanding. Nowhere else, for instance, is the cartoon affair to refer conventionally as the "Muhammad-crisis", and nowhere is the prime minister's spin version of the affair adopted by the Danes, but rejected in other countries (Hervik, 2008).

Writing within a Nordic setting but drawing analytical categories and historical comparisons beyond Europe, in the Nordic literature on racialization, whiteness, anti-racism, and post-colonialism, there is still both an ethno-centrist and a euro-centrist bias; little attention is being paid to racism toward aboriginal people, Islamophobia, anti-Semitism, and other forms of racist subordination. Moreover, there is also a striking absence of voices of non-Western people.

Robert Miles (1989) credits Frantz Fanon for having pioneered the work on "racialization of thought", which took place when colonialism erased differences among and within Africans and blacks in place of racial categories such as "Negro". The answers to race and racism, Fanon argues, are to be found in European models of thought, not in the assumed affinity between national cultures of the colonized but on the similar claims of colonialized nations (Murji & Solomos, 2005, p. 7). That belief started earlier than the Middle Passage, and it also exploded from within civilization during Nazism which holds a central racist force that cannot simply be reduced to colonialism.

By asking what people object to when people object to racism, Barnor Hesse reminds us that reducing racism to a linear story that starts with the theological reflections, kidnapping, torturing, and enslaving of black Africans from various different language groups and clans is insufficient to explain the dynamics of racism historically speaking. He therefore suggests we look closer at racism's alterities just like we have looked at nationalism's others (Hervik, 2011; Loftsdóttir & Jensen, 2012). Hesse does not deny, minimize, or reject the significance and horror of this part of history, but he argues that reducing racism to "Western Colonialism and White Supremacy" fails to acknowledge and integrate the dynamics of Nazism and the Holocaust. Where racism originates in Western colonialism of non-Western peoples, there is also a racism articulated very strongly in objection to Nazism and its extremist nationalism. The "first" racism comes from an articulation of the relationship between the "West" and the ("non-West") colonized people, and the "second" racism is a product of Western civilization and modernity. As Hannah Arendt reminds us, Jews objected to being stigmatized as racial-colonial subjects and insisted that "European Jews were undeniable white" (Arendt cit in Hesse, 2014).

Today, racialization studies of "European models of thought" have moved away from being synonymous with racism and the idea of a single monolithic racism (Goldberg, 1990), and the approach to different forms of discrimination studied as "distinct silos" (Meer, 2012, p. 2), or single-axis explanations that only focus on race but leaves aside the intersections of race with gender or class (Crenshaw, 1991).

For Miles, for instance, in a European context, ideologies of racism and nationalism are relational and the ideas of "race" and "nation" (the outcomes of racial discrimination and "nationalism") are categories of simultaneous inclusion and exclusion (1993, p. 55), while neo-nationalism itself builds on anti-migration and the idea of new foreign cultures threatening the coherence and cohesion of domestic cultural values.

Moreover, as Nasar Meer has noted, the academic literature on race, racism, and racialization lacks discussions of Islamophobia (cf. with the idea of "distinct silos") even though this has been changing within the last five years (see Bangstad, 2014; Hervik, 2015; Gardell, 2010 for Nordic exceptions).

A third example of Hesse's point is Robert E. Park's study of African-American migration to Chicago. The colonial conquest was not included, and with that the "enduring forms of white domination on which it was conceptually sustained" (Hesse, 2014). In fact, the study reproduced the idea that race is something only applied to non-white peoples, as long as white people are not racially seen and named" (ibid.). In this case, the racializing reactions concerned 10% of the African-American population in the South, who migrated toward a better more just and equal life (Anderson, 2016).

According to Nelson Maldonado-Torres the concept of "coloniality of being" was born in the early 1990s in conversations among Latin American scholars about the implications of the coloniality of power in different areas of society (2007, p. 242). These interlocutors found themselves breathing coloniality all the time, whether in authority, sexuality, knowledge, and the economy, as well as in the general understanding of being as well. Modern forms of exploitation and domination, and coloniality of knowledge and of being, had a primary reference through lived experience of coloniality of power (Maldonado-Torres, 2007). One should remember that coloniality studies grew out of activities connected to the marking of 1992 as being 500 years since Columbus "discovered" the new world. Indigenous associations and activists across the Americas met for the first time on a grand scale to share experiences and coordinate activities, which again attracted the attention of scholars (Urban & Sherzer, 1991; Warren & Jackson, 2002).

Where "Colonialism denotes a political and economic relation in which the sovereignty of a nation or a people rests on the power of another nation which makes such nation an empire", then coloniality "refers to long-standing patterns of power that emerged as a result of colonialism, but that define culture, labor, intersubjective relations, and knowledge production well beyond the strict limits of colonial administration" (2007, p. 242). In other words, coloniality is different from colonialism. It occurs in the absence of colonial administration (Maldonado-Torres, 2007) and it has a longer history.

De-coloniality scholars have re-defined racism to avoid the reductionism of existing definitions (single-axis): "Racism is a global hierarchy of human superiority and inferiority, politically, culturally and economically produced and reproduced for centuries" (Grosfoguel, Oso, & Christou, 2014, p. 3). They adopt Fanon's distinction between zones-of-being, as subjects on the superior side, and zones-of-non-being for those who live on the inferior side, where racialization occurs through the marking of bodies by colour, ethnicity, language, culture and/or religion (ibid., pp. 3–4). This division into zone-of-being and non-being is that of being considered "subhuman or non-human; that is, their humanity is questioned and, as such, negated" (Fanon in Grosfoguel et al., 2014, p. 3).

With this division, Grosfoguel and collaborators open up for various forms of racism, not only color racism but also Islamophobia, racism against aboriginal populations, and so on, although from a view of indigenous people of the Americas, there is little attention. With this opening, Grosfoguel goes on to argue that Islamophobia is an original racism that became particularly public in 1478 with the beginning of the Spanish Inquisition, when Spain began cleansing southern Spain from Muslims and Jews. After 700 years of presence, they were asked to convert to Catholicism or leave, based on the Western pre-nation idea of one culture, one religion, one language, and one territory, which can also be seen as a project of cultural homogeneity. Once this project was completed, Columbus would be allowed to set sails and cross the Ocean to India. In this endeavor, Christian/Catholic religion and culture was seen as superior to Islam and Judaism, yet recognizing these religions as within civilization.

At the risk of simplifying complex research, Grosfoguel explains that through an analysis of Colombus' diary when he reached the "new" land, the beings he encountered were not like the Muslims or Jews. Columbus wrote that these beings did not have souls and religion, and therefore they were not human beings. He did not concern himself with his own, white or brown, skin color or that of the people of the Antilles. Only years later in 1537, following long debates, did the Pope decide that "Amerindians" were humans (Grosfoguel, 2008; Maldonado-Torres, 2014). What this means is that racism as an idea and practice, with an ideology of superiority/inferiority along the lines of human vs. non-human, was present before the Middle Passage and had Catholic theology as a key rationalization.

The historical moment, or point zero of Eurocentrism, defined as the conflation of the historically specific European and the universal, can be found in Rene Descartes' philosophy, for instance.

Grosfoguel argues that Descartes:

> ...replaces God, as the foundation of knowledge in the theo-politics of knowledge of the European Middle Ages, with (Western) man as the foundation of knowledge in European Modern times. All the attributes of God are now extrapolated to (western) man. Universal truth beyond time and space, privilege access to the laws of the Universe, and the capacity to produce scientific knowledge and theory is now placed in the mind of western man...It is this "God-eye view" that always hides its local and particular perspective under an abstract universalism. (2008, p. 4)

The de-coloniality project is to identify and dismantle this "Capitalist/Patriarchal Western-centric/Christian-centric Modern/Colonial world-system" (ibid., p. 5). "European patriarchy and European notions of sexuality, epistemology and spirituality were exported to the rest of the world through colonial expansion as the hegemonic criteria to racialize, classify and pathologize the rest of the world's population in a hierarchy of superior and inferior races" (ibid., p. 7). These notions were naturalized in conflation of universal validity of Christianity and the universal validity of historical emergence of nationalism. This complex coloniality system is also present in post-colonialism to which Grosfoguel and Maldonado-Torres subscribe themselves. Post-colonialists must deconstruct their own Eurocentrism and, in addition, listen more carefully to the native voices wherever they go and at the level of everyday experiences of superiorizing and inferiorizing, which of course challenges the researcher to deconstruct his or her relations with people in the field. For a recent example of how de-colonization can be carried out in the academia and its efforts of participatory research, see Parker, Holland, Dennison, Smith, and Jackson

(2017). A modest start could be identifying the language spoken and written by these people and to what extent the researchers are familiar with this language. This de-colonilization struggles are of course not new to those who grew up in anthropology confronting the colonial encounter like no other discipline in the late 1960s, 1970s, and into the 1980s (see, for instance, Asad, 1973; Weiner, 1992; Wolf, 1982 and many others) and for a decade leaving it in a disciplinary identity crisis.

With coloniality scholars opening up for various forms of racism occurring at different historical conjunctures, we must ask the question in a Nordic context about what is the racism in "anti-racism" and "color-blind racism". Barnor Hesse has been particularly clear on this when he makes the opening statement: "Racism is more objected to than understood in sociology. When it is only as a result of the objection to it that racism becomes an object of analysis, then it is not racism itself that is being observed, but rather the objection which comes to stand in its place" (Hesse, 2014, p. 141). Anti-racists, he goes on to say, are more occupied in Black Sociology with "imaginaries of racism, rather than exposing racism" (ibid., p. 142). Hesse's lead may be helpful for looking at how racism, anti-racism, and racialization are approached and opposed in the Nordic societies.

## Positions of Engagement

The engagements in racism and racialization seem to fall into four inter-related positions in the Nordic countries, where two appear as popular social movements and two categories are more institutionally anchored. *First*, the legal framework of the law, often lying with the Ombudsman or with the Human Rights Institution, as well as some NGOs that prioritize the law as the point of departure. The legal framework is the least studied in this book. *Second*, we see anti-racism as a cluster, where members "object" to what they regard as racism, often revolving around a group or collective of people who experience being propelled into certain categories, or perhaps trash bins, full of prejudice and stigmatization. Or, people who act to enhance the interest of racialized or otherwise stigmatized individuals or groups. This includes the efforts of middle-class women in Finland, who are not unlike those white women Ruth Frankenberg wrote famously about (Frankenberg, 1994) as well as attempts to use anti-racism in discourses about national and racial exceptionalism (see Haavisto, this volume). For the Norwegian scene, Stokke discusses the anti-racism of

Muslim feminist groups (this volume). And 2000 km north of Oslo, local Norwegians turn to basic humanitarianism in their activism for a more equalitarian less humiliating treatment of asylum seekers in vulnerable situations (Boe and Horsti, this volume). In Denmark, anti-racism is currently most visible as a new social movement of anti-racists who seek "safe spaces" in closed social media groups and coordinate a series of activist initiatives that include targeting commentators and racial signifiers in the Danish public (Keskinen & Andreassen, 2017). With the Sweden Democrats' successful entrance into the Parliament (Riksdagen), Sweden has seen a drastic embracement of anti-racism, even if this may appear more an issue of branding than a direct countering of racial discrimination (Hübinette & Lundström, 2011). Also included—and well represented in this volume—is the emergence of new initiatives to combat racism, often phrased as post-colonial, structural discrimination, or color racism. The (in)efficiency of anti-racist initiatives is captured by Miri Song. Song has noted that in Britain the dominant understanding is still that a white person or institution is the perpetrator of racism with the implicit assumption that "almost any form of racial statement, made by anyone (of any hue), as automatically, and indiscriminately, 'racist'" (Song, 2014, p. 109). *Third*, color-blind racism to use the term suggested by Sayaka Osanami Törngren, in this volume (with a bow to Eduardo Bonilla-Silva). This approach is that of the hegemonic majority that dominates debates in the Nordic countries. While adhering to color blindness and the idea that racism only exists in "faraway places" and "in the past" fails to address the transparency of whiteness and its raciality (Nielsen, this volume), people within this group instead resort to an anti-anti-racism in order to elevate their interests, which then makes it difficult to talk about racism at all, since racism triggers "wrongful accusations". *Fourth*, the study of racism that is the research-based approach to racism, where racism is the point of departure, less so, than the mere objection to racism. When using much research on racism in the North American context, racism seems to be a master narrative, whereas racism in the Nordic context seems more to revolve around nationalism of the nation-state and the welfare state.

The most salient feature of anti-racism and color blindness is the focus on identity formation and identity politics based on a morally and emotionally driven force against inequalities rather than a legal one. While the rhetoric of 20 years ago (Hervik, 1999a, 2002) in media coverage and everyday conversations reveals similar attitudes and perceptions, the Nordic countries in the last years are characterized by a moralization. With longterm exposure to moralization and moralizing, affect builds up, not least as moral outrage. Then anxieties follows to the point, where arguments and listening are abandoned. At this point, "rage" in Carol Anderson's sense takes over, and arguments are reduced to positions and visual appearance. Anderson captures this well through the concept of the "white rage", which lingers behind the easy triggering of confrontational racist language and violent action:

> The trigger for white rage, inevitably, is black advancement. It is not the mere presence of black people that is the problem; rather, it is blackness with ambition, with drive, with purpose, with aspirations, and with demands for full and equal citizenship. It is blackness that refuses to accept subjugation, to give up. A formidable array of policy assaults and legal contortions has consistently punished black resilience, black resolve. (Anderson, 2016, pp. 3–4)

The identity politics of anti-racism is crucial for the claims of social justice, overcoming various forms of inequalities, and strives for recognition. However, identity politics is organized to advance the interests around who you (and your group) perceive yourself to be and are perceived by others and less about attempt to remove the political impact on identity, as, for example, the civil rights movement did in the USA. As Halleh Ghorashi points out, identity politics risk enhancing the divisiveness as it feeds stronger emotion and fear of what others do, whether domestic adversaries or incoming people. Apart from the work for social justice, she asked the difficult question as to what degree anti-racism in its current form is the most effective way forward in dismantling racism, "Race" as a social category may itself become a rallying point for creating community among the anti-racist rights movements. Anti-racism does not so much handle heterogeneity and needs to address issues of power (Ghorashi, 2017). Perhaps, racism may be fought more efficiently by taking a step back in order to look at the structures and coloniality complexes that produces racializing policies, media coverage, draconian security measures, as well as turning local policing into income-generating nightmares as in the case of Ferguson (United States Ministry of Justice, 2015).

Anti-racism and color-blind racism hold antagonistic relations to each other as they struggle for space on the news agenda and social media. Anti-racists generally turn to strategic racialization, whiteness, brownness, and emotional appeals of testimonies, while color-blind racism, in my view, works through either "race" or "nation" or both as master narratives evoking ultimate emotions, incompatible values, and non-negotiable entitlement. People in the color-blind racist group target Muslims, non-Westerners, and also the anti-racists and thereby become anti-anti-racist. On its side, anti-racists are at risk of taking their effort to the point of becoming anti-white.

Students of racism include activist approaches; it is difficult to imagine scholarly experts on racism not also being public intellectuals and community or organizational activists. Researchers will seek to analyze and dismantle the logics and mechanisms of racialization and racism. In this way, they take part in the anti-racism scheme. Similarly, anti-racist activists may also tap into the research-based approaches, if only sporadically, in order to provide documentation and a foundation upon which to forward their agenda of creating a more just society. Some scholars of the color-blind group do seek to influence the public agenda, but they are not racism scholars (see Danbolt & Myong, this volume; Gullestad, 2006), whereas racism scholars seldom join the color-blind racism groups. The legal and the scholarly based groups, ideally, seek a more universal perspective to racism, although human rights as a normative system is often associated more with the Western world than not.

Scholars of racism can be further roughly divided into clusters according to whether they, as Barnor Hesse suggests, continue to influence the legacies of colonialism in the contemporary world, radical nationalism, Nazism, anti-Black racism, anti-Semitism, and racism against aboriginal groups to mention some of the more salient racisms with distinct alterities.

## Overview of Parts and Chapters

The chapters are roughly divided into three parts plus a concluding chapter on "Whiteness and Racialization". Part I is on debates on racism and racialization, Part II on denials of these, and Part III on examining anti-racism more closely as research object.

On July 17, 2017, Danish television, TV 2, brought together in the studio three (white) "experts" that were to comment on the week's top stories as defined by the host. One of the themes discussed was a radio show for the younger generations of listeners. Listeners were asked to bring what they considered jokes that went beyond the limits of the acceptable, regardless if racial, sexual, religious, or other nature. One Danish anti-racist activist with a Ugandan background, Mary Namagambe, objected strongly to the program, and eventually the director of the program terminated the program. Now, speaking from another studio, Namagambe explained her experience, moral outrage, and criticism.

One of the experts in the studio is specialist in American politics and parliamentary candidate for the liberal party, Venstre, Mads Fuglede. Fuglede disagreed with Namagambe without acknowledging her experience. He went on by stating that "to be a racist is to believe there is a difference in different skin colour that shows different intelligence, and those rights that goes along with these differences, and I don't think that you necessarily believe in that because you tell bad jokes" (TV 2 News, 2017). In response to Namagambe feeling offended by the program, Fuglede answered, "I hope that we all feel that sometime". He then turned the experience of being offended by the vulgar jokes around and into a wish of using offendedness as the basis for a demand to stop the program, "to do this form of opinion censorship and judging taste, where you decide what you can say and what you cannot within the limits of freedom of speech" (ibid.).

This little glimpse of a recent media coverage may serve to illustrate how racism and racialization are debated in Denmark and the Nordic countries more generally:

1. The white expert in the studio rejected Mary's experience of being racially offended.
2. None of the experts in the studio were experts on racism, but spoke from a gut-level sense of what racism is. The statement of racism provided by one of the guests refers to a belief that was rejected by social science decades ago.
3. Despite being an expert on American issues, Fuglede showed little sense about non-white views and experience of racism.
4. The angle chosen to approach the theme is recurrent in most news media coverage: When is something racism and when is it not? May I say a given word or not (see also Ventilate and Hervik, this volume). This leads easily to a boxing match type of exchange and is a lost opportunity for a much needed, informed dialogue.
5. The white majority position includes articulating itself as a victim of attempts to limit its freedom of speech.
6. There is general agreement among US racism scholars and anti-racist activists that the "white supremacist" position has for more than 100 years in the USA included claims that it was offended, which in various ways was used to legitimize racialized treatment of blacks.

Throughout the Nordic countries, it is common to find that the white, hegemonic majority denying minority experiences of racial or other discrimination. Denials are present in public service as well as commercial television, when racialized experiences are presented in the studio, and/or with scholarly based research results with elaborate definitions and well inscribed into the research history, and opposed them to non-professional, politicians, who by definition speak from a normative position and spinning himself in the most favorable light. The result is disregard and ignorance of experiences and research, reduced to gut-level reactions of what people think about or like about them. While social scientists have to document as part of their work, the politicians are normative, often media-trained and in command of populist language. In whose interest then is the journalist and news agency working?

In Chap. 2, Myong and Danbolt analyze the news coverage of non-racist experts' denial and explaining away of racism in Denmark as it is analyzed by Danish researchers. The authors reveal the hegemonic conditions that shape the circulation of research-based knowledge of racism in Denmark and argue through the dismantling of the debate for a break with the historic and color-blind racism among the network of authors, journalists, and editors-in-chief in the news media coverage. Tuija Saresma analyzes the Kempele rape case in Finland in Chap. 3, which is an exemplary case to illustrate the mechanisms of racialization that is inseparable from gendering, sexism, misogynism, and much more. Like in the coverage of 22/7 in Oslo (Breivik's terrorist massacre), the lack of early information about the suspects of rapist automatically provided a schema-driven suspicion directed at two younger asylum seekers. With effects but no causes, prevailing hegemonic racialized views appear. The two boys were falsely accused. They were not present at the scene of the crime. Saresma analyzes the event and discusses the media rhetoric of rape as performative that brought all asylum seekers under suspicion. This rhetoric of rape and accusations of rape is particularly difficult to counter and nuance, due to its winning communication ability, you cannot meaningfully argue against rape cases. Therefore, the gendered rape speech and reasoning can be used as posing and enhance a threat to white women in particular while also offering protection from non-white potential rapists. In Chap. 4, Asta Smedegaard Nielsen identifies a similar racialization pattern in the public media as a performer of racialization in Danish journalism. She analyzes the Copenhagen mass shooting in 2015, where the threat of terror dominates the angle of coverage without providing alternative forms of particularly heinous crimes. The hegemonization of the event is dominated by a habitual whiteness which works to keep its privileged white position, through the logic of defending themselves against those threats inscribed on the bodies of "the other" and therefore leading to the new restrictive measures. In her study of how two British media (BBC and *The Guardian*) and two American media (CNN and *New York Times*) cover a local Swedish newspaper's publication of a controversial Muhammad cartoon caricature, Mahitab Ezz El Din further documents strong dichotomizations that help us to understand the logic of having two different standards for representing the same event. In Chap. 5, she identifies this dichotomy as a form of Orientalism and as such it is a binary division that is an ongoing identity narrative that builds on ideas of incompatibilities which are at odds with the experiences on the ground.

Closely related to debates about racialization, we find denials of racism and denials of experiences of racism and racialization (Part II), which is widespread in the Nordic world whether overtly as in the TV 2 incident above or hidden in habitual whiteness as argued by Nielsen. In Chap. 6, Sayaka Osanami Törngren focuses on attitudes toward mixed relationships. Her analysis brings out a conventional discourse celebrating free unrestricted choice of partners, yet reasoning about how actual mixed relations bring issues out that shows grave concerns about upholding Swedish gender equality norms. This reasoning, she finds, is based on a color-blind racism, where those who do not comply with the Swedish sacred values of especially gender equality are to be sanctioned. In Chap. 7, Mantė Vertelytė and Peter Hervik take issue with the moralizing of racial epithets in Danish media through an analysis of the unfolding debate on the use of the term *Neger*. The term is responded to through the use of the "N-word". The analysis of the arguments shows an incongruence between the different sides of the debate, which reveals a general lack of knowledge of racism's history and celebration of Danish racial exceptionalism that denies and trivializes racialization in Denmark. In Chap. 8, Carolina Sanchez Boe and Karina Horsti find that anti-racist and humanitarian initiatives are not solely found in urban centers in Europe but also in the most northern region of Europe. They tell the story of local Norwegian responses and circumstances of responses in relation to the "biking" Syrian and other asylum seekers from Russia via Norway-Russia border some 2000 km north of Oslo. Through the analysis, authors document that moral senses of right and wrong may challenge the legal framework and administrative routine practices in a way that better highlights human rights and fights inequalities in a process where they themselves are embedded through their precarious positions at the margins of Europe.

In the third part, four authors examine in three chapters cases of anti-racist initiatives while examining also the concept of anti-racism itself. Christian Stokke asks in Chap. 9 the question whether anti-racist efforts and policies have made a difference. By studying the media coverage and exchanges around the Norwegian cartoon affair in early 2006 and the hijab debates, Stokke first documents discourses in "Immigrant as a problem" and the "anti-Muslim" and then moves on to the core of his study, namely, the Muslim feminists and their anti-racist efforts to counter what goes on in the debates. The outcome of these efforts is found, he argues, in how the social democratic government has accommodated minority perspectives into multicultural education, potentially opening for a broader anti-racism education. In Chap. 10, Camilla Haavisto looks at anti-racism through four mediated events in Helsinki and Malmö. Haavisto finds "listening" and the proficiency in conveying experiences of racism and thereby the potential for genuine dialogue to be crucial for the anti-racism activism. This is where transformative power comes in and leads her to distinguish "critical events" from others. In Chap. 11, Kjetil Rødje and Tess Sophie Skadegård Thorsen analyze the racialized and racializing debate around a large Danish amusement parks' use of racial signifiers for some of its rides. The analysis reveals a by now recurrent pattern in such events that a majority subscribes, intentionally or habitually, to an entitled position that allows it to ignore and explain away critique of the park as well as arguments that claim experiences of racial offendedness. The lack of congruency in the debate implies that the event never becomes a "critical event", but remains yet another missed opportunity to seriously discuss the difficult issues of racism and national white self-understandings. One important absence in studies of Nordic racialization has been to understand how ideas of "Whiteness", which takes racialization as its starting point, relates to "Neo-Nationalism", which includes racialization but also draws on the generative power of defending the "nation". In Chap. 12, Nasar Meer offers a much welcome treatment of these relations from a broader analytical perspective. In this effort, he discusses the racialization of Muslim and the role of Islamophobia.

## References

Alexander, C. (2004). Writing Race: Ethnography and the Imagination of the Asian Gang. In B. Martin & J. Solomos (Eds.), *Researching Race and Racism.* London and New York: Routledge.

Ålund, A. (Ed.). (1998). *Mot ett normalt liv: bosniska flyktingar i Norden.* Copenhagen: Nord, 7 (in Swedish).

Anderson, C. (2016). *White Rage.* New York and London: Bloomsbury.

Andreassen, R. (2005). *The Mass Media's Construction of Gender, Race, Sexuality and Nationality: An Analysis of the Danish News Media's Communication about Visible Minorities from 1971 to 2004.* Unpublished Ph.D. dissertation, Department of History, University of Toronto.

Andreassen, R., & Henningsen, A. F. (2011). *Menneskeudstilling: Fremvisninger af eksotiske mennesker i Zoologisk Have og Tivoli [Human Exhibitions: Race, Gender and Sexuality in Ethnic Displays].* Copenhagen: Tiderne Skifter.

Andreassen, R., & Vitus, K. (Eds.). (2015). *Affectivity and Race. Studies from the Nordic Context.* Farnham: Ashgate.

Asad, T. (Ed.). (1973). *Anthropology & the Colonial Encounter.* London: Ithaca Press. Atlantic Highlands, NJ: Humanities Press.

Balibar, E. (1991). Is There a 'Neo-Racism'? In E. Balibar & I. Wallerstein (Eds.), *Race, Nation, Class: Ambiguous Identities* (pp. 17–28). New York: Verso.

Bangstad, S. (2014). *Anders Breivik and the Rise of Islamophobia.* London: Zed Books.

Barker, M. (1981). *The New Racism: Conservatives and the Ideology of the Tribe.* London: Junction Books.

Berg, B. (Ed.). (1998). *Kommet for å bli?: om integrasjon og tilbakevending blant bosniske flyktninger i Norden.* Nord, 1998, 8 (in Norwegian).

Boisen, S., & Hervik, P. (2013). Danish Media Coverage of 22/7. *Nordic Journal for Migration Research, 3*(4), 197–204.

Brochmann, G., & Hagelund, A. (Eds.). (2012). *Immigration Policy and the Scandinavian Welfare State 1945–2010.* New York: Palgrave Macmillan.

Butler, J., & Athanasiou, A. (2013). *Dispossession: The Performative in the Political.* Cambridge: Polity Press.

Carsten, J. (1995). The Substance of Kinship and the Heat of the Hearth: Feeding, Personhood, and Relatedness among Malays in Pulau Langkawi. *American Ethnologist, 22*(2), 223–241.

Crenshaw, K. W. (1991). Mapping the Margins: Intersectionality, Identity Politics, and Violence against. Women of Color. *Stanford Law Review, 43*(6), 1241–1299.

Danbolt, M. (2017). Retro Racism: Colonial Ignorance and Racialized Affective Consumption in Danish Public Culture. *Nordic Journal of Migration Research, 7*(2), 105–113.

Eide, E., Kjølstad, M., & Naper, A. (2013). After the 22 July Terror in Norway: Media Debates on Freedom of Expression and Multiculturalism. *Nordic Journal of Migration Research, 2*, 187–196.

Essed, P. (2013). Entitlement Racism: License to Humiliate. In *Recycling Hatred: Racism(s) in Europe Today: A Dialogue between Academics, Equality Experts and Civil Society Activists* (pp. 62–76). Brussels: European Network against Racism (ENAR).

Fadel, U. H. (1999). Skik følge eller land fly: Danske forståelser af kulturel forskellighed. In P. Hervik (Ed.), *Den generende forskellighed* (pp. 214–261). Copenhagen: Hans H. Reitzels Forlag.

Fadel, U. H., Hervik, P., & Vestergaard, G. (1999). De 'besværlige' somaliere. In P. Hervik (Ed.), *Den generende forskellighed* (pp. 171–213). København: Hans Reitzels Forlag.

Frankenberg, R. (1994). Whiteness and Americanness: Examining Constructions of Race, Culture, and Nation in White Women's Life Narratives. In S. Gregory & R. Sanjek (Eds.), *Race* (pp. 62–77). New Brunswick, NJ: Rutgers University Press.

Gaasholt, Ø., & Togeby, L. (1995). *I syv sind: Danskernes holdninger til flygtninge og indvandrere*. Århus: Politica.

Gadamer, H.-G. (2003) [1960]. Hermeneutical Understanding. In G. Delanty & P. Strydom (Eds.), *Philosophies of Social Science* (pp. 158–163). Maidenhead and Philadelphia: Open University Press.

Gardell, M. (2010). *Islamofobi*. Stockholm: Leopard Förlag.

Ghorashi, H. (2017). *Racism and Anti-Racism in the Nordic Societies*. Key Note Speech Held at the International Workshop, Rethinking Democracy and Solidarity in Late Modern. June 1–2, 2017, Södertörn University, Sweden.

Gingrich, A. (2006). Nation, Status and Gender in Trouble? Exploring Some Contexts and Characteristics of Neo-Nationalism in Western Europe. In A. Gingrich & M. Banks (Eds.), *Neo-Nationalism in Europe and Beyond: Perspectives from Social Anthropology* (pp. 29–49). Oxford: Berghahn Books.

Ginsburg, F. (2005). Media Anthropology: An Introduction. In E. W. Rothernbuhler & M. Coman (Eds.), *Media Anthropology* (pp. 17–25). Thousand Oaks, CA: Sage.

Glick-Schiller, N. (2014). *The Migration Debates: Thinking beyond Nationalism and Transnational Processes*. Inaugural Lecture, Aalborg University, October 21.

Goldberg, D. T. (Ed.). (1990). *The Anatomy of Racism*. Minneapolis: University of Minnesota Press.

Goldberg, D. T. (2006). Racial Europeanization. *Ethnic and Racial Studies, 29*(2), 331–364.

Goodman, A. H., Moses, Y. T., & Jones, J. L. (2012). *Race. Are We So Different?* Chichester, West Sussex: John Wiley & Sons.

Grosfoguel, R. (2008). *Transmodernity, Border Thinking, and Global Coloniality. Decolonizing Political Economy and Postcolonial Studies* [ORIG. Published in Portuguese Revista Crítica de Ciências Sociales 2008]. 1–23. Retrieved from http://www.eurozine.com/transmodernity-border-thinking-and-global-coloniality/

Grosfoguel, R., Oso, L., and Christou, A. (2014). Identities. Global Studies in Culture and Power, 1-23 (Online version), 22(6), 635-652 (print version, 2015).

Guenif-Souilamas, N. A. H., & Mohammed, M., et al. (2015). How Does It Feel to Be a Problem?: A Statement by French Social Scientists of Arab and African Origin Following the Paris Attacks. *Op-Ed, Truth-Out.* Retrieved January 26, 2015, from http://www.truth-out.org/speakout/item/28742-how-does-it-feel-to-be-a-problem-a-statement-by-french-social-scientists-of-arab-and-african-origin-following-the-paris-attacks

Gullestad, M. (2002). *Det norske sett med nye øyne. Kritisk analyse av norsk innvandringsdebatt.* Oslo: Universitetsforlaget.

Gullestad, M. (2006). *Plausible Prejudice. Everyday Experiences and Social Images of Nation, Culture and Race.* Oslo: Universitetsforlaget.

Gullestad, M. (2007). *Picturing Pity.* Oxford and New York: Berghahn Books.

Hansen, L. (2002). Introduction. In L. Hansen & O. Wæver (Eds.), *European Integration and National Identity. The Challenge of the Nordic States* (pp. 1–20). London and New York: Routledge.

Hansen, L., & Wæver, O. (Eds.). (2002). *European Integration and National Identity. The Challenge of the Nordic States* (pp. 50–87). London and New York: Routledge.

Harvey, D. (2003). *Accumulation by Dispossession: The New Imperialism.* New York: Oxford.

Hastrup, K. (Ed.). (1992). *Den Nordiske Verden I.* Copenhagen: Gyldendal.

Hebb, A., & Couldry, N. (2013) [Origl 2010]. *Introduction: Media Events in Globalized Media Cultures.* LSE Research Online. 1–38. Retrieved from http://eprints.lse.ac.uk/52468/1/__libfile_REPOSITORY_Content_Couldry%2C%20N_Introduction%20media%20events_Couldry_Introduction%20media%20events_2013.pdf

Heinö, A. J. (2009). Democracy between Collectivism and Individualism. De-Nationalisation and Individualisation in Swedish National Identity. *International Review of Sociology, 19*(2), 297–314.

Hellström, A., & Nilsson, T. (2010). We are the Good Guys: Ideological Positioning of the Nationalist Party Sverigedemokraterna in Contemporary Swedish Politics. *Ethnicities, 10*(1), 55–76.

Hervik, P. (1999a). *Den generende forskellighed. Danske svar på den stigende multikulturalisme.* Copenhagen: Hans Reitzels Forlag.

Hervik, P. (1999b). Ny-racisme—politisk og folkelig. In P. Hervik (Ed.), Chapter 4*Den generende forskellighed. Danske svar på den stigende multikulturalisme* (pp. 108–132). Copenhagen: Hans Reitzels Forlag.

Hervik, P. (2002). *Mediernes muslimer. En antropologisk undersøgelse af mediernes dækning af religioner i Danmark.* The Board for Ethnic Equality: Copenhagen. Retrieved from Mediernes Muslimer.pdf.

Hervik, P. (2004). Introduction: Anthropological Perspectives on the New Racism in Europe: Theme Issue "The New Racism in Europe". *Ethnos. Journal of Anthropology, 69*(2), 149–155.

Hervik, P. (2008). The Original Spin and Its Side Effects: Freedom Speech as Danish News Management. In E. Eide, R. Kunelius, & A. Phillips (Eds.), *Transnational Media Events. The Mohammed Cartoons and the Imagined Clash of Civilizations* (pp. 59–80). Gothenburg: Nordicom.

Hervik, P. (2011). The Annoying Difference. In *The Emergence of Danish Neonationalism, Neoracism, and Populism in the Post-1989 World.* New York and Oxford: Berghahn Books.

Hervik, P. (2014). Cultural War of Values: The Proliferation of Moral Identities in the Danish Public Sphere. In J. Tripathy & S. Padmanabhan (Eds.), *Becoming Minority: How Discourses and Policies Produce Minorities in Europe and India* (pp. 154–173). New Delhi, India: Sage Publications.

Hervik, P. (2015). Xenophobia and Nativism. In J. D. Wright (Ed.), *International Encyclopedia of the Social & Behavioral Sciences* (Vol. 25, 2nd ed., pp. 796–801). Oxford: Elsevier (org. 2001).

Hervik, P. (2017). Ten Years after the Danish Muhammad Cartoon News Stories: Terror and Radicalization as Predictable Media Events-Television and New Media. *Special Issue "Prime Time", 19*(1), 1–8.

Hesse, B. (2014). Racism's Alterity. The After-Life of Black Sociology. In W. D. Hund & A. Lentin (Eds.), *Racism and Sociology* (pp. 141–174). Wien and Berlin: LIT Verlag.

Hjarnø, J. (1995). Multiculturalism in the Nordic Societies. In *Proceedings of the 9th Nordic Seminar for Researchers on Migration and Ethnic Relations.* Tema Nord: Copenhagen.

Hjarvard, S., Mortensen, M., & Eskjær, M. F. (Eds.). (2014). Introduction. Three Dynamics of Mediatized Conflicts. In *The Dynamics of Mediatized Conflict* (pp. 1–16). New York: Peter Lang.

Hübinette, T. (2013). Swedish Antiracism and White Melancholia: Racial Words in a Post-Racial Society. *Ethnicity and Race in a Changing World, 4*(1), 24–33.

Hübinette, T., & Lundström, C. (2011). Sweden after the Recent Election: The Double-Binding Power of Swedish Whiteness through the Mourning of the Loss of 'Old Sweden' and the Passing of 'Good Sweden. *NORA—Nordic Journal of Feminist and Gender Research, 19*(1), 42–52.

Huntington, S. (1993). The Clash of Civilizations? *Foreign Affairs, 72*(3), 22–49.

Huntington, S. (1996). *The Clash of Civilizations and the Remaking of World Order*. New York: Simon & Schuster.

Jørgensen, R. E., & Søderhamn, V. B. (1999). Ali og de fyrretive k(r)oner: En analyse af Ekstra Bladets kampagne 'De fremmede'. In P. Hervik (Ed.), *Den generende forskellighed* (pp. 81–107). Copenhagen: Hans H. Reitzels Forlag.

Keskinen, S., & Andreassen, R. (2017). Developing Theoretical Perspectives on Racialisation and Migration. *Nordic Journal of Migration Research, 7*(2), 64–69.

Keskinen, S., Tuori, S., Irni, S., & Mulinari, D. (Eds.). (2009). *Complying with Colonialism: Gender, Race and Ethnicity in the Nordic Region*. Farnham: Ashgate.

Kundnani, A. (2015). *The Muslims Are Coming!: Islamophobia, Extremism, and the Domestic War on Terror*. London and New York: Verso.

Lähdesmäki, T., & Saresma, T. (2014). Reframing Gender Equality in Finnish Online Discussion on Immigration: Populist Articulations of Religious Minorities and Marginalized Sexualities. *NORA—Nordic Journal of Feminist and Gender Research, 22*(4), 299–313.

Lentin, A. (2008). *Racism: A Beginner's Guide*. Oxford: Oneworld.

Lewis, B. (1990). The Roots of Muslim Rage. *Atlantic Monthly, 266*(3), 47–60.

Loftsdóttir, K., & Jensen, L. (Eds.). (2012). *Whiteness and Postcolonialism in the Nordic Region. Exceptionalism, Migrant Others and National Identities*. London and New York: Routledge.

Lööw, H. (2009). Country Report Sweden. In Bertelsmann Stiftung (Ed.), *Strategies for Combating Right-Wing Extremism in Europe* (pp. 425–459). Gütersloh: Bertelsmann Stiftung.

Maldonado-Torres, N. (2007). On the Coloniality of Being. Contributions to the Development of a Concept. *Cultural Studies, 21*(2–3), 240–270.

Maldonado-Torres, N. (2014). AAR Centennial Roundtable: Religion, Conquest, and Race in the Foundations of the Modern/Colonial World. *Journal of the American Academy of Religion, 82*(3), 636–665. https://doi.org/10.1093/jaarel/lfu054

Meer, N. (2012). Racialization and Religion: Race, Culture and Difference in the Study of Antisemitism and Islamophobia. *Ethnic and Racial Studies, 36*(3), 1–14.

Miles, R. (1989). *Racism*. London: Routledge.

Miles, R. (1993). *Racism after Race Relations*. London and New York: Routledge.

Møller, B., & Togeby, L. (1999). *Oplevet diskrimination. En undersøgelse blandt etniske minoriteter*. Copenhagen: The Board for Ethnic Equality.

Mulinari, D., & Neergaard, A. (2017). Theorising Racism. Exploring the Swedish Racial Regime. *Nordic Journal of Migration Research, 7*(2), 88–96.

Murji, K., & Solomos, J. (Eds.). (2005). *Racialization: Studies in Theory and Practice*. Oxford: Oxford University Press.

Myong, L. (2009). *Adopteret—fortællinger om transnational og racialiseret tilbliv-else*. Ph.D. dissertation, Department of Learning, Aarhus University.

Norman, K. (2004). Equality and Exclusion: 'Racism' in a Swedish Town. *Ethnos*, *69*(2), 204–228.

Olwig, K. F. (2003). Narrating Deglobalization: Danish Perceptions of a Lost Empire. *Global Networks*, *3*, 207–222.

Parker, P., Holland, D., Dennison, J., Smith, S. H., & Jackson, M. (2017). Decolonizing the Academy: Lessons from the Graduate Certificate in Participatory Research at the University of North Carolina at Chapel Hill. *Qualitative Inquiry*, 1–14.

Rasmussen, K. S. (2004). *Hvad er Dansk Racisme?* Public lecture September 26, 2004, Århus. Retrieved from http://www.minority-report.dk/dansk/deltagere/kim_su_rasmussen.html

Rastas, A. (2012). Reading History through Finnish Exceptionalism. In K. Loftsdóttir & L. Jensen (Eds.), *Whiteness and Postcolonialism in the Nordic Region. Exceptionalism, Migrant Others and National Identities* (pp. 89–104). London and New York: Routledge.

Røgilds, F. (2002). Den nye racisme: aktører, forhistorie, modstrategier. *Dansk Sociologi*, *13*(3), 101–111.

Saresma, T. (2012). Miesten tasa-arvo ja kaunapuhe blogikeskustelussa [Equality for Men and Resentment Speech in Blog Discussions]. In H. Harjunen & T. Saresma (Eds.), *Sukupuoli nyt! Purkamisia ja neuvotteluja [Gender Now! Deconstruction and Negotiations]* (pp. 13–34). Jyväskylä: Kampus Kustannus.

Saresma, T. (2018). Gender Populism: Three Cases of Finns Party Actors' Traditionalist Anti-Feminism. In Kovala, E. Palonen, M. Ruotsalainen, & T. Saresma (Eds.), pp. 177-200. *Populism on the Loose*. Jyväskylä: Research Centre for Contemporary Culture.

Schierup, C.-U. (1993). *På Kulturens Slagmark. Mindretal og Størretal taler om Danmark*. Esbjerg: Sydjysk Universitetsforlag.

Schwartz, J. (Ed.). (1998). *Et midlertidigt liv. Bosniske Flygtninge i de Nordiske Lande*. Copenhagen: Nord 1998:9 (in Danish).

Song, M. (2014). Challenging a Culture of Racial Equivalence. *The British Journal of Sociology*, *65*(1), 107–129.

Standing, G. (2014). *A Precariat Charter: From Denizens to Citizens*. New York: Bloomsbury.

Statistics Sweden. (2016). *Party Preference Survey November 2015*. Retrieved October 1, 2017, from http://www.scb.se/Statistik/_Publikationer/ME0201_2016M11_BR_ME60BR1602.pdf

Stolcke, V. (1995). Talking Culture: New Boundaries, New Rhetorics of Exclusion in Europe. *Current Anthropology*, *36*(1), 1–24.

TV 2 News, News & Co. (2017). DR får kritik for racism. 16 July, 15.00.

United States Ministry of Justice. (2015). *Investigation of Ferguson Police Department.* Retrieved from https://www.justice.gov/sites/default/files/opa/pressreleases/attachments/2015/03/04/ferguson_police_department_report.pdf

Urban, G., & Sherzer, J. (Eds.). (1991). *Nation-States and Indians in Latin America.* Austin: University of Texas Press.

Warren, K. B., & Jackson, J. J. (Eds.). (2002). *Indigenous Movements, Self-Representation, and the State in Latin America.* Austin: University of Texas Press.

Weiner, A. B. (1992). *Inalienable Possessions. The Paradox of Keeping-While-Giving.* Berkeley: University of California Press.

Wigerfelt, A., & Wigerfelt, B. (2014). A Challenge to Multiculturalism. Everyday Racism and Hate Crime in a Small Swedish Town. *WOMEN'S. The Journal of Multicultural Society, 5*(2), 48–75.

Wigerfelt, B., & Wigerfelt, A. (2001). *Rasismens yttringar, exemplet klippan.* Lund: Studentlitteratur.

Wolf, E. (1982). *Europe and the People without History.* Berkeley, Los Angeles and London: University of California Press.

Wren, K. (2001). Cultural Racism: Something is Rotten in the State of Denmark. *Social and Cultural Geography, 2*(2), 141–162.

# CHAPTER 2

# Racial Turns and Returns: Recalibrations of Racial Exceptionalism in Danish Public Debates on Racism

## *Mathias Danbolt and Lene Myong*

In recent years, the Danish public has been embroiled in different yet entangled debates on racism and whiteness. One of the things that make these debates stand out from earlier ones is the increasing political mobilization of people of color in Denmark and their concerted attempts to influence public opinion and resist white dominance. In this chapter, we conceptualize the emergence of these debates as a set of racial turns and returns, which have produced ambiguous effects. On the one hand, these turns can be read as a break with historic and color-blind denials of racism; on the other hand, these turns have also given rise to multiple rejections and reproductions of racist logics. We refrain from evaluating these racial turns as predominantly negative or positive; instead, we wish to analyze

M. Danbolt (✉)
University of Copenhagen, Copenhagen, Denmark
e-mail: danbolt@hum.ku.dk

L. Myong
University of Stavanger, Stavanger, Norway
e-mail: lene.myong@uis.no

39

P. Hervik (ed.), *Racialization, Racism, and Anti-Racism in the Nordic Countries*, Approaches to Social Inequality and Difference,
https://doi.org/10.1007/978-3-319-74630-2_2

the productive dimensions of the intensified focus on race and racism. In particular we ask: how and to what effects has research-based knowledge on racialization and racism been circulated and (mis)construed as a consequence of these turns? In other words, we are interested in the epistemological processes that lend authority to some forms of scholarship/knowledge while marginalizing other forms of knowledge production.

This chapter belongs to a broader study of the Danish racism debates from 2012 to 2016. We surmise that during this period, knowledge production that points to racism as a systemic and structural problem has been cast as not only unscientific and ideologically driven but as a new form of what Alistair Bonnett (2005) calls "anti-racist racism". The framing of research on racism as a form of racism itself indicates a shift from previous patterns of "systematic, trivializing, and negligent denials of racism" in a Danish context (Hervik & Jørgensen, 2002, p. 84). In these recent media debates, the conceptualization of racism is reconfigured and displaced in paradoxical ways, as the debates, on the one hand, consolidate a restricted definition of racism centered on intentionality and "reasonability" and, on the other hand, position "well-meaning" and "anti-racist" researchers as the propagators of dangerous racist thinking with their insistent talk about racial difference. The effect of this epistemological framework is a delegitimation of research-based understandings of racism. We argue that these turns in the conceptualization of racism in Denmark have served to rearticulate and recalibrate notions of Danish racial exceptionalism.

## HENNING BECH AND MEHMET ÜMIT NECEF'S *ARE DANES RACIST?*

This section is based on extensive readings of newspaper reporting and opinion pieces on racism published in Danish newspapers during the years 2012–2016 but with a specific concentration on a debate that took off in early 2013 and continued for several months following the publication of the book *Are Danes Racist? The Problems of Immigration Research* [*Er danskerne racister? Indvandrerforskningens problemer*] by researchers Henning Bech and Mehmet Ümit Necef.[1] We have chosen this debate as

---

[1] The titles of and quotes from books and newspaper published in Danish have been translated into English by the authors, with original titles in brackets. See also the article's reference section for original titles of all the Danish publications.

a starting point because it marks an important shift in how research on racism is framed in Danish public debates. From being a relatively minor research field in terms of institutional support and media attention, the 2013 debate, as we will show, worked to present research on racism as holding a hegemonic position in the human and social sciences—as well as in the media—propagated by a self-enclosed clique of powerful academics eager to police knowledge production on immigration, racism, and cultural difference in Denmark.[2]

In their book, Bech and Necef seek to test the validity of what they claim to be a ubiquitous assertion made by what they call anti-racist researchers,[3] namely, that "the Danes are racist" (Bech & Necef, 2013, p. 22). Through a critical close reading of a selected number of research publications on immigration in Denmark, Bech and Necef argue that this research lacks proper documentation and uses improper research methods to support the claims of widespread "racism and the like" in Denmark (p. 10). By suggesting that anti-racist researchers have misinformed the public with their unfounded generalizations about the Danes' racist "foundational attitude" [grundholdning] (p. 327), Bech and Necef position themselves (and their book) in isolated opposition to what they see as a dominant, left-leaning, intersectional, and discourse-constructivist paradigm within scholarship on racism and migration (p. 335) that has come to "demonize the majority of the Danes by calling them racist" on unsolid ground (p. 342). In response to this, Bech and Necef argue for the importance of returning to a scientific, rational, and hermeneutic framework for analyzing racism, grounded in a restricted intentional-oriented definition of racism, and a methodology centered around keywords such as openness, patience, pragmatism, humor, and self-criticism (pp. 338–342).

In interviews about *Are Danes Racist?*, Bech and Necef make clear that they have written their study with "the general public" in mind, as they hope to make "both citizens, journalists, and politicians [beslutning-

---

[2] For a discussion on how research on racism has been neglected by governmental think tanks in their work on integration in the 1990s and early 2000s, see Hervik and Jørgensen (2002), p. 90.

[3] To our knowledge the terminologies of "anti-racist research" or "anti-racist researchers" do not reflect how most critical race scholars in Denmark have positioned their research or themselves over the past decade; it is, however, consistently used by Bech and Necef, and in the conclusion to the book, it is defined as a "designation for research, where there is a significant probability that unsubstantiated claims of widespread racism and the like are being put forth" (p. 326).

stagere] more critical towards research" (Necef quoted in Vind, 2013, p. 1). It is beyond the scope of this article to critically engage in depth with the claims put forward by Bech and Necef in their book. We have chosen to focus on the media debate generated by *Are Danes Racist?* rather than the book itself because we are interested in examining what kind of "critical" thinking the book generated among the general public of journalists and media-contributing citizens. When, in the following sections, we address these assertions and assumptions, and discuss how they have informed the discursive framing of racism in public debates, we are thus aware of the fact that researchers are never in full control of the presentation and reception of their research in the media.[4] But we argue that the discourse produced around the publication of this book, aided by the numerous interviews with the authors, has worked to establish and normalize an influential interpretive framework for dismissing Danish research on racism and discrimination—a framework that has gained force in the following years in which it has functioned as a touchstone that people of color, who articulate criticism of racism, are constantly measured against.

## THEORETICAL FRAMING: DANISH RACIAL EXCEPTIONALISM AND ANTI-ANTI-RACISM

The phrasing of the question that makes up the title of Bech and Necef's book *Are Danes Racist?* positions racism as a personalized trait in individuals or populations (i.e. racists). When seen in connection with the subtitle's indication of problematic research, it suggests that an affirmative response to the question is impossible and unconvincing. In other words, the title can be said to position the book in a tradition of what has been discussed as racial exceptionalism (Goldberg, 2006) in a Danish and Nordic context (Loftsdóttir & Jensen, 2012). The exceptional element pertaining to the presence of racism in the Nordic region has often been connected to ideas of the region's unique geographical and historical circumstances, as well as to the region's unique investment in a specific set of qualities and values. Within narratives of racial exceptionalism, the term *racism* is used to describe acts of discrimination based on a belief in the biological difference and inferiority of people of color (Goldberg, 2006; Gullestad, 2005; Hervik, 2011). This ideological framework has been

---

[4] In an interview, Bech attempted, for instance, to clarify what he considered to be a misinterpretation of an aspect of the argument in *Are Danes Racist?* (*Information*, 2013).

connected to historical episodes such as chattel slavery in the United States, the apartheid regime in South Africa, and the eugenic project of the Nazis in Germany. The long tradition for silencing and disavowing the Nordic countries' colonial involvements and "colonial complicities" (Vuorela, 2009), as well as the countries' investment in eugenic social projects far beyond WWII, has been central to the naturalization of a historical, imaginary Nordic region as an area of notable racial homogeneity. The framing of the Nordic region as a space without a history of racial difference and tensions, and the use of a definition of racism restricted to a biological and intentionalist ideology of racial differentiation, has enabled the creation of a narrative where racism proper is understood as something that primarily "exists 'far away', 'in the past', or 'on the extreme right wing'" in a Danish context (Myong, 2014, n.p., See also Danbolt, 2017).

The idea of racial exceptionalism in the Nordic countries has been central to the branding of the region's unprecedented commitment to equality, tolerance, and solidarity (Blaagaard & Andreassen, 2012; Browning, 2007; Danbolt, 2016; Gullestad, 2005; Habel, 2012; Hübinette, 2014; Mulinari et al., 2009; Myong, 2014; Rastas, 2012). The idea of historical innocence and a contemporary investment in equality has worked to foster what Ylva Habel terms "sanctioned ignorance" pertaining to racialized marginalization and racism in a Nordic context (Habel, 2012, p. 104). This ignorance has nurtured a culture of normative color-blindness, where the avoidance of "seeing" and verbalizing racialized signs, such as skin color, has been thought of as a non-racist strategy that works to turn race into a meaningless category (Andreassen, Henningsen, & Myong, 2008). This culture of racial silence (Myong, 2009) has served to obscure the ways in which race continues to operate as a biopolitical medium that produces and reproduces frames for understanding bodily difference in a Nordic context (Andreassen & Vitus, 2015). Furthermore, the normative culture of racial silence also ensures that those who criticize racism appear to be the ones who introduce racial thinking into the conversation, as the media debate on *Are Danes Racist?* demonstrates with great clarity.

The debate, as mentioned, is indicative of what we argue is a shift from a culture of racial silence toward new forms of racial engagement in Denmark. We conceptualize this shift in terms of racial "turns" and "returns" in order to underline the variegated processes at play in these debates, where established and well-known dynamics around race and racism turn up and get turned around in different ways with different results and by different actors. It is precisely the co-existence of repetition and renewal that we seek to draw attention to by tracking the ways in which racism is understood and discussed in Danish media. The delegitimation of and resistance to research on racism in Denmark bear structural similarities to the different upsurges of "anti-anti-racism" in the United Kingdom and the United States over the last decades (Bonnett, 2005). Focusing on different moments of backlash against racial equity across the 1980s and 1990s in the United Kingdom, Bonnett discusses a recurring pattern of instrumental media interventions aimed at construing anti-racism as "a superficial and discrete political agenda that can be humiliated or defeated" (Bonnett, 2005, p. 148). These interventions have had the effect of "establishing a cliché or [stereotypical] image that subverts the possibility of establishing [a] less parochial and more informed debate on the topic" of anti-racism (Bonnett, 2005, p. 149). The resistance to research on racism in the Danish cases we analyze can similarly be said to have worked against the development of more nuanced debates and discussions on the topic. Yet, the Danish cases do not mirror the narrative of backlash that frames Bonnett's analyses of "anti-anti-racism" in the United Kingdom in the 1980s and 1990s. Given the long-standing silence and ignorance surrounding the politics of race and racism in Denmark, the opposition to research on racism does not appear in response to a large-scale, progressive anti-racist movement, as in the United Kingdom. Yet, even if Danish debaters have sought to produce such phantasmic images of anti-racist dominance, the intensified focus on racism in the media over the last five years has also seemed to generate if not an anti-racist movement, then at least new openings for minority voices who address the effects of racism in Denmark.

## RACIAL ENGAGEMENT: DEBATING *ARE DANES RACIST?*

"We are not racists in Denmark" (Ritzau, 2013), "You're Not Racist After All" (Kamil, 2013b), "The Myth of the Danish Racist" (Kamil, 2013a), "Pseudo-Research" (Jalving, 2013a), and "Confronting the 'Demonization of the Danes'" (Schjørring, 2013) are but a few of the headlines in the newspapers that announced the publication of the book *Are Danes Racist?* in mid-January 2013. The news of the book's main message were, however, already circulated in Danish media as far back as September 2012 when *Kristeligt Dagblad* published an article on the forthcoming book as well as a longer interview with Necef called "Scrub the Myth of the

Victimized Immigrant" (Søndergaard, 2012a, 2012b).[5] From the days around the book's publication on January 14 and until mid-March 2013, we have identified 34 articles that relate to the book and/or its authors.[6] While this may seem a limited number of articles, it should be noted that during 2012–2016, no other research-based books on immigration or racism in Denmark have received the same level of attention nor have they been received with such widespread positive reinforcement from mainstream media outlets. The closest example in terms of media attention would be the publication of *The Pitfalls of Multiculturalism: Blackout and Moralizing in Media, Research, and Politics* [Multikulturalismens fælder: Mørklægning og moralisme i medier, forskning og politik] in April 2016, a collection of texts edited by Necef and Torben Bech Dyrberg that can be seen as a follow-up to *Are Danes Racist?*

The media texts that we analyze in this chapter have been found through searches in Infomedia, a database that provides electronic full-text articles from all Danish newspapers and a number of other media platforms. The 34 articles span different genres, such as feature articles, editorials, interviews, book reviews, opinion pieces, op-eds, and one blog entry, and they constitute the immediate or first cluster of the book's reception. The vast majority of the articles were published in leading national newspapers with regional newspapers running shovelware and syndicated versions of these texts. Conservative and right-leaning newspapers such as *Jyllands-Posten*, *Berlingske Tidende*, and *Kristeligt Dagblad* carried the reporting leading up to the book's publication. All three newspapers offered lengthy interviews with Bech and Necef that were supported by editorials on racism that positively reinforced the book's results. Thus, as the conservative parts of the media rallied around the book's message, the leading liberal newspaper, *Politiken*, kept a low profile choosing not to publish any articles on the book, whereas the left-leaning *Information* published a number of articles and interviews with the authors (Dandanell, 2013a, 2013b; Information, 2013). Generally, the reception was dominated by white male pundits, journalists, and experts; racialized minority voices were largely absent from the unfolding debate on racism.

---

[5] Other positive references to the forthcoming publication at the time also included Ritzau (2012), Nørgaard (2012), and Støvring (2012).

[6] This is not an exhaustive account of all the articles referencing the case in Infomedia. We have not included peripheral front-page references, brief mentions, online versions of printed articles, and shovelware versions of previously published articles, the latter occurring especially in regional media outlets.

As indicated by the newspaper headlines above, a number of ideas about the book quickly came to organize the media coverage: first, Bech and Necef's argument, of how dominant research on race and racism is void of scientific evidence of the existence of racism on any grand scale in Denmark, was presented in the media as evidence of how the idea of "the racist Dane" is a myth. In the journalistic framing of the book's message, individual researchers were named and identified as symptoms of this mythmaking. Second, the book's takedown of individual researchers was claimed to expose a structural problem inherent to the field of so-called anti-racist research in which scholars working within this field are guilty of scientific dishonesty given that their anti-racist values and ideological paradigms prompt them to ignore, cover up, or alter their research data. And third, the book demonstrated how the proliferation of unfounded accusations of Danes as racist unjustly demonizes the Danish (white) population, victimizes minorities, and thereby actively contributes to the production of ethnic and social antagonisms. Hence, the ideologically motivated criticism of racism in Denmark constitutes a problem equal to, if not larger than, the marginal phenomenon of racism itself.

## A CALL TO ACTION: CREATING VILLAINS AND HEROES

A few days before *Are Danes Racist?* was published, *Jyllands-Posten*[7] ran a lengthy article featuring an interview with Bech and Necef titled "A Call to Action Against the Good Intentions of Researchers" (Bonde Broberg, 2013a). The article focused on the failings and shortcomings of Danish research on racism, and it came to organize much of the subsequent reception, as quotes from Bech and Necef were widely circulated and picked up by other media platforms. In the article, the authors strongly reject the validity of research that point to the existence of anti-Islamic[8] sentiments and neo-nationalism in Denmark, or as Bech puts it: "Researchers have written numerous texts on Danes as being terribly racist, but when we analyzed those texts we did not find any evidence" (Bonde Broberg, 2013a, p. 8). To illustrate the point about the lack of evidence, the article refers to how Bech and Necef have caught one researcher in miscalculating percentages in relation to discrimination and how another has tampered

---

[7] *Jyllands-Posten* published the much-discussed 12 cartoons of the Prophet Muhammad in September 2005, leading to five months of globalized conflict (Klausen, 2009).

[8] Anti-Islamic is the terminology used in the article (and not, e.g. anti-Muslim).

with citations. However, within the context of the published interview, Bech and Necef are never asked to name the researchers that presumably committed these mistakes/offenses nor the ones who label Danes "terribly racist". On the contrary, Bech and Necef's criticism of researchers is articulated in general and elusive terms. According to Necef it is the good intentions of these researchers that constitute a problem:

> Researchers want to be good humans and protect minorities against majority violations. And if you feel that both your heart and intellect are in the right place, then you become blind to things that do not fit with your starting point. You ignore honor killings, forced marriages and that some Muslim men resist that their women will have to join the labor market. In this way scholarship disappears and you become an ideologue. (Bonde Broberg, 2013a, pp. 8–9)

In this quote the researchers are construed as driven by affective investments in doing good and rescuing minorities, a drive that also has the grave consequence of making them guilty of ignoring murder, sexism, and social coercion. While this logic positions the researchers in question as ideological and political *because* of their affective investments, it simultaneously construes Bech and Necef as rational scholars who are able to articulate a scathing criticism without having to resort to mudslinging and scapegoating despite the fact that their criticism is clearly personalized. In response to a question of why the problems with research on racism have not been discussed before, Necef says:

> Some researchers live in a closed circle, where they write to one another and confirm each other in these theories. They preach for the redeemed [frelste], and they are not as careful with their footnotes or arguments because they assume that no one will question them. Moreover, they use words that create fear or anxiety. If you go against them, one risks to be scandalized as a racist with no sympathy and empathy for the oppressed minorities. (Necef quoted in Bonde Broberg, 2013a, p. 9)

The presentation of the field of racism research as a closed choir of "redeemed" individuals underlines the personalized nature of the criticism. The endemic problems with anti-racist research are thus explained with reference to a research cult(ure) comprised of a group of self-righteous hypocrites, who want to "be good humans" but in reality "create fear and anxiety" in society (Bonde Broberg, 2013a, p. 9).

In the context of *Jyllands-Posten*, this personalization is executed in a shorter article published in connection with the interview (Bonde Broberg, 2013b) in which two of the main targets of the book's criticism are named and invited to comment, namely, Peter Hervik and Rikke Andreassen.[9] The juxtaposition of the interview and the shorter article works to construe the "problem" as systemic and general while also tied to specific individuals. The journalistic identification of Hervik and Andreassen—which exempts Bech and Necef from the burden of naming names—provides flesh, bones, and a face to the problem of the "closed circle" of influential and hegemonic researchers. Hence, the personalization assembles an easily identifiable starting point from where to be critical of the hegemonic ideology thought to structure research on racism.

The naming and shaming of Hervik and Andreassen also worked to establish Bech and Necef as *the* authoritative voices on racism in Denmark, voices that were not afraid to speak up against a dominant paradigm of so-called anti-racist research. Furthermore, the authorization of Bech and Necef was closely tied to how the media latched on to representations that portrayed them as dissenting and minoritized researchers oppressed by Cultural Radicalism[10] or as the conservative commentator Kasper Støvring phrased it in the commentary "Civil Courage":

> A few dissidents exist, such as, among others, the sociologists Mehmet Necef and Henning Bech. In a new book they have pulled the rug out from under the scholarship produced at universities that for years and entirely unfounded has accused Danes of being racists. Luckily, the two sociologists already hold tenured positions. (Støvring, 2013)

The quotation construes Bech and Necef as exceptional scholars, who are not afraid to diverge from the hegemony of anti-racist research. Yet, the

---

[9] Peter Hervik and Rikke Andreassen were not the only scholars accused of unscientific misconduct in *Are Danes Racist?* In a front-page interview published in *Weekendavisen* (Vind, 2013), Henning Bech launched a scathing attack on Professor Jytte Klausen (Brandeis University) for connecting *Jyllands-Posten*'s Muhammad cartoons (published in 2005) with anti-Semitic iconography promoted by the Nazi regime.

[10] Cultural Radicalism is a translation of the Danish word "kulturradikalisme" that denotes a movement among Danish intellectuals that emerged in the 1870s. The heyday of Cultural Radicalism is often ascribed to the interwar period. The movement was revitalized during the 1960s and 1970s, and it is often associated with a politics of tolerance and anti-authoritarian views, for example, in relation to child rearing and sexuality. Historically, conservatives have perceived Cultural Radicalism as a form of cryptocommunism (Duelund, 2001).

quote also implies that if they were not already tenured, their opinions would prove to be an obstacle for tenure and promotion within the context of Danish academia. Bech and Necef are thus positioned as dissenting and brave scholars vulnerable to expulsion. However, the vulnerability articulated through Støvring's quote sticks to Bech and Necef's opinions and not their biographies; they have, after all, held privileged tenured positions as, respectively, professor and associate professor for many years. Thus, the articulation of Bech and Necef's opinions as dissenting, vulnerable, and under threat worked to cement a notion of the anti-racist paradigm as powerful and hegemonic in danger of restricting the academic freedom of speech. This personalized criticism of individual researchers became a stepping stone for journalists and commentators to call for the entire field of research on racism to be dismantled, as we will discuss in the following section.

## Dislodging the Concept of Racism

It is telling that, among the articles that constitute the immediate reception, we have found few examples of public support for the work of Hervik and Andreassen.[11] The wider communities of scholars working within related fields of anthropology, gender studies, media studies, and migration studies—including ourselves—remained conspicuously silent in regard to the personalized attacks on Hervik and Andreassen. These scholars may of course have harbored a diversity of opinions on Bech and Necef's criticism as well as Hervik and Andreassen's work, yet the overall passivity and silence was noteworthy. Even though the immediate reception primarily worked to delegitimize Hervik's and Andreassen's research under the auspice of scientific misconduct, a much broader process was under way, namely, the dismantling of racism as an analytic term and a relevant field of research.

---

[11] We have only been able to find a few examples such as Anna Rytter's (2013) op-ed, "We are all racists". At the time Rytter was a parliamentary candidate for the Red-Green Alliance. Her op-ed is critical of the broader reluctance to address racism in Danish society. Bech and Necef's book is briefly mentioned as carrying a message that suits the anti-immigration agenda of the Danish Peoples Party. For another example, see Jonas Christoffersen's (2013) blog post "Danes are racist...". Christoffersen, at the time executive director for Danish Institute of Human Rights, aligns himself with Bech and Necef's argument that racism by and large has been eradicated from Danish society, but he is critical of their argument concerning how society occasionally needs to act based on generalizations (in Danish, gennemsnitsbetragtninger).

Bech and Necef's conceptualization of the term racism is central in this regard. In the media, Bech and Necef were never asked to respond to the fact that their definition of racism differs dramatically from the definitions at play in the research they criticized. Bech and Necef merely claimed to be using *the* scientifically agreed upon meaning of racism: "The definition of racism is an unjust denigration in action or words to people who have a different race, ethnicity or culture" (Bech & Necef, 2013, pp. 11, 126–130; Bonde Brobjerg, 2013a, p. 9). This narrow definition boils the question of racism down to intentional acts of unreasonable behavior, which, in turn, reduces research on racism to the act of assessing whether an alleged racist expression can be proven to be unjust or not. Bech and Necef's use of this constricted definition enabled them to claim that many, if not most, of the practices and situations that were analyzed in terms of racism were never proven to be based on intentional "unjust denigration" of people with a different background. Instead, they argued that most of these acts could easily or, even better, be understood as "well-founded worries" of immigrant groups with a "well-deserved" bad reputation (Bonde Broberg, 2013a, p. 9; Schjørring, 2013). Bech and Necef did, in this way, never flat out deny the existence or gravity of racism; instead they questioned the lack of hard *evidence* of a situation being racism proper.

Importantly, few, if any, research texts analyzed by Bech and Necef in *Are Danes Racist?* operate with such a restricted and intentionalist definition of racism. Some of the research texts they analyze do not even use the term racism at all. In the book, Bech and Necef use the phrase "racism and the like" when discussing the analyses and "accusations" put forth by the so-called anti-racist researchers. This phrase functions as an umbrella for more than 30 terms that Bech and Necef suggest to operate relatively synonymously with racism in the research literature they analyze (including radically different concepts such as colonialism, culturalism, homogenizing, nationalism, discrimination, and populism) (Bech & Necef, 2013, pp. 10–11). Yet, the validity of the research literature is measured with reference to Bech and Necef's narrow definition of racism.

In the media debate, the fact that researchers such as Hervik and Andreassen operated with a radically different theoretical framework for analyzing racism than Bech and Necef's was never discussed.[12] Yet, this

---

[12] Information did include one article where researchers questioned Bech and Necef's definition of racism, but it focused on how their conceptualization related to the definition of racism in Danish jurisdiction (Dandanell, 2013b).

unmentioned conceptual and epistemological incompatibility was clearly relevant to their inability to find any valid "evidence" for racism in research texts operating with different theoretical frameworks (Jensen, 2014, p. 105). Given the opportunity to present their own restricted definition of racism as scientifically sound, commonsensical, and universal, Bech and Necef were able to claim that anti-racist researchers' use of "racism" was nothing but an ideological catchall phrase with little or no scientific value, except to function as an invective that unjustly "demonizes the Danes" (Bonde Broberg, 2013a, p. 9; Søndergaard, 2013, p. 2; Vind, 2013, p. 6).

## Anti-Racist Bullies: Abusing the Term Racism

In the days leading up to the publication of *Are Danes Racist?* three newspapers published editorials (*Berlingske Tidende*, 2013; *Jyllands-Posten*, 2013; *Kristeligt Dagblad*, 2013) promoting intentionalist definitions of racism akin to Bech and Necef's definition.[13] Similar to Bech and Necef, the editorials did not reject the existence of racism, but their narrow definition paved the way for the argument that the concept of racism has been abused. As the editorial in *Berlingske Tidende* put it: "[t]he word racism has, during the past decades, been abused to such an extent that it has become an empty concept that is used automatically and without consideration" (*Berlingske Tidende*, 2013, p. 2). These sentiments resonated with *Kristeligt Dagblad*'s editorial that was published on the same day: "The concept of racism has been used and abused to the extent that it has lost its independent force and in some instances it says more about the person using the word" (*Kristligt Dagblad*, 2013, p. 16). The framing of racism as an abused concept does not only work to reinstate a specific definition of racism, it also construes those who use the concept of racism "incorrectly" as abusers. Within this logic of abuse, it is not only the concept of racism that is cast as the object/victim of abuse but also the greater Danish population who is facing unfounded accusations of racism and xenophobia.

This line of thought was also pursued by a number of influential, white conservative commentators and journalists who used the publication of the book as a stepping stone to repudiate the entire field of research on

---

[13] To support their definitions of racism, the editorial in *Berlingske Tidende* (2013) referenced *The Danish Dictionary*, while the editorial in *Kristeligt Dagblad* (2013) referenced *The Great Danish Encyclopedia*, thus signaling that encyclopedic knowledge is authoritative and final.

racism (Beinov, 2013; Blüdnikow, 2013; Jalving, 2013a, 2013b; Wivel, 2013; Støvring, 2013). In an opinion piece, conservative pundit Mikael Jalving (2013a) made the argument that scholars of immigration[14] notoriously belong to the political left and that the field of immigration research in general is to be considered "pseudoscience", as the title of his opinion piece phrased it. A few weeks later, the notion of fraudulent research was echoed in a longer piece by the conservative journalist Klaus Wivel (2013) in *Weekendavisen*:

> With such a lethal criticism [i.e. in Bech and Necef's book] of twenty years of Danish research on racism overseen by the central administration and universities alike one should think that secretaries of state, department chairs, and others would demand the entire field turned upside down. When Milena Penkowa was accused of fraud we saw how expensive investigative committees were appointed. (Wivel, 2013, p. 4)

In this passage Wivel seems to call for the entire field of critical race studies to be investigated, and he invokes the high-profile case of the lauded neuroscientist Milena Penkowa, who was suspended from her professorship at University of Copenhagen in 2010. The Penkowa case unfolded over several years, and it saw her convicted of fraudulent conversion and forgery in relation to her research.[15] In 2012, the Danish Committees on Scientific Dishonesty found her guilty of deliberate scientific malpractice. Wivel's invocation of the Penkowa case works to arouse suspicion (of criminal acts), but it also produces a notion of double standards and conspiracy; if Penkowa was investigated and subsequently stripped of all titles and honors, then why not researchers on racism? The idea that Bech and Necef's criticism should prompt the Danish authorities to launch a formal investigation of critical race studies forecloses any attempts to understand the debate as an epistemological struggle. Instead the distribution of suspicion and the call for an investigation effectively feed into the idea that those scholars, who have used racism "incorrectly", could very well be guilty of scientific malpractice, if not a crime.

This reductive reconfiguration and displacement of racism from an analytic category to an abused concept worked to delegitimize not only the

---

[14] Immigration research is a direct translation of Jalving's use of "indvandrerforskningen", an outdated term which is no longer used within the context of Danish academia.

[15] For a summary of the Penkowa case, see University of Copenhagen's updated summary of the case: http://nyheder.ku.dk/penkowa (Last accessed January 1, 2017).

researchers in question—Hervik and Andreassen—but any researcher that used or wanted to use racism as a critical analytic. By presenting anti-racist research in Denmark as a form of bullying of the Danes, Bech and Necef's intervention effectively dislodged racism from its function as an analytic of power, structures, institutions, and history; instead it became framed as a divisive concept used against the Danish majority population.

## Resurrecting Denmark as a Tolerant Nation

Bech and Necef's central claim that unfair accusations of racism are just as harmful as racism itself demonstrates the larger stakes in the search of a "scientific" answer to the question "are Danes racist?"[16] The logic at play implies that if Danes cannot be proven to be racist, then so-called anti-racist researchers are guilty of an act analogous to racism proper: demonizing an "innocent" population. This notion of "unjust demonization" came to organize the initial reporting on the book's publication, and it was intimately connected to the discourse of Denmark as an open and tolerant society in need of immigration-skeptical politics. A lengthy feature article published in *Berlingske Tidende* (Kamil, 2013a) illustrates how the argument about demonization was accentuated and brought forward. The article opens with quotes from Erik Meier Carlsen, a conservative commentator and journalist, who aligns himself with the view that Danes are not racist. According to Meier Carlsen, "somebody has nurtured a political interest in confusing concern about immigration with racist convictions: However, international research shows that Danes are at the top when it comes to tolerance" (Kamil, 2013a, p. 6). According to Meier Carlsen's argument, concern about immigration must not be conflated with lack of tolerance or racist convictions. It is quite the opposite. Meier Carlsen suggests that the intensified critique of immigration that unfolded through the 1990s[17] actually worked to *strengthen* tolerance in Denmark: "It was a purification. The harshness of the debates has mellowed the population" (Kamil, 2013a). This cleaving of (harsh) immigration-skeptical debates from racism was echoed by other commentators, such as

[16] In *Are Danes Racist?* Bech and Necef position the act of unjustly calling someone a racist as analogous to racism proper. According to Bech and Necef, it is "*just as* [emphasis added] unwise to in advance demonize the old-danes as racist, xenophobic and islamophobic" as it is to "talk about immigrants and refugees, as if they are retarded and criminal" (p. 12).

[17] For an analysis of the debates on immigration in the 1990s and early 2000s, see Hervik (2011).

the conservative editor Jesper Beinov. In an opinion piece, also published in *Berlingske Tidende*, Beinov argued that prior to 2000, it was falsely believed that those who called for stricter regulation of migration were driven by "wicked motives", and he gives thanks to Bech and Necef for dismantling this type of "demonization" (Beinov, 2013). Beinov's opinion piece, entitled "The Hospitable Denmark", ends with the conclusion that Danes are open people.[18]

The opinion of Meier Carlsen and the writing of Beinov serve as examples of a dominant discourse in which immigration-skeptical sentiments are separated and isolated from the question of racism. This logic upholds the notion of Denmark as an open and tolerant (non-racist) society or, as Meier Carlsen suggests, a tolerance which has only been purified and enhanced through the unleashing of immigration-skeptical debates. Yet the discursive cleaving also secures the framework which posits a tolerant white majority population as victims and so-called anti-racist researchers as ideologues who contribute to polarization and radicalization of the public sphere.

In the years following the debate on *Are Danes Racist?*, the argument of anti-racist researchers as bullies that threaten the cohesion of Danish public culture has been reiterated numerous times in different versions (Esholdt, 2015; Hauge, 2014a, 2014b; Rebensdorff, 2015; Villemoes, 2015). An elaborate continuation of this discourse can be found in the book *The Decent Ones* [*De anstændige*], published by Jens-Martin Eriksen and Frederik Stjernfelt in the late summer of 2013. In the chapter "Filtering of Information", they write at length about Bech and Necef's important "exposition of the filter of decency" that anti-racist researchers, such as Hervik, deploy in order to retain their so-called multicultural world view (Eriksen & Stjernfelt, 2013, pp. 264, 266). According to Eriksen and Stjernfelt, this group of researchers—labeled the Decent Ones—do not shy away from falsifying and fabricating quotes and facts in order to make it fit their value system properly. This alleged filtering of information has grave consequences. Besides spreading lies about Denmark nationally and internationally, the Decent Ones also work to "to pit social groups against each other" (Eriksen & Stjernfelt, 2013, p. 267): "The bottom line seems to be that the Decent Ones, who in their own self-understanding are angels, so morally superior in relation to

---

[18] According to Beinov this point is scientifically proven, but there is no reference to the studies/researchers in question.

their opponents, in reality more than anyone contribute to the splitting up of society" (Eriksen & Stjernfelt, 2013, p. 271).

One of the most recent attempts to present anti-racist scholars as polarizing and destabilizing figures can be found in the anthology *The Pitfalls of Multiculturalism* (Necef & Dyrberg, 2016). In many of the book's chapters, multiculturalism is operationalized as a sweeping term that groups together a variety of journalists, scholars, artists, and politicians that have been critical of racism in Denmark and the strict Danish immigration politics. These critical positions are framed as politically correct and left wing, informed by a problematic identity politics and Cultural Radicalism. In the book's introduction, Dyrberg and Necef argue that democracy, and not least the fundamental right to freedom of speech, is under threat from this ideology of multiculturalism. They proceed to ask the questions:

> Could it be that the most prolific threat to democracy does not originate from violent and extremist Islamists? Maybe it originates from those who applaud freedom rights and who appear as tolerant, humane and forthcoming, but whom, at the end of the day, cannot and dare not defend these rights and instead are busy criticizing those who insist on exercising these rights for being right wing and callous freedom-of-speech-fundamentalists. (Dyrberg & Necef, 2016, p. 11)

As seen in this quote, the so-called multiculturalists (a category resembling Eriksen and Stjernfelt's use of the "Decent Ones") are construed as the biggest threat to liberal democracies in this moment of time. The severity of the threat is exacerbated through the comparison with the threat from Islamist extremism. Furthermore, Dyrberg and Necef argue that the ideology of multiculturalism represents a form of soft totalitarianism that implies "control of the mind, conformity, blacklisting of problems not deemed 'politically correct', and moralism" (Dyrberg & Necef, 2016, p. 16). The chapters of the anthology thus seek to build a case against "multiculturalists" and how they have actively silenced and ignored problems related to immigration and migrants (Dyrberg, 2016; Eriksen, 2016) and/or demonized and excluded scholars with diverging opinions (Esholdt, 2016; Mørck, Danneskiold-Samsøe, & Sørensen, 2016).

While *The Pitfalls of Multiculturalism* thus builds on the frameworks propagated by *Are Danes Racist?* and *The Decent Ones*, it intensifies this criticism through the accusation of anti-racist totalitarianism and the danger it poses to democracy. It is also worth noting that one of the significant aspects about this intervention is how it works to invoke this political stance as relevant for a broader political landscape. Even though Necef and Dyrberg primarily criticize what could be called radical left-wing positions, they are eager to stress that the problems should not be understood within a traditional right-wing/left-wing framework. Instead they argue that criticism of multiculturalism is also of importance for the liberal parts of the left-wing spectrum. Over the last five years, this interpretive framework that positions so-called anti-racist research and critique as a new form of racism can be found across the spectrum of political positions in media debates.

## RECALIBRATIONS OF RACIAL EXCEPTIONALISM

Anti-racist research has rarely been the subject of serious scholarship. As Bonnett notes, anti-racist work has often been seen "fit only for platitudes of support or denouncement" (Bonnett, 2005, p. 2). Bech and Necef's book could be seen as an attempt to counter this tendency with its intention of delivering a critical examination of research they call "anti-racist". But Bech and Necef's use of "anti-racist research" as an imprecise umbrella term in their critique of a broad spectrum of researchers with different theoretical and conceptual repertoires worked against such an aim. Their lacking attention to the difficulty or even "impossibility of speaking of anti-racism as a unity or unproblematic phenomenon", to borrow Alana Lentin's words (Lentin, 2004, p. 6), is central in this regard. Instead of creating a framework for nuanced discussions, the debate generated by the book created yet new opportunities for denouncing platitudes about this type of research, platitudes that now were seen to be given a scientific legitimacy. Thus, the debate emerging in the wake of *Are Danes Racist?* reads less as a criticism of a specific *body* of research in the spirit of academic debate—although this is what Bech and Necef claimed to be doing—and more as an attempt to disqualify specific *traditions* of research and their conceptualizations of racism.

Significantly, recognition of racism does not disappear from this debate. Bech and Necef, as well as most of the commentators, are not denying that racism might occur in Denmark. But their circumscribed definition of racism works to mobilize a demand to distinguish between "real racism" and "pseudo-racism" and, in extension of that, between "real researchers" and "pseudo-researchers". This call to clean up the field is central to the ways in which racism as a concept gets dislodged from operating as an analytic to appear as a form of bullying of—or direct threat to—Danish society. This discursive figuration of anti-racist critics as catering to hatred and social destabilization set the tone for the debates that were to follow in the winter and spring of 2014, when critics of color voiced opposition to structural racism.

The racism debates between 2012 and 2016 ought to be seen in relation to a longer process of what Hervik has discussed as the "emergence of Danish neonationalism, neoracism and populism in the Post-1989 world" (Hervik, 2011), including the 2001 election of the Anders Fogh Rasmussen government and the cartoon crisis in 2005–2006. While the racial turn suggests a shift from an investment in color-blindness to one of increasing racial engagement, this move should not be seen as a *break with* but rather as a *recalibration of* the established configuration of Danish racial exceptionalism. One of the most striking elements of the 2013 debate is not the large-scale rejections of the alleged claim that "Denmark is racist". Rather, the importance of this debate—and the ways in which it can be said to recalibrate racial exceptionalism—lies in how it sets the stage for a larger claim for the political urgency of dismantling Danish research on racism. The debate was marked by a widespread recognition of the existence of racism as a marginal, contained, controllable, and intentional phenomena, and of anti-racist research and knowledge production as a destructible, oppressive force that has gone too far. According to this framework, what needs to be kept on a tight rein is no longer racism as such but anti-racist researchers with their epistemological framework that wrongly demonizes the Danes by calling them racist.

## References

Andreassen, R., Folke Henningsen, A., & Myong, L. (2008). Indledning [Introduction]. *Kvinder, Køn og Forskning, 3*, 3–8.

Andreassen, R., & Vitus, K. (2015). *Affectivity and Race. Studies from Nordic Contexts*. London & New York: Routledge.

Bech, H., & Necef, M. U. (2013). *Er danskerne racister? Indvandrerforskningens problemer [Are Danes Racist? The Problem of Immigration Research]*. Frederiksberg: Frydenlund.

Beinov, J. (2013, January 15). Det gæstfri Danmark [The Hospitable Denmark]. *Berlingske Tidende*, 26.

Berlingske Tidende. (2013, January 11). Racisme [Racism]. *Berlingske Tidende*, 3.

Blaagaard, B., & Andreassen, R. (2012). Disappearing Acts: The Forgotten History of Colonialism, Eugenics and Gendered Othering in Denmark. In B. Hiplf & K. Lofstdóttir (Eds.), *Teaching 'Race' with a Gendered Edge* (pp. 81–95). Utrecht & Budapest: ATGENDER.

Blüdnikow, B. (2013, January 21). Tavshedens rige [The Kingdom of Silence]. *Berlingske Tidende*, 21.

Bonde Broberg, M. (2013a, January 8–9). Til kamp mod forskernes gode viljer [A Call to Action Against the Good Intentions of Researchers]. *Jyllands-Posten*, 8–9.

Bonde Broberg, M. (2013b, January 11). Ny bog møder modstand [New Book Meets Resistance]. *Jyllands-Posten*, 9.

Bonnett, A. (2005). *Anti-Racism*. New York and London: Routledge.

Browning, C. (2007). Branding Nordicity: Models, Identity, and the Decline of Exceptionalism. *Cooperation and Conflict, 42*(1), 27–51. https://doi.org/10.1177/0010836707073475

Christoffersen, J. (2013). Danskerne er racister [Danes Are Racists]. Retrieved from http://www.menneskeret.dk/nyheder/blog-danskerne-racister

Danbolt, M. (2016). New Nordic Exceptionalism: Jeuno JE Kim and Eva Einhorn's *The United Nations of Norden* and Other Realist Utopias. *Journal of Aesthetic and Culture, 8*(1). https://doi.org/10.3402/jac.v8.30902

Danbolt, M. (2017). Retro Racism: Colonial Ignorance and Racialized Affective Consumption in Danish Public Culture. *Nordic Journal of Migration Research, 7*(2), 105–113. https://doi.org/10.1515/njmr-2017-0013.

Dandanell, N. (2013a, January 12). Ny bog: Kun intellektuelle kan være racister [New Book: Only Intellectuals Can Be Racists]. *Information*, 3.

Dandanell, N. (2013b, January 16). Kan negative stereotyper også være racisme? [Do Negative Stereotypes Also Count As Racism?]. *Information*, 7.

Duelund, P. (2001). Cultural Policy in Denmark. *The Journal of Arts Management, Law, and Society, 31*(1), 34–56.

Dyrberg, T. B. (2016). Venstrefløjens selektive og moraliserende tolerance [The Left Wing's Selective and Moralizing Tolerance]. In M. U. Necef & T. B. Dyrberg (Eds.), *Multikulturalismens fælder. Mørklægning og moralisme i medier, forskning og politik [The Pitfalls of Multiculturalism: Blackout and Moralizing in Media, Research, and Politics]* (pp. 165–185). Frederiksberg: Samfundslitteratur.

Dyrberg, T. B., & Necef, M. U. (2016). Kritiske fortolkninger af multikultural-isme og racisme [Critical Interpretations of Multiculturalism and Racism]. In M. U. Necef & T. B. Dyrberg (Eds.), *Multikulturalismens fælder. Mørklægning og moralisme i medier, forskning og politik [The Pitfalls of Multiculturalism: Blackout and Moralizing in Media, Research, and Politics]* (pp. 9–35). Frederiksberg: Samfundslitteratur.

Eriksen, J.-M. (2016). Er indvandrere racister? [Are Immigrants Racist?]. In M. U. Necef & T. B. Dyrberg (Eds.), *Multikulturalismens fælder. Mørklægning og moralisme i medier, forskning og politik [The Pitfalls of Multiculturalism: Blackout and Moralizing in Media, Research, and Politics]* (pp. 131–146). Frederiksberg: Samfundslitteratur.

Eriksen, J.-M., & Stjernfelt, F. (2013). *De anstændige [The Decent Ones].* Copenhagen: Gyldendal.

Esholdt, H. F. (2015). *Når humor, leg og lyst er på spil: Social interaktion på en multietnisk arbejdsplads [When Humor, Play and Desire is at Play: Social Interaction on a Multi Ethnic Workplace].* Ph.D. dissertation, Lunds University, Lund, Sweden.

Esholdt, H. F. (2016). Styres forskningen af frygten for at blive kaldt racist? praksisnære overvejelser [Are Research Controlled By the Fear of Being Called Racist? Praxis-Oriented Considerations]. In M. U. Necef & T. B. Dyrberg (Eds.), *Multikulturalismens fælder—mørklægning og moralisme i medier, forskning og politik* (pp. 189–206). Frederiksberg: Samfundslitteratur.

Goldberg, D. T. (2006). Racial Europeanization. *Ethnic and Racial Studies, 29*(2), 331–364. https://doi.org/10.1080/01419870500465611.

Gullestad, M. (2005). Normalising Racial Boundaries. The Norwegian Dispute about the Term *Neger. Social Anthropology, 13*(1), 27–46. https://doi.org/10.1111/j.1469-8676.2005.tb00118.x

Habel, Y. (2012). Challenging Swedish Exceptionalism? Teaching While Black. In K. Freeman & E. Johnson (Eds.), *Education in the Black Diaspora: Perspectives, Challenges, and Prospects* (pp. 99–122). New York and London: Routledge.

Hauge, H. (2014a, March 10). Strukturel racisme [Structural Racism]. *Berlingske Tidende,* 22.

Hauge, H. (2014b, April 3). Antiracisternes hærgen [Antiracists Causing Havoc]. *Berlingske Tidende,* 26.

Hervik, P. (2011). *The Annoying Difference: The Emergence of Danish Neonationalism, Neoracism, and Populism in the Post-1989 World.* New York and Oxford: Berghahn Books.

Hervik, P., & Jørgensen, R. E. (2002). Danske benægtelser af racisme [Danish Denials of Racism]. *Sociologi i dag, 32*(4), 83–102.

Hübinette, T. (2014). Racial Stereotypes and Swedish Antiracism: A Swedish Crisis of Multiculturalism? In *Crisis in Nordic Nations and Beyond* (pp. 69–85). Surrey & Burlington: Ashgate.

Information. (2013, January 19). Læserne spørger: HenningBech [Readers' Questions: Henning Bech]. *Information.* Retrieved from https://www.information.dk/moti/2013/01/laeserne-spoerger-henning-bech

Jalving, M. (2013a, January 13). Pseudoforskning [Pseudo-Research]. *Jyllands-posten,* 28.

Jalving, M. (2013b, February 3). Eliterne og lilleputfolket [The Elites and the Lilliput People]. *Jyllands-Posten*, 30.

Jensen, S. Q. (2014). Kritik af dansk racismeforskning—og kritik af kritikken [Criticism of Danish Research on Racism—and Critique of the Critique]. *Dansk sociologi, 25*(1), 103–110.

Jyllands-Posten. (2013, January 12). Linguistic Poison [Sproglig Gift]. *Jyllands-Posten*, 20.

Kamil, C. (2013a, January 11). Myten om den racistiske dansker [The Myth of the Racist Dane]. *Berlingske Tidende*, 6–7.

Kamil, C. (2013b, January 11). Du er ikke racist alligevel [You're Not Racist After All]. *Berlingske Tidende*, 1.

Klausen, J. (2009). *The Cartoons that Shook the World*. New Haven, CT: Yale University Press.

Kristeligt Dagblad. (2013, January 12). Racismeforskning kræver omhu [Editorial: Research on Racism Should be Done with Due Care]. *Kristeligt Dagblad*, 16.

Lentin, A. (2004). *Racism and Anti-Racism in Europe*. London and Ann Arbor: Pluto Press.

Loftsdóttir, K., & Jensen, L. (Eds.). (2012). *Whiteness and Postcolonialism in the Nordic Region: Exceptionalism, Migrant Others and National Identities*. Farnam: Ashgate.

Mørck, Y., Danneskiold-Samsøe, S., & Sørensen, B. W. (2016). Æresrelateret vold som kulturaliserende diskurs? kritik af en udbredt forskningstilgang [Honour Violence as a Culturalizing Discourse? Criticism of a Widespread Research Approach]. In M. U. Necef & T. B. Dyrberg (Eds.), *Multikulturalismens fælder. Mørklægning og moralisme i medier, forskning og politik [The Pitfalls of Multiculturalism: Blackout and Moralizing in Media, Research, and Politics]* (pp. 245–272). Samfundslitteratur: Frederiksberg.

Mulinari, D., Keskinen, S., Irni, S., & Tuori, S. (2009). Introduction: Postcolonialism and the Nordic Models of Welfare and Gender. In S. Keskinen, S. Tuori, S. Irni, & D. Mulinari (Eds.), *Complying with Colonialism: Gender, Race and Ethnicity in the Nordic Region* (pp. 1–16). Burlington: Ashgate.

Myong, L. (2009). *Adopteret: Fortællinger om transnational og racialiseret tilblivelse [Becoming Adoptee. On Transnational and Racialized Subjectification]*. Ph.D. dissertation, Aarhus University, Copenhagen.

Myong, L. (2014, December 15). Frihedens racistiske præmis [The Racist Premise of Freedom]. Peculiar.dk. Retrieved from http://peculiar.dk/frihedens-racistiske-praemis

Necef, M. Ü., & Dyrberg, T. B. (Eds.). (2016). *Multikulturalismens fælder. Mørklægning og moralisme i medier, forskning og politik [The Pitfalls of Multiculturalism: Blackout and Moralizing in Media, Research, and Politics]*. Frederiksberg: Samfundslitteratur.

Nørgaard, L. (2012, September 5). En forsker fremturer. Når virkeligheden lader sig forme [A Researcher Insists: When Reality Is Manipulated]. *Kristeligt Dagblad*, 11.

Rastas, A. (2012). Reading History through Finnish Exceptionalism. In K. Loftsdóttir & L. Jensen (Eds.), *Whiteness and Postcolonialism in the Nordic Region: Exceptionalism, Migrant Others and National Identities* (pp. 89–104). Farnham: Ashgate.

Rebensdorff, J. (2015, February 2). 'Perker' kan være kærligt ment [Saying 'Paki' Can Be Affectionately Intended]. *Berlingske Tidende*, 9.

Ritzau. (2012, August 31). Forskere fremstiller indvandrere som ofre [Researchers Portray Immigrants as Victims]. DR. Retrieved from http://www.dr.dk/Nyheder/Politik/2012/08/31/0831234053.htm

Ritzau. (2013, January 10). Ny Bog: Danskere meget lidt racistiske [New Book: Danes Are Rarely Racist]. *Ritzau*.

Rytter, A. (2013, January 15). Vi er alle racister [We Are All Racists]. *Information*, 18–19.

Schjørring, E. (2013, January 11). Opgør med dæmoniseringen af danskerne [Confronting the Demonization of the Danes]. *Berlingske Tidende*, 27.

Søndergaard, B. (2012a, September 1). Drop myten om de stakkels indvandrere [Scrub the Myth of the Victimized Immigrant]. *Kristeligt Dagblad*, 2.

Søndergaard, B. (2012b, September 1). Ny bog: Indvandrerforskningen har gjort nydanskere til sagesløseofre [New Book: Immigration Research Has Turned New-Danes into Innocent Victims]. *Kristeligt Dagblad*, 1.

Søndergaard, B. (2013, January 12). Sociologer hudfletter indvandrerforskning [Sociologists Castigates Immigrant Research]. *Kristligt Dagblad*, 2.

Støvring, K. (2012, September 4). Når indvandrere siger sandheden om forfejlet integration [When Immigrants Speak the Truth about Unsuccessful Integration]. Retrieved from http://kulturkamp.blogs.berlingske.dk/2012/09/04/nar-indvandrere-siger-sandheden-om-forfejlet-integration

Støvring, K. (2013, February 22). Debat: Civilcourage [Debate: Civil Courage]. *Berlingske Tidende*, 31.

Villemoes, S. (2015, February 13). Sort-hvid forskning [Black-White Research]. *Weekendavisen*, 7.

Vind, J. (2013, January 11). Når man prædiker for de frelste [Preaching to the Choir]. *Weekendavisen*, 1, 6.

Vuorela, U. (2009). Colonial Complicity: The "Postcolonial" in a Nordic Context. In S. Keskinen, S. Tuori, S. Irni, & D. Mulinari (Eds.), *Complying with Colonialism: Gender, Race and Ethnicity in the Nordic Region* (pp. 19–34). Burlington: Ashgate.

Wivel, K. (2013, January 25). Mavefornemmelser [Gut Feelings]. *Weekendavisen*, 4.

# CHAPTER 3

# Politics of Fear and Racialized Rape: Intersectional Reading of the Kempele Rape Case

*Tuija Saresma*

## RAPING WHITE WOMEN

On November 24, 2015, accusations were broadcast in the Finnish media that a suspected rape of a young girl by two refugees based at a newly established immigration detention center had occurred in the small town of Kempele in Northern Ostrobothnia. Two young men "with a foreigner background" were blamed for raping a 14-year-old girl. Immediately after the news about the suspected rape was released, a huge media panic erupted concerning the safety of Finnish girls and women. It was claimed that no female was safe since "floods of asylum seekers" (allegedly all men) are occupying the country and raping whomever they encounter in the streets of even the smallest, formerly peaceful villages.

Soon, one of the two suspects—both 17-year-old boys—was released because he had not even been near the crime scene. The other was found to have known the raped girl before the rape took place. Nevertheless, the

T. Saresma (✉)
University of Jyväskylä, Jyväskylä, Finland
e-mail: tuija.saresma@jyu.fi

P. Hervik (ed.), *Racialization, Racism, and Anti-Racism in the Nordic Countries*, Approaches to Social Inequality and Difference, https://doi.org/10.1007/978-3-319-74630-2_3

huge media excitement continued, blaming the refugees and also accusing politicians of irresponsibility for allowing the "flows of refugees" to come to Finland via northern Sweden.

Much of the anxiety, hatred, and fear felt toward asylum seekers as racialized others that had been aroused and incited during the summer and autumn of "the refugee crisis" of 2015 crystallized in the Kempele rape case. It is an extremely illuminating example of how race and ethnicity intertwine with gender in contemporary media discussions that take place in both the traditional and social media (Keskinen, 2013; Lähdesmäki & Saresma, 2016). Yet, the trope of the immigrant rape does not come out of nowhere. It has a long history. Discourse on "immigrant rape" prevails in the Nordic countries, as Karina Horsti (2016) suggests. She has traced the trope to Fjordman's blog on December 12, 2005, where the blogger claims that "many of the Muslims in Europe view themselves as a conquering army and that European women are simply war booty," and Atlas Shrugs's blogging on December 15, 2005, which claims that "Muslim violence infects, spreads across continents."

In Finland, former member of the Finnish Parliament (currently MEP) Jussi Halla-aho wrote in his blog—characterized by anti-immigration-minded opinions as well as explicit Islamophobia, homophobia, and misogyny—on December 20, 2006:

> There will be a significant increase in the number of rapes [due to immigration]. As more and more women will be raped, I ardently hope that the *right* women are raped. The green-leftist do-gooders and their voters. Rather them than anybody else. Nothing else works on them but that multiculturalism hits them.

Halla-aho thus claimed that multiculturalism and immigration will evidently lead to more rape. He is thus an advocate of the "rape culture" that refers to "a social reality where it is assumed that sexual violence is a fact of life, inevitable as death and taxes" (Ferreday, 2015, p. 22, as cited in Herman, 1984). What is noteworthy is that he hopes this "rape wave" will turn against the leftist defenders of multiculturalism. In his blog, the politician actually reveals his wish that some women, "the right women," are raped.

Since then, the aggressive, racialized discussion about rape has nothing but strengthened in the Nordic mediascape. The contemporary media buzz about the recurrent discursive trope of "Muslim rape" is only the tip of the iceberg. Rape has been and is constantly used for both racist and misogynous propagandas. Suvi Keskinen (2013, pp. 225–226) suggests that:

> ...constructions of political antagonisms are the result of an intertwining of two kinds of anxieties related to societal changes in the current Nordic countries—anxieties over the future of the "white nation" fantasy and changing gender and sexual relations.

Due to these anxieties, "articulations of multiculturalism, feminism, and race are intertwined in the more mainstream discourses" (Keskinen, 2013). Based on Horsti's and Keskinen's ideas, my hypothesis is that the talk about immigrant rape has two discursive aims. On the one hand, rape as a threat and a violent physical act targeted at women is a powerful means to show women who "really" rules and a way to keep women in their place. On the other hand, however, in contemporary multicultural societies, rape talk in the media is also used to achieve racist goals, such as inciting xenophobia. This is nothing new, as Richard Dyer (1997, p. 26) points out: the motif of (non-white) rape in white race fiction commonly "displaces attention from the routinised misuse of non-white women by white men" and "threatens white men's control over their property" as their women as chattels and menaces white reproduction. Interracial rape is also "represented as bestiality storming the citadel of civilization."

In this chapter I analyze the dual functions of racialized and gendered rape speech: it simultaneously poses a threat to and promises to "protect" (white) women.[1] My aim is to show that racism and racialization are intertwined with sexism and misogyny. Besides analyzing the media discourse on racialized rape, I ask how Islamophobia and xenophobia are promoted by linking a certain racialized ethnic background and rape in the media. I also wish to add to the understanding of the workings of repressive ideologies by analyzing the relationship between racialization and both misogyny and sexism. I seek to do this by using intersectionality as my methodological tool.

In analyzing the dual functions of the media panic about a case of racialized rape, I take rape as a "particularly versatile narrative element" that "often addresses any number of social themes and issues" (Ferreday, 2015,

[1] This work was supported by the Academy of Finland under Grants SA21000019101 and 309550 (Populism as movement and rhetoric and Mainstreaming Populism) and by Kone Foundation (projects Arts of Belonging and Intersecting Mobilities).

p. 21, citing Sarah Pjojansky). Here, my aim is to show that in these discussions, racialization functions first in constructing the racialized "other" as the enemy of the seemingly nonracial (white) "us," and second, it intersects inextricably with gendering both "us" and "others" in a way that positions the members of the "unmarked categories" of whiteness and maleness at the top of the power hierarchy (Choo & Marx Ferree, 2010). These intersectional power hierarchies are seen especially through the victims' gendered (females as victims that need protection) and aged (young girls in need of special protection) position.

Besides analyzing the construction of intersectional power hierarchies, I look at the rhetoric of the media texts, which utilizes the image of Finland as a nation at war, for example, in the article "Framing the War Against Terrorism" (Ryan, 2004). What interests me especially is the affective logic of the rhetoric, and how the *economy of fear* (Ahmed, 2004) is utilized and the *politics of fear* (Wodak, 2015) is exploited in the wider context of the *culture of fear* (Chomsky, 1996, citing Gleisejes, who states that "peace and order were guaranteed by ferocious repression") in using the trope of "immigrant rape" as a means to control women and to feed the nationalist, racist ideologies of right-wing populists. Thus, I suggest that despite the explicit message of both politicians and online debaters, the trope of immigrant rape is used more to threaten than to "protect" Nordic women.

## Gendered Violence, Racialized Rape, and the Affective Politics of Fear

It is mostly women that are the victims of sexual violence. Sexual violence takes place in all societies (WHO, 2013). However, there is a long history of white men mistreating "their" (allegedly subservient) women, be they their wives, servants, or slaves. Thus, the (ancient) gender order that places the man at the top of the family and society is based on the question of ownership (Saresma, 2017c).

Finland has a reputation of being a state where gender equality is a commonly shared value and where women's position in society has been more equal in terms of education, employment, and wage level than elsewhere across Europe (Norocel, Saresma, Lähdesmäki, & Ruotsalainen, 2017). Yet, the level of violence against women in Finland has traditionally been one of the highest in Europe. In a large survey conducted by the EU

2014, only Danish women were more likely to encounter physical or sexual violence (HS, 2014). The prevalence of gendered violence against Finnish women by Finnish men has, however, been quite a taboo. The discussion on sexual violence burst in the media in the aftermath of the so-called refugee crisis of 2015, during which Finland, a relatively ethnically (and racially) homogeneous country until then, received 32,000 asylum seekers in a couple of months, whereas earlier Finland had received approximately only 3000 refugees yearly. Citing chief secretary of the Home Office Päivi Nerg (2017), establishing almost 200 reception centers around Finland was a shock, especially to the inhabitants of small villages that had never hosted any foreigners before the sudden encounter with "young men from Iraq."

Against this backdrop, it is perhaps no wonder that the rise of the right-wing populism across Europe gained ground and prominence in Finland as well. The media and the politicians soon adopted the discourse of the "immigration critical" far-right fragment of populist Finns Party (Saresma, 2017a; Ruotsalainen & Saresma, 2017) that draws from xenophobia and anti-feminism in legitimating Islamophobia (Saresma, 2017d). Simultaneously, the Nordic gender equality ideals are harnessed for the same cause; despite the generally shared understanding and discourse of Nordic gender equality (Lähdesmäki & Saresma, 2014), a certain backlash can be sensed in the contemporary opinion climate that seems to be yearning for the allegedly lost gender order (Saresma, 2014a, 2017c). It can also be interpreted as a part of a broader change in the public opinion; for example, Suvi Keskinen (2013, p. 226) finds the backlash argument simplified and suggests that the question is more about reimagining both whiteness and masculinity in a changing societal setting. I agree with her and thus focus on not only gender but the intersections of gender, race, and sexuality (see also Lähdesmäki & Saresma, 2014a, 2014b; Saresma, 2012, 2014a, 2017b).

Traces of the attitude atmosphere that support backlash and anti-multiculturalism can be observed in sexist attitudes. Sexism, by definition, usually refers to "a historically and globally pervasive form of oppression against women" (Cudd & Jones, 2005). Rosalind Gill (2011, p. 67) calls for a revitalization of a notion of sexism to be studied "not as a stand-alone ideology, but rather to reassert its place through intersectional analysis and politics." In this chapter, I answer her call "to think sexism with racism, ageism, classism, homophobia, and (dis)ableism."

Sexism is obviously intertwined with misogyny and, as I hope to show, racialization and racism. Rape, on its part, is a violent act of power; it is about men exercising authority over women (or, rarely, over other men). Rape is often considered a public secret that, as Carolyn Nordstrom (1996, p. 147) says, "spans arenas from public war to private life." According to her, rape is "imbued with relationships of domination, contestation, and resistance." Although rape is intertwined with sexism, it has to be emphasized that it has nothing to do with sex: it is an aggressive and malicious deed that aims at subordination of the raped. It is also worth noting that rape *is* culture:

> The very term 'rape culture' indicates the need to understand rape *as* culture; as a complex social phenomenon that is not limited to discrete criminal acts perpetrated by a few violent individuals but is the product of gendered, raced, and classed social relations that are central to patriarchal and hetero-sexist culture. (Ferreday, 2015, p. 22)

The mere threat of rape is a powerful tool in inciting anxiety and fear. The economy of fear refers to the emotional atmosphere that the more or less imaginary threat of terror causes (Ahmed, 2004). According to Sara Ahmed, fear has been at the forefront of public discourses of the Western world ever since 9/11—the time that brought the Western countries "the war on terror," as was overdramatically declared by then-president George W. Bush (Ryan, 2004). This "politics of fear," as Ruth Wodak (2015) puts it, is based on dividing people into "us" and "them" and creating threats.

The contemporary talk about "floods of refugees" and the "refugee crisis" in the media draws from the same affective sources. Fear is the emotion that seems to occupy the current "landscape of risk" up to a point where "fear is now aggressively (over)determined and distributed" via values, ideas, technology, and politics (Flaxman & Rogerson, 2010, p. 333). In the Nordic countries, fear is incited exactly through the threat posed by immigrants and asylum seekers as racialized others.

Karina Horsti (2016, p. 10) analyzes the "culture or race war" that is being constructed in the blogosphere, where (white) women represent the body of the nation, the nation's "daughters" who are in need of protection:

> In these narratives, the white female represents the border of territory, family, race, culture, and identity.... Feminist scholars have analyzed such connections of gender and sexuality to citizenship, nationalism, and nation-building in

various contexts.... This body of research explains how women are often, in a very banal way, represented as embodying the nation, or the nation is imagined as a family, and therefore women represent the threshold of what belongs to men.

In analyzing racialized rape and why it is such a powerful and widely circulated trope, I also draw from the study of affects and emotions, especially from Sara Ahmed's concept of affective economy of fear (2004) and Ruth Wodak's newest book *The Politics of Fear* (2015). In her analysis, Wodak calls the fringe voices of populist right-wing political discourse the politics of patriarchy, which has "become a central frame for mainstream media debates in the situation where nationalistic, xenophobic, and racist rhetoric affects 'the social divides of nation, gender, and body.'" I also draw from Iris Marion Young's (2003) idea of the masculine protector of the "weak" (women and children): it is "the gendered logic of the masculine role of protector in relation to women and children" (Young, 2003) that applies here especially well, since the Kempele rape case victim was not only female but also an underage child. As Young (2003) suggests, in this patriarchal logic that "expects obedience and loyalty at home... the role of the masculine protector puts those protected, paradigmatically women and children, in a subordinate position of dependence and obedience." In this logic, as Young puts it,

> [t]he "good" man is one who keeps vigilant watch over the safety of his family and readily risks himself in the face of threats from the outside in order to protect the subordinate members of his household. The logic of masculinist protection, then, includes the image of the selfish aggressor who wishes to invade the lord's property and sexually conquer his women. These are the bad men. Good men can only appear in their goodness if we assume that lurking outside the warm familial walls are aggressors who wish to attack them. The dominative masculinity in this way constitutes protective masculinity as its other. (p. 18)

In what follows, I show how the division of good and evil men is racialized and draws from (fantasies of) violence against women and girls as the fuel for inciting the atmosphere of fear.

The affective politics of fear that encompasses the "immigration rape in Kempele" commotion in contemporary Finnish media publicity is an illuminating example of how rape has been and is used as a means to exercise and abuse the power of privileged white men, to control women and refugees as ethnicized or racialized others. Rape, as "one of the most common terror tactics in war" (Nordstrom, 1996, p. 147) and as a form of sexual assault, is powerful also in the racist discussion about the white nation and its enemies that is increasingly taking place in the traditional and social media. In what follows, I present the media material that I analyze, focusing on the intersections of race and gender. Before going into the material, I will briefly introduce my methodological framework.

## INTERSECTIONAL ANALYSIS OF THE KEMPELE CASE IN THE MEDIA

Even in the Nordic countries, anti-immigration-minded and xenophobic views have gained ground in public discussion. Conservative, anti-progressive thoughts affected by far-right ideologies are propagated especially in the social media after the rise of right-wing populist parties in the Nordic counties (Herkman & Matikainen, 2017). In the blogs published on the internet, discussion about immigration has turned into an exchange of affective arguments that include racialization and racism (Lähdesmäki & Saresma, 2014a). Often these "critical" voices also promote homophobic, misogynist, and sexist opinions, and are pointed against sexually, ethnically, religiously, or otherwise "different" others. In these discussions, there has been a "shift from classic, scientific racism to culturalist rhetoric in relation to extra-European immigrants," in which the term "culture" has often replaced "race" (Gullestad, 2006, p. 26). What's more, religion is often used as "...a new 'cultural' justification of racialization" (ibid.).

The social media are renowned for their capacity to incite hate speech, aggressive and hostile rhetoric against women, immigrants, and sexual minorities (Ruotsalainen & Saresma, 2017; Saresma, 2014b). However, this populist discourse, characterized by black-and-white rhetoric, stereotypification, and scapegoating, is eventually oozing all over the contemporary mediascape (Horsti, 2015; Palonen & Saresma, 2017; Saresma, 2016, 2017a). Here, I analyze mainstream media texts collected a week after the Kempele rape case, using intersectionality as a methodological tool (Karkulehto, Saresma, Harjunen, & Kantola, 2012; Lähdesmäki & Saresma, 2014b). With intersectional analysis, I refer to integrating race/ethnicity and gender with other axes of power and difference, such as age, and (here to a lesser extent) also sexuality and social class. To be more specific, I understand intersectionality as performative (Karkulehto et al., 2012) in the sense that the processes of racialization and gendering that are intertwined and take place in the media discussions position subjects in various locations in the webs of power and subordination.

In my analysis, I follow the theme of racialized rape and the recurring trope of immigrant rape in the texts produced in the media commotion, which I call the Kempele case, during a span of eight days from November 24 to December 2, 2015. The material analyzed here comprises altogether 72 media texts from various sources, including the main daily newspapers, internet news, and video clips broadcasted by the publicly funded Finnish broadcasting company Yle. I go through them in chronological order to show how the narrative around the trope of immigrant rape is constructed. I describe the newsfeed about the rape and analyze the most distinguishable discourses in the material. After going through the news material through an intersectional lens, I briefly turn to an internet discussion in the open discussion forum Suomi24 to show how the discourses in the print media and the social media reflect and affect each other.

My analysis is based on the presumption that the rhetoric used in the media is performative—that by using particular words, certain effects are produced and realities constructed. Thus, I agree with social media researcher Helen Nissenbaum (2009) that (digital) media texts are about both politics and rhetoric, both information and influencing. I hope to demonstrate that the discourses used in discussing rape circulate in the Finnish mediasphere and more broadly in the Nordic mediasphere, that "man" and "woman" are not coherent categories but are constantly defined and redefined in relation to other hierarchical categories of power such as race, and that a power imbalance based on ethnicity intersects with other hierarchical categories of difference and discrimination (gender, sexuality, social class). I also wish to uncover the paradox of rape discussion where, on the one hand, the so-called immigration critical or anti-immigration-minded discussants claim there is an increase in the rape statistics due to immigration, and, on the other hand, they deny the idea of rape culture altogether. As a conclusion, I would also like to suggest some ways of talking back at hate speech toward racialized others and to make space for intersectional discussion on ethnicity, gender, and sexuality.

## The Rape Narrative in the Media: A Chronological Account with Interpretative Comments

The first newsflash about the Kempele case is published in the tabloid *Ilta-Sanomat* on Tuesday, November 24, 2015, at 9:58, reporting that on Monday night at half past ten, a 14-year-old Kempele girl was raped in the open air on Asemantie Street. The police report that "two persons with a foreign background [had] offended her [and] at last one of the two men had raped her." Later, "a police dog patrol followed the traces of the offenders [and] caught up with two young men" who are now "arrested as suspects of aggravated rape and aggravated sexual abuse of a child." It is reported that the suspects are 15–17 years old and that there was a police operation at the immigration detention center late Monday night that is related to the crime investigation, but the interviewed inspector "cannot confirm the reason for the suspects' stay in the country" (*Ilta-Sanomat*, 2015a, November 24, 9:58).

The 14-year-old girl that was raped is described as being shocked about the event and thus unable to discuss it with the authorities in its entirety. The suspects have not been heard from yet on Tuesday afternoon, as there are no interpreters available to help the police: "the interpreters are fully employed with other duties at the moment." The police emphasize that because the investigation is in its early stage, the victim is underage, and the crimes under investigation, as well as the "foreign issues" related to the case, are confidential, no more information can be given about the matter. As the rape case has aroused a massive flow of comments in the social media, the police "express their hope that people would contain themselves regarding this inflaming issue and avoid all kinds of excesses" (*Ilta-Sanomat*, 2015b, November 25, 16:44; *Karjalainen*, 2015, November 25, 16:12).

Soon after the first news, the media report new leads about the background of the suspects. *MTV News* 2015a publishes a newsflash already at 12:37, saying:

> According to the information we have acquired, the two young men with a foreign background suspected of raping the 14-year-old girl are asylum seekers coming from Afghanistan.… Chief inspector Seppo Leinonen from the Oulu police department has not commented on this information.

The next newsflash on the national broadcasting company Yle web page is published in the afternoon with the headline "The rape of the young girl raises hatred and fear in Kempele" (*Yle*, 2015e, November 24, 16:17). The tone of the news is affective. The introduction in its entirety says:

> The rape case of the Northern Ostrobothnian girl has been reacted to with varying feelings: the action has aroused worries about safety, but at the same time, it is feared that it stigmatizes all asylum seekers.

In the photograph attached to the story, there is a gloomy underpass in the midst of a snowy gray landscape; behind it, a lonely man is leading his bicycle away from the viewer. It is said in the caption that "A young girl was raped in Kempele on Monday evening. The deed has aroused hatred and fears in the population." In this short newsflash (altogether 224 words), the affective atmosphere of the small town of Kempele is painted by repeating affective words such as fear (mentioned seven times), hatred (mentioned two times), irritation (mentioned two times), anxiety, and shock. The need for discipline and courage is mentioned in the couple of comments cited, as well as pepper spray and avoiding being out in the darkness of the night. All this is contrasted with the previous peacefulness of Kempele. The fear is also spreading, as one of the interviewees claims:

> [The name of the older woman], who is visiting Kempele from Muhos, has never been afraid thus far in the rural parish of Muhos.... But now they are even there, [the name] ponders. (*Yle*, 2015e, November 24, 16:17)

In this newsflash, the rapists are not identified, but asylum seekers and immigrants are talked about on a more general level. In the citation above, it is explicitly insinuated that it is "they," the asylum seekers, who are the reason for the current fearful atmosphere.

The thread of this story, emphasizing the affective response of the people of Kempele to the rape, is the idea that is later repeated in the material several times. It is the discourse of "telling them how to behave." Here, a male inhabitant of Kempele says:

> The morning did not start well as I heard this news. After my morning routine, I went to the place of the rape and thought that if I met any immigrants, I could teach them how to keep their friends in their place. (*Yle*, 2015c, November 24, 16:17)

In the citation, it is assumed that the immigrants are a coherent group that just doesn't know how to behave in Finland.

After the news about the rape had been broadcast, a comment by the Kempele municipal council party groups was published in which they demand that "it has to be made clear that it will be safe to live in Kempele also in the future" (*Kaleva*, 2015, November 24). The same afternoon, STT (Oy Suomen Tietotoimisto, Finska Notisbyrån AB, Finnish News Bureau) releases an announcement in which Prime Minister Juha Sipilä "summons a crisis meeting because of the Kempele rape case" (*Iltalehti*, 2015, November 24).

*Yle Uutiset* announces in the news on November 24, 2015, at 15:10, that "Prime Minister Sipilä organized a crisis meeting about the Kempele rape." In what follows, I quote the newsflash in its entirety:

> Prime Minister Juha Sipilä (Center party) condemns the Kempele rape and wants to find out as soon as possible, whether the laws need to be altered. Sipilä summoned a crisis meeting on Tuesday with the Minister of Justice and the Minister of the Interior. Sipilä intends to find out very soon whether the rape of a teenage girl in Kempele will cause changes in the legislation. He reminds that people have tried to explain to asylum seekers in the immigration detention centers how women in Finland should be treated. Information has also been given about the constitutional state.
>
> Sipilä is shocked about the Kempele case. "It is serious, revolting, and reprehensible if the information given in public holds true," Sipilä says.
>
> A 14-year-old girl was raped in Kempele on Monday. Two young foreign men are suspected. According to MTV News, the suspects are refugees from Afghanistan. The Prime Minister himself has his home in Kempele. In September, he promised to open his home to asylum seekers to use.

This lengthy quotation contains many details that are of interest when discussing racialized rape. First, approximately a thousand Finnish women and girls are raped every year by ethnically Finnish men (Tilastokeskus, 2017). This has never been the subject of a media commotion, not to mention a crisis meeting by the government. Second, legislative reform seems to be quite an enormous effort after one suspected rape. Third, by saying that the refugees have been taught how to treat women and how to live in a constitutional state, the PM makes a clear distinction between Finland and "less civilized" countries. Fourth, the tone of Sipilä's announcement is very affective. He is shocked, he finds the case revolting and reprehensible, and later, it is hinted that the PM was almost crying while giving his statement. Such affectivity is not usually expected from the prime minister; politicians, especially heads of state, are allowed to show their feelings and emotional turmoil in natural catastrophes such as the tsunami of 2004 or terrorist attacks such as the 9/11 or Charlie Hebdo incidents. Previously, no politician has stated his shock after a single rape. It is not my intention to denigrate the effects of the rape on the victim and her circle of acquaintances but to point out that rape is usually considered perhaps a personal tragedy but still a minor occasion from the governmental perspective.

The fifth and perhaps most important detail here is that although the PM hastened to deem the case repulsive and actually brought all asylum seekers under suspicion based on this one case, he admits he does not know whether the news is accurate or true at all. This is obviously against the UN's Declaration of Human Rights article 11, the European human rights agreement (article 6, chapter 2), and the Finnish preliminary investigation law (chapter 4, § 2), which state that every suspect must be treated as innocent until proven and judged otherwise. This presumption of innocence also covers the ethical journalistic practices that all the media should follow.

As mentioned earlier, Kempele is the town where PM Juha Sipilä was born and where he used to reside before his appointment to be the leading politician of the country. His promise to settle asylum seekers to his now empty house, just before this media panic about the alleged rape, was received with mixed feelings.

A rectification of this announcement by the PM is published late the next day. The news about the theme of the crisis meeting is corrected, and it is declared that the idea of having a meeting focusing on the situation with the refugees had been discussed already *before* the Kempele case took place and that the rape case was only one of the issues related to the agenda of the meeting on the situation of asylum seekers (*Ilta-Sanomat*, 2015c, November 25, 22:06). Despite the rectification and despite the correction of the news headlines afterward, the news about the crisis meeting of the government dealing with the Kempele rape is the main news of the media landscape.

The headlines of the related news on the Yle news page illustrate the fearful atmosphere: "The rape of a young girl incite hatred and fear in Kempele" (*Yle*, "Nuoren tytön raiskaus," 2015e); "PM Sipilä organizes a crisis meeting due to the Kempele rape" (*Yle*, "Pääministeri Sipilä järjesti," 2015c); "Housing unit for asylum seekers evacuated during the night for security reasons" (*Yle*, "Turvapaikanhakijoiden asumisyksikkö," 2015b); "Tempers flared at the asylum demonstration: 'field court-martial demanded'" (*Yle*, "Tunteet kuumenivat," 2015f). So, it can be seen that the Kempele rape case has had vast consequences in the atmosphere and that besides affective rhetoric, there is also affective, aggressive movement targeted toward the racialized others, despite the fact that they are underage.

While the issue of gender is not explicitly discussed in the rape case reporting, the idea of women and girls being in need of male protection (Young, 2003) is implicitly present. The widespread idea of gender equality in the Nordic countries is utilized in the media texts (de los Reyes, Molina, & Mulinari, 2003; Keskinen, 2010, 2013; Lähdesmäki & Saresma, 2014a) to the extent that makes it possible to provide "ground for the creation of self-images as modern, progressive, and advanced nations through a juxtaposition with migrant 'others'" (Keskinen, 2013, p. 226). Islamophobia expresses itself in argumentation that emphasizes the Western values of gender equality and tolerance toward sexual "others" (e.g., "homonationalism," Puar, 2007), although its ideological base is actually traditional heteronormative anti-feminism (Lähdesmäki & Saresma, 2014b).

Interestingly enough, it is only when the rapists come from somewhere else that rape becomes a question of gender equality. Despite the universal nature of sexual violence and sexism, the image of a victimized white woman, as Horsti (2016) suggests, has been used throughout the centuries in Western countries to wage war, "to persuade men to fight 'the enemy' and exercise masculinity." In the ideology of masculinist protection (Young, 2003), the "weaker," that is, women and children, are in need of protection. In the media buzz, it is exactly white women that need protection, young girls even more so. This makes the 14-year-old girl an "ideal victim" (Lindgren & Lundström, 2010, p. 301). To illustrate the gendered nature of the media coverage of the Kempele rape case, I will turn briefly to a video clip by Yle.

### Four Interviews

The media landscape after the Kempele rape is filled with affective responses: fear, hatred, and anxiety. The national broadcasting company broadcasts on its web page video footage that is titled "The Shocked Atmosphere in Kempele" (*Yle*, "Tunteet kuumenivat," 2015f). The video clip lasts 1 minute and 11 seconds, and four Kempele inhabitants are interviewed by a female voice: a middle-aged male with a mustache, a younger male with long hair and a fur cap, and two girls, apparently friends, one of them a blond and the other a brunette. A female reporter asks the questions, and the interviewees answer respectively:

Interviewee #1:  A middle-aged white, chubby man with a moustache looks at the ground very seriously. "I don't understand this, this that... something like this happens *here*. This has been a very peaceful area to live in and... to be and..." [looks at the ground again, sniffing]

Reporter:  Are you afraid? Yourself?

Interviewee #1:  [defiantly, looking at the interviewer and raising his voice] Well I'm not scared. I am not afraid, but on behalf of them, the elderly and the young.

Speaking himself from the position of a middle-aged white man, the interviewed man does feel dread, but he brings up the issue of age, suggesting that others may be afraid. It is as if the situation, as difficult and hard as it may be, does not really concern him, except for shaking the peaceful atmosphere of his hometown.

Interviewee #2:  A long-haired, thin young white man wearing an old fur cap.

Reporter:  How do you feel, on behalf of the young girls? Is it still safe to move around here?

Interviewee #2:  [squinting his eyes] Well yeah, sure but... perhaps one should consider a bit about where to go and maybe take something with them, pepper spray or... and whether to take men with them when going somewhere... I dunno. Hard to say. It is so very case-specific, all this [pointing around him].

The interviewee, perhaps ten years older than the raped girl, thinks it is still safe for young girls to move around Kempele. Although he tries to mitigate the fear-inciting discourse of the interviewer, taking into account the case specificity and the context of the rape, the fearful tone is sticking in his reply as he admits that perhaps the girls should walk armed or accompanied by men. This is an example of what Sara Ahmed (2004) calls the stickiness of feelings. However, it is noteworthy that interviewee #2 refuses to submit to the demands of all-embracing fear or blaming of all refugees.

In the third video clip, two girls, apparently friends, perhaps the same age as the rape victim, stand side by side outside a shopping mall. A blond girl, resembling the Maid of Finland, if you wish, is asked (again inciting a fearful atmosphere):

Reporter:        So does one dare go out alone any more in the dark, or does one have to have a friend with her or something like that?

Interviewee #3:  Well at least I would rather go with a friend so that.... And I also think parents would not like to let anyone go by herself.

The second girl, not as blond, but still white, agrees but also adds:

Interviewee #4:  Well, yes, I'm like the same but then again it's like also Finnish men can do things like this and it has always been a possibility. This time the situation just happened to be like this now so.... There is like always danger of such a thing so.... So I don't think I will now become especially, especially careful now.

All the earlier news clips were from the perspective of someone else, but in the last clip, two young girls, whom the viewer eagerly interprets as peers of the victim, are finally allowed to speak themselves. The first of these girls is keen to lean on friends or parents, but the latter—who is the last interviewee in the news clip—takes another stand, suggesting that the situation is really not that different now, even though the (suspected) perpetrator is not an "insider" of the community this time. Her point of view is valuable in the media commotion that is focused on the foreign background of the suspect and the alleged difference, reminding the viewer that, indeed, rape has always been there as a threat to girls and women. Although the reporter started the interviews with perhaps a fear-mongering attitude, it must be emphasized that this viewpoint was the last and thus the most notable opinion.

## *Commentaries*

Soon after the actual news, various commentaries on the case are published. Already the same night, during prime-time news, the broadcasting company MTV interviews the chief of the crime editorial office Jarkko Sipilä, who claims that the Kempele case was to be expected to happen. It is also announced that according to the police and the Home Office report, disturbances and unrest have increased in and around the detention centers, and it is feared that the Kempele case will increase the problems even more. In his interview, inspector Sipilä claims: "This is the kind of event that we have actually been afraid of. This may tighten the situation around detention centers further." He emphasizes that there is "no need to hush up about what has happened, but also no need to generalize so that all asylum seekers are blamed for this" (*MTV*, 2015b, November 24, 22:14). This means of course that *some* of the refugees are to be blamed—even before there has been any judgment.

In Jarkko Sipilä's opinion, echoes from the culture of fear, as well as the politics of fear, can be traced. The inspector has been pondering how to prevent "cases like this"—which obviously refers to the rape of the Finnish girl by racialized others—and has come to the conclusion that the most essential thing is "to make the asylum seekers realize that Finland as a country is different from the country they have left. Here all, both women and men, have the very same rights. If we could get this message through, it would help a lot" (*MTV*, 2015b, November 24, 22:14).

Thus, again, the fact that Finnish men rape Finnish women does not seem to mean anything in this othering and racializing discourse of (cultural) difference. The voices that try to emphasize that gendered violence has a long history and has happened before the "immigrant or Muslim rape," but that there has been no commotion about it, are silenced.

Also, other kinds of voices are gradually emerging. Instead of invoking affects such as fear and anxiety, news such as "Experts: Education is the best way to diminish incidents of harassment by asylum seekers" (*Yle* 24.11., Asiantuntijat: Valistus on paras tapa) or "Rumors around the rape case have incited feelings of insecurity" (Salovaara, 2015) try to tackle the rape case more analytically.

Critical voices also start to emerge: comments by an Amnesty International expert (*Yle* 26.11., Amnestyn asiantuntija Kempeleen, 2015d) asking why hasn't there been such rage and crisis meetings incited by rape crimes before the Kempele rape; The National Councli of Women of Finland, see http://www.naisjarjestot.fi/100-tasa-arvotekoa/ylavalikko/in-english/ noting that the victim has been forgotten in the media panic (*Yle* 26.11., Naisjärjestöjen mielestä uhri, 2015a); and Member of Parliament, Anna Kontula, claiming that no such interest has been shown toward raped women (*MTV, 3* 2015c, 27.11., Kansanedustaja Kontula: Eipä). Thus, in the mainstream media, there is an effort to show fairness and impartiality, although it is not always successful. What is of interest here is the quality of the discussion on the internet.

## AN EXCURSION INTO SOCIAL MEDIA

To cite Debra Ferreday (2015, p. 24), "the internet has become a site of struggle over sexual violence." It is thus crucial to also take a look at the discussion about the Kempele rape case in a discussion forum. To mirror the previously analyzed and described material, I take an example from the most popular internet discussion forum in Finland during the Kempele rape case, namely, *Suomi24* (Finland24). Whereas the news in the mainstream media is usually—although not always, as we saw above—based on facts, the internet forum discussions many times lean on exaggeration, if not pure lies (Hirsjärvi, 2018), and they utilize and generate gossip.

The case aroused much discussion in the social media. To give an overview, here are some of the titles of discussion threads during the first day of the media panic in the Suomi24 forum: "A rape in Kempele"; "A rape in Kempele! Will the PM resign?"; "Rauno Varis says: Kempele rape is a sham"; "Safety is demanded in Kempele"; "A Police announcement about the Kempele youngsters[2]"; "The god-daughter of Sipilä raped in Kempele?"; "Immigrants[3] raped in Kempele"; The intruders[4] raped a 14-year-old in Kempele"; "A 14-year-old raped in Kempele—it's the fucking intruders"; Sipilä's protégé raped a 14-year-old?"; and so on.

In the media material analyzed above, the tone is more "neutral," although names such as "refugee" and "foreigner" are used. The tone is harsher in the social media forums. As an example, I will present some quotations from the first discussion, "A rape in Kempele! Will the PM resign?" In the discussion, PM Sipilä is framed as a scapegoat that is to

---

[2] In the Finnish term "KEMPELELÄISNUORUKAisisTA," the letters _isis_ are written with small letters, whereas the other words are written with capital letters.

[3] Originally Mamut = ma̲a̲hanmu̲u̲ttajat, a pejorative abbreviation for the word immigrant.

[4] The original word in Finnish is "matu" as a pejorative abbreviation of the words ma̲a̲hantu̲nkeutuja, (foreign) intruder.

blame for these horrible deeds. Simultaneously, the victim is denied her agency; she is depicted as someone whose life is inevitably ruined:

> Sipilä will not understand until a member of his family is raped. A 14-year-old girl's life was ruined. (Pseudonym erittäinkriittinen [verycritical], *Suomi24*, 24 Nov 2015)
>
> Sipilä betrayed the citizens of his own hometown. My regards to the raped girl and her family. This is an experience that will haunt her for the rest of her life; she will never be the same again. Our politicians are responsible for this. (Vihastunutäiti [angrymother], 2015)

In the following two quotations, the victim is given some—yet very restricted—agency:

> (...) now Sipilä's nephew has ruined her life forever (...). She will most definitely commit suicide after realizing what Sipilä did (...). She lost her life in all ways. (Sipiläeiymmärrä [sipilä doesn't get it], 2015)

Only in this quotation is the victim given some, albeit dubious agency: the discussant sees the rape victim as an agent in her own faith. The rarity of this kind of commenting is remarkable, since the discourse is a very common one when (seldom) a rape committed by a Finnish white man is discussed:

> This hen [tytteli] was familiar with this wog. Thus playing with fire. The consequences are known, the dick of the darkie was erect. Consequence: rape. (sdfdv, 2015)

In this discussion thread, the accused and, besides him, all refugees—and sometimes even all immigrants—are called "barbarians," "animals," "intruders," "wealth refugees," "darkies," "wogs," "monkeys," "sloths," "dumb, lazy, and ugly wanderers," although only one commentator mentions Muslims. As Karina Horsti (2016) summarizes, the globally shared trope of "immigrant rape," also called "immigrant rape wave," "Muslim rape," "Muslim gang rape," "Muslim rape epidemic," "Muslim rape wave," or "rape jihad," has become prominent in the "counter-jihad" movement as a part of the feared "Islamization" of Europe in the last decades. Counter-jihadism relates to and fuels Islamophobia as an emerging trend in racist discourse. Islamophobia is, as Karina Horsti defines it (referring to Werbner, 2013; and Taras, 2013), "a form of culturalized racism that includes persistent Orientalist myths about Islam and Muslims." It comprises beliefs about Islam as a patriarchal, sexist, misogynist, violent, anti-rational, and anti-democratic religion or culture (Horsti, 2016; Kumar, 2012, pp. 42–60), and positions Western cultures as the opposite—as equal, democratic, liberal, and rational (see Lähdesmäki & Saresma, 2014b).

The threat is also exaggerated in the discussion, inciting fear of the rape wave that will spread over Finland. The tone of the comments follows MEP Jussi Halla-aho's prophesies cited in the beginning of the chapter:

(…) and this is not the last rape that is going to happen in Kempele, just so you know. (Erittäinkriittinen [verycritical], 2015)

Something will happen soon if there is no change in this. (pilattuelämä-työllä [liferuinedwithwork], 2015)

(…) the minister will not understand before his own children are raped; as bad as this sounds, yet they will understand only then! (sierjeg, 2015)

These animals should be shot in the head. (tämäkinköyksittäistapaus [isthistooanindividualcase], 2015)

Is it finally time for direct action? (hgghkll, 2015)

If these comments are read from an intersectional viewpoint, it becomes apparent that the rape case is heavily racialized—rapists are foreigners, strangers, even barbarians, or animals—but it is also gendered: it is the women or girls that are the victims, and men's role is to serve as their protectors. In this duty, the Prime Minister and the government have deceived the trust of the citizens, and this is why the discussants are very angry and boasting about taking justice into their own hands.

But intersectional reading also allows social class to be taken into account. It has been noted several times that it is usually the poorest and least educated people that have the most racist opinions (Deary, Batty, & Gale, 2008; Wodtke, 2016). Here, the concern for well-being and wealth is also presented even in the selection of pseudonyms such as "liferuined-withwork." This writer was especially worried about the refugees coming to Finland and getting for free what s/he has had to work hard for all her/his life. Also, a certain hatred of the elite—characteristic of populist rhetoric—can be sensed in the scapegoating of the Prime Minister.

I wanted to take this discussion as an example of racialization on the internet, not because it is the "worst" or most aggressive example (which it is not!) but because it was the first discussion thread after the news of the rape. It is important to take a look at it because much of contemporary opinion shaping takes place in the discussion forums and social media. Rosalind Gill (2011, p. 66) states:

> [T]he rapid expansion of DIY media via the blogosphere, social networking, and other features of Web 2.0 necessarily complicates much of the existing literature... because of the proliferation of representations that are self-produced and could be considered "freely chosen."

In this case, it means that although moderated, the comments published in this discussion forum reflect the "true" opinions of the "people" better than the filtered opinions published in the main media analyzed above. Thus, it is worthwhile to take a brief look at this discussion and see whether it really differs that much from the mainstream media discourses on racialized rape.

Despite the affective and aggressive discourse, the discussants avoid words like "race" or referring to the biological characteristics of the others, thus avoiding the label of "racist." However, othering people based on the religion or culture of a certain ethnic group is racist. Thus, I suggest that what we are witnessing in the discussion fora on the internet is a subtler form of racism, cultural racism. Using names such as wog, coon, and darkie exemplifies how "the idea of whiteness is essential for national identities in the Nordic countries [and] those marked by their non-white bodies are referred to as "immigrants" or "foreigners" and subjected to racializing processes" (Keskinen, 2013, p. 226). This process is going on in the mainstream media in a subtle way and in the internet discussions in a very striking manner.

At the very core of the Kempele rape case is the question of race and the process of racialization. Sara Ahmed (2004) takes as her starting point Frantz Fanon's description of "the fear of the black man" to show the power of racialized stereotypes and how they stick to certain bodies. She explains in her work how in the post-9/11 politics of fear, this fear has been channelized to equate looks (of a stereotypical Muslim) to possible acts ("could be a terrorist"). In the media buzz about the Kempele "immigrant rape" case, this false equation has been made between asylum seekers and "could-be rapists." Horsti (2016) suggests, referring to Mitchell (1996, p. 74): "...if in Franz Fanon's words, blackness is a 'corporeal malediction' that emerges in a visual encounter, Swedish whiteness, especially blondness, is a 'corporeal blessing' that allows social prestige."

Thus, the affective politics of fear aims (allegedly) to protect women from the threat of potential Muslim/immigrant/refugee rapists; yet it simultaneously limits the freedom of women and girls to move within the public space, challenging the autonomy of the female body. The rhetoric of "protecting" *our* women is fundamentally tied with the anti-feminist aim of restricting women's agency via the politics of fear, scapegoating the racialized and aged other—the young, male refugees—and the exaggerated threat of gendered violence.

## DISCUSSION

The definition of rape culture, cited in the beginning of this chapter, emphasized the need to understand rape *as* culture. If rape is understood culturally as a complex social phenomenon, it is inevitably seen as "the product of gendered, raced, and classed social relations that are central to patriarchal and heterosexist culture" (Ferreday, 2015, p. 22). The media narrative about the Kempele rape is an example of racialization in the gendered politics of fear.

Intersectional reading of the Kempele case illuminates that rape is not only a question of gender; the power hierarchies produced in the media texts are thoroughly racialized. The racialized discourse aims at othering asylum seekers, presenting them as a threat to the white nation. It also aims at controlling women. The textual organizing of power relations in the media according to various differences, both traditional and social, has to do with racialization and racism, misogyny, sexism, and ageism. Based on the quotations of the police inspectors and politicians above, it is not far-fetched to argue that structural racism has an indisputable position in the institutions of politics, police, and law. The tiny rhetorical choices made by the representatives of the police and the government reveal structural racism behind the politically correct discourse that denies any racial discrimination. Racialization is thus the active form of existing structural racism that is embedded in the media. Racialization is performative; it is an act with consequences that the media participates in on a daily basis. The quotations also suggest that although the traditional media aim at "neutrality," the tone is racist, and the suspected perpetrator is clearly racialized.

Thus, in the discourse on racialized rape, racialization is as important a factor as is gender and age. These categories of power and subordination intersect in a way that positions the white middle-aged male at the top of the hierarchy, as the norm, and the racialized and gendered others under his control. The strong connection between the neo-nationalist struggle to "maintain" the white nation white and the "protection" of women crystallizes in the discussion of raping the white woman. Rape as such is an "inevitable" act that is seldom brought into publicity. However, a huge commotion is fired up when the suspected rapist is "the other."

To adapt Rosalind Gill's (2011, p. 65) idea of the "profoundly classed, racialized, and heteronormative framing of the debates themselves, whose privileged object of "concern" has been the white, western, middle-class [man]," I wish to conclude that the emergent rape speech is not a sign of men wanting to protect women per se but of white men wanting to protect what they perceive as "their property," namely, the body of the white woman and thus the borders of the white nation, from the racialized "intruders." This, of course, is not a new phenomenon but an ancient strategy of reinforcing the populist division of people into "us" and "them." In the modern, racialized version of this strategy, the real "others" of the privileged white men are both the construction of the group of white women as those who allegedly need protection and the racialized "enemy" men.

What's more, the politics of fear is based on an alleged threat and incorrect accusations. The problem of fear—the stickiness of it, as Sara Ahmed would say—is that it does not follow rational logic but is spread just like in the media panic. As Flaxman and Rogerson (2010, p. 334) aptly describe:

> Most of us will never encounter terrorism [or rape], but what's most interesting (and alarming) about fear is that this truth is utterly irrelevant. The disproportion between the statistical improbability of such a threat and the pervasiveness of a real affect constitutes the very space in which the problem of fear emerges.

Fear is contagious, and what's more, it induces silence (Chomsky, 1996). One of the aims of the media buzz around the Kempele rape case might be the effort to silence the so-called tolerant flower hat ladies that stand for multiculturalism and immigration by using the threat of being raped. However, in this case, this didn't succeed, as is seen in the analytical critical responses from various agents such as Amnesty International, Women's Organizations United, and some female Members of Parliament.

The disproportion of the actual threat and the threat constructed pervasively is exactly the ground where the politics of fear is fueled in the media panic about the "immigrant rape" in Kempele. It is challenging to try to block the affective flows that take over people only by reasonable argument. Instead, a sense of security should be rebuilt instead of using the discourse of crisis and war. The first step is to deconstruct the affective trope of "immigrant rape" and start talking about rape as gendered violence aimed at harming women, executed by men that feel insecure, in order to bolster their vulnerable sense of self, no matter what ethnicity or religion, culture, or race they represent. Racializing rhetoric, explicit in the internet discussion forums, although more vaguely expressed by the mainstream media, is performative: it has its material consequences. Words have their effects, so the responsibility of the media in not inciting fear, and aggression should be taken seriously.

## References

Ahmed, S. (2004). *Cultural Politics of Emotion*. London: Routledge.

Chomsky, N. (1996). *The Culture of Fear*. Retrieved from Chomsky.info/199607.

Choo, H. Y., & Marx Ferree, M. (2010). Practicing Intersectionality in Sociological Research: A Critical Analysis of Inclusions, Interactions, and Institutions in the Study of Inequalities. *Sociological Theory, 28*(2), 129–149.

Cudd, A. E., & Jones, L. E. (2005). *Sexism. A Companion to Applied Ethics*. London: Blackwell.

Deary, I. J., Batty, G. D., & Gale, C. R. (2008). Bright Children Become Enlightened Adults. *Psychological Science, 19*(1), 1–6.

de los Reyes, P., Molina, I., & Mulinari, D. (2003). *Maktens (o)lika förklädnader. Kön, klass & etnicitet i det postkoloniala Sverige*. Stockholm: Atlas.

Dyer, R. (1997). *White*. London and New York: Routledge.

erittäinkriittinen. (2015, November 24, 12:23). *Message Posted to Discussion Eroaako pääministeri?* Retrieved from http://keskustelu.suomi24.fi/t/13962748/kempeleessa-raiskaus!-eroaako-paaministeri

Ferreday, D. (2015). Game of Thrones, Rape Culture and Feminist Fandom. *Australian Feminist Studies, 30*(83), 21–36.

Flaxman, G., & Rogerson, B. (2010). The Economy of Fear. *Symploke, 18*, 1–2 & 333–336.

Gill, R. (2011). Sexism Reloaded, or, It's Time to Get Angry Again! *Feminist Media Studies, 11*(1), 61–71.

Gullestad, M. (2006). *Plausible Prejudice. Everyday Experiences and Social Images of Nation, Culture and Race*. Oslo: Scandinavian University Press.

Herkman, J. & Matikainen, J. (2017). Neo-Populist Scandal and Social Media: The Finnish Olli Immonen Affair. *Political Scandal, Corruption, and Legitimacy in the Age of Social Media* (p. 24). IGI Global. Retrieved from http://www. igi-global.com/chapter/neo-populist-scandal-and-social-media/173993

Helsingin Sanomat. (2014, March 5). Tutkimus: Suomi on naisille EU:n toiseksi väkivaltaisin maa. *Helsingin Sanomat.* Retrieved from http://www.hs.fi/kotimaa/art-2000002714270.html

hgghkll. (2015, November 25, 9:27). *Message Posted to Discussion Eroaako pääministeri?* Retrived from http://keskustelu.suomi24.fi/t/13962748/kempeleessa-raiskaus!-eroaako-paaministeri

Hirsjärvi, I. (2018). Rattaissa on käen muna. Rasistisen meemin levittäminen internetissä. In E. Palonen & T. Saresma (Eds.), *Kulttuurinen populismi ja populismin valtavirtaistuminen.* Manuscript submitted for publication.

Horsti, K. (2015). Techno-Cultural Opportunities: The Anti-Immigration Movement in the Finnish Mediascape. *Patterns of Prejudice, 49*(4), 343–366.

Horsti, K. (2016). Digital Islamophobia: The Swedish Woman as a Figure of Pure and Dangerous Whiteness. *New Media and Society.* Retrieved from https://doi.org/10.1177/1461444816642169

Iltalehti. (2015, November 24, 14:48). *Sipilä kutsui koolle ministereitä keskustelemaan turvapaikanhakijoista.* Retrieved from http://www.iltalehti.fi/uutiset/2015112420719886_uu.shtml

Ilta-Sanomat. (2015a, November 24, 9:58). *Poliisi tutkii: 14-vuotias tyttö raiskattiin Kempeleessä—epäillyt 15–17 -vuotiaita.* Retrieved from http://www.iltasanomat.fi/kotimaa/art-1448331557423.html

Ilta-Sanomat. (2015b, November 25, 16:44). *Poliisilta lisätietoa Kempeleen raiskausepäilyn tutkinnasta.* Retrieved from http://www.iltasanomat.fi/kotimaa/art-1448341117051.html

Ilta-Sanomat. (2015c, November 25, 22:06). *Oikaisu STT:n juttuun Sipilän kokouksesta.* Retrieved from http://www.iltasanomat.fi/kotimaa/art-1448370589653.html

Kaleva. (2015, November 24). *Kempeleen valtuustoryhmät vaativat turvallisuutta alueelle.* Retrieved from http://www.kaleva.fi/uutiset/oulu/kempeleen-valtuustoryhmat-vaativat-turvallisuutta-alueelle/713202/

Karjalainen. (2015, November 24, 16:12). *Poliisi Kempeleen tapauksesta: Ihmiset, älkää sortuko ylilyönteihin.* Retrieved from http://www.karjalainen.fi/uutiset/uutis-alueet/kotimaa/item/91025-poliisi-kempeleen-tapauksesta-ihmiset-alkaa-sortuko-ylilyonteihin

Karkulehto, S., Saresma, T., Harjunen, H., & Kantola, J. (2012). Intersektionaalisuus metodologiana ja performatiivisen intersektionaalisuuden haste. *Naistutkimus—Kvinnoforskning, 25*(4), 16–27.

Keskinen, S. (2010). Sukupuolistunut väkivalta. In T. Saresma, L.-M. Rossi, & T. Juvonen (Eds.), *Käsikirja sukupuoleen* (pp. 243–254). Tampere: Vastapaino.

Keskinen, S. (2013). Antifeminism and White Identity Politics. Political Antagonisms in Radical Right-Wing Populist and Anti-Immigration Rhetoric in Finland. *Nordic Journal of Migration Research, 3*(4), 225–232.

Kumar, D. (2012). *Islamophobia and the Politics of Empire*. Chicago: Haymarket Books.

Lindgren, S., & Lundström, R. (2010). Inside Victims and Outside Offenders: Dislocations and Interventions in the Discourse of Rape. *Social Semiotics, 20*(3), 309–324. https://doi.org/10.1080/10350331003722885

Lähdesmäki, T., & Saresma, T. (2014a). Re-Framing Gender Equality in Finnish Online Discussion on Immigration. *NORA—Nordic Journal of Feminist and Gender Research, 22*(4), 299–313.

Lähdesmäki, T., & Saresma, T. (2014b). The Intersections of Sexuality and Religion in the Anti-Interculturalist Rhetoric in Finnish Internet Discussion on Muslim Homosexuals in Amsterdam. In G. Strohschen & J. Gourlay (toim.), *Building Barriers and Bridges: Interculturalism in the 21st Century* (pp. 35–48). Oxford: Inter-Disciplinary Press.

Lähdesmäki, T., & Saresma, T. (2016). Emotive Strategies and Affective Tactics in 'Islam Night'. In E. Devereux, A. Haynes, & M. Power (Eds.), *Public and Political Discourses of Migration* (pp. 57–71). London: Rowman & Littlefield.

Mitchell, W. J. T. (1996). *What Do Pictures "Really" Want?* (pp. 71–82). Cambridge, MA: The MIT Press.

MTV. (2015a). *14-Vuotiaan tytön raiskauksesta epäillyt ovat afganistanilaisia turvapaikanhakijoita.* Retrieved from http://www.mtv.fi/uutiset/rikos/artikkeli/14-vuotiaan-tyton-raiskauksesta-epaillyt-ovat-afganistanilaisia-turvapaikanhakijoita/5575018

MTV. (2015b). *MTV:n Jarkko Sipilä Kempeleen tapauksesta: tällaista on pelätty.* Retrieved from http://www.mtv.fi/uutiset/rikos/artikkeli/mtv-n-jarkko-sipila-kempeleen-tapauksesta-tallaista-on-pelatty/5576028

MTV. (2015c). *Kansanedustaja Kontula: Eipä ole ministereitä naisten raiskaukset ennen kiinnostaneet.* Retrieved from https://www.mtv.fi/uutiset/kotimaa/artikkeli/kansanedustaja-kontula-eipa-ole-ministereita-naisten-raiskaukset-ennen-kiinnostaneet/5581108#gs.Ht4zOzU

Nerg, P. (2017, May 11). *Pitkä matka Suomeen.* Oral Presentation, Zonta International Occasion. Jyväskylä, Finland.

Nissenbaum, H. (2009). *Privacy in Context. Technology, Policy, and the Integrity of Social Life.* Palo Alto: Stanford University Press.

Nordstrom, C. (1996). Rape: Politics and Theory in War and Peace. *Australian Feminist Studies, 11*(23), 147–162.

Norocel, O. C., Saresma, T., & Lähdesmäki, T. & Ruotsalainen, M. (2017). *Intersectional Performances of 'Us' and 'Other' in Right-Wing Populist Media in Finland and Sweden.* Manuscript submitted for publication.

Palonen, E., & Saresma, T. (2017). Perussuomalaiset ja populistinen retoriikka. In E. Palonen & T. Saresma (Eds.), *Jätkät ja jytkyt. Perussuomalaiset ja populistinen retoriikka* (pp. 13–44). Tampere: Vastapaino.

pilattuelämätyöllä. (2015, November 24, 12:58). *Message Posted to Discussion Eroaako pääministeri?* Retrieved from http://keskustelu.suomi24.fi/t/13962748/kempeleessa-raiskaus!-eroaako-paaministeri

Puar, J. K. (2007). *Terrorist Assemblages: Homonationalism in Queer Times.* Durham: Duke University Press.

Ruotsalainen, M., & Saresma, T. (2017). Suvivirrestä maahanmuuttajamyyttiin. *Helsingin Sanomien ja Perussuomalaisen monikulttuurisuuskeskustelu.* In E. Palonen & T. Saresma (Eds.), *Jätkat ja jytkyt. Populismin retoriikka* (pp. 151–180). Tampere: Vastapaino.

Ryan, M. (2004). Framing the War against Terrorism. US Newspaper Editorials and Military Action in Afghanistan. *Gazette: The International Journal for Communication Studies, 66*(5), 363–382.

Salovaara, O. (2015, November 25). Kempeleen kunnanjohtaja: Huhumylly Kempeleen raiskaustapauksen ympärillä on lietsonut turvattomuutta. *Helsingin Sanomat.* Retrieved from http://www.hs.fi/kotimaa/art-2000002868673.html

Saresma, T. (2012). Miesten tasa-arvo ja kaunapuhe blogikeskustelussa. In H. Harjunen & T. Saresma (Eds.), *Sukupuoli nyt! Purkamisia ja neuvotteluja* (pp. 13–34). Jyväskylä: Kampus Kustannus.

Saresma, T. (2014a). Maskulinistiblogi feministidystopiana ja kolonialistisena pastoraalina. In T. T. Saresma & S. Jäntti (Eds.), *Maisemassa. Sukupuoli suomalaisuuden kuvastoissa* (pp. 249–284). Jyväskylä: Nykykulttuurin tutkimuskeskus.

Saresma, T. (2014b). Sukupuolipopulismi ja maskulinistinen standpoint-empirismi. *Sukupuolentutkimus—Genusforskning, 27*(2), 46–51.

Saresma, T. (2016). *'Close the Borders!' Affective Nationalism in the Digital Echo Chambers.* Retrieved from http://www.inter-disciplinary.net/critical-issues/wp-content/uploads/2016/08/TuijaSaresma-sp7-dpaper.pdf

Saresma, T. (2017a). Sananvapaus, vihapuhe ja sananvastuu. In K. Enqvist, I. Hetemäki, & T. Tiilikainen (Eds.), *Kaikki vapaudesta* (pp. 35–53). Helsinki: Gaudeamus.

Saresma, T. (2017b). Väkivaltafantasiat ja pelon politiikka (pp. 221–246). Helsinki: Suomalaisen Kirjallisuuden Seura.

Saresma, T. (2017c). The Concept of Love in Masculinist Blogs: A Strategic Ideal. In D. Byrne & W. M. Yong (Eds.), *Fluid Gender, Fluid Love.* Leiden: Brill.

Saresma, T. (2017d). Gender Populism. Three Cases of Finns Party Actors' Traditionalist Anti-Feminism. In U. Kovala, E. Palonen, M. Ruotsalainen, & T. Saresma (Eds.), *Populism on the Loose.* Jyväskylä: Nykykultuuri. Retrieved from http://urn.fi/URN:ISBN:978-951-39-7401-5

sierjeg. (2015, November 24, 14:25). (2015, November 24, 12:23). *Message Posted to Discussion Eroaako pääministeri?* Retrieved from http://keskustelu. suomi24.fi/t/13962748/kempeleessa-raiskaus!-eroaako-paaministeri

Sipiläeiymmärrä. (2015, November 24, 20:43) (2015, 24.11. 12:23). *Message Posted to Discussion Eroaako pääministeri?* Retrieved from http://keskustelu. suomi24.fi/t/13962748/kempeleessa-raiskaus!-eroaako-paaministeri

Suomi24. (2015, November 24). *Suomen suurin verkkoyhteisö [The Largest Internet Community in Finland].* Retrieved from http://www.suomi24.fi/ sdfvd. (2015, November 24, 18:21). *Message Posted to Discussion Eroaako pääministeri?* Retrieved from http://keskustelu.suomi24.fi/t/13962748/kempeleessa-raiskaus!-eroaako-paaministeri

tämänkinköyksittäistapaus. (2015, November 24, 14:33). *Message Posted to Discussion Eroaako pääministeri?* Retrieved from http://keskustelu.suomi24. fi/t/13962748/kempeleessa-raiskaus!-eroaako-paaministeri

Taras, R. (2013). 'Islamophobia Never Stands Still': Race, Religion and Culture. *Ethnic and Racial Studies, 36*(3), 417–433.

Tilastokeskus. (2017). *Suomi lukuina. Tuotteet ja palvelut. Oikeus.* Päivitetty March 23, 2017. Retrieved May 12, 2017, from http://tilastokeskus.fi/tup/ suoluk/suoluk_oikeusolot.html

vihastunut äiti. (2015, November 24, 12:30). *Message Posted to Discussion Eroaako pääministeri?* Retrieved from http://keskustelu.suomi24.fi/t/13962748/ kempeleessa-raiskaus!-eroaako-paaministeri

Werbner, P. (2013). Folk Devils and Racist Imaginaries in a Global Prism: Islamophobia and Anti-Semitism in the Twenty-First Century. *Ethnic and Racial Studies, 36*(3), 450–467.

WHO. (2013). *Global and Regional Estimates of Violence Against Women: Prevalence and Health Effects of Intimate Partner Violence and Non-Partner Sexual Violence.* Geneva: WHO Press.

Wodak, R. (2015). *The Politics of Fear. What Right-Wing Populist Discourses Mean.* London: Sage.

Wodtke, G. T. (2016). Are Smart People Less Racist? Verbal Ability, Anti-Black Prejudice, and the Principal-Policy Paradox. *Social Problems, 63*(1), 21–45.

Yle. (2015a, November 26, 06:25). *Naisjärjestöjen mielestä uhri unohtuu rais- kauskeskustelussa.* Retrieved from https://yle.fi/uutiset/3-8481451

Yle. (2015b, November 28, 14:17). *Turvapaikanhakijoiden asumisyksikkö Kempeleessä tyhjennettiin yöllä Turvallisuussyistä.* Retrieved from https://yle. fi/uutiset/3-8488939

Yle. (2015c, November 24, 15:10). *Pääministeri Sipilä järjesti kriisikokouksen Kempeleen raiskauksesta.* Retrieved from https://yle.fi/uutiset/3-8478553

Yle. (2015d, November 26, 16:00). *Amnestyn asiantuntija Kempeleen rais- kausepäilyistä: "Missä ovat olleet raivo ja kriisikokoukset aikaisemmin?"* Retrieved from https://yle.fi/uutiset/3-8482346

Yle. (2015e, November 24, 16:17). *Nuoren tytön raiskaus herättää vihaa ja pelkoja Kempeleessä.* Retrieved from https://yle.fi/uutiset/3-8478754

Yle. (2015f, November 28, 16:34). *Tunteet kuumenivat Kempeleen turvapaikkamielenosoituksessa: "Kenttäoikeus käytäntöön".* Retrieved from http://yle.fi/uutiset/kempeleessa_jarkyttyneet_tunnelmat__video/8479438

Yle. (2015g, November 24, 20:39). *Asiantuntijat: Valistus on paras tapa turvapaikanhakijoiden häirintätapausten vähentämiseksi.* Retrieved from https://yle.fi/uutiset/3-8479543

Young, I. M. (2003). The Logic of Masculinist Protection: Reflections on the Current Security State. *Signs: Journal of Women in Culture and Society, 29*(1), 1–25.

# CHAPTER 4

# News Media Racialization of Muslims: The Case of *Nerikes Allehanda*'s Publishing of the Mohamed Caricature

*Mahitab Ezz El Din*

## INTRODUCTION

In July 2007, almost a year and half after the 2005 Danish cartoon crisis,[1] the Swedish artist Lars Vilks made several drawings depicting the Prophet Mohamed's face on the body of a dog and wanted to show them at a local exhibition. The organizers and most art galleries refused to show the drawings for security reasons, based on the fear of an angry Muslim reac-

---

[1] The Danish cartoon crisis goes back to September 2005 when the Danish daily *Jyllands-Posten* published 12 anti-Muslim cartoons depicting Prophet Mohamed in a polarized insulting manner, arguing that it was an attempt to open debate about Islam. The cartoons evoked Muslim anger around the world and caused violent demonstrations and boycotting of Danish products in Muslim states. The Danish Prime Minister, Anders Fogh Rasmussen, refused to meet with the Muslim ambassadors in Denmark, ignoring Muslim anger and leading to a major controversy and political tension between Denmark and the Muslim world (Eide, Kunelius, & Phillips, 2008).

---

M. Ezz El Din (✉)
Örebro University, Örebro, Sweden
e-mail: mahitab.ezzeldin@oru.se

© The Author(s) 2019
P. Hervik (ed.), *Racialization, Racism, and Anti-Racism in the Nordic Countries*, Approaches to Social Inequality and Difference,
https://doi.org/10.1007/978-3-319-74630-2_4

tion. This response led the Örebro-based local newspaper *Nerikes Allehanda* (*NA*) to publish one of the drawings on August 18, 2007, together with an opinion piece on freedom of expression. Although several other Swedish newspapers published the drawings, the controversy drew international attention following the *NA* publication. This publication triggered protests and official and non-official condemnation from Muslims in Sweden and in the Muslim world. Further, the Swedish flag and a doll depicting Swedish Prime Minister Reinfeldt were burned during one of the protests in Pakistan. On September 15, the *Al Qaeda*-affiliated militant group, the *Islamic State of Iraq*, issued a death threat and offered a bounty of $100,000 and $50,000 on Vilks and Johansson's heads, respectively.

The Swedish Prime Minister quickly addressed the issue and presented dialogical initiatives in an attempt to de-escalate and calm the crisis; these included a visit to a mosque and a meeting with 22 ambassadors from the Muslim world. These initiatives distinguished Sweden's stand on the crisis from that of its neighbor Denmark, which did not demonstrate any dialogical initiatives to quell its own earlier crisis (Hervik, n.d.).

This chapter aims at discussing in what ways media contributes to the racialization of Muslims and how the Muslim identity is constructed in their reporting by creating various forms of "us" versus "them." I use critical discourse analysis (CDA) to study the media coverage of the Swedish newspaper *Nerikes Allehanda*'s (*NA*) in two UK online mainstream outlets (BBC News and *The Guardian*) and two online mainstream US outlets (CNN and *The New York Times [NYT]*) over a six-month period.

## MEDIA, RACIALIZATION, AND IDENTITY CONSTRUCTION

In today's globalized world, there is an enormous change in the mobility map due to wars, conflicts, and deteriorating economic conditions. Racialization is observed with the influx of migrants. There is an increase in the fear from the Other, especially the Muslim Other, who are assumed to be different and construct a threat to the European identity. Gans (2017) suggests that newcomers who "differ phenotypically" are "probably the first targets of the racialization process" (345). Racialization can be seen as a process of exclusion of the racialized (Gans, 2017). Media, in this process, also contributes to the construction of the racialized as a threat to society.

News media plays a key role as mediators and cultural translators during times of conflict (even creating conflicts that are not really there), contributing to the dramatization of conflicts and consequently to their escalation (Cottle, 2006; Hafez, 2000; Spencer, 2005). The articulation and reproduction of discourses in news give rise to various types of stereotyped representations. Polarized positions of "us" versus "them" tend to become prevalent in news reporting. Dramatized and polarized news discourse can then lead to (mis)representations—racialization—of some ethnic groups (Cottle, 2006; cf. Tehranian, 2002).

The media's promotion of polarization may reinforce historic hostilities, racialization, and stereotypical perceptions of, and between, cultures. This is particularly true of perceptions of parts of the East (Islam and Islamic countries) and the West (mainly Europe, the USA, Canada, and Australia). The polarization of the East and West tends to enhance an Orientalism versus Occidentalism dichotomy (Hafez, 2000).

Scholars appear to agree, by and large, that Islam represented as an enemy and a threat to the West is a central element in reporting about Islam and Muslims (Jayyusi, 2012; Lewis, Mason, & Moore, 2009; Manning, 2004; Martin & Phelan, 2002; Ridouani, 2011), especially after the 9/11 terror attacks. The media, hence, plays a crucial role in racializing Muslims and communicating fear and in aligning Muslims with the threat of global and transnational terror networks (Nohrstedt & Ottosen, 2008; Spencer, 2005).

Racialization can be understood as a form of Othering (Gans, 2017), it builds on a binary opposition that divides people into "us" and "them," and thus it is pivotal to study identity in relation to Othering. Racialization is distinctive in the sense it can be sometimes harsher leading to permanent mistreatment (Gans, 2017; Hall, 1996). As a point of departure for the discussion, one needs to understand Othering as a type of social representation that is tied to stereotypes characterized by various levels of negativity (Jackson, 2012; Tekin, 2010). Othering is conventionally used in reference to the repressed and marginalized side, and "when the Other is being judged, the emphasis is on what differentiates instead of what connects" (Creutz-Kämppi, 2008, p. 297). Hence, Othering makes it possible for people to construct similarities and differences and then to confirm their own identity in relation to an Other (Jackson, 2012).

Othering and identity are not separate. Identity is often constructed in relation to an Other. On many occasions, identities are constructed not based on one's "own sense of belongingness and solidarity arising out of shared life worlds" but rather through a focus on "opposition to an Other" (Neumann, 1999, p. 13). Othering builds on a binary opposition that divides people into "us" and "them": the "us" refers to a segment that belongs to one's group and shares similar characteristics, a sense of superiority or views, while the "them" are considered to be the "opposite," that is, those who do not belong to the group. Identity, therefore, is constructed through difference and centers around Othering by showing opposition, particularly exclusion and inclusion, encompassing polarized ideas on what we are and are not (Delanty, 1995; Schöpflin, 2001; Woodward, 1997). This type of construction may also be described as "hierarchical Othering," where the "we" places the Other in a "down under" position (Eide, 2011, p. 93).

In these hierarchical levels, struggles are apparent; the "them" is excluded and is hence constructed, especially in the media, as culturally "lower," "the enemy," or a "threat." The "us" and "them" dichotomy is thus relevant when studying the reproduction of cultural identities and in situations of mediated intercultural conflict.

## RACIALIZATION WITHIN THE LENS OF ORIENTALISM AND OCCIDENTALISM

Orientalism and Occidentalism are the core concepts in the discussion of racialization and Othering in this chapter. The theories of Orientalism and Occidentalism examine and explain the essentializing, hierarchical identity constructions that began developing in the context of relations between the European colonial powers and the colonized societies and their cultures. They are tied to the process of racialization since people who are phenotypically different tend to be racialized (Gans, 2017).

### Orientalism

Although Orientalism as a term has historically been used to refer to scholars who studied the Orient (Hübinette, 2003), Edward Said (1978) and others (Abdel-Malek, 1963; Tibawi, 1964) used it as a critical concept to underline the historical and ideological trends in representations of the Orient. Orientalism, as it appeared in the colonial and postcolonial eras, captures the hierarchical Western constructions of the Orient as connected to the representation of the "privileged" Occident over the "weak" Orient

(Moosavinia, Niazi, & Ghaforian, 2011). It has been suggested that the West is unable to interact with dissimilar cultures (Spivak, 1988). The Orientalist discourse, constructing the East as the Other, reflects how the West presents Islam as a threatening Other who is incompatible with Western ideals. This representation satisfies specific political and psychological needs beneath the Western identity (Lueg, 1995).

The relationship between the Occident and the Orient can be described as a relationship between a hegemonic power that constructs a binary opposition between itself (the West, i.e., Occident) and the Orient (Said, 1978). In that respect, Said argues that Orientalism can serve as legitimation for hegemony and war, suggesting that the "us" and "them" dichotomy legitimizes wars (Said, 1978). The idea that they are "not like 'us' and didn't appreciate 'our' values" is considered to be "the very core of traditional Orientalist dogma" (Said, 2003, p. xv).

This discussion on Orientalism is based on Said's arguments about the construction of the Muslim Other. Said found from his intensive study of the image of the East represented in the West, especially of the Western construction of Arabs and Islam, that Arabs and Muslims have been represented as violent and underdeveloped as well as threatening to Western values (Said, 2003). This representation can be easily seen in the polarized construction of Arabs presented in the Western media (cf. Bullock & Jafri, 2000; Martin & Phelan, 2002; Kabir, 2006; Shaheen, 2009/2012; Sadar, 2014).

Said's work enabled further investigation of Orientalist discourses, allowing his theory to be examined in different disciplines and discourses (Abu-Lughod, 2001). Hence, Orientalism can be a useful theory for analyzing news media constructions of the Other, as it offers a foundation for analyzing the relationships between the West and the East.

That said, Said has been criticized for only telling "half of the story" (Varisco, 2007, p. 26) when discussing representations of the Orient. He is accused of a heavy focus on Muslims and of excluding Christians in the region and the Arab Maghreb nations, which were under French rule (Rassam, 1980; Walker, 1991). He is also criticized for blaming the Orientalist for "essentializing the Orient," while he himself essentialized the West (Varisco, 2007, p. 252). Further, he is criticized for not suggesting alternatives to the Oriental Other and for being biased in concentrating on the negative influences of the West on the East, using concepts such as imperialism and racism without referring to any Western contributions (Rassam, 1980).

Bernard Lewis,[2] one of Said's major critics, found Said's discussion on Orientalism to be limited to the Middle East and narrowed to the Arab world. Lewis also criticizes Said for ignoring other relevant scholarly work, delimiting discussion of the Orientalists to British and French examples and excluding others such as Germans and Russians. Said, Grabar, and Lewis (1982) respond to the accusations as "anti-Western," and he describes the West as a "collective" entity, arguing that it is "idiotic to say that Orientalism is a conspiracy or to suggest that 'the West' is evil: both are among the egregious fatuities that Lewis has the gall to ascribe to me" (p. 4). However, Said describes it as "hypocrisy to suppress the cultural, political, ideological, and institutional contexts in which people write, think, and talk about the Orient, whether they are scholars or not" (Said et al., 1982, p. 4). He argues that it is relevant to understand contemporary discourse as about power and that this discourse constructs Islam as "monolithic"; ultimately, he states that "The discourse of modern Orientalism [has] a chronic tendency to deny, suppress or distort the cultural context of Orientalism in order to maintain the fiction of its scholarly disinterest. It is precisely this tendency that Lewis's rejoinder to me exemplifies" (Said et al., 1982, p. 4).

One can see that both Lewis and Said openly express their disagreements and that each accuses the other of allowing his work to be driven by ideological reasons. Said (2001) accuses Lewis of being biased and of treating Islam in a "monolithic" manner. He further ties Lewis's "monolithic" approach to Huntington's "Clash of Civilizations" where neither scholar examines the diversity and plurality of each civilization, and Said accuses them of being ignorant. He also defends *Orientalism* in an afterword in (1994), where he argues that his study is a "testimony" on the status of the subaltern and is seen by many scholars to be stressing "multiculturalism, rather than xenophobia and aggressive, race-oriented nationalism" (Said, 2003, p. 336).

However, given the optimism of "cultural globalism," some scholars believe that Said's thesis is no longer valid and only valid for the past. The global world is said to have dissolved the boundaries between the Eastern and the Western worlds and hence created a "global culture" (Walker, 1991). In that sense, Walker sees Said's arguments as developed in his discussion on *Orientalism* to be invalid in a global world.

[2] Lewis (1990) suggested the idea of a clash between cultures. He introduced the term "Clash of Civilizations" that was later developed by Samuel Huntington (1993, 1996).

## Occidentalism

Occidentalism is also a relevant theory that can complement the understanding of how both the Orient and the Occident are represented. The term "Occidentalism" refers to stereotyped views of the Western world developed in the East. The term was mentioned in Said's 1978 study, in Carrier (1995), and in Chen (1995, 2002), and was popularized in Ian Buruma and Avishai Margalit's *Occidentalism: The West in the Eyes of its Enemies* (2004), in which the authors treated Occidentalism as the reverse of the Orientalism introduced in Said's works.

Similar to Orientalism, the "us" and "them" are fundamental to Occidentalism. In fact, in Occidentalism, the "we" and the Other are key issues, but in this context, the Other is the enemies of the East, that is, the West. Here, the West is not the traditional geographical European West but is rather seen as an Anglo-American notion (Buruma & Margalit, 2004). The West has been linked to money worship and modern capitalism, which according to Buruma and Margalit (2004) are considered to be a sign that the West is "forging a global civilization"; this view contributes to the so-called conspiracy theory discussions. "Roman imperialism," "Anglo-American capitalism," "Americanism," "crusader-Zionism," and "American imperialism" are a few examples of the different names that have been used to refer to the West (Buruma & Margalit, 2004, p. 32).

Occidentalism first appeared in developing countries to "complete the process of decolonization" in an attempt to study the colonial Other (Hanafi, 2005, p. 1). However, it is argued that due to the unequal distribution of global power, with the better position of the West, the West had more power in constructing the East as the Other than the East had in constructing the Western Other (Woltering, 2011). The representation of the West in the Middle East is not unitary. Sometimes the West is constructed as a symbol of technological advancement, economic development, and freedom of speech, but when considering Western control and influence over the Middle East, the West becomes a symbol of frustration and colonization, and the discourse of Western imperialism appears (Funk & Said, 2004). Tracing the origins of both discourses, the Oriental and Occidental images have been developed in many literary works in the West and East, respectively, hence contributing to constructions of the Other in both worlds. Occidentalism was represented as a cultural divide between the East and the West, confirming the pre-existing stereotyped representations of the West (El-Enany, 2012). The study of Occidentalism from an

Arab perspective can be traced back to its appearance in Arabic literature starting with the French occupation of Egypt in 1798 (Casini, 2008; El-Enany, 2012).

## RACIALIZATION OF MUSLIMS IN THE *NA* CASE

### *Muslims as the "Distant Other"*

The results of the *NA* case analyses show that there are two forms of constructions of Muslim identity: a conventional and a new non-conventional one. The conventional identity is the most dominant form of the Other. The traditional Orientalist polarized "uniform" representations are evident in the conventional construction of the Other in the selected Western media. This racialization of Muslims exists in articles that take a monological culturalist view of cultural differences and is tied to the Islamophobic constructions of Muslims.

Muslims are racialized and distanced. They are constructed to be the "opposite" "threatening" Other. They are manifested in two forms: a culturally incompatible "distant Other[3]" and a threatening "distant Other." This identity is conveyed when ideologies and cultural differences are represented in a culturalist discourse discussing Western ideologies. The conventional threatening stereotypical construction of Muslims is present in the texts characterized by insecurity and fear of the Other as shown in the Islamophobic discourse. Those constructions of Islam/Muslims connote the image of a threat to Western societies.

---

[3] I distinguish between two types of Other: the polarized relation with an "external" Other, that is, the Oriental and Occidental Others, on the one hand, and on the other hand, the more ambivalent relation to "internal" Oriental or Occidental Others (see Camauër, 2010). The idea of "internal" and "external" Others appeared in a study by Camauër (2010), where she refers to them as the "close" and the "distant" Other (pp. 147–149). In her study, Camauër found representations of the "close" Muslim, who has a dialogical approach and a problem-solving orientation to conflicts, with views that are closer to Swedish values. Moreover, the "distant" Muslim, who is often but not always geographically far away, is represented through traits and values that appear to be incompatible with those conventionally ascribed to the Swedish "we." In brief, "close" and "distant" Others not only refer to physical or geographical distance but also to compatible values. It is different from Mamdani's (2004) "bad" and "good" Muslim. The "good" Muslim here is not just against terror, but in this chapter the "close" Muslim is visible in the multicultural discourse where the terror aspect is not necessarily present in the news article.

I find the culturalist "distant Other" identity is marked by the absence of dialogue. A clash is conveyed when the discussion addresses what can be understood as culturally rooted Western values, through an emphasis on freedom of expression being at stake. At this point, the Western democratic values are represented as being incompatible with Islam and Muslims. The hierarchical construction of what can be understood as culturally rooted Western values as being superior is used as a strategy in this discourse. Identity differences are therefore highlighted when arguments about freedom of expression versus religious tolerance in the West are manifested. In those cases, a dichotomy is represented between the Orient and the Occident in which the West places the Other in a "down under" lesser position.

The "distant Other" also appears in articles that express an Islamophobic discourse, which is a monological discourse characterized by insecurity and fear of the "opposite" Other, that is, the threatening Other. Namely, the "distant Other" constitutes an identity that depicts the Muslim Other as a threat to Western society.

The monological Islamophobic discourse is the dominant discourse across the articles analyzed in the selected Western media. The Orient is depicted as an "enemy" Other, and the focus in the news articles can be related not only to the traditional Orientalist and Occidentalist constructions but also to a Global War on Terror (*GWT*) narrative. Elevating the "threat image" of Islam and the victimization of the West represent two strategies that manifest this discourse. The most common constructions of the "us" and "them" binary opposition within the Islamophobic discourse are the "threatening" East and the West as its "victim." These articles cover the case in such a way that the text indirectly aligns itself with the *GWT* narrative. The dominant depiction in the articles constructs Islam as a threat and represents it as the "distant" and "enemy" Other.

The death threat, as reported in the articles, shows Muslims as "violent" and as a "threatening enemy.[4]" The articles also focus on the violent and threatening rhetoric introduced by conservative voices, while the voices of moderate Muslims are absent. The newspaper articles in this group do not contextualize the death threat. They do not present any background on this threat or on the terrorist group. They take it for granted that this terrorist group exists and is active.

The CNN coverage promotes Muslims as a "threat" to society, especially through the reference to an anonymous woman dressed in a black

---

[4]On September 15, the Al Qaeda-affiliated militant group, the Islamic State of Iraq, issued a death threat and offered a bounty of $100,000 and $50,000 on Vilks and Johansson's heads, respectively.

burqa, without bringing in other voices. I find that the unnecessarily detailed description of this woman's outfit and also the publishing of her picture could implicitly foster hostility about veiled women in general along with an assumption that they are terrorists and not open to dialogue. This single story published by CNN presents unequal power relations. Voices that show respect for Muslims are absent. The story represents only particular conservative voices and promotes the *GWT* narrative; the quotations from the Muslim actors convey a threat image only. Through the selection of those voices, the text presents Muslims as aggressive.

The visual representations of Muslims and the textual constructions support Edward Said's argument about the media's "uniform[5]" coverage regarding the representation of Islam. The texts reflect the stereotypical representation of Muslims as violent barbarians. This also goes in line with Gans's (2017) argument on racialization of Muslims. He describes how Muslims are seen as a potential threat and "potential Jihadists" especially that terrorism today is tied to a certain religion and thus Muslims are perceived to be terrorists.

The results, finally, show unequal power relations in the representation of voices and actors in the Western media. Power relations refer to ways in which the article writers establish specific intra-textual patterns and are manifested within texts by the inclusion/exclusion of actors. Most of the articles include only conservative unofficial Muslim voices or official Muslim voices. The articles represent these actors' anger and condemnation without any reference to Arab and Muslim dialogical initiatives such as those that appear in the Arab media articles (Ezz El Din, 2016). These unequal power relations between actors might contribute to the overall shaping of the articles as predominantly revealing a discourse of insecurity. Indeed, in direct binary opposition to the construction seen in the Arabic articles, the Western media represents.

## (De)Racialization of Muslims in the *NA* Case

### *Muslims as the "Close Other"*

The new non-conventional form of identity is the "close Other." It is tied to a multicultural discourse and Muslims are (de)racialized. They are not distanced from the Swedish community. Although this discourse is barely

---

[5] Said (1997) argues that "the picture of Islam (and of anything else, for that matter) is likely to be quite uniform, in some ways reductive, and monochromatic" (pp. 48–49).

present in the Western media sample of this case,[6] it is still manifested in the text covering Swedish attempts to calm the situation. Bridging gaps is a strategy used to manifest a discourse of multiculturalism.

The text constructs a dialogical narrative. The article explicitly represents the PM's meeting with the Muslim ambassadors as an "effort to defuse a row," thus suggesting that a dialogue has been opened between Sweden and the Muslim world, in which Sweden is willing to calm down the situation.

The article draws on voices from both Sweden and the Muslim world to highlight the importance of mutual understanding and dialogue as a solution to the conflict. Although in the culturalist discourse constructed in other articles, the Swedish PM is shown as prioritizing freedom of expression in his relationship with the East, within this multicultural discourse, his statements are used to clarify that he is "not allowed to interfere in the media." This idea has not been developed in the Arab media, where the stories failed (except in a quote in one article) to explain the position of the Swedish PM in relation to media freedom.

In summary, the multicultural "close Other" is constituted by a focus on active action that bridges gaps, "promotes dialogue," and serves to "defuse a row." Differences are not discussed in the texts, and when the text brings the value of press freedom into the discussion, it does so to clarify the government's position and relationship to the media. The unofficial voice of Muslim protestors is absent; the only representation is visual in the single use of a picture of local protests in Örebro. The protestors are not interviewed, but the official Swedish voice and the official Muslim representative are present in the texts to convey dialogue.

Thus this conflict as covered in the Western media barely contains a multicultural form of identity in comparison to the Arab media coverage of the same case (see Ezz El Din, 2016). I find the lack of more articles promoting dialogue in the Western media notable in two ways. On the one hand, although the potential for dialogue exists on only one occasion, it still supports the idea that there are alternative ways to report on mediated intercultural conflicts. On the other hand, the reporting in this particular article does not strongly reflect these alternatives, and the two conflicting sides are still essentially represented as the dichotomous East and West.

[6] The multicultural discourse is found on a larger scale in other case studies (see Ezz El Din, 2016).

Generally, the overall representation, in which Muslims are racialized and constructed as being in conflict with freedom of expression, tends to evoke the image of Muslims as violent. This construction is solidified through the absence of dialogical attempts from the Muslim world. These attempts are only seen as coming from the West, which contributes to reinforcing the classic dichotomy between the East and the West and the construction of Muslims as "angry" by ignoring those voices offering dialogical initiatives.

## Problems of Racialization in a Global Society

The conventional construction of Muslims manifested in the continuous reproduction of what Edward Said describes as uniform stereotypical images is seen to be problematic. Horsti (2016, p. 3) discussed Islamophobia and the incompatibility of cultural values as a form of "culturalized racism," where the alleged incompatibility focuses on cultural differences. Such unseen or "hidden" beliefs and gendered/Islamophobic ideologies are reproduced in this discourse. Emphasizing ideologies can be seen as a problem in the media because it contributes to the reproduction of the same stereotypical images (van Dijk, 1988, 1995; Wodak & Meyer, 2006/2009). As stated by van Dijk (1995), the dichotomy of the "us" and "them" discourse is also evident here when outlining the negatives of the "them" in relation to the positives of the "us." In such "hierarchical Othering," the "we" positions the Other in a "down under" position (Eide, 2011). The reproduction of the same forms of racialized stereotypical identity can be attributed to the use of (only) certain voices. This silencing of certain alternative voices—including the voices of those involved as objects of the media reports—can, to some extent, explain why identities are reproduced the way that they are in the media today.

The types of racialized stereotypical or conventional identities found are also consistent with the discussion in Altheide's (2002) *Creating Fear* and in what Nohrstedt (2010) describes as the "culture of fear." The media depends on the construction of a fear discourse and represents social problems in terms of victims and threatening stereotypical enemies. A fear discourse is argued to serve elite interests by legitimizing unequal power relations in society (Altheide, 2002).

The reproduction of the racialized stereotypical Muslim when reporting conflicts can be connected to what Galtung (1990) describes as "cultural violence." Cultural violence refers to cultural aspects that legitimize violence or to what I relate here as the Othering of a group based on their religion or culture, which can lead to more racism and xenophobia. "Cultural violence" can be considered to be a form of "emotional" violence, which in my two cases is exemplified when Muslims are described as expressing that they are "hurt," "disrespected," "insulted," and so forth. Such emotional attributions to a collective "they" (who do not think or feel as "we" do) can be understood as a factor that may hinder integration in many Western societies.

The "fear of Islam," that is, Islamophobia, can be seen as a new form of racism, and as Kumar (2012) explains, it is used by elites to serve a particular agenda. If media practitioners become more aware of how their writing can change stereotypical images, hostility against migrants can be lessened and our world can become less racist.

## Beyond the Binary: Post Racial-Hybrid Identity and the Global World

In contemporary global society, one can argue that homogenous identities have been replaced by hybrid identities, in which a person has the right to "include in what he regards as his own identity a new ingredient, one that will assume more and more importance in the course of the new century and the new millennium: the sense of belonging to the human adventure as well as his own" (Maalouf, 2011, pp. 132–133).

In line with Maalouf's argument, Stuart Hall argues that the West can be found everywhere, as can the East (Hall, 1990). Therefore, the global world must incorporate the global Other, and thus cosmopolitanism is suggested as the new alternative (Beck, 2002, 2014). Cosmopolitanization can be used as a frame of reference that helps us to understand social conflicts, their dynamics, and their structures, and it can offer an alternative way of life that integrates the "otherness of the other" (Beck, 2002, p. 18). Cosmopolitanism does not indicate a homogenous world; Beck in fact argues that the world should still have diversity and uniqueness (Beck, 2005). He further explains that concepts such as multiculturalism only indicate and recognize that different ethnic groups live together within the same state and that tolerance means acceptance and putting aside differences. However, Beck (2014) suggests that cosmopolitan tolerance is an active concept that opens one to the world of Others, recognizing that difference enriches society and leads one to treat the Other on equal footing. As he describes it, the "either-or" logic is replaced by a cosmopolitan vision of a "both-and" logic. The media reporting of the Other should be consistent with Beck's "both-and" logic. I see that the dichotomous Orientalism or Occidentalism constructions will result in "either-or" racialized identities, while in this global age, there are more opportunities for alternative hybrid identity constructions.

## References

Abdel-Malek, A. (1963). Orientalism in Crisis. *Diogenes, 11*(44), 103–140.

Abu-Lughod, L. (2001). Orientalism and Middle East Feminist Studies. *Feminist Studies, 27*, 101–113.

Altheide, D. L. (2002). *Creating Fear: News and the Construction of Crisis.* Transaction Publishers.

Beck, U. (2002). The Cosmopolitan Society and Its Enemies. *Theory, Culture & Society, 19*(1-2), 17–44.

Beck, U. (2005). *Power in the Global Age.* Cambridge: Polity.

Beck, U. (2014). We Do Not Live in an Age of Cosmopolitanism but in an Age of Cosmopolitization: The 'Global Other' Is in Our Midst. In *Ulrich Beck* (pp. 169–187). Springer International Publishing.

Bullock, K., & Jafri, G. (2000). Media (Mis)Representations: Muslim Women in the Canadian Nation. *Canadian Women Studies, 20*(2), 35–40.

Buruma, I., & Margalit, A. (2004). *Occidentalism: The West in the Eyes of Its Enemies.* London: Atlantic.

Camauër, L. (2010). Constructing 'Close' and 'Distant' Muslim Identities. The Mohamed Cartoon in the Swedish Newspaper Nerikes Allehanda. In S. Nohrstedt (Ed.), *Communicating Risks: Towards the Threat Society* (pp. 137–160) (1st ed.). Göteborg: Nordicom.

Carrier, J. G. (1995). *Occidentalism: Images of the West: Images of the West.* Clarendon Press.

Casini, L. (2008). *Beyond Occidentalism: Europe and the Self in Present-Day Arabic Narrative Discourse* [Online]. Mediterranean Programme Series EUI RSCAS; 2008/30. Retrieved December 5, 2015, from http://hdl.handle.net/1814/9367

Chen, X. (1995). *Occidentalism: A Theory of Counter-Discourse in Post-Mao China.* Cary, NC: Oxford University Press.

Chen, X. (2002). *Occidentalism: A Theory of Counter-Discourse in Post-Mao China.* Rowman & Littlefield.

Cottle, S. (2006). *Mediatized Conflict.* Maidenhead, Berkshire, UK: Open University Press.

Creutz-Kämppi, K. (2008). The Othering of Islam in a European Context: Polarizing Discourses in Swedish-Language Dailies in Finland. *NORDICOM Review: Nordic Research on Media & Communication, 29*(2), 295–308.

Delanty, G. (1995). *Inventing Europe.* New York: St. Martin's Press.

Eide, E. (2011). *Down There and Up Here: Orientalism and Othering in Feature Stories.* Hampton Press.

Eide, E., Kunelius, R., & Phillips, A. (2008). *Transnational Media Events.* Göteborg: Nordicom.

EL-Enany, R. (2012). *Arab Representations of the Occident: East-West Encounters in Arabic Fiction.* London: Routledge.

Ezz El Din, M. (2016). *Beyond Orientalism and Occidentalism: Identity Constructions in Arab and Western News Media.* Doctoral dissertation, Örebro University.

Funk, N., & Said, A. (2004). Islam and the West: Narratives of Conflict and Conflict Transformation. *International Journal of Peace Studies, 9*(1), 1–28.

Galtung, J. (1990). Cultural Violence. *Journal of Peace Research, 27,* 291–305.

Gans, H. J. (2017). Racialization and Racialization Research. *Ethnic and Racial Studies, 40*(3), 341–352.

Hafez, K. (2000). *Islam and the West in the Mass Media.* Cresskill, NJ: Hampton Press.

Hall, S. (1990). Cultural Identity and Diaspora. In J. Rutherford (Ed.), *Identity: Community, Culture, Difference* (pp. 222–237). London: Lawrence & Wishart.

Hall, S. (1996). Introduction: Who Needs Identity? In S. Hall & P. Du Gay (Eds.), *Questions of Cultural Identity* (1st ed., pp. 1–17). London: Thousand Oaks Sage.

Hanafi, H. (2005). From Orientalism to Occidentalism. *Studia Philosophiae Christianae, 40,* 227–237.

Hervik, P. (n.d.). Danish Cartoon Crisis/Controversy. In *Oxford Islamic Studies Online.* Retrieved September 8, 2016, from http://www.oxfordislamicstudies.com/article/opr/t343/e0198

Horsti, K. (2016). Digital Islamophobia: The Swedish Woman as a Figure of Pure and Dangerous Whiteness. *New Media & Society,* 1–18.

Hübinette, T. (2003). Orientalism Past and Present: An Introduction to a Postcolonial Critique. *The Stockholm Journal of East Asian Studies, 13,* 73–80.

Huntington, S. (1993). The Clash of Civilizations? *Foreign Affairs, 72*(3), 22.

Huntington, S. (1996). *The Clash of Civilizations and the Remaking of World Order.* New York: Simon & Schuster.

Jackson, J. (Ed.). (2012). *The Routledge Handbook of Language and Intercultural Communication.* London: Routledge.

Jayyusi, L. (2012). Terror, War & Disjunctures in Global Order. In D. Freedman & D. Thussu (Eds.), *Media and Terrorism: Global Perspectives* (1st ed.). London: Sage.

Kabir, N. (2006). Representation of Islam and Muslims in the Australian Media, 2001–2005. *Journal of Muslim Minority Affairs, 26*(3), 313–328.

Kumar, D. (2012). *Islamophobia and the Politics of Empire.* Chicago: Haymarket Books.

Lewis, B. (1990). The Roots of Muslim Rage. *The Atlantic Monthly, 266*(3), 47–60.

Lewis, J., Mason, P., & Moore, K. (2009). Islamic Terrorism's and Repression of the Political. In L. Marsden & H. Savigny (Eds.), *Media, Religion and Conflict* (pp. 17–38) (1st ed.). Farnham: Ashgate Publishing Limited.

Lueg, A. (1995). The Perception of Islam in Western Debate. In J. Hippler & A. Lueg (Eds.), *VV. AA. The Next Threat. Western Perceptions of Islam* (pp. 7–31). London: Pluto Press y TNI.

Maalouf, A. (2011). *On Identity*. Random House.

Mamdani, M. (2004). Good Muslim, Bad Muslim: Post-Apartheid Perspectives on America and Israel. *PoLAR, 27*(1).

Manning, P. (2004). *Reporting Arabic and Muslim People in Sydney Newspapers*. Sydney: Southwood Press.

Martin, P., & Phelan, S. (2002). Representing Islam in the Wake of September 11: A Comparison of US Television and CNN Online Messageboard Discourses. *Prometheus, 20*(3), 263–269.

Media, 2001–2005. Journal of Muslim Minority Affairs, 26 (3), 313-328.

Moosavinia, S. R., Niazi, N., & Ghaforian, A. (2011). Edward Said's Orientalism and the Study of the Self and the Other in Orwell's Burmese Days. *Studies in Literature and Language, 2*(1), 103–113.

Neumann, I. (1999). *Uses of the Other: The "East" in European Identity Formation*. Manchester: Manchester University Press.

Nohrstedt, S. (2010). Threat Society and the Media. In S. Nohrstedt (Ed.), *Communicating Risks: Towards the Threat Society?* (pp. 17–51) (1st ed.). Göteborg: Nordicom.

Nohrstedt, S., & Ottosen, R. (2008). War Journalism in the Threat Society: Peace Journalism as a Strategy for Challenging the Mediated Culture of Fear? *Conflict & Communication Online, 7*, 1–17.

Rassam, A. (1980). Comments on Orientalism. Two Reviews: Representation and Aggression. *Comparative Studies in Society and History, 22*(04), 505–508.

Ridouani, D. (2011). The Representation of Arabs and Muslims in Western Media. *RUTA: Revista Universitària de Treballs Acadèmics, 3*, 7–15.

Sadar, P. (2014). Exotic Beauties, Victims and Terrorists: Representations of Veiled Women in the British Press (2001–14). *Journal of Arab & Muslim Media Research, 7*(1), 59–73.

Said, E. (1978). *Orientalism*. London: Penguin.

Said, E. (1994). *Culture and Imperialism*. Vintage.

Said, E. (1997). *Covering Islam: How the Media and the Experts Determine How We See the Rest of the World*. Random House.

Said, E. (2001). Adrift in Similarity. *Al-Ahram Weekly*, 11–17.

Said, E. (2003). *Orientalism: Western Conceptions of the Orient*. London: Penguin.

Said, E., Grabar, O., & Lewis, B. (1982). Orientalism-An Exchange. *New York Review of Books, 29*(13), 44–48. Retrieved September 8, 2016, from http://www.nybooks.com/articles/1982/08/12/orientalism-an-exchange/

Schöpflin, G. (2001). *The Construction of Identity.* Österreichischer Wissenschaftstag.

Shaheen, J. (2009/2012). *Reel Bad Arabs.* New York: Interlink Publishing.

Spencer, G. (2005). *The Media and Peace.* Basingstoke, UK: Palgrave Macmillan.

Spivak, G. C. (1988). Can the Subaltern Speak? In C. Nelson & L. Grossberg (Eds.), *Marxism and the Interpretation of Culture* (pp. 271–313). Basingstoke, UK: Macmillan Education.

Tehranian, M. (2002). Peace Journalism: Negotiating Global Media Ethics. *The Harvard International Journal of Press/Politics, 7*(2), 58–83.

Tekin, B. Ç. (2010). *Representations and Othering in Discourse: The Construction of Turkey in the EU Context, 39.* John Benjamins Publishing. The Standard Eurobarometer 2014 Report. *Europa.eu.* Retrieved from http://ec.europa.eu/public_opinion/archives/eb/eb82/eb82_anx_en.pdf

Tibawi, A. L. (1964). English-Speaking Orientalists: A Critique of Their Approach to Islam and Arab Nationalism. *Islamic Quarterly, 8*(1), 25.

Van Dijk, T. (1988). *News Analysis. Case Studies of International and National News in the Press.* Hillsdale, NJ: Erlbaum.

Van Dijk, T. (1995). Discourse Analysis as Ideology Analysis. In C. Schäffner & A. Wenden (Eds.), *Language and Peace* (1st ed., pp. 17–33). Aldershot: Dartmouth.

Varisco, D. (2007). *Reading Orientalism.* Seattle: University of Washington Press.

Walker, K. (1991). *Orientalism and the "Other." Towards a New Anthropology of the Middle East.* Berkeley: University of California.

Wodak, R., & Meyer, M. (2006/2009). *Methods of Critical Discourse Analysis.* London: Sage.

Woltering, R. (2011). *Occidentalisms in the Arab World.* London: I.B. Tauris.

Woodward, K. (1997). *Identity and Difference.* London: Sage in Association with the Open University.

# CHAPTER 5

# White Fear: Habitual Whiteness and Racialization of the Threat of Terror in Danish News Journalism

*Asta Smedegaard Nielsen*

In October 2015 a white, young man, the 21-year-old Anton Lundin Pettersson, with knife and sword attacked pupils and employees at a school in Sweden killing three people. Afterward, the police shot the perpetrator who shortly after died in the hospital. According to the police, the attack was motivated by racism. As a reaction to the attack, users of Danish social media sites started a debate, which was later picked up by parts of the mass media about why it was labeled as a hate crime and not as terror by police, media, and other authorities when a similar attack earlier the same year, in February in Copenhagen, Denmark, was labeled as terror from most sides. Similarly, the perpetrator of this attack was a lone young man, namely, the 22-year-old Omar Hamid El-Hussein, who, wielding a gun, attacked a cultural center hosting a meeting with the Swedish Muhammad cartoonist Lars Vilks, and a guard at the Jewish synagogue, killing two people, one at each location. Also in this case, the perpetrator was shot and killed by the

A. S. Nielsen (✉)
Aalborg University, Copenhagen, Denmark
e-mail: nielsen@cgs.aau.dk

P. Hervik (ed.), *Racialization, Racism, and Anti-Racism in the Nordic Countries*, Approaches to Social Inequality and Difference,
https://doi.org/10.1007/978-3-319-74630-2_5

police. However, the ideological motive behind the attack was different as it was Islamist, as was the racial identity of the perpetrator, who was of Arab descent and "appearance." One answer to the difference in interpretation to the two attacks is that the post-2001 terror paradigm has consolidated an interpretative frame of terror as referring to almost exclusively Islamist-motivated terror present in much news media and in the mindsets of many journalists (Smedegaard Nielsen, 2014). This paves the way for a ready interpretation of Islamist-motivated violence as terror and a simultaneous hindrance of recognizing other types of ideologically motivated violence as terror. Furthermore, it involves a racialization of the threat of terror, in terms of the construction of a terror potential at young men of what is often termed "Middle Eastern or Arab appearance" (Smedegaard Nielsen, 2014). However, the main focus of the chapter will be to turn the point of view away from the position of the terror threat and the potential terrorist and seek to consider how the addressing of the public in the news is at work in processes of racialization. That is, to consider how the journalists' addressing and representation of the public works to perform, and thus create a particular image of, the public (Chouliaraki, 2013), and in which ways these particular constitutions of the public are informing the racialization of the threat of terror.

When considering the phenomenon of the threat of terror, it is the premise of this chapter that the way that fear is at work affectively to shape social space is of crucial significance. This chapter seeks to unfold the argument that when some kinds of violence, and not others, are interpreted as terror, it does not only have to do with the installed enemy image of "the Muslim terrorist" (although, of course, this also plays a significant role), but investigates the significance of the ways fear is accumulated in the public and its inhabiting of space, turning some bodies' fear into a general, common fear and others' not. Thereby, it sets the frame for which danger is seen as general and indiscriminate—and thus interpreted as terror—and which danger is interpreted in more specified terms. Here and in earlier work (Smedegaard Nielsen, 2014, 2015), I study journalistic discourses on the threat of terror against Denmark. But, where, in my earlier work, I found that on the interpretative level, then, to some extent, the *threat of terror* can only be brown, here I want to consider if *fear of terror* can only be white. For this purpose, I will use Sara Ahmed's (2004, 2006) works on both fear and whiteness as the main inspiration for my framework of analysis.

I will consider my research question through both a revisiting of empirical data I have gathered earlier and which consists of Danish newscasts about terror and interviews with producing journalists (Smedegaard

Nielsen, 2014), as well as analyze new material in the form of more recent news and other media material about terror. The new material is news coverage and debates related to the attacks on the cultural center *Krudttønden* and the Jewish synagogue in Copenhagen in February 2015, and the media coverage of a case from August 2014 in which a young innocent man, as a terror suspect, was hunted down in Copenhagen after a train passenger had reported his behavior as suspicious. Both old and new materials are from the Danish public service media DR and TV2.

In Danish media research there has generally been significant attention toward how social problems are racialized as well as media's constructions of the Muslim minority as a problem identity have been critically examined (Andreassen, 2007; Hervik, 2002; Smedegaard Nielsen, 2014; Yilmaz, 2006). Less—although some—attention has been given to how the production of whiteness plays into these processes of racialization and minoritization. Inspired by Ahmed's (2006) work on spatial orientation, I wish to address this issue by considering if and how the threat of terror can be considered an affective force that is working to organize social space racially by orienting and distributing subjects, objects, bodies, and "things" more generally. I will ask if the mediation of fear of terror in the news can be understood as a mechanism working through affects to occupy social space with whiteness and thus restrict the movement of bodies not resonating with the idea of whiteness. The study is, thus, based on the hypothesis that the production of whiteness is related to the way the public, represented and addressed in the news, gets constituted. As I study news production of national Danish public service media, it is evidently the constitution of the Danish public I consider. This implies that when I study the production of whiteness, I study the specific form that the idea of "whiteness" undertakes in the Danish context. Hence, by my analyses I wish to contribute to the field of critical race and whiteness studies with insights into the specificities of the production of whiteness within the Danish context.

## WHITENESS: METHODOLOGICAL AND THEORETICAL CONSIDERATIONS

With its non-essentialist conceptualization of whiteness, my study places itself within the tradition of critical whiteness studies. The field has its grounds in early US-based scholars' studies of white supremacy and racism (Allen, 1975; Du Bois, 1969/1920; Wellman, 1977) and has, in particular, gained ground since the 1990s with the works of, for example, Toni

Morrison (1992), Ruth Frankenberg (1993), and Richard Dyer (1997). In Europe, the critical study of race and whiteness has a shorter research history than in the USA. This may be caused by the historic experiences of World War II and the Holocaust, which meant that race, for a long time, has been surrounded by a taboo in a continental European and Nordic context, considered to be something we have gotten over. From good antiracist intentions, a "colorblind" ideology has fostered a view of race as having no significance (Doane & Bonilla-Silva, 2003; Goldberg, 2006; Hübinette, Hörnfeldt, Farahani, & Rosales, 2012; Myong, 2009). However, within recent years, Nordic scholars from different fields of research have stressed the importance of reinventing race as a theoretical and analytical concept, and whiteness has gained increased attention as well (see Andreassen, 2014; Andreassen & Vitus, 2015; Blaagaard, 2009; Hübinette & Lundström, 2011; Hübinette et al., 2012; Keskinen, Tuori, Irni, & Mulinari, 2009; Loftsdottir & Jensen, 2012; Myong, 2009; Smedegaard Nielsen, 2014). The insistence on making race and whiteness objects for research can be regarded as a response to the ideology of colorblindness, which involves a blinding of ourselves to acknowledging and understanding those structures and processes that form the lived experiences of discrimination, othering, or differentiation, conditioned by the visibility of racialized bodily signs. As part of this turn, I will, in this chapter, present a critical study of whiteness.

I view race and whiteness as intertwined concepts unthinkable without one another. As such, I conceptualize whiteness as a producing power struggling to let some bodies pass as racially unnoticed, and others not, and thus consequently, to subject some bodies to the processes of racialization and others not. The production of race and whiteness takes place in the contact between this structural power and the performativity of the bodies in terms of their ability to inhabit whiteness or not (Butler, 1990, 1993a; Smedegaard Nielsen, 2014, pp. 63–64). It works to create social relationships between people that are bodily manifested and recognizable. That it is meaningful to conceptualize this power as whiteness, and not, for example, blackness or brownness, has historical reasons. Historically, the power of racial whiteness has been expanded alongside European colonialism through the racialization of non-white bodies, as being made objects for white Europeans' civilization and capturing of the world (Dyer, 1997, p. 30; Goldberg, 2006). Although it is important to note that the bodily signs recognized as white are historically and situationally changeable, history has illustrated that some bodily signs will more easily than

others pass as white. Richard Dyer (1997, pp. 12–13) refers to a hegemonic whiteness to which the idea of the Northern European body most
easily lay claim. This implies that, although whiteness comes in different
degrees, some characteristics such as blue eyes and blond hair are uniquely
white, and assembled at one body will thus signify the whitest and
undoubted whiteness (Dyer, pp. 42–43). Furthermore, these characteristics are often used to refer to a certain Nordic whiteness (Sawyer, 2008,
p. 90; Smedegaard Nielsen, 2014, pp. 257–258). Hence, in a Danish context, it can be safe to assume that the public space to some degree is regu-
lated by the power of whiteness.

Empirically, whiteness mostly appears at one of the two extremes of
being hypervisible or invisible, depending on the gaze (Brander Rasmussen,
Klinenberg, Nexica, & Wray, 2001, p. 10; Frankenberg, 2001). In 1920,
W. E. B. Du Bois (1969/1920, p. 29) wrote about "the souls of white
folks":

> Of them I am singularly clairvoyant. I see in and through them. I view them
> from unusual points of vantage. Not as a foreigner do I come, for I am
> native, not foreign, bone of their thought and flesh of their language.

On the other hand, whiteness can be difficult to get a grip on, as it often
stands out as "just" human, in contrast to the racialization of people of
color (Dyer, 1997, p. 1–2). This has made way for the conceptualization
of whiteness as invisible, but as Ruth Frankenberg (2001) points out, the
invisibility of whiteness might be a white delusion, as it is indeed visible for
most racialized people. Rather, the hyper-/invisibility of whiteness is
closely connected to the body's capability of inhabiting whiteness or not,
and its consequential lived experiences of whiteness and race (Du Bois,
1969/1920; Frankenberg, 2001). Hence, when whiteness manifests itself
as "natural" and invisible, it must be thought of as being embodied practices, of *some* bodies, what could be termed, a habit (Ahmed, 2006,
p. 129f). Bourdieu views an agent's habitus, that is, its dispositions for
praxis, beliefs, and preferences, as formed by their social position and their
experiences (Bourdieu, 1998, pp. 6–9). Within this line of thought, a
habitual whiteness can be viewed as part of a racialized habitus for those
who inhabit whiteness or "...for those who get so used to its inhabitance
that they learn not to see it," as Ahmed (2006, p. 133) puts it. So, how
can I, as inhabiting whiteness, study whiteness? I need to believe that
when the habit of whiteness can be learned by those who do not inhabit

whiteness, there must also be a way to learn to see whiteness while inhabit-ing it. At least, I will make an effort. I can do this by learning from racial-ized people's experiences and reflections on whiteness. And, I can make an effort to derogate myself from my own habitual whiteness and address my own whiteness within the analytical object of whiteness that I study. I can do this by drawing on my lived experiences of how whiteness becomes a habit, for example, through the comfortableness and easiness that comes with letting one's whiteness pass unnoticed (Ahmed, 2006, p. 132). Moreover, exactly this experience makes me acknowledge and accept that, for me as researcher, it demands a coming to terms with feelings of unease and uncomfortableness to confront whiteness and the privileges it pro-duces for bodies like my own that pass as white. Awaking to her own whiteness and racism, Frankenberg (2001, p. 77) states that: "White anti-racism is, perhaps, a stance requiring lifelong vigilance," meaning that white habitus has to be continuously shaken in order to keep an antiracist stance. So, put shortly, I will try to continuously stir up my bad habit of whiteness, in the study of it.

To guide my search for and analysis of whiteness in my data, I will take hold of this conceptualization of whiteness as a habit. Inspired by Sara Ahmed (2004, 2006) and Ghassan Hage (1998), I will furthermore relate it to the analysis of how whiteness takes up space. Whereas Ahmed (2006) works with the notion of space within an abstract theoretical thinking, Hage (1998) puts his focus on the work of whiteness in the constitution of the nation and the national space. Hage finds that white Australians tend to view the national territory as a space whereto whites have a more "natural" and innate right than others like "Third World-looking people" and Aboriginal people. He sees this as part of a "white nation fantasy," which also shows itself through a conception that white Australians think that they are entitled to regulate non-whites' access to the nation (Hage, 1998, p. 18–19). Ahmed (2006, p. 109) views whiteness as a social and bodily orientation in space and argues that when a space, or the world at large, is made white, for example, through the history of colonialism, then bodies that can inhabit whiteness will be and feel at home, whereas other bodies will not. Hence, similar to Hage's thoughts, whiteness implies an idea of some bodies' more "natural" or habitual (Ahmed, 2006, p. 129) belonging and access to the considered space. A sense of the habitualness of whiteness can also be recognized from Hage's (1998) notion of the white nation fantasy, insofar as he disconnects this fantasy from the ques-tion of having racist intentions or not, as he identifies it as white Australians of both racist and multiculturalist ideological beliefs (p. 18). Thus, at some points, these two views of whiteness as being habitual or a white nation fantasy have some similarities. Nevertheless, I find Ahmed's notion of habitual whiteness a bit more adequate for my analytical purpose, as "the habit" implies an embodiment as routines or other forms of praxis, whereas the notion of fantasy can more easily risk being seen as isolated to the minds of people. Hence, the habit as analytical tool opens the gaze for the importance of bodily performances of whiteness. However, in order to capture the habitualness of whiteness in a specific analytical context, Hage's thoughts are very useful. From a Bourdieu-inspired point of view, he argues that the Australian national space is governed by a field of whiteness, where the accumulation of national capital is limited by a person's non-white appearance and thus the appearance of not being a "natural" white Australian. Hence, when addressing whiteness as habit, it is of great significance to consider how it informs habits of nationality, in my case the habits of Danishness. For my analytical purpose, in particular, habitual ideas or performances concerning the constitution of the Danish public are of interest.

Having, thus, argued for an approach to the Danish public space as being informed by habitual whiteness, it is next relevant to consider how the spatial occupation by whiteness is produced and maintained. It is here that I will address the affectivity of fear and, thus, follow an affect-analytical framework for analysis, mainly inspired by Ahmed's (2004, 2006) works on affect. She (2006, pp. 134–135) points out that to maintain its habitual inhabitance of space it is crucial for whiteness to expand itself. She views white bodies as comfortable, by which she refers to that "whiteness may function as a form of public comfort *by allowing bodies to extend into spaces that have already taken their shape*" (Ahmed, 2006, p. 135, emphasis in original). Hence, it comes about with greater ease to let whiteness expand itself within an already white space than to let other bodies take up space. But, the expansion of whiteness will always restrict other bodies. I will study how the affectivity of fear influences the inhabitance and expansion of whiteness within the Danish national space. I will address what Ahmed (2004, p. 68) terms "the spatial politics of fear" which says that "fear works to restrict some bodies through the movement or expansion of others" (p. 69). When studying discourses of "the threat of terror," the affective work of fear is of great relevance to address, as fear may be the most common way that threat is "felt into being" (Massumi, 2010, p. 54).

To sum up, I will let my analysis be guided by the two main characteristics of whiteness outlined above. That is, first, to search for the presence of a habitual whiteness, identified through, for example, an unreflected experience of the Danish public as white, a sense of naturalness related to the belonging of white bodies to the national Danish space, and processes of racialization or "othering," that is, the constitution of bodies as nonwhite and/or non-Danish. Second, I will study the movement of fear and conduct analyses of how this movement relates itself to the racialized organization of space, including considerations of whether whiteness can be seen to expand itself through fear.

Lastly, it should be mentioned that my theory-driven approach, which I find inevitable when addressing whiteness, means that my analyses will not expose every detail of scientific interest that might be found in the empirical material. However, as I have elsewhere done a comprehensive analytical work on the presence of the terror threat in Danish television news, with a particular focus on its significance for the racialized structurings of Danish society, the analyses presented in this chapter will be contextualized within a sensitivity toward the broader picture of newsmaking on the threat of terror that I have exposed in earlier studies (Smedegaard Nielsen, 2014).

## *Threat as News*

The fact that I study public service news production sets some particular conditions for my analyses. First, the news are produced by professional journalists, working within professional media institutions, and thus expected to follow those ideals and norms that are regulating the journalistic profession, such as objectivity and the view of news as a transmission of information about reality (Chouliaraki, 2013; Tuchman, 1972; Wien, 2005). Second, the public service status entails that the journalists in their news production have an obligation to address and represent the broader general public and its interests. With the public service media, DR and TV2, being institutionalized as national Danish media, the general public is here conceived of as a national Danish public. Furthermore, the increasing commercialization of media, and in a Danish context the competition of attracting viewers between DR and TV2, might foster an even more intense effort to address the national public in its broadest sense in order to attract as many viewers as possible. Following Lilie Chouliaraki (2013), I view journalism as a performative practice, and thus I study the specificities of professional public service journalism in terms of how it works to perform the public it claims to represent. Hence, my focus is on how the public is performed in news journalism about the terror threat with particular attention set on how the affectivity of fear informs this performative practice.

My affect-analytical framework is inspired by Sara Ahmed (2004, 2006) and her "model of affect as contact" (2006, p. 2). She holds that "...fear opens up past histories of association" (2004, p. 63) and argues that when, for example, a child fears a bear, it must be explained by the fact that the child has already learned that the bear is fearsome. However, she does not thereby argue that the child's immediate reaction is based on a conscious reflexivity about the bear as fearsome. Instead, she argues that past histories of contact between the bear and the child shape a bodily knowledge in the child of the bear as fearsome (2004, p. 7). In this view she differs from other approaches to affect like Brian Massumi (2010), who distinguishes between referential language *about* danger and performative signs *of* danger, where the latter will trigger an automatic bodily response independent on our consciousness, and thus conceptualizes this response as affective (pp. 59,63). Within this approach, affect is seen as detached from the level of consciousness and signification. This issue, whether affect should be thought of as detached from or closely interrelated with signification and consciousness, is disputed among scholars of affectivity and thus leaves the field more or less divided between these two understandings of affect (Hemmings, 2005; Leys, 2011a, 2011b). By more or less adapting Ahmed's conceptualization of affect, I position myself in the camp of the latter. I agree with Ruth Leys (2011a) who argues that the separation of bodily affect and conscious emotions installs an inadequate dualism suggesting a splitting in the human between different levels, such as the conscious and the unconscious, the bodily and the cognitive. Hence, in order to fully understand how affects and emotions shape social life, I find it inevitable to consider its mutual interrelation to signification and social structures. Following Ahmed's (2004, 2006) model of affect as contact, then, when some sign or object triggers an affective response it has to do with the way we come into contact with it, and how the history of meaning it carries with it invites us to orient ourselves toward it. Nevertheless, I also draw inspiration from Massumi (2010) and Richard Grusin (2010), whose conceptualizations of affect differ from mine, as they have made valuable contributions to the research on fear and mediation of terror, respectively.

In interviews with news journalists from the Danish public service television stations, DR1 and TV2, I found that they come into contact with signs of the threat of terror in other ways than they expect their viewers to come into contact with them. Whereas they conceptualized their audience, the Danish public, as a fearing public, fear was not the primary affective response they expressed toward the threat of terror themselves. Rather, they expressed a sense of excitement when thinking about their important societal role as being obliged to news coverage of the events in case of a future terror attack (Smedegaard Nielsen, 2014, p. 294). One of the interviewed journalists put it like this:

> ...we, who cover it, would know, that it would make history. In contrast to almost everything else we make, which is more day-to-day, then it would be historic the moment it happens. So, that's where we are, that's why we clear the schedule.

Massumi (2010, p. 54) suggests viewing threat as an affective fact that is being felt into being as fear. However, as the quote illustrates, threat is not only felt into being in the form of fear but, in the case of the journalists, felt it as excitement. Furthermore, this suggests that it can be fruitful to study the performativity of affects, in the sense that the expression of particular emotions entails a performance of particular subjectivities. When the interviewed journalists felt the threat into being through excitement, they simultaneously constituted themselves as important societal actors taking the responsibility of informing a fearful public about the terror threat. The constitution of a fearful public made them able to position themselves in the important role of handling terror by informing the public about it (Smedegaard Nielsen, 2014, p. 283). Hence, the affectivities of excitement and fear together let the journalists perform themselves as capable and responsible and the public as passively fearing in need of the journalists' work.

Besides the specifics of the journalism of public service news, the newsmaking on the threat of terror must also be studied with sensitivity toward its socio-historical context of the paradigm of an ever-present threat of terror against the West, which has arisen since the 9/11 attacks in 2001. With his concept *premediation*, Richard Grusin (2010) argues that after 9/11 the media have contributed to link 9/11 to the future by "making itself felt" (p. 8) as event, thereby justifying the regime of preemptiveness and the anticipation of security against future terror. By this effort the media have worked to prepare the public for future terror in order to not be caught unaware, as was the case in 2001 (Grusin, 2010, pp. 2, 4, 8–9, 141). When a journalist at DR, after the attacks in Copenhagen in 2015 with reference to debates on social media, assesses that people were not shocked by the attack because "they had expected that...a shooting like this *would* happen in Denmark, in Copenhagen, at some point" (DR1, 2015a), it can be regarded to reflect this point from Grusin. Hence, the premediation of terror comes to confirm the attacks as an incident of exactly the premediated terror, although it has, afterward, been disputed in public debates if the attacks rightfully could be defined as terror (Khader, 2015a, 2015b; Wilhjelm, 2015). Moreover, the interpretative logic at work in the journalist's assessment of the public expecting an attack like this—immediately interpreted as terror—also becomes self-causal because it refers back to the past by its confirmation that the public *has* been pre-pared to expect what was actually going to happen. Hence, a self-referential logic is at work, where it is the expectedness of terror that both marks the attacks as terror and constructs the public as one expecting exactly this kind of attack and, thus, is expected to fear it. Additionally, when the jour-nalist suggests that "people were not shocked," it points at that exactly the premediation of the threat might have a bigger impact on the constitution of society than actual terror attacks themselves. This illustrates the societal significance of the phenomenon of "the threat" and its close relation to the affectivity of fear as is the analytical focus of the chapter.

Grusin (2010) could be criticized for holding an unconscious US-centric view on the work of the media, as he does not clarify which public or publics are objects for the media's affective work. Thus, he lacks consideration of the significance of the more specific local contexts within which the media content is produced and received. In a Danish context, the crisis of the Muhammad cartoons, and not 9/11, stands out as the event that most insistently continues to "make itself self" (Grusin, 2010, p. 8) as what is justifying preemptive measures of controlling the threat of terror, as well as the mediated awareness of it (Smedegaard Nielsen, 2014). This was evident in the immediate response to the attack on *Krudttønden*. Precisely because the center hosted a meeting about "freedom of speech" with the participa-tion of the Swedish Muhammad cartoonist, Lars Vilks, the attack was inter-preted as an ongoing terror attack, calling for the police to preemptively secure the city for further attacks—regretfully, the police did not manage to avoid the other tragic attack where a young man, guarding the Jewish syna-gogue, was killed. Also, in the following days, "Middle Eastern-looking" men were reported to have been unlawfully held by the police for suspicion of terror, and Muslims reported having been harassed, as well as having violence committed against them, from white Danes (Christiansen, 2015; Larsen, 2015).

Ahmed (2004, 2006) suggests that it is valuable to address affect by studying it as something working *between* bodies or subjects, and thus in their contact with each other (Ahmed, 2006, p. 2). She argues that affect circulates in both backward historic and sideways movements between signs, objects, and bodies, making them relate to each other in terms of linking them together or differentiating between them. In their circulation, affects accumulate over time and thus work to make more persistent bindings and blockages between signs, objects, and bodies (Ahmed, 2004, pp. 44, 64, 89). Thereby, affects can work as a structuring force for the spatial organization of society. By adding the model of affect as contact, as Ahmed (2004, 2006) offers, premediation can be reworked as a concept referring to the media presence of an anticipation of future terror, but which needs to be further considered in terms of how it is formed by the circulation of affect in and between different contexts or zones of contacts between signs of terror and the fearing, excited, or otherwise affected subject. Hence, both the situational contexts, the pointing out of particular signs of terror, and the ways subjects orient themselves toward the threat, all form part of the affective work of the mediated threat.

### Their Terror, Our Fear

The post-2001 premediation of terror does not just anticipate any kind of terror, as it is an *Islamist*-motivated terror that is expected to come. This is in itself an important element in how the premediation of terror can be thought of. In my analyses of both newscasts and interviews, exactly the *non*-Islamist motive behind the Norwegian July 22, 2011, terror attack stood out as surprising and as a contrast to the journalists' preconceptions of terror. Hence, for the journalists, the right-extremist terror of July 22nd was not something that formed part of the premediation, that is, it was not the *kind* of terror that was expected. Rather, July 22nd stood out as an incidence of exception, as a deviation from the expected path of history (Smedegaard Nielsen, 2014, 2015). Thus, rather than terror, as such, being premediated, it is more accurate to talk about a premediation of Islamist terror. This marks a significant twist, as it makes the threat hinge on "the Islamist" rather than on "terror" in itself.

Being linked to "the Islamist," the threat of terror becomes a threat stemming from something that has to do with particular ideologies, cultures, and bodies. This was also reflected in the news coverage of July 22nd, in which Breivik's appearance as white was what first cast doubt about the expected Islamist motive behind the attacks, and the perpetrator's identity as "Muslim" (Smedegaard Nielsen, 2015, pp. 46–48). In the interviews with journalists, conducted a few months after the attacks, the significance of the premediated *Islamist* terror was evidently demonstrated by their spontaneous comparisons of the actual scenario of the July 22nd terror attack and the imagined scenario of *if* it had been conducted by "a Muslim." They judged that two such attacks, being similar in their scope of dead and injured, would have had totally different societal consequences due to the difference of identities and motives of the perpetrators (Smedegaard Nielsen, 2015). As one of the journalists put it: "if it had been a Muslim then it would have had terrible consequences" (Smedegaard Nielsen, 2015, p. 48). Accordingly, when considering the affective work of mediated threat, it cannot *just* be evaluated in terms of if it generates affects at the public such as an affectivity of security, as Grusin (2010, p. 141) argues. It must also be evaluated in terms of how it interacts with structures of signification in its affective orientation of bodies, signs, and objects. In short, it must be considered why the interviewed journalists judge that "Muslim terror" would generate fear and societal division, while the right-wing, white, Christian terror is not considered to do so (Smedegaard Nielsen, 2015). Arjun Appadurai (2006, pp. 8, 78–79, 92) argues that minorities, however small they may be, remind the national majority of its incompleteness, and thus, can cause fear of a possible future numerical turnaround of the majority-minority relation. Hence, "the Muslim terrorist" living among "us" might trigger this anxiety of incompleteness, which can be read as both the fear of future terror from minorities, and as the worry that the terror attack will be followed by anger toward the terrorist's fellow minority members, as some of the interviewed journalists express. Both fear of and the concern for the minority group of the terrorist express the idea that "the Muslim terrorist" has something to do with and somehow relates itself to the societal constitutions of majority and minorities, whereas the white, ethnic Norwegian terrorist does not. Ahmed (2004, p. 72) argues that rather than viewing fear as something just being there, what should really be considered is how a "language of fear" works to draw boundaries between those who threaten and those who are under threat. Thus, when the journalists judge that the July 22nd terror attack will not cause further fear, it must be because right-extremist, white, Christian terror is not part of a language—or discourse—of fear, that can work to mark it as a threat. On the contrary, the Islamist terror is. As a journalist in one of the analyzed newscasts expresses it, had it been Al-Qaeda, "…one [could] never know where it ended" (Smedegaard Nielsen, 2014, p. 201), and by this he marks the imagined Islamist attack as an incident of a lasting, continuous threat.

In his reflections on the phenomenon of "threat" Massumi (2010) points out that when signs alert us that a danger *could* happen in the future, it commands an affective response in the present. Hence, expectations of the future are at work as something structuring the present. As hinted at above, the way the Islamist terror is imagined by the journalists involves a sense of could-be-ness concerning the future, whereas the actual right-wing terror does not. Consequently, also the could-be-ness of future danger hinges on "the Islamist" rather than on "terror" in itself, as the Islamist terror is represented as continuously ongoing, whereas the right-extremist terror Breivik represents has ended with the termination of his specific attacks. Thus, when the could-be-ness of future terror is involved in discourse, it might not only, or even primarily, have to do with the danger of terror and our sense of security. Rather, we have to do with discourses that, as Ahmed (2004, p. 72) points out, work to intensify threats in its pointing out of bodies, signs, and objects of *the present* as respectively threatening and threatened. As a threat concerns what to come in the future—that we cannot know of—it needs to be reframed in terms of knowledge of the present—as what we *can* know of.

In my earlier work, I found that the produced knowledge of the present, in terms of identifying the threat in order to avoid it, involved a racialization of terror. Not least through a discourse on radicalization, the threat was inscribed on young, male Muslim/immigrant bodies as a terror potential (Smedegaard Nielsen, 2014, p. 106). This racialization of the threat as non-white goes hand in hand with the avoidance of acknowledging Breivik's white terror as a threat. Thus, the threat of terror seems to make a division between a racialized threat against a non-racialized public and thus points to the presence of a habitual view of the Danish/Norwegian/Nordic space as white. This point can be further strengthened from the considerations of how the journalists relate themselves to the addressed public when considering how to handle the threat. The racialization of the threat as inscribed on young, male Muslim/immigrant bodies must be considered in close relation to the journalists' positioning of other Muslim/immigrant bodies—male and female—in more positive affective relations to the public "us." In the news they are, for instance, positioned as useful resources, where the journalists on behalf of the public turn to the Muslim/immigrant in order to provide knowledge about this racialized other to the public "us." In other instances they are represented as law-abiding citizens showing their gratitude to the Danish society (Smedegaard Nielsen, 2014, p. 106). Hence, discourses of fear, as, for example, radicalization discourses, do not only work to point out the threatening and the threatened, as Ahmed suggests. They also work to relate bodies to each other with regard to how the threat can be handled. Here, the journalists stand out as acting on behalf of the addressed "we," which on its side is expected to fear. Thus, the journalists are represented as those who can represent "us" in the non-fearful orientations toward "the others" in order to use them as resources for handling the threat and to generate a more accurate picture of who to fear (Smedegaard Nielsen, 2014, p. 208).

As I see it, the spatial politics of fear, as outlined above, involve the expansion of whiteness. Fear is positioned at the public and works to connect the public to the journalists. However, this binding process does not go through the sharing of a common fear, but through a self-positioning of the journalists as authorities able to represent the public and take care of its fear through an addressing of those racialized others, who are not a threat. But still, the journalists' mediation between them and the public seems to go through an expectation that the public nevertheless might fear approaching them, or at least that they are not part of the public, on behalf of which the journalists exactly have to approach them. Thus, the public is performed through the expectation of a habitual white fear of a threat from racialized others, which works also to distance it to other non-threatening racialized others who consequently are excluded from the performed public. Moreover, it involves an expansion of whiteness, which though does not happen through an accumulation and expansion of a common fear, but rather through the journalists' representation of the public fear in a racialized orientation of non-white bodies as devices for the handling of the white fear. Hence, here the expansion of whiteness involves a racialization of bodies not recognized as white, where they are spatially restricted, by functioning as orientation devices for the white body (Ahmed, 2006, p. 128). It can be read as a way of countering an anxiety of incompleteness of the white nation (Appadurai, 2006), insofar as the non-white minority bodies work in favor of the expansion of whiteness.

These bodies work as orientation devices for the expansion of whiteness through a positioning of them as having a special connection to that threat that is to be handled in order to counter the white public fear. As such, whiteness is expanded through the restriction of these othered bodies, being retained in those specific positions. Hence, within the theoretical approach inspired by Ahmed (2006) and Hage (1998), the journalists' news communication on the threat of terror stands out as guided by a fantasy or habit of viewing the national Danish public as inhabited by white bodies that fear the racialized other from where the terror stems. In the following section, I will go deeper into the work of fear for the racialized regulation of space by considering other more recent cases related to the phenomenon of the terror threat.

### White Fear as Common Fear

On August 28, 2014, a train passenger traveling in the Copenhagen area felt threatened by the presence of another passenger, who was reportedly acting nervous and carrying a suitcase, and he was described as male of Middle Eastern appearance and having a beard. The passenger alarmed the police, and a manhunt of the suspected terrorist began, which included that the central train stations and other central areas in Copenhagen were cordoned off and guarded by heavily armed police. It was all intensively followed by the media, which apart from covering the activities of the police's action also distributed the police's description of the suspect and their warning against a "suspicious man," as well as the distributed surveillance photo of him, and speculated that he might have a bomb (Christiani, 2014; Thorsen, 2014). When the young man—who had been attending a university exam and had nothing to do with terrorism—found out he was being hunted and suspected of terror, he locked himself in a public restroom. He feared that the search for him could cause a citizen's arrest or other kinds of attacks against him.

In this case, the train passenger's fear of the man, as being a sign of terror, became "our" fear in its expansion in public space through the police's actions as well as the media's coverage. In this way, the fear of terror worked to spatially expand the bodies of those fearing terror, in the simultaneous restriction of those bodies being associated with terror. The young man's fear of being made an object for preemptive measures or attacks was very illustratively locked into a toilet. "Our" fear took up all space to such an extent that it hindered his fear to exist at all outside of his place of escape. And, it is worth bearing in mind that this work of fear happened in a situation where there turned out to not be any danger of terror to the public "us," whereas it seems a reasonable calculation of the young man that he might have been in danger due to the suspicions against him.

The example illustrates that the spatial politics of fear are racially structured. The racial component of the man's "Middle Eastern appearance" was a prominent element as to why he could be publicly perceived as endangering "us" (Butler, 1993b), as terror is ascribed as a potential of the male body of "Middle Eastern appearance" (Smedegaard Nielsen, 2014). On the other hand, his fear of preemptive measures against him was not directed toward publicly conceived endangering bodies. It became his specific individualized fear, which worked to further restrict his movement in space (Ahmed, 2004, p. 69). Thus, if the potentiality of terror inscribed on the racialized body of "Middle Eastern appearance" is what legitimizes the restriction and control of it as a matter of self-defense, it is simultaneously what gives way to the comfortable spatial expansion of whiteness in its presence as a generalized public fear (Ahmed, 2006, p. 129). Exactly the comfort of expanding whiteness can be recognized in this case. It would come about with much less ease to let the young man's fear of racialized violence accumulate, as it would question the fantasy of white supremacy within space (Hage, 1998). It would represent the non-whiteness, represented by the young man, as having an equal right to inhabit space, by letting its fear become public fear. And it would question the police's and media's reactions to the fear experienced by the train passenger, in the form of the hunt-down of the young man. If they should have reacted in the same way to his fear, it had demanded reflections about where the threats to him could stem from, reflections that might have questioned the rightfulness of the white public, and the legitimacy of the police and media as its representatives. Then, as Ahmed (2006, p. 135) suggests, it comes about with much more comfort and ease to allow "bodies to extend into spaces that have already taken their shape." It does not place uncomfortable questions to the status quo of the racialized shape of space.

In the case of the February 2015 attacks in Copenhagen on *Krudttønden* and the Synagogue, fear was also represented as a common fear in the media coverage, as well as the attacks being generalized as an example of the well-known terror threat. The fear was rather explicitly expanded from the specific locations of the attacks to the broader public addressed in the newsmaking. For instance, this came about in both DR's and TV2's coverage on February 14, where journalists in live reportages from location described their own emotional experiences of being there (DR1, 2015a, appr. 6:30 min; TV-2, 2015a, appr. 13:00 min). One journalist highlighted the proximity of the crime scene to a children's playground and further described how the families at the playground had experienced the atmosphere as "strange" and "unsafe" when they heard gunfire and saw the police coming (DR1, 2015a, appr. 6:30 min). TV2 transmitted an interview with a witness who appeared very emotionally touched and shocked, and the viewers were impressed by her emotions, when she said: "I saw the one who collapsed, I saw he was shot. I saw two people with guns and rifles, and then I saw the one who was shot. He collapsed. Outside" (TV-2, 2015a, appr. 12:25 min).

Also other emotions than fear worked to perform the Danish public as such as being under attack. Helle Thorning-Schmidt, the Danish Prime Minister, expressed a common mourning and loss: "Today all Danes' thoughts go to the victims and their families. We have all lost today" (DR1, 2015b, appr. 29:00 min). Furthermore, she coupled the loss with the struggle for "our" values and society, when she regarded the attacks as a reason for:

> us [...] as Danes to say [clearly] that this is not the Denmark we wish to have. We are a peace loving people, we love our democracy and everything we stand for, and we shall continue to be who we are, so to speak. Live as we are, meet and debate, go celebrate as the Jewish society did yesterday. And this is also the message we should send today in the midst of the grief. (TV-2, 2015b, appr. 11:45 min)

Judith Butler (2004, p. 19) argues that the mourning of some lives, and not others, is at work in the building of communities by its pointing out of which lives are grievable and thus count as real lives. My analysis suggests that similar affective work is done by fear. Those who are constituted as fearing must also be those lives that would be grievable if lost in a terror attack. Hence, where mourning is at work in the constitution of communities concerning those lives that have already been lost, fear is pointing at the future, constituting the community of those lives that should be protected against threats.

Such a linking of the mourned lost lives and the fearful protection of the lives feared to be lost in the future happened through a generalization of the case as part of a broader terror threat by references to other terror attacks (DR1, 2015b, appr. 18:00 min; TV-2, 2015a, appr. 18:15 min;

TV-2, 2015b, appr. 31:45 min), and by referring to the attacks as "a scene we know all too well" (DR1, 2015b, appr. 18:00 min). Apart from the premediation and expectedness of Islamist terror, the generalizations also worked to establish the threat, and thus, our fear as continuous, and thus as a condition for the constitution of society, rather than just being an isolated event. Hence, also in this case the affective work of the news seemed to take the comfortable way to expand in space those bodies that already inhabit space, by their fear of the Islamist terror.

As mentioned in the introduction, this stands in contrast to a comparable, but racist motivated, attack on a Swedish school, where the threat from racist violence was not generalized or accumulated as public fear. However, in later debates in Danish media, this was actually problematized, in terms of the questioning of the reasonableness of labeling the Copenhagen attacks as terror, but not the school attacks. This discussion mostly concerned the question why only Muslims with Islamist motives are recognized as terrorists. However, as I have tried to shed light on, I will hold that it also, and maybe even to a greater extent, can be explained by the fantasy of white supremacy (Hage, 1998), which only lets white fear be recognized. By habit, we only see white fear as fear, whereas brown or black fear disappears in its restriction fostered by the expansion of whiteness. Thus, fear can be seen as being at work in the constitution of reality. When we are not able to see the precariousness of non-white lives, it can be explained by those lives already being negated (Butler 2004, p. 33). They are not part of that reality, we—by habit—perceive as white. The use of the terror-label does in itself also contribute to this process. Terror is, per se, a threat against society and it implies indiscriminateness with regard to its victims, which makes the threat point at the public as such. By labeling that, which in the same token is implied as generating fear at white bodies, as terror, thus, works to generalize this specific white fear as a generalized human fear. In contrast, by the restriction of non-white people's fear (or of a fear that might not be habitually recognized as white, as, for example, the fear of right-extremist attacks that Social Democrats or others engaged in politics might have felt after the July 22nd terror attack), it is left as a specific fear, as an individual fear, or a fear just concerning particular groups or minorities and thus not concerning society at large. Consequently, those groups are exactly kept as minorities leaving the white nation fantasy intact.

To sum up, when the premediation of Islamist terror is at work within a setting of habitual whiteness (Ahmed, 2006, p. 129)—as the Danish public sphere—fear works to let white bodies expand in space through the restriction of other bodies. As such, threat can be regarded as a racialized feature keeping whiteness in a privileged position, through the logic of defending "ourselves" against those threats inscribed on the bodies of "the other." The habitual view of the public as white, in the newsmaking expressed through the journalists' fantasy of a white fearing public, is of crucial significance for the racialization of terror, involving the incapability of seeing white terror as threatening—if as terror at all. If it was not so, then racialized people's fear of racist attacks, the student's fear, or the fear generated by the racist killings of youngsters in the Swedish school could be accumulated into a common, public fear, allowing bodies not adhering to whiteness to take up space and resist the domination of whiteness within space. It could make way for the ability to recognize also the white terror faced by non-white people (hooks, 1992, p. 174). However, this was not what happened in these cases, as the Danish public space stands out to already having taken the shape of whiteness and thus has great difficulties of letting other bodies than whites expand into it.

## Conclusions and Perspectives

In this chapter, I have addressed the affective work of fear in news communication about the threat of terror in the post-9/11, 2001 climate, which in a Danish context has intensified after the crisis of the Muhammad Cartoons in 2005–2006. Although the focus on securitization against terror has undoubtedly increased significantly since 2001, I am not so confident that the post-2001 terror paradigm has caused fundamental shifts when considering the racialized structuration of space. As shown, it is not "terror" as threat in itself that is the image of the future being primarily involved in how the present is perceived. Rather it is "the Islamist" and its slidings to "the Muslim," "the immigrant," and all those histories of association it carries with it that are at work when the threat of future terror is made of significance for the present through the affectivity of fear. The media's work in the racializing processes of inscribing a potentiality of danger on the racialized—and mostly male—bodies has a much longer history. Even when considering "the Muslim or Middle Eastern body" (see Andreassen, 2007; Hervik, 2002).

Rather, the strong affectivity of the threat of terror might express an intensification of the work of whiteness to continuously expand itself in space in order to uphold its privileged position. If it is so, that whiteness must intensify its inhabitance of space, it could be interesting to consider why. Could it be that whiteness is threatened on its naturalized right to the national Danish space? Do we witness a greater visible presence of non-white bodies as part of the Danish public, and does it work to remind us that the world is not white and thus challenges the habitual whiteness? That is, is white fear, after all, the fear of losing white privilege? It could be considered if such a challenge to the habitual whiteness is what fosters an affectively intensified spatial expanding of whiteness, causing harsh restrictions of non-white bodies. But it could also be questioned if it is met by other more inclusive ways of performing the public. In the aftermath of the terror attacks in Bruxelles in 2016, DR's web news site brought a reportage from the neighborhood Molenbeek (which is suspected of housing terror cells) under the heading: "Muslim in Molenbeek: I'm just as frightened as anybody else" (Thomsen, 2016). This can of course be read as the exception that proves the rule of the fear of terror as white—after all, the newsworthiness of the quote must rely on an expectation that the audience would not expect "a Muslim" to fear terror. However, through a more optimistic lens, it might also be read as the humble beginnings of a more inclusive performance of the public in news journalism, where, as here, the "Muslim" fear of terror works to perform "the Muslim" as part of the public. However, in this case it is still "our" white fear that is adapted by "the Muslim," and not, for example, a non-white fear of racist attacks made public.

## REFERENCES

Ahmed, S. (2004). *The Cultural Politics of Emotion*. Edinburgh: Edinburgh University Press.

Ahmed, S. (2006). *Queer Phenomenology: Orientations, Objects, Others*. Durham & London: Duke University Press.

Allen, T. W. (1975). *Class Struggle and the Origin of Racial Slavery: The Invention of the White Race*. The New England Free Press.

Andreassen, R. (2007). *Der er et yndigt land. Medier, minoriteter og danskhed*. København: Tiderne Skifter.

Andreassen, R. (2014). Response: The Nordic Discomfort with 'Race'. *Nordic Journal of Migration Research, 4*(1), 42–44.

Andreassen, R., & Vitus, K. (Eds.). (2015). *Affectivity and Race. Studies. The Nordic Context*. Farnham: Ashgate.

Appadurai, A. (2006). *Fear of Small Numbers. An Essay on the Geography of Anger*. Durham & London: Duke University Press.

Blaagaard, B. B. (2009). *Journalism of Relation: Social Constructions of 'Whiteness' and Their Implications in Contemporary Danish Journalistic Practice and Production*. Ph.D. thesis, University of Utrecht, Utrecht, Netherlands.

Bourdieu, P. (1998). *Practical Reason. On the Theory of Action*. Cambridge: Polity Press.

Brander Rasmussen, B., Klinenberg, E., Nexica, I. J., & Wray, M. (2001). Introduction. In B. Brander Rasmussen et al. (Eds.), *The Making and Unmaking of Whiteness* (pp. 1–23). Durham & London: Duke University Press.

Butler, J. (1990). *Gender Trouble*. New York & London: Routledge.

Butler, J. (1993a). *Bodies that Matter: On the Discursive Limits of "Sex"*. New York & London: Routledge.

Butler, J. (1993b). Endangered/Endangering: Schematic Racism and White Paranoia. In R. Gooding-Williams (Ed.), *Reading Rodney King. Reading Urban Uprising* (pp. 15–22). New York & London: Routledge.

Butler, J. (2004). *Precarious Life. The Powers of Mourning and Violence*. London & New York: Verso.

Chouliaraki, L. (2013). Re-Mediation, Inter-Mediation, Trans-Mediation: The Cosmopolitan Trajectories of Convergent Journalism. *Journalism Studies, 14*(2), 267–283.

Christiani, S. G. (2014, August 28). Politiet advarer central steder i København mod mistænkelig mand. *DR.DK*, Copenhagen: DR. Retrieved from http://www.dr.dk/nyheder/indland/politiet-advarer-centrale-steder-i-koebenhavn-mod-mistaenkelig-mand.

Christiansen, M. S. (2015). Terror-tjekket for tredje gang: Jeg kræver en undskyldning. *Ekstra Bladet*, 12 March, Copenhagen: JP/Politikens Hus. Retrieved from http://ekstrabladet.dk/112/terror-tjekket-for-tredje-gang-jeg-kraever-en-undskyldning/5478959

Doane, A. W., & Bonilla-Silva, E. (Eds.). (2003). *White Out. The Continuing Significance of Racism*. London & New York: Routledge.

DR1. (2015a, February 14). TV-Avisen 18.30, Copenhagen: DR (Television Broadcast).

DR1. (2015b, February 15). TV-Avisen 18.30, Copenhagen: DR (Television Broadcast).

Du Bois, W. E. B. (1969/1920). The Souls of White Folks. In *Darkwater: Voices from within the Veil* (pp. 29–55). New York: Schocken Books.

Dyer, R. (1997). *White*. London & New York: Routledge.

Frankenberg, R. (1993). White Women, Race Matters: *The Social Construction of Whiteness*. Minneapolis: University of Minnesota Press.

Frankenberg, R. (2001). The Mirage of an Unmarked Whiteness. In B. Rasmussen et al. (Eds.), *The Making and Unmaking of Whiteness* (pp. 72–96). Durham & London: Duke University Press.

Goldberg, D. T. (2006). Racial Europeanization. *Ethnic and Racial Studies, 29*(2), 331–364.

Grusin, R. (2010). *Premediation. Affect and Mediality after 9/11*. Hampshire & New York: Palgrave Macmillan.

Hage, G. (1998). *White Nation. Fantasies of White Supremacy in a Multicultural Society*. New York & London: Routledge.

Hemmings, C. (2005, September). Invoking Affect. Cultural Theory and the Ontological Turn. *Cultural Studies, 19*(5), 548–567.

Hervik, P. (2002). *Mediernes Muslimer. En antropologisk undersøgelse af mediernes dækning af religioner i Danmark*. København: Nævnet for Etnisk Ligestilling.

hooks, b. (1992). *Black Looks. Race and Representation*. Boston: South End Press.

Hübinette, T., Hörnfeldt, H., Farahani, F., & Rosales, R. L. (2012). *Om ras och vithet i ett samtida Sverige*. Botkyrka: Mångkulturellt centrum.

Hübinette, T., & Lundström, C. (2011). Sweden after the Recent Election: The Double-Binding Power of Swedish Whiteness Through the Mourning of the Loss of 'Old Sweden' and the Passing of 'Good Sweden'. *NORA—Nordic Journal of Feminist and Gender Research, 19*(1), 42–52.

Keskinen, S., Tuori, S., Irni, S., & Mulinari, D. (Eds.). (2009). *Complying with Colonialism: Gender, Race and Ethnicity in the Nordic Region*. Farnham: Ashgate.

Khader, N. (2015a, May 9). Jo, gu' er det terror. *Politiken*, Copenhagen: JP/ Politikens Hus. Retrieved from http://politiken.dk/debat/ECE2661843/jo-gu-er-det-terror/

Khader, N. (2015b, May 22). Preben Wilhjelm er blind for den indre fjende, vi står overfor. *Politiken*, Copenhagen: JP/Politikens Hus. Retrieved from http://politiken.dk/debat/ECE2680909/preben-wilhjelm-er-blind-for-den-indre-fjende-vi-staar-over-for/

Larsen, J. B. (2015, February 20). Danske muslimer melder om hadske overgreb efter terror. *DR.DK*, Copenhagen: DR. Retrieved from http://www.dr.dk/ nyheder/indland/danske-muslimer-melder-om-hadske-overgreb-efter-terror

Leys, R. (2011a). The Turn to Affect: A Critique. *Critical Inquiry, 37*(4), 434–472.

Leys, R. (2011b). Affect and Intention: A Reply to William E. Connolly. *Critical Inquiry, 37*(4), 799–805.

Loftsdottir, K., & Jensen, L. (2012). *Whiteness and Postcolonialism in the Nordic Region: Exceptionalism, Migrant Others and National Identities*. Farnham: Ashgate.

Massumi, B. (2010). The Future Birth of the Affective Fact. The Political Ontology of Threat. In M. Gregg & G. J. Seigworth (Eds.), *The Affect Theory Reader* (pp. 52–70). Durham & London: Duke University Press.

Morrison, T. (1992). *Playing in the Dark: Whiteness and the Literary Imagination*. Cambridge, MA: Harvard University Press.

Myong, L. (2009). *Adopteret. Fortællinger om transnational og racialiseret tilblivelse*. Ph.D. thesis, Institut for Læring, Danmarks Pædagogiske Universitetsskole, Aarhus Universitet, Copenhagen.

Sawyer, L. (2008). Engendering 'Race' in Calls for Diasporic Community in Sweden. *Feminist Review, 90*, 87–105.

Smedegaard Nielsen, A. (2014). *De vil os stadig til livs: Betydningskonstruktioner i tv-nyhedsformidling om terrortruslen mod Danmark.* Ph.D. thesis, Department of Media, Cognition and Communication, Københavns Universitet, Copenhagen.

Smedegaard Nielsen, A. (2015). If It Had Been a Muslim. Affectivity and Race in Danish Journalists' Reflections about Making News on Terror. In R. Andreassen & K. Vitus (Eds.), *Affectivity and Race. Studies from Nordic Contexts* (pp. 43–58). Farnham: Ashgate.

Thomsen, P. B. (2016, March 24). Muslim i Molenbeek: Jeg er lige så bange som alle andre. *DR.DK*, Copenhagen: DR. Retrieved from https://www.dr.dk/ nyheder/udland/muslim-i-molenbeek-jeg-er-lige-saa-bange-som-alle-andre

Thorsen, K. R. (2014, August 28). Tidligere PET-chef: Derfor begynder politiet menneskejagten. *TV2.DK*, Odense: TV-2. Retrieved from http://nyheder.tv2. dk/krimi/2014-08-28-tidligere-pet-chef-derfor-begynder-politiet-menneskejagten-0

Tuchman, G. (1972). Objectivity as Strategic Ritual: An Examination of Newsmen's Notions of Objectivity. *The American Journal of Sociology, 77*(4), 660–679.

TV-2. (2015a, February 14). *Nyhederne 19.00*, Odense: TV-2 (Television Broadcast).

TV-2. (2015b, February 15). *Nyhederne 19.00*, Odense: TV-2 (Television Broadcast).

Wellman, D. T. (1977). *Portraits of White Racism.* Cambridge: Cambridge University Press.

Wien, C. (2005). Defining Objectivity within Journalism. *Nordicom Review*, (2), 3–15.

Wilhjelm, P. (2015, May 12). Attentatet på Krudttønden var hadforbrydelse ikke terror. *Politiken*, Copenhagen: JP/Politikens Hus. Retrieved from http:// politiken.dk/debat/debatindlaeg/ECE2665502/attentatet-paa-krudttoen-den-var-hadforbrydelse-ikke-terror/

Yilmaz, F. (2006). *Ethnicized Ontologies: From Foreign Worker to Muslim Immigrant. How Danish Public Discourse Moved to the Right through the Question of Immigration.* Ph.D. thesis, University of California, San Diego.

# Denials of Racism and Racialization

PART II

Uptake of Cadmium and Radiocesium

# Talking Color-Blind: Justifying and Rationalizing Attitudes Toward Interracial Marriages in Sweden

*Sayaka Osanami Törngren*

## INTRODUCTION

Even though Sweden played a leading role in the development of race biology in the beginning of the twentieth century, the usage of the concept and categories of race is not widely accepted in the twenty-first-century Sweden. The word *race* is most often replaced with words such as "origin" or "ethnic groups," and differences between the majority and minority are discussed by using ambiguous terms such as "immigrants," "country of birth," or "persons with immigrant background."

Color-blindness, "a mode of thinking about race organized around an effort to not "see," or, at any rate, not to acknowledge, race differences" (Frankenberg, 1993, p. 142), is prominent in Sweden (Hübinette, Hörnfeldt, & Rosales, 2012). Swedish integration policy is based on the color-blind ideology, which revolves around the idea that everybody is

S. Osanami Törngren (✉)
Malmö Institute for Studies of Migration, Diversity and Welfare,
Malmö University, Malmö, Sweden
e-mail: sayaka.torngren@mau.se

© The Author(s) 2019
P. Hervik (ed.), *Racialization, Racism, and Anti-Racism in the Nordic Countries*, Approaches to Social Inequality and Difference,
https://doi.org/10.1007/978-3-319-74630-2_6

137

equal regardless of their cultural or ethnic background. Swedes understand themselves as being "democratic, liberal, equal, tolerant and individualist"; highly value "anti-racism, universalism, secularism and gender equality"; and realize these values to a great extent (Heinö, 2009, p. 303). It is interesting that color-blindness is so embedded in the integration policy in Sweden, considering that the country officially embraces multiculturalism, which recognizes distinctiveness of different ethnic and racial groups. Swedish multiculturalism has centered around the idea of taking measures "positively," providing minorities' right to state support independent of ethnic and cultural background rather than promoting "negative" policies that give minorities the right to exemptions from state intervention (Borevi, 2013). In the most recent reform of 2009, the goal of integration policy included the same rights, duties, and possibilities for everyone irrespective of ethnic and cultural background, with a focus on individuals. Access to the labor market is a central feature of integration policy, which derives from a belief that the labor market is color-blind and rational (Heinö, 2009; Mattsson, 2004; Rakar, 2010). Because Swedish multiculturalism is based on the idea that everybody should be able to access institutional policies and all should be treated equally independent of ethnicity and race, multiculturalism can coexist with color-blindness.

Instead of specifically referring to race or visible differences, the concept of ethnicity and culture is widely accepted and applied to analyze and understand contemporary racism, anti-racism, and racialization in Sweden (Hübinette et al., 2012). Despite the prevailing color-blind ideal in politics and in academia, research shows that visible differences matter in Sweden and how whiteness and racial differences shape the definition of Swedishness and non-Swedishness (Osanami Törngren, 2011; Hübinette & Lundström, 2011; Mattsson, 2005; Runfors, 2006, 2016). Many researchers illustrate that it is not the individuals' ethnicity and culture that matter but rather their visible differences such as skin color and other physical markers, that is, race that matter. African, Asian, Latin American, and Middle Eastern identities are developed through interaction and contact with the majority society, through which they become aware of their skin and hair color being different (Kalonaityte, Kwesa, & Tedros, 2007; Khosravi, 2006; Lundberg, 2014; Lundström, 2007; Nam, 2007; Trotzig, 2001). Moreover, the concept of ethnicity is solely used when discussing the situations of Muslims, Africans, or Latin Americans in Sweden and never applied to discuss the situations of white Danish, Norwegian, or German immigrants. Perception of racial differences leads to the idea of ethnic and cultural differences that may or may not exist. The terms *ethnicity* and *culture* therefore are actually used as a means of referring to people who are nonwhite, in other words, racial minorities, without referring to the racial and visible differences.

This chapter problematizes this color-blind approach in Sweden and analyzes the way white Swedes talk color-blindly. Apfelbaum et al. address how color-blindness is strategically used in the effort to appear unbiased and unprejudiced during social interaction and needs more examination (Apfelbaum, Sommers, & Norton, 2008). Based on interview results, this chapter addresses how attitudes toward interracial marriages are justified, rationalized, and normalized through color-blind expressions. Expressing reservations toward interracial marriages in color-blind manners is seen in previous studies in the US (Bonilla-Silva, 2010; Frankenberg, 1993; Moran, 2001), and this chapter explores whether the equivalent can be observed in the Swedish context. The analysis shows that the interviewees' words reflect two broad ways of color-blind explanations of the racial preference of a marriage partner and attitudes toward interracial marriages: rationalization of attitudes as natural through the values of liberty and equality focusing on individual choice and gender equality and arguing for the problems that can arise in marriages focusing on culture and welfare of the couple and the children. Especially the idea of individual choice and gender equality defined as part of Swedish culture and value becomes a very powerful way of naturalizing and rationalizing the choice and preference of a marriage partner in a color-blind manner. These two ways of explaining the attitudes emerge as a rational way of understanding the attitudes and make the preference of a marriage partner as reasonable rather than prejudiced. At the same time, these justifications mark a strong distinction and separation of "we" Swedes and "others," which indicate a strong racial divide.

## THEORETICAL PREMISES

### *The Idea of Race*

The concept of race evolved theoretically as a biological category first, until science proved that there is no such thing as biological racial categories explaining inferiority and superiority. Up to the late nineteenth to the early twentieth century, European researchers, including prominent Swedish scholars, engaged in studies dividing human beings into different races. In the beginning, this was conducted supposedly without any racist implications; however, a racist ideology was introduced into the division of human "race" by scholars like Gobineau and those who promoted social Darwinism. Through social Darwinism, cultural, social, and moral differences were explained by biological racial differences, which entailed superiority and inferiority. Studies of racial biology and eugenics flourished with this idea. Sweden played a central role in the evolving understanding of race, from biological to social categories. Herman Lundborg, for example, who was strongly influenced by Gobineau's idea of race, played a prominent role in the development and the construction of the idea of the Swedish race as "the pure race." He was deeply concerned that the Swedish race was threatened by degeneration and promoted Eugenics and advocated that the pureness of the Swedish race should be maintained through prohibiting immigration and racial mixing. Sweden established the world's first governmental institute engaged in racial biology in 1922, and Lundborg became the head of the institute (Broberg & Tydén, 2005; Furuhagen, 2007; Gustafsson, 2007; Hagerman, 2007; Jacobsson, 1999).

The scientific value of dividing humans in different races proved to have little meaning and already by the 1920s. In 1936, when Gunnar Dahlberg became the head of the National Institute for Racial Biology, Sweden took on a different turn: Dahlberg maintained that there was no evidence of racial difference when only looking at visible features such as skin color and facial forms and that there was no reason to believe that one race was better than the other. The idea of biological race was officially dismissed worldwide in 1950 after World War II in a declaration made by UNESCO, which affirmed that there was no biologically superior or inferior human race. The Swedish scholars Gunnar Dahlberg and Gunnar Myrdal were among the scholars who signed the declaration (Jacobsson, 1999).

Even though race bears no biological significance, the social reality and meaning of race, that is, idea of race and stereotypes and prejudices against certain groups of people, remain alive in contemporary societies. Therefore, today in the field of social science, race is commonly understood as a socially constructed idea evoked by visible differences. Race is something that exists not as a biological reality but as a social reality because racism and discrimination based on the idea of race still prevail. Race as a social construct means that the meanings and categories of race are constructed in a specific context and vary according to place, society, and over time. Although a social construction, race is socially real for some groups of people and "affect[s] their social life whether individual members of the races want it or not" (Bonilla-Silva, 1997, p. 473).

## The Idea of Color-Blindness

Race is a product of thought that is culturally, socially, and historically determined. Therefore, the Swedish involvement in the development of the idea of race should not be forgotten and erased. However, today, Sweden is reluctant to admit the fact that racism and discrimination are based on the idea of race that exists in society. Many Swedish scholars cling to the idea of ethnicity, culture, and citizenship to explain racism and discrimination in Sweden and avoid discussing discrimination in terms of racial and visible differences, with a strong belief that "race does not exist" (Hübinette et al., 2012). Brekke and Brochgrevink (2007) write about the ambiguous categorization of people in Sweden according to the color of the skin and state that "[t]he sensible approach to the issue, which is also the official Swedish approach, is to consider color irrelevant to the appraisal of an individual" (79). It is obvious that the idea of color-blindness established with the belief that "racial group membership and race based differences should not be taken into account when decisions are made, impressions are formed, and behaviors are enacted" (Apfelbaum, Norton, & Sommers, 2012, p. 205) is prevailing. The logic motivating the belief is simple and straightforward: if people or institutions do not even notice race, then they cannot act in a racially biased manner, and therefore the practice reduces prejudice and discrimination.

However, research repeatedly shows that racially visible differences are one of the first things people notice and perceive together with gender differences (e.g. Apfelbaum, Sommers, & Norton, 2008; Bronson & Merryman, 2009; Katz, 2003; Osanami Törngren, 2013). Color-blind politics "proscribe discrimination rather than actively intervening in the market or other putatively private behavior to rectify racial imbalances" (Lieberman, 2006, p. 13); at the same time, color-blindness enables people to believe that discrimination based on race is not an issue because it is illegal for individuals to be treated differently according to their race, ethnicity, or religion (Gallagher, 2003). As Ferber (2012) states, exercising color-blindness is a practice of defending the "culture of privilege," being unaware of how race impact peoples' daily lives. In fact, studies in the US show that color-blindness, which emphasizes minimization of group differences, reinforces minority marginalization, and engaging in color-blindness may actually undermine interracial interactions in a negative manner (Apfelbaum, Sommers, & Norton, 2008; Plaut, Thomas, & Goren, 2009).

As mentioned earlier, color-blindness is deeply embedded in the integration policy of Sweden. The idea of color-blindness is officially applied, to such an extent that there are efforts to eliminate the word "race" in Sweden. A parliamentary decision to abolish the word "race (ras)" from official language in 2001 was followed by the removal of race as a basis of discrimination in 2009 (Hübinette & Hylten-Cavallius, 2014). In 2014, the Swedish government announced that the word "race" should be erased from all existing legislation in Sweden and should be replaced with another word (Hambraeus, 2014). The rejection of the term race has been at the very core of the Swedish anti-racist movement as well. Hübinette and Hylten-Cavallius (2014) write: "Color-blindness in the Swedish contemporary context means that for many Swedes it is even difficult to utter the word 'race' in everyday speech, and it is equally uncomfortable to talk about white and non-white Swedes" (30).

The same year as the Swedish government announced the replacement of the word race with another word, the word "racialized (rasifierad)" was officially recognized as a new Swedish word to refer to a person who is categorized as belonging to certain racial groups because of the visible differences. While the acknowledgment of the word should be marked as the first step toward recognizing the racial problems in Sweden, the color-blind idea is still dominant. In academia, the opinions are polarized between those who advocate talking about race and those who deny it. Whether to register ethnicity and race in the Swedish population statistics or not is debated by Demker and Johansson Heinö (2013) and Jebari and Magnusson (2013), which well depicts this polarization of whether we should or should not talk about race in Sweden. They debate over two opposite opinions presented by Swedish scholars on whether the statistical category "Swedes with foreign background" should be abolished in the Swedish statistics. Demker and Johansson Heinö (2013) argue that the term lumps a wide variety of individuals in one collective category therefore making a political decision based on such a category is harmful, and therefore, only categories such as "the place of birth" and "citizenship," which are categories that are "individual," should be used as statistical categories. On the other hand, Jebari and Magnusson (2013) agree that the term "Swedes with foreign background" lumps together a wide variety of individuals that do not necessarily share common social characteristics and argue that ethnicity and race, which are self-claimed categories of "individuals" that can be hidden in categories such as "the place of birth" or "citizenship," should be registered in the population statistics.

The two distinct stands of whether to recognize racial and ethnic differences or not are clearly seen also in the debate concerning Botkyrka commune announcing the suggestion to establish equality data based on race and religion in 2015 (Botkyrka kommun, 2015; Hübinette, 2015). Equality data will register individuals' skin color and religion based on anonymous self-reporting, contrary to the existing categories of "place of birth" or "citizenship" that are automatically registered without the individuals' choice and become the basis of ethnic groups today. The statistics should help identify which specific groups of people face discrimination and social problems. While the Afro-Swedish association supports this initiative, other political institutions and debaters show strong disagreement toward gathering such statistics (Baker, 2016; SVT Nyheter Stockholm, 2015). In Feburary 2018, the Left Party announced the support for gathering equality data which accelerated debates reflecting various voices for and against the data in media outlets (e.g. Dinamarca et al., 2018; Ismail, 2018; Osanami Törngren & Wigerfeld, 2018).

Moras (2010) argues that color-blindness is "a language of liberalism" (235). Moreover, it is neoliberalism based on the moral, political, and legal claims of the individual over the collective itself, with its principles of liberty, equality, and fraternity (Harvey, 2007) that actually give credence to the idea that race is irrelevant and society is color-blind (Bonilla-Silva, 2000, 2010; Goldberg, 1993; Tigervall, 2008). Bonilla-Silva argues that this focus on the individuals is one of the ways color-blindness is incorporated in explaining racial inequality within the liberal thoughts: individuals are seen as having choices, and through naturalization of differences, racial phenomena can be considered as natural occurrences. Ideas of different cultures are used in arguing why some groups are not as well-off as others, and racism and discrimination are neglected as a central factor affecting life chances (Bonilla-Silva, 2010, pp. 28–29).

### Color-Blind Talk

Apfelbaum, Sommers, and Norton (2008) propose the idea of "strategic colorblindness," a strategy whites adopt in order to avoid talking about race and acknowledging racial difference in an effort to escape sounding biased when faced with ambiguous and often threatening contexts of race-relevant social interactions. So how is color-blindness strategically used in social interactions? Bonilla-Silva (2015) writes that whites' contemporary racial discourse makes them "look good" as they no longer sound "racist."

He proposes four mental models and ways of talking color-blind (Bonilla-Silva, 2010; Hughey & Embrick, 2015). The first model is "abstract liberalism," which focuses on individuals and equal opportunities to explain existing racial status quo (Bonilla-Silva, 2010, p. 30). A typical way of talking in a US setting will be to claim support for equal opportunity while opposing affirmative action, which gives special treatment to racial minorities. This way of talking allows people to appear reasonable and moral while denying measures to eliminate the racial inequality that exists. The second mental model is "naturalization" (Bonilla-Silva, 2010, p. 34). People can argue that "that's the way it is"; things should be kept the way they are and should not be forced upon people, by claiming that, for example, segregation is a self-choice, or bussing of school children is forcing people to mingle, or that people have individual choice. This way of talking rationalizes segregation and inequality as natural and thus has nothing to do with race. The third mode is "cultural racism" (Bonilla-Silva, 2010, p. 39). This way of color-blind talk blames the minorities for the social outcomes that they face that the cultural practices and preferences of the minorities are putting them in the position they are in. The last mental model is "minimization of racism" (Bonilla-Silva, 2010, p. 43), which argues "it's better than the past"—that racism is a thing of the past and declines the significance of race.

Previous qualitative studies in the US show clearly how the idea of color-blindness is reflected in the discourse of interracial marriages. In Bonilla-Silva's (2010) study, the idea of abstract liberalism and naturalization comes to surface when discussing difficulties in accepting interracial marriage. Interviewees would describe such marriages as a matter of love and articulate the acceptance of others getting involved in interracial marriage by focusing on individual choice. In these cases, hesitation about getting involved in an interracial relationship was articulated as a matter of attraction. In Moran's study (2001), it also becomes clear that Americans with a norm of color-blindness believe that race is irrelevant for marital choice, and this idea was utilized to legitimize the high rate of same-race marriages. The contradicting idea of "I have no problem with interracial marriages but I am only attracted whites" came out clearly (Bonilla-Silva, 2010). Moreover, reservations toward interracial marriage are also explained through the ideas that those marriages were more "difficult" and entailed "problems" because of cultural differences. Those who were opposed to interracial marriage referred to the racism that exists in society and accused people of being selfish and not thinking about the consequences for the children born into such a relationship (Bonilla-Silva, 2010).

In Frankenberg's study (1993), the preference of a partner in a relationship was largely discussed through the notion of cultural proximity and the degree of similarities and dissimilarities. When examining discourses against interracial marriage, "the racial construction of masculinity and femininity," "the construction of race difference as 'real', 'essential', and based on 'biology' and the construction of racial and cultural groups as entirely and appropriately separate from one another" are apparent (Frankenberg, 1993, p. 75).The color-blind idea was communicated through expressions such as "race makes, or should make, no difference between people," while others "discussed the significance of race in terms of cultural differences or economic and sociopolitical differences" (Frankenberg, 1993, p. 138). The women Frankenberg interviewed outlined their concern for the interracial couple and their children that they would experience issues related to cultural belonging and difficulties in society and defended their reservations to such marriages. Their opinions were justified through projection and articulating concerns for children or family reactions, and the existence of racist beliefs about interracial marriage was admitted by focusing on other people's racism. She argues that this concern for the welfare of the couple and their children only strengthens the idea that racial differences are ascribed with visible differences. Frankenberg complements this argument by presenting how a person of mixed heritage is always identified with the nonwhite racial or ethnic group rather than being white (Frankenberg, 1993, pp. 93–95).

Rosenblatt et al. also studied black and white biracial couples and analyzed the concerns that white families raised in their opposition to such marriages. They conclude that there is a wide range of "racist feelings, assumptions and fears at the heart of the discourse of opposition" to interracial marriages (Rosenblatt, Karis, & Powell, 1995, p. 98). Issues such as societal and surroundings disapproval and problems the children may face were recurring themes underlying the opposition. Frankenberg and Rosenblatt et al.'s studies crystalize the aspects of cultural racism and naturalization that are integrated in color-blind talk.

Root's study (2001) examines how "open" and "closed" families react and accept interracial marriages differently. While "closed" families object to interracial marriages by maintaining the boundaries of "us" and "them," "open" families keep "the clear sense of boundaries between individuals" and respect their choice. As abstract liberalism highlights, respecting individual choice does not automatically mean that "open" families were completely engaged with positive attitudes toward interracial marriages.

Interracial marriage was accepted on the basis of respect toward the family members' choice and the personality of the individuals. Root explains that the families maintain the idea that it is "them" who need to accommodate "us." Instead of race, cultural or class background was in the center of the objection toward interracial marriages (Root, 2001, pp. 97–98). Root's study also highlights how abstract liberalism, naturalization, and cultural racism are embedded in the color-blind discourse toward attitudes toward interracial marriages.

Analysis on color-blindness and examination of color-blind talk are scarce in Swedish context. Based on 30 interviews with Swedes, the following section will analyze how different mental models of color-blindness are communicated when expressing attitudes toward interracial marriages.

## Color-Blind Explanations of Attitudes Toward Interracial Marriages

The following analysis is based on 30 interviews carried out from September to December 2009 as a follow-up to the postal survey on attitudes toward interracial marriage conducted in December 2008 to February 2009.[1] Three of the informants volunteered to be interviewed, while others were systematically and randomly selected from those who have answered the survey and have given consent for a further contact. Following the systematic random sampling, the gender ratio was fairly maintained (17 female and 13 male), and interviewees were selected from diverse residential areas. The average age for female interviewees was 42.9 and 46.5 for men, and the interviewees engaged in diverse occupations and socioeconomic status, from being a student, a highly qualified professional, to currently unemployed, although most of the interviewees were white-collar workers, especially the women.

Interview questions were formulated based on the results from the survey. Interviews were semi-structured and were carried out in Swedish; eight interviews were conducted face to face and others on the telephone. The interviewees were asked to react and respond to the factual survey

---

[1] For detailed results see Sayaka Osanami Törngren, *Love Ain'T Got no Color?: Attitude Toward Interracial Marriage in Sweden* (Malmö; Norrköping: IMER/MIM/Malmö högskola; Migration och Etnicitet/REMESO/Linköpings universitet, 2011); Sayaka Osanami Törngren, "Attitudes Toward Interracial Marriages and the Role of Interracial Contacts in Sweden," *Ethnicities* (2016), https://doi.org/10.1177/1468796816638400.

results spontaneously rather than to articulate their own personal thoughts on the issue. This was an intentional choice and attempt to eliminate the effect of social desirability needs and race of interviewer that can be experienced by the informants. Besides, as Ehn (1996) writes, when people make comments on actual societal questions, such as immigration and immigrants, people tend to give answers based on how others act and think instead of answering how they themselves actually think; therefore, to formulate questions that put focus on the general result and how interview informants perceive the public would react to interracial marriage becomes even more reasonable. Ehn states that this enables interpretation of the interview results not only as pure information on what the individuals think and what they have experienced but also as a social construction of meaningful experiences and cultural identity (173).

Informants commonly responded to the questions first by expressing their agreement or disagreement to the results and then formulated their thoughts on why survey respondents answered in the way they did. Projection technique did not inhibit interviewees from referring to their own opinions, experiences, and thoughts on interracial marriages. There were clear distinctions in the way informants articulated their own opinion and their thoughts on others' opinions, for example, by the usage of pronouns "I" and "they."

### The Idea of Individuals and Individual Choice

Bonilla-Silva (2010) proposes that one of the ways to talk color-blind is to focus on individuals and equal opportunities to justify racial status quo (30). The contradicting idea of interviewees saying that they have nothing against interracial marriages but at the same time would not want to engage in such marriages was observed repeatedly. For example, Karl, a 48-year-old, said, "You can be quite positive towards red-haired people but you don't necessarily want to get married with them," and continued by saying:

> I believe also that if someone gets married, it's a very personal thing, and people should do what they want. It's another thing if we the society should accept it. If my neighbor is in it [interracial relationship] and if that's what they want [they should have it like that] […] it's what I think, I think it creates a problem with the community or other things concerning the cultural things. At the end of the day I don't care about their marriage because it's not of my concern, it's just their preference you know.

Karl's quotes are a typical example of "I am not racist but...," high-lighting the contradiction of showing tolerance at the same time endors-ing the existing racial hierarchy, which allows him to sound reasonable and moral and less prejudiced. Interviewees employed projection and expressed that they themselves do not have anything against interracial marriages; however, they know that there are people who are against it. This dis-course coincides with the previous studies where informants sometimes admitted the existence of racist beliefs on interracial marriage by focusing on other people's racism (Bonilla-Silva, 2010; Frankenberg, 1993; Moran, 2001; Rosenblatt et al., 1995). In fact, many interviewees referred to the racism and discrimination that exist in society as reasons not to get involved in interracial marriages. Karin, a 30-year-old, clearly stated her position and that of others by saying:

> I think also, personally, that I have nothing against [interracial marriage] but my understanding is that there are attitudes in society, which are trouble-some for persons who choose to live in an interracial marriage or relationship.

Confronted with the survey results, which showed that survey respon-dents did not think that it was negative that Swedes marry interracially but at the same time Swedish society did not accept such marriages to the same extent, 24-year-old Louise reasons:

> I believe that many Swedes think, as I said, that you should do whatever you want and you should be allowed to decide over yourself, you should have freedom. At the same time, you also know that there are attitudes in society and that there is racism and prejudice. So, I think that for my own part it maybe is easier to say that it is okay but then you at the same time know that in society there are people who don't think that it's okay.

Louise's words depict the contradiction that arises from abstract liberal-ism, which shows both openness and hesitance to interracial marriages. The idea of individuals and reference to racism that exists in society was also utilized when explaining the survey results, showing more negative atti-tudes toward interracial childbearing compared to dating. Instead of stat-ing that it becomes a problem for informants themselves, some projected the problem to the welfare of the couple and children. Several informants expressed that when you are just dating or living together, it is only about yourself, that is, your own choice; however, when you have children, it is not just about your choice, but it also involves others. The idea that mixed children will face racism and problems was used to justify the unwillingness to have mixed-race children, as in previous studies (Bonilla-Silva, 2010; Frankenberg, 1993; Rosenblatt et al., 1995). Anna, 41-year-old, said:

> For me it is a much bigger thing to have children with someone compared to living together as a couple. When you live together as a couple I think that it can be a little bit exotic to live with someone from another country and another background, and then you think about yourself. It's just about what you want to do.

Reference to the other people's prejudice and racism was prominent also when interviewees talked about how they would react if their family members choose to intermarry. For example, a 47-year-old Marie who has a daughter says:

> It would not be easy to have a relationship with two different cultures and it would not be easy either to cope with how the surroundings would react to your relationship. It is two problems you have to deal with and because of that reason I would try to inform her [my daughter], as a mother who wants to protect her children, that it's not just experiencing strange things in your relationship but it's also how people around would react to you because you are together with someone or married to someone who comes from another country.

Naturalization that "that's the way it is" was also noticeable through the idea of individual choice and attraction and that nobody should be forced. The focus on individual choice was prominent when interviewees expressed their thoughts on the result that shows that survey respondents were less negative to the idea of family and other members of society getting involved in interracial marriages, compared to the respondents' own preference of a marriage partner. Even though one-fourth of the interviewed informants stated that they would have initial reservations, they still stated that they would, from the perspective of individual choice, accept and respect their family members' choice of a partner. Lars, 35-year-old, says:

> I believe that they [the respondents who have answered the questionnaire] think that they cannot influence what their family members think, therefore they have to accept it, but if it is about yourself then they can say no, not me.

As in Bonilla-Silva's study (2010), focus on individuals and individuals' choice can be observed in comments that marriage partner choice is a matter of attraction and not about origin. The idea that it is a matter of attraction and not about the origin minimizes the significance of race as well. For example, 45-year-old Johan said "I think that it's about the person and not about where you come from or what color of skin or which religion you have. It's about the person."

Forty-seven-year-old Linnea's words clearly depict the idea of individual choice and focus on the personality of the person rather than the origin. Discussing how she would react if her brother chose to be together with someone of non-Swedish origin, she says:

> I rather accept a Chinese who is very nice than a Swede who is not nice if you understand what I mean [laughs]. It is not about the nationality but about personality. If they are both nice and kind to my brother and if I believe that he would be a better person not worse, then it doesn't matter for me. [...] there is a difference between having someone with you every day who shares your life with and having siblings. You don't decide over your siblings in this culture [Swedish].

As Bonilla-Silva argues (2010), mental model of abstract liberalism and focus on individual choice can be seen throughout the interview materials. Attitudes are explained as natural through these ideas, and a color-blind argument is established. Moreover, this color-blind discourse makes the interviewees "look good" as they do not sound racist (Bonilla-Silva, 2015). An individual choice is explained as a choice that individuals have in wanting and not wanting to marry someone of another origin and at the same time a choice others have in wanting and not wanting to marry someone of another origin. The idea of individual choice functions as a defense mechanism for respondents' own opinion of interracial marriage at the same time as a sign of tolerance toward others who get involved in interracial marriages.

### The Idea of Cultural Differences

When the question "what do you think about or associate when you hear the word mixed marriage" is asked, it became obvious that the majority of interviewees seemed to share the idea that interracial marriages are controversial and entail problems because of the cultural differences. Preference of a partner in a relationship was naturalized through the notion of familiarity and degree of cultural and religious proximity. Interview informants argued that couples who are involved in intermarriage might need extra help because of the differences they might have, and they may experience a cultural clash. Helena, a 24-year-old, says:

> The thing that I have problems with concerning interracial marriage is the cultural clash, that I don't have the energy to take the confrontation every time something happens. Therefore, I can be a bit traditional and rather want someone who comes from my culture.

The idea of interracial marriages as a problem is oriented by a strong idea that having an origin in another country than Sweden is equal to social and religious differences that are difficult to bridge. This becomes a legitimate color-blind argument against interracial marriages, shifting the focus from and minimizing the significance of race. However, looking closer at the idea of cultural differences and the notion of that culture, it becomes prominent that interviewees refer to culture as something different from the Swedish or the Western ones. For example, several interviewees expressed how a marriage between a Swede and a Dane is not a mixed marriage. The idea of cultural differences shifted the focus from race and thus established a color-blind argument; however, in fact, the cultural differences were only attached to people of nonwhite origins. This point becomes clearer when Helena discusses why there is no attitudinal difference toward someone of immigrant background and nonwhite adoptees:

> It must be about prejudice and the physical appearance. Because culture, I mean adoptees have the same culture, it's impossible to argue that it is the culture [that is the reason behind the negative answers]. So, it must be that you take one step further that you want someone who looks like yourself, not only the same customs and values. It's sad but it's a little bit like that, if I choose someone who looks like me, I'm playing the safe card. I don't know if this person is adopted or not before I have asked. It can also be that people can't carry on like that.

The interviewees referred to different degrees of cultural differences, which they believed affect attitudes toward interracial marriages. When informants talked about Latin American and Central/East European, the central argument was on the cultural similarity, while for other racial groups, especially for Middle Eastern, focus was on differences. Interviewees reasoned that because persons of Latin American and Central/East European origin were considered to be culturally similar, they were more preferred as a marriage partner. Below is a quote from a 44-year-old Peter, which is interesting in many different dimensions. First, he says that Central/East Europeans are similar to Swedes. When he specifies what similarities he is talking about, he first focuses on the physical appearance, indicating the aspect of attraction, and then connects it to cultural similarities.

Interviewee:   It can be that people think that they [CEE] are similar to us. It is also an important thing, you know. They are rather like us. Of course, it plays a role when you imagine what you think when you answer these questions.

Interviewer:   What do you mean "similar to us"?

Interviewee:   I don't know, physical appearance you want to keep. Because when it comes to relationships you can say that it's about the physical appearance. If you like this person it doesn't matter but maybe people believe that there are cultural similarities [when you have similar physical appearance] even though there might not be [in reality]. They are like European, not West European but still [....]

Thirty-four-year-old Anders also engaged in the discussion of cultural similarities and differences, and his opinion clearly depicted the pattern of abstract liberalism. He claims that he is not racist and at the bottom of a partner choice are individual preference and attraction, which contradicts his statement that he cannot imagine being together with someone of Middle Eastern origin. His argument is naturalized through the idea of cultural and religious differences:

Anders:   I can imagine being together with somebody of another origin, except for Middle Easterner.

Interviewer:   Why?

Anders:   Because I believe that the religious and cultural differences would just be too difficult. You can imagine meeting a Middle Eastern woman who is very liberal towards the religion and culture she comes from, but I would still believe that her family [would be a problem], I mean if you get married and have children and so on you would associate a lot with the family and I believe that there would be trouble, somewhere. That's why I would be careful, but I am not a racist so if you fall in love you fall in love.

Anders' thoughts were very typical among interviewees when talking about someone of Middle Eastern background. Negative attitudes toward Middle Easterners were effectively rationalized and naturalized through references to religion and Islam. Johanna, a 50-year-old, explains the negative attitudes toward Middle Easterners as following:

> I am not so surprised. I think the results for Middle Easterners are so negative probably because of the low status that Islam currently has. [....] It has to do a lot with the fact that the further away you are religiously and geographically the less inclined you are to accept or understand the culture.

The idea of cultural differences was given also as a reason why survey respondents might have been more negative toward interracial childbearing compared to dating or marriages. In this discourse the idea of culture as something essential and unchangeable emerges. For example, a 32-year-old Mikael says:

> [...] maybe more cultural clashes may arise when you have children. [....] If you don't have children, you can partly continue with your own culture. I mean, of course if you have children the question becomes what you should teach to the children and what you want to pass on. So, I can imagine that culture can be the reason [for people being more negative to having children with].

In fact, mixed children always seem to be attached with the idea of cultural differences rather than them being Swedish. Here again, as mentioned earlier, the argument that there are racism and prejudice in society and among people, and not because of your own prejudice, is effectively used to explain the more negative attitudes toward childbearing than marriage. Jan explains:

> [...] you maybe think about how the child will be looked upon from the surroundings when he or she grows up, that people will be prejudiced towards the children. Even though they may speak perfect Swedish, it doesn't always protect the child from prejudice. I think thoughts like this may be a reason.

Attitudes toward interracial marriages were explained in a color-blind manner through the mental model of cultural racism, by blaming the minorities for the social outcome that they face as well. It is "their" cultural preference that makes interviewees not willing to marry someone of another origin. The idea that "that's the way it is" and things should not be forced on anyone was obvious when interviewees explained their own marriage preferences. This argument again was targeted mainly toward someone of Middle Eastern background. A 41-year-old Anna was particularly engaged in this type of argument, stating that people with an immigrant background who accepted and adjusted to the cultural norms of Sweden were not problematic, while those who did not accept and adjust were questionable: "If you have a problem with Swedes and how Swedes are, why do you move here?" Anna's idea is that "you can resist but you should accept." Anna said, "if the region I move to requires me to have a head scarf, I would do it even though I would resist otherwise." Eva, 65-year-old, also used the same example as Anna that if she was in an Arabic country, she would wear a head scarf. She wondered why women could not take their head scarves off when they were in Sweden. Underlying is the idea that cultural differences can be compromised if immigrants change their behavior. In this way, cultural differences are projected as a sign of unwillingness from the immigrants' side that they choose to be so. Through the projection, the problem of culture and religious differences can be justified and naturalized as an explanation as to why intermarriage with Middle Easterners is difficult.

The survey results showed that male respondents, in general, are more positive toward interracial marriages than female respondents. More than half of the interviewees found gender equality standard in Sweden as the reason for the gender discrepancy in attitudes toward interracial marriage. Moreover, interviewees expressed that gender equality is the main cultural difference that exists between Swedes and those who have origins in another country. This corresponds with previous studies, which show that gender equality is understood as part of a strong Swedish national identity (Hübinette & Lundström, 2011; Keskinen, 2009; Mulinari, 2008; Rabo, 1997). Mikael says:

> [...] maybe it is perceived that other cultures are more male-dominated. [....] I still believe that Sweden, the Swedish culture is pretty equal and gender equality is something important.

In Mikael's words, the idea of gender equality has a clear dichotomy; Swedes have the gender equality ideal and have achieved it to a great extent, while in other cultures, people are not as gender-equal as Swedes. Jan argues the same, by using the words "view of women":

I can imagine that it has to do with the view of women, I mean, view towards women is not equal you can say, not the same as we have in Sweden. I can imagine that it's such things that affect the answer. You are afraid of the negative view of women which you can see some people have [...] some countries have not come as far when it comes to the view of women as we have come in Sweden I think at least.

However, the dichotomy that can be seen in the issue of gender equality is not always just a simple racialization but also gendered. Many interview informants reasoned that immigrant men and especially Middle Eastern men are not desirable for Swedish women because of the religious differences and because they do not share the view of our gender equality. Marie says:

I believe that a large number of Muslims would not accept that women keep her and daughter's gender equality, actually. I think that people have thought a lot about gender equality [when answering the questionnaire].

Even though gender equality is claimed as a Swedish value, some interviewees reason that some Swedish men desire immigrant women because they rather want a relationship that is not gender-equal. For example, Linnea argues:

There are so many guys who travel to Thailand and I have a neighbor who has just moved in, I just see him from distance but he looks quite old, like around retired age, and he has like two five-year-old children, a boy and a girl and the woman, I have no idea how old she can be but she is not much older than thirty at least. Many Swedish men have it easier. And also women in Sweden have had a tradition for the last several decades to become successful in professional life and have not been interested in staying at home and taking care of the children and can't even imagine having a man do that work. So if you are traditional and you want to have a career yourself then they should choose women from another culture.

Especially South/East Asian women are the focus in this discourse. Interviewees expressed, referring to the survey results that show that male survey respondents were significantly more positive toward marrying South/East Asian than female survey respondents, that a marriage between a South/East Asian woman and a Swedish man entails less conflicts and problems because South/East Asian women are not striving after a gender-equal relationship. Johanna, for example, articulates:

Firstly, I think it is frightful that Swedish men's attitudes towards women are still so out-of-date. It is my spontaneous reaction. [....] I think there are too many Swedish men who want to look for a wife from the Far East because it is too much with a Swedish woman who has lots of demands, while it's more comfortable to have women from countries where they don't have the same level of freedom and gender equality as Swedish women have. Too many Swedish men think that it is comfortable to find women from there.

Similarly, Karl also takes the idea of the gender equality ideal among Swedish women for granted, although this desire for gender equality is not applicable for South/East Asian women and Swedish men:

[...] if you see a South/East Asian woman, if you come from there, she is culturally or not, often below the man so to speak, not like Swedish men and women who should be somewhere 50–50 and sometimes even too much on one side or the other. So there is no conflict.

As in previous studies, oppositions and reservations toward interracial marriage were expressed through focusing on cultural and sociopolitical differences, which effectively enable interviewees to avoid the racial language (Bonilla-Silva, 2010; Frankenberg, 1993). The idea of cultural proximity and differences naturalizes the racial preferences, at the same time making clear the racial divide by defining what Swedish culture and values are. As in Frankenberg's study, there seems to be a racial construction of masculinity and femininity through the idea of gender equality (Frankenberg, 1993). Even though informants believed that gender equality is a Swedish value, they did not seem to question the inconsequence between the Swedish gender lines. This indicates that the racialization of the gender values is profound and the gender equality of immigrant women is not questioned. As Bonilla-Silvia states, color-blindness works as "collective representations" that have been developed to explain and justify the inequality (Bonilla-Silva, 2010, p. 262).

### Minimization of Race

The analysis above illustrated how interviewees minimized the significance of race by engaging in a color-blind talk, through the idea of individual choice and cultural differences. When their color-blind argument was contested with survey results, interviewees simply could not find a word to express their opinion, or they expressed their disagreement with the survey results and stressed the significance of choice and cultural differences even more. Such strategies were seen when interviewees were faced with the survey results showing that nonwhite adoptees, growing up with Swedish parents and culture, are not preferred as a marriage partner, as much as Swedes and other Europeans were. For example, Anders responded:

> Because then it only has to do with the physical, like skin color and appearance, hair color, whatever it might be. And for me it plays a very small role, and I think it is sad that it is like that.

Stressing cultural differences and extending the idea of cultural differences to mixed children and their status are also seen. Lennart, a 63-year-old, even justified and naturalized the attitudes showing more positive attitudes toward someone of European origins compared to Middle Eastern, South/East Asian, and African, by referring to the visible differences. His words depict the idea that differential preferences cannot be helped and it is the individuals' choice to avoid "problems":

> You can say that in Sweden people have stretched out what is considered to be Swedish and we recognize Europeans as Swedes you know. Wherever in Europe you come from you are accepted as a Swede. [....] It is obvious, because then the children or the grandchildren will look like yourself [laugh]. You skip that problem you know.

Some informants explained their personal reservations about interracial relationships using comparisons with other social problems such as domestic violence. These explanations draw attention to the idea that partner choice is based on the personality of the individuals and not about their racial background. Comparison of interracial marriages with social problems functions not only as a tool to justify and rationalize their opinions but also as a modifier, which makes the interviewees' opinions sound insignificant and unproblematic. Furthermore, drawing a comparison between social problems and interracial marriage shifts the focus from and minimizes the issue of visible differences. An example can be seen in Anna's argument:

> It can be for example that my younger sister may meet somebody who beats her. I mean, it doesn't have to be an immigrant, it can be a Swede. It does not matter because you never have a guarantee ever. You don't know and that's why you should not be negative directly to it [interracial relationship]. But I would probably react if she took home someone who is a Muslim who acts oppressive towards women in an obvious way.

Comparing social problems and choice to intermarry also shifts the focus from groups to individuals. Marie's words depict this color-blind talk clearly:

> I would want to learn about the person before I [make a judgment]. I don't care so much; I would be more worried if someone took home a person who has some kind of drug abuse problem or something similar.

Minimization of race arguing that racism is a thing of the past was not noticeably observed. However, Johanna did talk about how the idea of "mixed marriages" and reacting toward such marriage is a thing of the past and something out of date, moreover something that happens outside of the Swedish context. Johanna, referring to the 1960s in the US, says:

> For me, it sounds like the U.S.A. in the 60s, then you talked about interracial marriage. For me it is an outdated word. [....] Interracial marriage, I felt, was something that you talked about between the blacks and whites in 50s, 60s and something you were afraid of back then. Today it feels like we don't react over it [interracial marriage].

In the Swedish context, minimization of race was seen not so much as a denial of the extent of racism in society itself but rather as a continuation of the claim and reassurance of interviewees themselves not being prejudiced or racist contra the wider society and people in general being prejudiced. Moreover, through referring to the individual qualities of someone of minority background, color-blindness was established and the racial aspect of the individuals minimized.

## CONCLUDING REMARKS

Color-blindness is prominent in Swedish integration policies and ideologies; however, how the color-blindness works and is communicated among people has been seldom analyzed so far. This chapter showed how racial preferences in choosing a partner are justified and explained in a color-blind manner by different mental models and ways of talking color-blind. The ways people talk color-blind overlap with the previous research results from the US. Color-blind arguments focusing on individual choice, gender equality, cultural differences and proximity, and minimization of race effectively and rationally justify racial preference in a marriage partner. Especially the idea of individual choice and gender equality was strongly connected to Swedishness, which created a dichotomy of "us" and "them" vividly. In this sense, color-blindness truly works as a language and culture of privilege and collective representation (Bonilla-Silva, 2010; Ferber, 2012).

## References

Apfelbaum, E. P., Norton, M. I., & Sommers, S. R. (2012). Racial Color-Blindness Emergence, Practice, and Implications. *Current Directions in Psychological Science, 21*(3), 205–209.

Apfelbaum, E. P., Sommers, S. R., & Norton, M. I. (2008). Seeing Race and Seeming Racist? Evaluating Strategic Colorblindness in Social Interaction. *Journal of Personality and Social Psychology, 95*(4), 918.

Baker, J. (2016). *Jämlikhetsdata Och Identitetsvänsterns Obehagliga Debatt.* Retrieved August 15, 2017, from http://moderaterna.net/botkyrka/2016/04/jamlikhetsdata-och-identitetsvansterns-obehagliga-debatt

Bonilla-Silva, E. (1997). Rethinking Racism: Toward a Structural Interpretation. *American Sociological Review, 62*(3), 465–480.

Bonilla-Silva, E. (2000). 'This Is a White Country': The Racial Ideology of the Western Nations of the World-System. *Sociological Inquiry, 70*(2), 188–214.

Bonilla-Silva, E. (2010). *Racism without Racists: Color-Blind Racism and the Persistence of Racial Inequality in the United States* (3rd ed.). Lanham: Rowman & Littlefield Publishers.

Bonilla-Silva, E. (2015). The Structure of Racism in Color-Blind, "Post-Racial" America. *American Behavioral Scientist, 59*(11).

Borevi, K. (2013). Understanding Swedish Multiculturalism. In P. Kivisto & Ö. Wahlbeck (Eds.), *Debating Multiculturalism in the Nordic Welfare States* (pp. 140–169). New York: Palgrave Macmillan.

Botkyrka kommun. (2015). *Jämlikhetsdata.* Retrieved August 15, 2017, from https://www.botkyrka.se/kommun--politik/hallbar-utveckling-och-manskliga-rattigheter/ett-interkulturellt-botkyrka/jamlikhetsdata.html

Brekke, J.-P., & Brochgrevink, T. (2007). *Talking about Integration—Discourses, Alliances and Theories on Labour Market Integration in Sweden.* Institute for Social Research, Oslo. Retrieved August 15, 2017, from http://www.temaasyl.se/Documents/Brekke2.pdf

Broberg, G., & Tydén, M. (2005). *Oönskade i Folkhemmet: Rashygien Och Sterilisering i Sverige.* 2, [utök] uppl ed. Stockholm: Dialogos.

Bronson, P., & Merryman, A. (2009). *NurtureShock.* London: Ebury.

Demker, M., & Johansson Heinö, A. (2013). Slopa Kollektiva Identiteter i Den Officiella Statistiken. *Dagens Nyheter,* 07/21.

Dinamarca, R., Jallow, M., & Riazat, D. (2018). Antirasism är inte att förneka att färger finns. *Expressen.* Retrieved June 1, 2018, from https://www.expressen.se/debatt/antirasism-ar-inte-att-forneka-att-farger-finns/

Ehn, B. (1996). *Vardagslivets Etnologi: Reflektioner Kring En Kulturvetenskap.* Stockholm: Natur och kultur.

Ferber, A. L. (2012). The Culture of Privilege: Color-Blindness, Postfeminism, and Christonormativity. *Journal of Social Issues, 68*(1), 63–77.

Frankenberg, R. (1993). *White Women, Race Matters: The Social Construction of Whiteness.* London: Routledge.

Furuhagen, B. (2007). *Den Svenska Rasbiologins Idehistoriska Rötter, En Inventering Av Forskningen.* Stockholm: Forum för levande historia.

Gallagher, C. A. (2003). Color-Blind Privilege: The Social and Political Functions of Erasing the Color Line in Post Race America. *Race, Gender & Class, 10*(4), 1–17.

Goldberg, D. T. (1993). *Racist Culture: Philosophy and the Politics of Meaning.* Oxford: Blackwell.

Gustafsson, T. (2007). *En Fiende Till Civilisationen: Manlighet, Genusrelationer, Sexualitet Och Rasstereotyper i Svensk Filmkultur Under 1920-Talet.* Lund: Sekel.

Hagerman, M. (2007). *Det Rena Landet: Om Att Uppfinna Den Svenska Nationalmyten.* Stockholm: Nordstedts.

Hambraeus, U. (2014). Rasbegreppet ska bort ur lagen. *SVT Nyheter.* Published July 30, 2014. Retrieved August 15, 2017, from https://www.svt.se/nyheter/inrikes/rasbegreppet-ska-bort-ur-lagen

Harvey, D. (2007). Neoliberalism as Creative Destruction. *The Annals of the American Academy of Political and Social Science, 610*(1), 21–44.

Heinö, A. J. (2009). Democracy between Collectivism and Individualism. De-Nationalisation and Individualisation in Swedish National Identity. *International Review of Sociology, 19*(2), 297–314.

Hübinette, T. (2015). *Vad Är Jämlikhetsdata?* Tumba: Mångkulturellt centrum.

Hübinette, T., Hörnfeldt, H. F., & Rosales, R. L. (Eds.). (2012). *Om Ras Och Vithet i Det Samtida Sverige.* Tumba: Mångkulturellt centrum.

Hübinette, T., & Hylten-Cavallius, C. (2014). *White Working Class Communities in Stockholm.* Open Society Foundations.

Hübinette, T., & Lundström, C. (2011). Sweden after the Recent Election: The Double-Binding Power of Swedish Whiteness through the Mourning of the Loss of 'Old Sweden' and the Passing of 'Good Sweden'. *Nordic Journal of Feminist and Gender Research, 19*(1), 42–52.

Hughey, M. W., & Embrick, D. G. (2015). Paving the Way for Future Race Research Exploring the Racial Mechanisms within a Color-blind, Racialized Social System. *American Behavioral Scientist, 59*(11), 1347–1357.

Ismail, Evin (2018). Lögn, förbannad lögn och statistik. *Arbetarbladet.* Retrieved June 1, 2018, from https://www.arbetarbladet.se/artikel/opinion/ledare/logn-forbannad-logn-och-statistik-7

Jacobsson, I. (1999). *Kan Man Vara Svart Och Svensk?: Texter Om Rasism, Antisemitism Och Nazism.* 1. uppl ed. Stockholm: Natur och kultur.

Jebari, K., & Magnusson, M. (2013). En Färgblind Stat Missar Rasismens Nyanser. *Tidskrift För Politsk Filosofi*, 2, 2013–2012.

Kalonaityte, V., Kwesa, V., & Tedros, A. (2007). Att Färgas Av Sverige: Upplevelser Av Diskriminering Och Rasism Bland Ungdomar Med Afrikansk Bakgrund i Sverige.

Katz, P. A. (2003). Racists Or Tolerant Multiculturalists? how do they Begin? *American Psychologist*, 58(11), 897–909.

Keskinen, S. (2009). *Complying with Colonialism: Gender, Race and Ethnicity in the Nordic Region*. Aldershot: Ashgate.

Khosravi, S. (2006). Manlighet i Exil: Maskulinitet Och Etnicitet Hos Iranska Män i Sverige. In Simon Ekström and Lena Gerhlm (Eds.), *Orienten i Sverige: Samtida Möten Och Gränssnitt* (pp. 77–104, 1. uppl ed.). Lund: Studentlitteratur.

Lieberman, R. C. (2006). 'The Storm Didn't Discriminate' Katrina and the Politics of Color-Blindness. *Du Bois Review*, 3(1), 7–22.

Lundberg, P. (2014). *Gul Utanpå*. Stockholm: Raben & Sjögren.

Lundström, C. (2007). *Svenska Latinas: Ras, Klass Och Kön i Svenskhetens Geografi*. Göteborg, Stockholm: Makadam.

Mattsson, K. (2004). 'Den Färgblinda Marknaden' Och Välfärdens Rasifiering. In K. Mattsson, F. Anthias, & I. Lindberg (Eds.), *Rasismer i Europa: Arbetsmarknadens Flexibla Förtryck: Rapport Från Forskarseminariet* (pp. 98–126). Agora and Agora forskarnätverk. Stockholm: Agora.

Mattsson, K. (2005). Klonad Skönhet—Fröken Sverige Och Andra 'Missar' i Kritisk Belysning. In G. Forsberg & C. Grenholm (Eds.), *Och Likväl Rör Det Sig: Genusrelationer i Förändring* (pp. 191–202). Karlstad: Karlstad University Press.

Moran, R. F. (2001). *Interracial Intimacy: The Regulation of Race & Romance*. Chicago: University of Chicago Press.

Moras, A. (2010). Colour-Blind Discourses in Paid Domestic Work: Foreignness and the Delineation of Alternative Racial Markers. *Ethnic and Racial Studies*, 33(2), 233–252.

Mulinari, D. (2008). Women Friendly? Understanding Gendered Racism in Sweden. In K. Melby, A.-B. Ravn, & C. Carlsson Wetterberg (Eds.), *Gender Equality and Welfare Politics in Scandinavia: The Limits of Political Ambition?* (pp. 167–182). Bristol: Policy Press.

Nam, D. (2007). *P3 Special: Mamma Kines*. Pappa Japan: Sveriges Radio.

Osanami Törngren, S. (2011). *Love Ain't Got no Color?: Attitude Toward Interracial Marriage in Sweden*. Malmö; Norrköping: IMER/MIM/Malmö högskola; Migration och. Retrieved from Etnicitet/REMESO/Linköpings universitet.

Osanami Törngren, S. (2013). Ras Och Etnicitet. In B. Petersson & C. Johansson (Eds.), *IMER Idag: Aktuella Perspektiv På Internationell Migration Och Etniska Relationer* (pp. 90–111). Liber.

Osanami Törngren, S. (2016). Attitudes Toward Interracial Marriages and the Role of Interracial Contacts in Sweden. *Ethnicities, 16*(4), 568–588.

Osanami Törngren, S., & Wigerfeld, A. S. (2018). Det är inte alltid fel att kategorisera människor. *Svenska Dagbladet.* Retreived June 1, 2018, from https://www.svd.se/det-ar-inte-alltid-fel-att-kategorisera-manniskor

Plaut, V. C., Thomas, K. M., & Goren, M. J. (2009). Is Multiculturalism or Color-Blindness Better for Minorities? *Psychological Science, 20*(4), 444–446.

Rabo, A. (1997). Free to Make the Right Choice? Gender Equality Policy in Post-Welfare Sweden. In C. Shore & S. Wright (Eds.), *Anthropology of Policy: Critical Perspectives on Governance and Power.* London: Routledge.

Rakar, F. (2010). *Ökad Inkludering Genom Språk—Förslag Och Underlag Till Insatser Inom Fokusområde Språk i Skåne Län.* Retrieved August 16, 2017, from http://www.lansstyrelsen.se/skane/SiteCollectionDocuments/Sv/manniska-och-samhalle/integration/mottagning-och-etablering-av-nyanlanda/Avslutade%20aktiviteter/Forstudie_Okad_inkludering.pdf

Root, M. P. P. (2001). *Love's Revolution: Interracial Marriage.* Philadelphia, Pennsylvania: Temple University Press.

Rosenblatt, P. C., Karis, T. A., & Powell, R. D. (1995). The White Partner's Family. In P. C. Rosenblatt, T. A. Karis, & R. D. Powell (Eds.), *Multiracial Couples: Black and White Voices* (pp. 63–99). Thousand Oaks: Sage.

Runfors, A. (2006). Fängslande Frihet: Paradoxer Och Dilemman i Den Moderna Frihetsvisionen. In S. Ekström & L. Gerholm (Eds.), *Orienten i Sverige: Samtida Möten Och Gränssnitt,* (p. 329, 1. uppl ed.). Lund: Studentlitteratur.

Runfors, A. (2016). What an Ethnic Lens Can Conceal: The Emergence of a Shared Racialised Identity Position among Young Descendants of Migrants in Sweden. *Journal of Ethnic and Migration Studies, 42*(11), 1846–1863.

SVT Nyheter Stockholm. (2015). *Alice Teoderescu Och Kitimbwa Sabuni i Debatt Om Jämlikhetsdata.* Retrieved August 16, 2017, from https://www.svt.se/nyheter/lokalt/stockholm/alice-teoderescu-och-kitimbwa-sabuni-i-debatt-om-jamstalldhetsdata?

Tigervall, C. (2008). Samtal Med Adoptivföräldrar Om Diskriminering Och Motståndsstrategier. In T. Hübinette & C. Tigervall (Eds.), *Adoption Med Förhinder: Samtal Med Adopterade Och Adoptivföräldrar Om Vardagsrasism Och Etnisk Identitet.* Tumba: Mångkulturellt centrum.

Trotzig, A. (2001). *Blod Är Tjockare Än Vatten.* Ny utg. ed. Stockholm: En bok för alla.

# CHAPTER 7

# The Vices of Debating Racial Epithets in Danish News Media Discourse

*Mantė Vertelytė and Peter Hervik*

During the last decades, Danish public mediatized arenas (TV news, radio, newspapers, social media platforms) have recurrently engaged in discussing the use of the contested Danish racial epithet and a slur "neger" (in English, "negro"). The first notable discussion took place in 1995, relating to the use of the word by a Danish police officer to refer to a person who wished to report an offense of racial discrimination. It was followed by the statements of the police chief who insisted on the right to use the word based on the argument that it is neutral. From then until the present day, the discussion has been sporadically occurring in the Danish mass media platforms in relation to issues such as the use of the word in the name of the Danish pastry "negerkyss" or "negerbolle" (in English, "negro kiss" or "negro buns"), the word used to name the famous Swedish character Pippi Longstocking's father as "Negerkongen" (in English, "the Negro king"), as well as in connection to discussing the usability of other racialized words such as "eskimo", "gypsy", "indio", "Caucasian", "hottentot", "oriental",

M. Vertelytė (✉) • P. Hervik
Department of Culture and Global Studies, Aalborg University,
Aalborg, Denmark
e-mail: vertelyte@cgs.aau.dk; hervik@cgs.aau.dk

© The Author(s) 2019
P. Hervik (ed.), *Racialization, Racism, and Anti-Racism in the Nordic Countries*, Approaches to Social Inequality and Difference,
https://doi.org/10.1007/978-3-319-74630-2_7

and the racialized Danish word "perker", which particularly targets people associated with Middle East or Arab backgrounds in Denmark. The controversy surrounding the use of the word, however, is not peculiar to Denmark. Neither is the debate restricted to these controversial categories but includes images loaded with racialized colonial relations. What is being generally referred to as "N-word debates" have been present in other European and non-European countries such as Norway (Gullestad, 2005), Germany, France, UK, Sweden (Hübinette, 2013), and Iceland (Loftsdóttir, 2013), while in the USA, the N-word debates mainly refer to the epithet "nigger" and seldom to "negro" (Moses, 2016). In the USA, the historical meaning progressed roughly from "colored" to "negro", to "black" and to "people of color", which indicates decades of struggle to grasp with processes of racialization (Moses, 2016). Even if European histories and contexts of race relations may differ from the ones in the USA, Moses reminds us that "our language continues to reflect our ongoing attempts to grapple with that reality" (2016). As in Kristin Loftsdóttir's account, these debates in Europe "reaffirm the importance of analysing majority or 'native' population perceptions of immigration and multicultural issues [and] shifting conceptions of 'race'" (2013, pp. 296–297).

In Denmark discussion of the usability of the word has been predominantly centered around the simplified binary morally laden questions, such as *may we say it or not, is it offending or not,* is the usage of the word *racist or not?* In this chapter, we wish to examine underlying processes of racialization that shape the debates of racializing epithets. We argue that the simple binaries of the debate are characterized by a rhetoric of moralization and warlike arguing between alarmists and deniers (Hunter, 1991), which upon closer analysis are far more complex. By looking into the recurrent arguments of the unfolding debate, we argue that racialization extends to include the belief that Denmark has moved beyond racism. Regardless of people's articulation of "I don't see color" and "racism only occurs if it is intentional", there is a color-blind racial ideology behind denials of racialization and brushing over of racial awareness of both African American history and Danish colonial and postcolonial relations.

The debate does not have, in our examination, a clear stage of culmination where issues of contestation are solved or put to rest. Neither do we observe particular alteration points where new narratives, argumentative structures, and contestations emerge. On the contrary, today, after close to 25 years of on-and-off exchanges between journalists, politicians, academics, activists, and news media and social media commentators, the morally laden question "may we use it or not" still remains at the center of attention. However, its sporadic time span allows us to see the perseverance of the dominant discourses that are being evoked throughout the years, particularly from our choice of starting point in 1995 and until 2016. In the analysis of the debate, we limit our empirical data to print media, mainly newspaper articles and commentaries, that we have been following in the past few years through Danish media data platform *Infomedia*. These include leading newspaper editorial articles, commentaries, interviews, and op-ed articles, including the statements by experts in Danish language and history. Since 1995 until 2016, approximately 4000 newspaper articles and commentaries were devoted to discussing the question "Can one say the word or not?", including the voices of those who support and oppose the use of the word. In the analysis of the debate, we look at major argumentative structures and logics used to debate the contestation of the word.

If the word is used in a quote or in a text, and if this word comes out of the mouth of a politician, then we do not change the quote to something else. In this article, we use the word in quotation marks when dealing explicitly with the debate about the word and in people's direct use of it. Recognizing the derogatory value, racialized history, and the advancement of racial and historical awareness in the USA and Europe, none of us (text authors) use the term in conversations or in writing. However, after long debates, considerations, and talks with colleagues in Europe and the USA, we come to the agreement that replacing the word with an N-word is also not an option. We derive from the argument that it is not the "N-word" that is being debated. The use of the "N-word" is a replacement that serves to distance oneself from the initial use of the word and as such works as a code word that signifies ones' position toward the issue at hand. When politicians, journalists, or media commentators use the word, they do not use it from the N-word position. Even so, only at the first glance, the Danish N-word may simply appear also to substitute the initial version of the word. However, it can also refer to the same basic negative understanding and end up, as some critics say, giving white persons a legitimate way to use the word without saying it. Using the N-word in this sense conveys, "You know what I mean" (Information, 2014). In this article, where the word is the topic of analysis or the reference point, we use it when we refer to the media debate in its actual use. When we refer to the word from our writing of the statements, we use "the word".

## EMERGENCE AND DEVELOPMENT OF THE DEBATE

The first significant debate regarding the usability of the word, in our analysis, took place in 1995. The head of *Dokumentations og rådgivningscenteret om racediskrimination* (DRC) (the Documentation and Advisory Centre on Racial Discrimination) went with a client to the police in order to register a complaint about racial discrimination. The former police chief of Copenhagen, Poul Efsen, responded to the DRC claim that the police used the word to refer to the asylum seeker in relation to reporting a case of racial discrimination. Poul Efsen argued, based on the knowledge from a language dictionary, that the word is a neutral Danish designation that defines people with black or dark brown skin color. People of African descent, according to Efsen, must recognize that, in Denmark, the word is used to refer to black or dark brown people. The case was brought up in the Parliament, and *Det Danske Sprognævn* (*DDS*) (the Danish Language Committee [DLC]) was asked for advice. In 1995, Jørgen Schack, a researcher at the DLC, wrote the report. According to Schack, most of the Danes who use the word do not use it derogatorily; however, he advised using "black" instead, arguing that it is a more neutral term (Ritzau's Bureau, 1995). The debate has intensively continued throughout several months and has been actively debated by journalist and media commentators and civil society activists, among others, covered by headlines such as "A Sensitive word" (Politiken, 1995b) or "Can a negro be called a negro" (Dagbladenes Bureau, 1995). Similar headlines have continued to be used throughout the years. For example, "Can one say negro?" is asked in 1998 (Politiken, 1998), "Black or Negro" in 1999 (B.T.), and "Negro or no" in 2004 (Information); from the headlines of the newspapers, it seems as though that the question that was still debatable in 1999 or 2004 has found more steady position in 2008, such as "'Negro' is an absolutely neutral word" in 2008 (Ugebrevet A4) or "The right to say negro" in 2008a (Information).

In 2012, the Danish newspaper *Dagbladet Roskilde* used the word in the article reporting a stolen car from an 80-year-old (Dagbladet Roskilde, 2012). The use of the word by the newspaper was taken up to social media and criticized. In the response to the critique, the editor of the newspaper, Steen Østbjerg, stated that the choice of the word:

> is an intentional choice since the police use the word in their profile of the man. I don't believe that it is an offensive word. This is a piece of information that makes it easier to find the man. If he had red hair, I would have written it. If he had been fat, I would have written so. (Journalisten.dk, 2012)

In relation to this discussion, newspapers *Dagbladet* and *Frederiksborg Amts Avis* organized a questionnaire asking their readers if they agree or disagree with the use of the word in the newspaper. Out of 108 answers, 75 agreed and 24 disagreed with the use of the word, and 9 persons remained neutral (Dagbladet Køge/Ringsted/Roskilde, 2012).

The coverage of the use of the word exploded again in 2014 when a representative for right-wing party *Venstre* and a member of the Danish Parliament, Esben Lunde Larsen, stated:

> If I in the future must refer to a person, who is black, then I will call him Negro, because that is what the word rightfully covers, and we shall stop making it odious to refer to a person from Africa as either black or Negro, because the meaning is the same. (Jyllandsposten, 2014)

Once again, the same arguments are put in the forefront: the word is a neutral categorization. However, under journalistic pressure, Larsen is reluctant and evasive when it comes to the use of the word about President Barack Obama, Martin Luther King, and Tiger Woods while maintaining that the word is applicable and neutral in an African setting. A year and a half later when Larsen became a minister in the new government, he declared that he now no longer would use the word to name dark-skinned people.

In 2016, again, two notable flare-ups of the debate involved politicians. In May 2016, the Danish People's Party launched a new campaign called *Our Denmark—there is so much we need to take care of* ("Vores Danmark— der er så meget, vi skal passe på"). The campaign used the signature image of a Danish family depicted with eight members (B.T., 2016). It was criticized and ridiculed on social media for the whiteness of the family. In response to the party campaign, new members with different than white backgrounds replaced family members instead, which was seen as another outburst against foreigners. After this critique, Søren Espersen, of the Danish People's Party, went out and said:

> Me, I am colorblind, so I don't know what color they have. We could easily have added a negro and then what? How would that have changed anything? Take for instance someone like Obama—what is he? We all know what this is about. We are talking about the first negro in the Presidency of the USA. (Nyheder TV2, 2016a)

One of the Social Democrats and European Parliamentarians, Jeppe Kofod, took up the latter statement in his own way, in what became known as the N-word tweet. Kofod tweeted "DF Chair of Danish Parliament Foreign Policy Committee calls @BarackObama first nigger President. Scandal!" (Nyheder TV2, 2016a). Soon after, Søren Espersen found out that he would not be traveling with the Foreign Policy Committee to the USA because of the tweet. The Danish news media again and again repeated the story between the two conflicting politicians. There were, to our knowledge, no attempts made to confront Espersen with the question whether he, when he was supposed to meet President Obama in the White House, would use the word to refer to the President. In the USA, the term is indisputably derogatory and even deemed immoral (Bonilla-Silva, 2014, p. 103). One should also note that the Danish People's Party since 2013 has recommended its party leaders not to use the term any longer, presumably for communicative reasons since its associations are only negative (Nyheder TV2, 2016b).

Soon after, yet another dispute relating to the use of the word came out. This time the word was used in the art exhibition titles and descriptions at the Danish National Art Museum. After the criticism, the museum decided to remove the word from the exhibition. On June 10, 2016, journalist Jesper Termansen of Denmark's Radio wrote yet another piece of "may we say it or not" once again successfully turning the issue into a moral one (DR.dk, 2016). Moreover, continuing this moralization, Termansen lumps the term and the issue into a whole box of terms, should we (as DR journalists) use "Islamic State" or "Daesh", "Elder burden", "terrorist", and "migrant".

These are just few instances illustrating the ongoing debate in Denmark throughout the last two decades. Interestingly, we see that the arguments pertaining to the neutrality of the word due to its long time use in Denmark as well as an argument that the word is a tool of political correctness have been pervasive throughout these years. What these arguments have in common is that they are solely based on drawing on the experiences and opinions of white Danes, to whom the claims of the offensiveness of the word is somewhat an indication of the national threat to their right to use the word. These claims, though, did not come without opposition. We found some articles by racialized minorities or scholars explaining the problematics of using the word. Notably, in a response to the debate, the activist campaign "N-Word that hurts" (N-ordet, det gør ondt) conducted the survey on

Facebook among Danes with an African background, showing that the use of the word is completely unacceptable for the ones who are exposed to it (Berlingske, 2016).

In the following section, we analyze more in detail two predominant claims made in the debate: (1) the claim of neutrality projected through the argument of the semantics of the word and (2) the claims of the threat to freedom of speech projected through the notions as Denmark being a postrace society.

## Maintaining the Right to Neutrality

In Danish media debates surrounding the word, one of the most prevalently evoked arguments is the one of the semantics. The argument proposes that the word is neutral because etymologically it derives from the Latin use of the word which semanticaly simply means the color black.

The explanation that the word comes from the Latin word *negro*, which simply means black, is used in the Danish debate as an absolute and ultimate evidence proving the neutrality of the word (Politiken, 1995a). This particular argument evoked on multiple occasions is further accompanied by arguing that because of its etymology and because of a different historical context, the Danish word does not have the same negative connotations as it has in the USA. However, paradoxically, Danish public debate often still refers to Reverend Martin Luther King as using the word, particularly in his "I Have a Dream" speech of 1963.

Upon closer look, there is more to the meaning of the word than a simple reference to color in Latin, Spanish, and Portuguese. The people of the Canaries and Western Africa were conceived as idolaters and devil-worshippers in the fifteenth century but nevertheless as having a (false) religion. They were seen as Moors or Muslims. "The expansion of the category "Moor" to include Africans was not strange, since *moro* is etymologically related to the Latin term for *negro* or black" (Maldonado-Torres, 2014, p. 650).

Maldonado-Torres argues that the skepticism of the humanity of indigenous people in the Americas (without religion) was transposed and readapted to the Africans. "Negro" and "Negra" used for "blacks" became the only legitimately enslavable category (2014, p. 654) and "represent a symbolic category denoting radical dispensability, suspicion, violence, and hate. As a result 'Negro' would become an establish way of referring to violent natives and other racialized subject in the modern/colonial world"

(2014, p. 657). In other words, the original reference to "black" people refers to people considered and treated as inferior beings along the lines of their perceived degree of humanity. The reference to black as a neutral word for color in Spanish and Portuguese, we argue, leaves out the social character of words, where the use of a term can also constitute a reality, in this case of superiority and inferiority relations. Instead, it can be seen as an attempt to recruit easy argument for upholding ideas of neutrality but does not hold the test of critical analysis.

When the debate started in 1995, the case was brought up in the Parliament, and the DLC (DDS) was asked for advice. Jørgen Schack, a researcher at the DLC, wrote the report. Schack went on to explain the use of the term. To do so, despite the prevalent argument used in the media that the word in the USA and Denmark does not bear the same connotations, Schack turned to American linguist Geneva Smitherman's work (1991) that deals with the use of the identity terms since Africans were first brought to the Americas. Schack thus notes that black Americans used the word themselves, particularly from 1920 to 1965. While in Schack's interpretation the shift to "black" signaled a new and stronger racial awareness (1995), for Smitherman it "signals an ideological shift, a repudiation of whiteness and the rejection of assimilation" and an attempt to eradicate "the negativity and self-hatred" (1991, p. 12). Yet, even if Smitherman wrote a fine article (and so did Schack), both are linguistically oriented with little information on the structural conditions and embodied experiences of racism of blacks in the USA and racialized groups in Europe. From the writings of Eduardo Bonilla-Silva, we know that after slavery was abolished and after the Jim Crow laws were discontinued, people of color have been:

> three times more likely to be poor than whites, earn about 40 percent less than whites, and have about an eighth of the net worth that whites have. They also receive an inferior education compared to whites, even when they attend integrated institutions. In terms of housing, black owned units comparable to white-owned ones are valued at 35 percent less. (2014, p. 2)

However, when Schack and Smitherman explain that black Americans also used the word from 1920 to 1965 without controversy, they fail to convey that this use took place with rigid segregation and race riots, not with much political awareness of shared black identity and strong prevailing views that blacks were less morally and mentally developed (hooks, 1994;

Ritchey, 2015; Smedley, 1993). Reverend Martin Luther King repeatedly urged the world to stand up against segregation reflecting the inferiorized positions of black Americans in the racial hierarchy, which indicates that the very use of the term is much more than semantics. At the same time and as noted above, there were times of radical change, change that includes the shift to "black" and the introduction of Afro-American and African American.

The attempts to find reasoning in semantic and etymological explanations and in bringing up the assumingly uncontroversial use of the word in the context of the USA, such as the Jørgen Schack account, become an empty slope that dis-attaches the language from the lived life practices and hegemonic discourses with its underlying structures of power relations. The sociological and anthropological researches from a critical race perspective provide many examples showing how linguistic categories of color and otherness are constructed through power relations. For example, Karen Brodkin Sacks writes about how Jews became white folks. Historically, the USA has a history of anti-Semitism and beliefs of seeing Jews as belonging to an inferior race (Sacks, 1996, p. 79); yet following WWII, Jews and Eastern and Southern Europeans were part of a larger whitening process (Sacks, 1996, p. 97). Virginia Dominguez (1986) has followed the official recognition of the Louisiana Creoles as an official minority group in the USA, which sparked strong reactions that they could not as a white group be a minority. More recently, Deepa Kumar (2012) has documented how Arab Americans could pass as whites prior to 9/11 and after as Arabs or Arab Americans (see also Meer, this volume).

Despite some critical voices of scholars and activists who took an active part in the debate, providing accounts that showed that the word is not unattached from larger colonial and postcolonial structures of racism, the argument that the word is semanticaly rooted in a Latin word which means black and thus neutral has persisted to be one of the main bottom-line rationales of the debate. Hence, skipping hundreds of years of historical aspects of power relations, including the slavery, caste-like segregation, and being at the bottom of the international hierarchy of race, color, and culture (Trouillot, 1991). Gullestad, for instance, in the analysis of the Norwegian media debate surrounding the word has shown how popular understanding of history in Norway is used to support the argument that the word is a traditional Norwegian and as such has no negative connotations. As Norway distances itself from the history of European imperialism and denies any responsibility toward the colonialism, to maintain the image as a tolerant and liberal nation, where issues of race are deemed to be irrelevant, becomes preconceived (Gullestad, 2005).

The parallel argumentation is apparent in Danish media debates. For instance, Danish active participation in transatlantic slave trade in the Virgin Islands (former Danish West Indies) in the seventeenth and eighteenth centuries and human exhibitions of "exotic" people in the Danish zoos in the nineteenth century is not included in the debate. Andreassen and Henningsen's historical study on human exhibitions in Denmark points to the everything-but-neutral uses of words and bodies at a time when evolutionary racial thinking peaked (Andreassen & Henningsen, 2011).

Audrey Smedley writes that in the minds of whites the cognitive perceptions and understandings of cultural differences were reduced to a single causative factor, namely, race (1993, p. 181). Within these enduring beliefs of white superiority and black inferiority, Smedley adds, blacks were seen as not really humans (pp. 181–182), perceived as being devoid of intellect, lacking moral restraints, and prone to idleness and thievery (p. 183). In the late nineteenth century, Du Bois was hired to carry out a study in a famous ghetto area of Philadelphia and find out why African Americans were so overwhelmed with poverty, crime, and drug addiction. After a pioneering and grounded study, he deduced that "the Negro problem looked at in one way is but the old-world questions of ignorance, poverty, crime, and the dislike of the stranger" (Du Bois, 1899, p. 385). From this perspective, it becomes problematic to see the word as only a linguistic term and as a word whose usage could be simply explained by its etymology or semantics. The word has never been neutral. It has always signified colonialism, with an idea of the inferiority of races. In the context of colonialism and postcolonialism, the word appears as a conception that refers to racial discrimination, slavery, colonialism, antiblack prejudice, and the perceived idea of racially divided societies across the globe. In other words, the debate is not a debate about linguistic legitimacy or the right to preserve the traditional language. Reducing the debate to the issue of language fails to recognize implicit postcolonial power relations and fails to discuss the contemporary meanings of race and racialization.

In the Danish debate, the persistence to hold on to the semantical argument comes together with the claims of generational durability of the neutrality of the word and neutral intentions of the ones using it. Such a position is being expressed in statements such as "I believe that elder people should be allowed to use a word that they have used all their lives without intending anything derogatory" (Politiken, 1995a). Furthermore, it is followed by slippery-slope moral panic narratives that if "we" cannot use the word, then soon "we" won't be able to use "black" or use the name in the Danish candies, pastries, children books, and so on (Ekstra Bladet, 1995, 2001). Mathias Danbolt, in the analysis of the debate surrounding the racialized representations on Danish food commodities, shows how similar discourses of "nostalgia" and "generational use" are evoked to reproduce the ideas of Danish cultural heritage, making what he coins as a *retro racism*—"the 'historical' displacement of racism, in which racism is figured retrospectively inscribed by 'antiracist' critics: a *retrospective* inscription that demonstrated that the criticism of racism is obviously a *retrograde* move, historically and politically" (2017, p. 119).

The insistance to maintain a national linguistic right to neutrality of the word speaks not only to the lack of the knowledge or ignorance toward the Danish active involvement in the colonial past and the general global colonial history (Blaagaard & Andreassen, 2012) but also in Gullestad terms, points to the reaffirmation of the "symbolic hegemony of majority" within the framework of the nation-state (2005, p. 42). The debate, thus, is not framed in terms of whether we should listen to people with different visible histories and account for their experiences of racialization in order to employ an inclusive vocabulary. The debate, instead, carries a distinction of us and them maintaining the boundaries between Danes and non-Danes as well as between politically correct and the ones that protect the rights to Danish racial nostalgia.

## DENYING EXPERIENCES OF RACIALIZATION

The question may we use the word or not in Danish public debate is the question of if there is racism in Denmark. When, in 1995, the police chief, Poul Efsen, was confronted with the use of the word by DRC, the assertion of DRC was not only not to use the word but also to draw attention to the presence of racial discrimination in Denmark. One of the apparent notions that goes along the lines of the debate is the question whether the use of the word is racist and if the one using the word should then be considered as racist. This line of logic points to the persistent idea that racism is legitimate only if it is intentional. Similar ways of reasoning are also found in other Danish public debates where the question of race and racism becomes central (see also Rødje & Thorsen, this volume).

In 2008 a race and discrimination scholar, Mira C. Skadegård, wrote an account "If I am a negro—are you racist?" (Information, 2008b). In her article, Skadegård highlighted important academic knowledge-based facts, such as that race is not a biological category but rather a social construction historically designated to establish white privilege and classify people into humans and nonhumans, which nevertheless, in spite of its fictional construction, still is an embodied notion for people who experience structural racial discrimination and everyday racism. The critical academic accounts, such as Skadegård's, are rarely used to move the debate forward. Instead, they are being followed by journalist and media commentators with resistance to accept that there is racism in Denmark and an insistence to see race as a biological category and reality.

These notions that race is real, and therefore the word is an objective classification of different races, come together with claims that the opposition to the use of the word and claims that it is an indication of racism bears a danger to Danish democracy (Ugebrevet A4, 2008). As one of the commentators of the debate, a lawyer Vagn Greve stated:

> It is immensely dangerous for the development of the democracy, if there isn't unlimited freedom to express oneself, but this is not to say that the language should be practiced at its lowest level. An awful change in the tone of language has taken place in the last 10–15 years in most political parties …. This is a dangerous fundamentalism that does not belong in a democracy. (Ugebrevet A4, 2008)

The narrative of political correctness is abruptly used not only as a tool to down tone the voices of those who oppose the use of the word, but also it forms a framework of explanation delineating the larger shift from a seemingly neutral word to the word that is inscribed in the ideology of political correctness. For example, in the Danish dictionary *Den Store Danske*, the entry to the word explains the occurring contestations as a result of political correctness and not as a result of the opposition of radicalized minorities, race scholars, and anti-racism activism (Sjørslev & Nielsen, 2017).

The political correctness in the debate is treated as a bottom-line argument, a showstopper for serious discussion and critique, and appears in most instances when race, tolerance, understanding, and other alleged "soft" measures are brought into the debate (Boisen & Hervik, 2013; Hervik, 2011). Once the PC-word is evoked, the possibility of serious debate diminishes. Basically, you cannot really argue against accusations of political correctness. More than anything, it is an empty signifier, a bad word, or an insult, "you are just politically correct", that you throw at your opponent (Gullestad, 2002, pp. 18–19). The term political correctness builds on some inner contradictions and semantic transformations. Originally political correctness emerged as a term to name the efforts to avoid negatively loaded use of the language addressed to different disadvantaged cultural groups and with the recognition of the historical injustice they have suffered (Hervik, 2002). In its original meanings, it expresses a particularly positive attention to underprivileged social groups, and the relationship is scrutinized for discriminatory rhetoric, practices, and policies. Especially feminists, multiculturalists, and other minorities and supporters of minorities are typically criticized for taking special positions (in neoliberal logic "special interests") as politically correct. However, much of the practices of euphemism and the choice of positively loaded words rather than negative ones come from the communication industry and not least military warfare. But the premise is a different one when it comes to the use of racial epithets, as they are signifiers of the continuous racial system and majority of people being called the words, indirectly or directly, strongly express their opposition.

The claims of the endangered freedom of speech and the threat of political correctness are built on the post-racial image of the nation—an idea that Denmark has nothing to do with race or racism. This post-racial thinking detaches the debate from the problems of race and racialization in Denmark and makes them fictional rather than real. In such cases the very mention of race and racially loaded words serves as an invitation to refute its relevance (Lentin & Titley, 2012) or transform it into accusations of bringing the danger to democracy and freedom of speech. While at the same time, the question of why do people insist on using the word when it hurts remains undiscussed.

The denial of racial ideology and racial system in the use of these racially loaded epithets is a good example of what Philomena Essed has named as entitlement racism. After the Muhammad cartoon crisis did she take this further and suggested the term *entitlement racism* (Essed, 2002, 2013). With the territorial and Western claim to a superior position, entitlement racism is based on the belief that one has the right to insult and humiliate others. With reference to the privileged position, the right to publish the cartoons or use racial epithets is defended while accusing their opponents of restricting freedom of speech. According to Essed, the very motivation or inclination to publish is the enactment of an entitlement—the perpetrators know, or could have known, that their portrayals are offensive, but they did not see any reason to apologize or change their behavior. They insist on the right to offend in the name of freedom, regardless of its impact on others. At the very core of this racism is the humiliation of the other in order to elevate the self (Essed, 2013).

## MEDIATING FOR MORALIZATION

Hervik argues that Danish public debates and conversations about immigration issues reveal a certain indignant form used across topics and functioning as a means to appeal to the moral outrage (2018). In this manner, the debate ties into one of the dominant discourse and social values characterizing the 2000s, namely, turning serious social issues and lightweighting alike items into questions of moralization: what you like and what you think is ugly or beautiful, right or wrong, unnatural or natural, racist or not racist (Zigon, 2008). In the light of are we racist or not debates (such as described in Danbolt and Myong chapter in this volume), the critical voices of activist and race scholars pointing to the problems of contemporary forms of race and racialization are being lost between the claims of anti-intellectualism and post-factual constructivist reasoning.

Such a discourse is repeating itself across terrains. We see no real difference between the moralizations of other issues. What is the difference between asking may I say the word or not and debating may *Jyllands-Posten* publish the infamous cartoons or not? Deciding whether a publication of a cartoon and a use of the word that carry racialized connotations is a blind alley. Questions like may I say the word, is it racist, or are the Danes racists are the kinds of questions that thrive in the binary logic of the commodified news media that simplify, create confrontation, and create moral panic between two radically opposed adversaries. Entering the "offended-not-offended" positions, the possibility of the serious debate is rather being turned into a non-debate. This type of debating, we argue, centers morally laden binary questions which evoke further polarization and hinder the dialogue. Serious and affirmative critique has little chance of evolving from the debate, where the question itself becomes the inclined framework of the potential discussion rather than the initiation of the critique and knowledge. What kinds of knowledge and critique could the debate produce if instead of asking may we use the word or not, one would ask what does the use of the word do to people or what happens when it is being used? Instead of deriving from the arguments of semantics and political correctness, one could rather ask what has been the role of the word in the production of the racial system.

Instead of approaching the debates from a moral perspective, which is dominating public and popular discussions, or a "who-wins-the-debate perspective", we invoke a simple basic premise developed in linguistics and anthropology. The study of meaning cannot be reduced to semantics, that is, roughly equivalent to the meanings of words as looked up in dictionaries but must include the pragmatics, that is, what goes on in social communication (Hanks, 1996). In communication, not only messages are being conveyed but also claims of social positions relative to one another. Accordingly, the claim that racial epithets are neutral is a false one, as it belies on who is claiming the neutrality. Categories, by definition, can never be neutral, since they are always offered by someone about someone else. Racial epithets, such as the word in question, have always been used about people in inferior positions by the ones with superior power. The word, as we showed, refers in unison to inferior bodies who lack humanness. Neither would that mean that other words such as "black" or "Afro-Dane" or "person of color" would be somewhat less neutral, as they would nonetheless serve as a markers of skin color and the assigned difference.

The commentators of the debate are right in saying that the DRC's proposed use of "black" as a more neutral term can nonetheless also be understood as a negative one. However, these claims fall short as it stems from the idea that there is the ultimate neutral word to be used and that it is up to the Danes to decide on it rather than listening to the voices of people to whom these words are directed to and who protest the use of the word as a means to oppose racism. Historically, we know that the positive shift of the negative association of "black" to the positive one was intentionally done by African Americans through the Black Power Movement under slogans like "Black is beautiful". It is not the word and its semantics that matters, but the struggles to reclaim or resist racial epithets by the communities who are objected to the very use of these words. The serious dialogue and the critique can only emerge departing from the point of view of the racialized and not the superior power of the racializer.

## CONCLUDING REMARKS

The use of racial epithets, such as the Danish word "neger", evokes a historically laden construction of inferiority and superiority, humanness and non-humanness. This word with its connotations has a long, complex history, which is only beginning to make inroads into the public opinions in Denmark. The debate about the use of the word in Danish news media holds statements about the neutrality of the contentious words, confrontational attacks on opponents accusing them of political accusations and treason, while they themselves hold on to normative principles of post racism and Danish-tolerant exceptionalism. In this chapter, we argued that there is no such thing as a neutral category, that is, categories that exist in vacuum, without any group of persons using it about others. The debate that is centered around the question of what is neutral or not, thus we argue, is a failed opportunity for society to discuss some of the most important issues of the last decades. Instead of discussing overt and not-so-overt forms of racialization, discrimination, racism, and exclusion, they are trivialized, explained away, and outright rejected in contemporary society, which in itself is regarded as a post-racial color-blind society.

The Danish hegemonic majority reacts in larger numbers and also with moral outrage. Their stance to the use of the racial epithets as non-intentional and post-racial is not the one of racial awareness. Faced with contestations of the use of the word, they react not on the content of the criticism but on the ideas of Danish exceptionalism as well-intended and post-racialist conviction. Framing the debate as a moral issue, whether one may or may not say the word, is beneficial for what we call media's non-debate. It reflects the attempts to frame issues of "integration" and multiculturalism as occurring moral panics, but it is unsolvable and misses an opportunity to seriously talk about the inferiorization of one group and the superiorization of another as the basis for policy, popular consciousness, violence, and, for that matter, research-based knowledge of racism and its history.

Adding it up, we argue that it is not so much the moralization that is relevant, or whether some legal standard or moral norm is broken, but what white persons' insistence of using the racial epithets and what it says about the racial formation of Danish society, where the racial categories never come without claims of a hierarchical relationship along the lines of superiority and inferiority.

## REFERENCES

Andreassen, R., & Henningsen, A. F. (2011). *Menneskeudstilling: Fremvisninger af eksotiske mennesker i Zoologisk Have og Tivoli* [Human Inhibitions: Race, Gender, and Sexuality in Ethnic Displays]. København: Tiderne Skifter.

Berlingske. (2016, May 31). Vi vil ikke kaldes negre. *Berlingske*.

Blaagaard, B., & Andreassen, R. (2012). Disappearing Acts: The Forgotten History of Colonialism, Eugenics and Gendered Othering in Denmark. In

B. Hilplf & K. Lofstdottir (Eds.), *Teaching 'Race' with a Gendered Edge* (pp. 81–95). Utrecht & Budapest: ATGENDER.

Boisen, S., & Hervik, P. (2013, December). Danish Media Coverage of 22/7. *Nordic Journal for Migration Research, 3*(4), 197–204.

Bonilla-Silva, E. (2014). *Racism without Racists: Color-Blind Racism and the Persistence of Racial Inequality in America* (4th ed.). Lanham, Boulder, New York, Toronto, Plymouth, UK: Rowman and Littlefield Publishers, Inc.

B.T. (1999, September 12). Sort eller neger. *B.T.*

B.T. (2016, May 17). Søren Espersen Efter Kritik Af DF-Kampagne: Vi Kunne Have Sat En Neger Ind. *B.T.*

Dagbladenes Bureau. (1995, August 1). Må en neger kaldes neger. *Dagbladenes Bureau.*

Dagbladet Køge/Ringsted/Roskilde. (2012, April 30). Læserne har intet imod oder "neger". *Dagbladet Køge/Ringsted/Roskilde.*

Dagbladet Roskilde. (2012, April 18). Neger stjal bil fra 80-årig. *Dagbladet Roskilde.*

Danbolt, M. (2017). Retro Racism: Colonial Ignorance and Racialized Affective Consumption in Danish Public Culture. *Nordic Journal of Migration Research, 7*(2), 105–113.

Domínguez, V. R. (1986). *White by Definition. Social Classification in Creole Louisiana.* New Brunswick: Rutgers University Press.

DR.dk. (2016, June 10). Må man sige 'neger' i DR? *DR.dk.*

Du Bois, W. E. B. (1899). *The Philadelphia Negro.* New York: Lippincott.

Ekstra Bladet. (1995, October 2). Neger-snak. *Ekstra Bladet.*

Ekstra Bladet. (2001, April 1). Neger-bolle. *Ekstra Bladet.*

Essed, P. (2002). Everyday Racism. In D. T. Goldberg & J. Solomos (Eds.), *A Companion to Racial and Ethnic Studies* (pp. 202–216). Malden, MA: Blackwell.

Essed, P. (2013). Entitlement Racism: License to Humiliate. In ENAR (Ed.), *Recycling Hatred: Racism(s) in Europe Today: A Dialogue between Academics, Equality Experts and Civil Society Activists* (pp. 62–76). Brussels: European Network Against Racism (ENAR).

Gullestad, M. (2002). *Det Norske Sett Med Nye Øyne Kristisk Anayse Av Norsk Innvandringsdebatt.* Oslo: Universitetforlaget.

Gullestad, M. (2005). Normalising Racial Boundaries. The Norwegian Dispute about the Term Neger. *Social Anthropology, 13*(1), 27–46.

Hanks, F. W. (1996). *Language and Communicative Practices.* Boulder, CO: Westview Press, A Division of Harper Collins Publishers.

Hervik, P. (2002). *Mediernes muslimer. En antropologisk undersøgelse af mediernes dækning af religioner i Danmark.* The Board for Ethnic Equality: Copenhagen. Retrieved from Mediernes Muslimer.pdf

Hervik, P. (2011). *The Annoying Difference. The Emergence of Danish Neonationalism, Neoracism, and Populism in the Post-1989 World.* New York and Oxford: Berghahn Books.

Hervik, P. (2018, June). Afterword. In Special Issue: "Moral Outrage as a Mobilizing Force to Action." *Conflict and Society*.

hooks, B. (1994). *Teaching to Transgress: Education as the Practice of Freedom*. New York: Routledge.

Hunter, J. D. (1991). *Cultural Wars: The Struggle to Define America*. New York: Basic Books.

Hübinette, T. (2013). Swedish Antiracism and White Melancholia: Racial Words in a Post-Racial Society. *Ethnicity and Race in a Changing World, 4*(1), 24–33.

Information. (2004, October 21). Neger eller ej, *Information*.

Information. (2008a, February 14). Retten til at sige neger, *Information*.

Information. (2008b, November 25). Hvis jeg er neger, er du racist? *Information*.

Information. (2014, January 18). Kvinder, der bruger N-ordet.

Journalisten.dk. (2012, April 27). Dagbladet Roskilde står ved ordet 'neger'. *Journalisten.dk*.

Jyllandsposten. (2014, January 22). Folketingsmedlem vil sige 'neger' I Protest. *Jyllandsposten*.

Kumar, D. (2012). *Islamophobia and the Politics of Empire*. Chicago, IL: Haymarket Books.

Lentin, A., & Titley, G. (2012, July 13). Racism Is Still Very Much with Us. So Why Don't We Recognise It? *The Guardian (Opinion)*. Retrieved from https://www.theguardian.com/commentisfree/2012/jul/13/racism-public-discourse-power-to-define

Loftsdóttir, K. (2013). Republishing 'The Ten Little Negros': Exploring Nationalism and 'Whiteness' in Iceland. *Ethnicities, 13*(3), 295–315. https://doi.org/10.1177/1468796812472854

Maldonado-Torres, N. (2014). AAR Centennial Roundtable: Religion, Conquest, and Race in the Foundations of the Modern/Colonial World. *Journal of the American Academy of Religion, 82*(3), 636–665. https://doi.org/10.1093/jailer/lfu054

Moses, Y. T. (2016). 'Race': Is the Term 'People of Color' Acceptable in This Day and Age? Retrieved from https://www.sapiens.org/column/race/people-of-color/

Nyheder TV2. (2016a, May 18). Søren Espersen vil ikke undskylde: 'Neger' ligger dybt i mit vokabularium. *Nyheder TV2*.

Nyheder TV2. (2016b, May 17). Koks i Dansk Folkeparti – Næstformand brugte forbudt n-ord. *Nyheder TV2*.

Politiken. (1995a, October 1). At være eller ikke være neger. *Politiken*.

Politiken. (1995b, September 22). Følsomt ord. *Politiken*.

Politiken. (1998, October 7). Må man ikke sige 'neger'? *Politiken*.

Ritchey, K. (2015). Black Identity Development. *The Vermont Connection, 35*(12), 99–105.

Ritzau's Bureau. (1995, November 1). De færreste bruger order 'neger' racistisk, siger sprognævn. *Ritzau's Bureau.*

Sacks, K. B. (1996). How Did Jews Become White Folks? In S. Gregory & R. Sanjek (Eds.), *Race* (pp. 78–102). New York and London: Routledge.

Schack, J. (1995, December 4). Om Ordet Neger. *Nyt Fra Sprognævnet.*

Sjørslev, I., & Nielsen, P. (2017). Neger. *Den Store Danske, Gyldendal.* Retrieved September 20, 2017, from http://denstoredanske.dk/index.php?sideId=130790

Smedley, A. (1993). *Race in North America. Origin and Evolution of a Worldview.* Boulder, CO: Westview Press.

Smitherman, G. (1991). What Is Africa to Me?: Language, Ideology and African American. *American Speech, 66*(2), 115–132.

Trouillot, M.-R. (1991). Anthropology and the Savage Slot. In R. Fox (Ed.), *Recapturing Anthropology: Working in the Present* (pp. 1–33). Santa Fe, New Mexico: SAR Press.

Ugebrevet A4. (2008, March 31). 'Neger' er et helt neutralt ord. *Ugebrevet A4.*

Zigon, J. (2008). *Morality: An Anthropological Perspective.* Oxford and New York: Berg.

# CHAPTER 8

# Anti-Racism from the Margins: Welcoming Refugees at Schengen's Northernmost Border

*Carolina S. Boe and Karina Horsti*

## INTRODUCTION

Images of men, women, and children riding bicycles in a snowy white Arctic landscape wearing sneakers, jeans, and light jackets captured international media attention in the autumn of 2015, as they crossed the northernmost external Schengen border from Russia to seek asylum in Norway. In a community of some 3500 inhabitants, 5542 asylum seekers arrived within a time period of a few months.

The so-called refugee crisis had already been a daily news topic in Europe for several years. The attention had, however, so far, been drawn further south, on fishing boats and rubber dinghies crammed with people in the Mediterranean Sea. This form of irregular border crossing had

C. S. Boe (✉)
Aalborg University, Aalborg, Denmark
e-mail: boe@cgs.aau.dk

K. Horsti
University of Jyväskylä, Jyväskylä, Finland
e-mail: karina.horsti@jyu.fi

© The Author(s) 2019                                                      183
P. Hervik (ed.), *Racialization, Racism, and Anti-Racism in the Nordic Countries*, Approaches to Social Inequality and Difference,
https://doi.org/10.1007/978-3-319-74630-2_8

perhaps become such a familiar visual trope that it had become a normal-ized part of the refugee experience in the eyes of the public in the global North. Were the images of Syrian, Afghan, and Iraqi asylum seekers cycling in the Arctic landscape necessary to wake these public up to realize how bizarre European refugee politics were becoming? Just as the progressive closure of the border between Morocco and Gibraltar led smugglers to charge more money and migrants to take higher risks, leading to inflations of deaths by drowning (Andersson, 2014; Migreurop, 2009, pp. 116–118; 2017; Pian, 2009), the building of fences by Balkan and Eastern European countries led migrants and human smugglers to find alternative routes. The images of Arctic border crossers, hence, also symbolized the creativity of smugglers who organized flight tickets from Istanbul to Moscow, from Moscow to Murmansk, and adapted to local legislation by providing their clients with overpriced bicycles to cross the border. The banal reason for the necessity of the bicycle was a 70-year-old ban by Russians to pedestrian traffic on the border and a recent threat from Norwegian authorities to prosecute drivers who would transport passengers without visas.

As the inhabitants of the Norwegian border town Kirkenes discovered through news media that refugees had started crossing the border a few kilometers away from their town, completely unprepared for the arctic winter, several groups organized to gather warm clothing and other basic necessities to welcome the refugees. Their solidarity network soon expanded to networks in other regions of Norway and of Europe, through social media. Sympathizers, from as far as Italy, sent boxes with clothes and toys. Solidarity messages, but also hate mails, arrived from other parts of Norway. Not everyone in these regions is supportive of refugees, and the communities are divided on how the so-called refugee crisis should be dealt with. Also, the nationalist populist Progress Party in Norway has grown in popularity in the North. Hate mail either was anonymous or came from people who didn't know those who welcomed refugees.

Two years later, in February 2017, we were among nine academics of the Nordic network Borderscapes, Memory and Migration who visited Kirkenes and had the chance to meet Eirik Nielsen, a former miner, and Merete Nordhus, a nurse, and other inhabitants of the region. When we met them, the Russian authorities had started to control the border again, and there were no longer any asylum seekers cycling to Kirkenes. The municipal sports hall, which had been a temporary shelter for the refugees, was back in use for the local Taekwondo and handball teams. Some refugees had been relocated in the town, but most had been sent to various reception centers elsewhere in Norway.

The memory of the event, however, was still vivid. It had forged friendships, solidarity networks, and a new geography of affect. Local people in Kirkenes told us how they now perceived news from afar much differently, whether bombings in Syria, bomb attacks in Iraq, or the war in Afghanistan (in spite of the involvement of Norwegian troops) were no longer distant events but touched them because the arrival of refugees to Kirkenes had created knowledge of and affective ties to these regions. Kirkenes was built around an iron ore mine in 1906, and just before the arrival of the refugees, in 2015, the local mining company Sydvaranger Gruve had gone bankrupt (Gullvik & Mortensen, 2016). All the miners, including Eirik, lost their jobs. Meeting the inhabitants of Kirkenes, an economically challenged region of Europe reminded us of encounters we have had with locals who have mobilized to help refugees in Lampedusa, Calais, or the marginalized neighborhoods of Paris (Boe, in press; Boe & Mainsah, 2017; Horsti & Neumann, 2017).

Through the case of Kirkenes, we will first analyze some more general trends that relate to the analysis of humanitarian actions and solidarity with asylum seekers and refugees. We will then analyze what happens when citizens discover and act upon law and legal practice, which they find unfair, engaging in moral arguments, illegalities, and legal struggles to redefine justice. Finally, we will discuss the pitfalls of explaining racism with social class: white working class or persons with shorter education from rural or formerly industrialized regions of the Nordic countries are often represented as allegedly more prone to xenophobia and racism. A common analysis is that their experiences of dispossession and marginalization go hand in hand with xenophobia and a feeling of threat from sexual minorities, women, migrants, and the specter of a multiculturalist society that has taken away their former privileges. Politicians, at least, often argue that it is to protect these voters that they are forced to become more and more populist and create increasingly repressive laws that favor border control and strict immigration policies. Yet, the example of Kirkenes tells us another story. Drawing on the analysis of French collective Cette France-là (2012), we ask, what if xenophobia stems less from "below" than from "above"?

## FROM HUMANITARIAN INVOLVEMENT TO MORE POLITICAL HUMAN RIGHTS ACTIVISM

Merete Nordhus was one of the first locals of Kirkenes to start organizing a solidarity network. When she learned of the refugees from the media, she was shocked that they weren't dressed appropriately for the weather: "I saw them on the news at the Storskog Border, and thought, 'these people must be freezing to death.'" She started to collect winter clothes and boots through Facebook and donated them to those who had arrived and those who were waiting for the border crossing in Nikkel on the Russian side. As an inhabitant of the border region, Merete has a multiple-entry border visa that makes it possible for her to travel 30 kilometers into the Russian side as often as she wishes to. Such visas allow frequent border crossings for Norwegians and Russians of the region alike. While the Norwegians mostly use the visas to buy certain commodities such as cheaper petrol, alcohol, and cigarettes in Russia, Russians from the other side of the border enter Norway regularly to sell their handicrafts on the market square in Kirkenes. As Merete and others responded to the arrivals of refugees, their visa took on new significance and provided invaluable support for their humanitarian effort.

Humanitarian responses to the arrivals or transits of refugees in local communities had been happening across Europe that same summer and autumn. A regional group, Refugees Welcome to the Arctic, followed the Refugees Welcome movement that was spreading across Europe, and their reactivity was often made possible by the swift constitution of groups on various social media. The stencils of a family holding hands and running started to appear not only in the liberal neighborhoods in Berlin, Copenhagen, and London, nor just at border localities such as Calais or Idomeni, but also in small towns in the Nordic countries.

The group continued their engagement with those who had crossed the border or were about to do so. Donating clothes to the aspiring asylum seekers who were staying at a run-down hotel in Nikkel was only the beginning for Merete and several others from Kirkenes. While doing their humanitarian work, they became more and more engaged with the legal conditions of the people whom they were helping. As Merete says, she has two lives, the one before refugees and the one with them. As she became more engaged, then friends, with some of the asylum seekers, it was soon obvious to her that warm clothes were not enough. The gap between the helper and the helped can be, at least partly, bridged by the encounter and engagement.

Another major change occurred as she and the other inhabitants of Kirkenes became witnesses of the treatment of asylum seekers whether by human smugglers, corporations, or state authorities. The more they knew, the more unjust they found the position of the asylum seekers. One of the issues that shocked Merete and others in the Refugees Welcome to the Arctic movement was the poor housing conditions of the asylum seekers. The reception of asylum seekers was organized by a private company, Hero, which the Norwegian state had hired. The Hero is the largest private operator of asylum reception centers in the Nordic countries. They run centers in Sweden, Norway, and Germany. What disturbed the activists was that the asylum seekers were stored in an unused military camp next to the airport, 15 kilometers from the town. By isolating them, they thought, the Norwegian state tried to make the asylum seekers invisible for the locals and for the tourists who had come for the Arctic experience. The asylum seekers had no access to the internet, were served insufficient food, and had few toilets and only two showers that could provide a maximum of 40 liters of hot water a day for 200 persons. They had no space except their bunk beds, as the cold weather made it impossible to stay more than a few minutes outside of the center.

Inhabitants from Kirkenes started to visit the center and drive some of the asylum seekers to town for coffee and a shower in their private homes. One of the former asylum seekers, an economist Ashraf Alio from Syria, told us, these small actions of solidarity were very important, as they gave hope and warmth and countered the dehumanizing effects produced by state bureaucracies and the privatized reception system at an individual and a one-to-one level. Attentiveness to asylum seekers as human beings was driven by humanitarian ideals but also by solidarity in front of injustice. And those engaging with the refugees felt that the injustice by the state, the European Union, and by the industry profiting from the crisis was directed also to them and their community.

The volunteers in Kirkenes increasingly wanted to express their concerns in more public ways, and they staged a protest on 23 January 2016 in freezing −30 °C weather "to show our solidarity," as Merete describes. A group of about 50 locals dressed up in their outdoor outfits, drove to the camp, and approached the gates holding torches and signs saying "Not Us and Them but We," "UNJUST" (URETT), "Not Human," and "How is it with human rights?". Silently they waited at the fence, and the asylum seekers began to come out, join them, start conversations, and hold torches. The volunteers took pictures and videos of the event and published them on the Refugees Welcome to the Arctic Facebook group, from which they were spread to other social media sites and in the general media. While the first demonstration with torches at the camp was a peaceful expression of solidarity, a performance where the locals expressed that they were with the asylum seekers and that they didn't accept the private company's and the government's treatment of them, it prepared for a second moment of public and mediated protest, which was more confrontational. Moreover, another turn had come when the local authorities took a stance against national policy and supported the activists' position. The mayor of Kirkenes, Rune Rafaelsen, publicly stated that he was "ashamed" of the ways in which the asylum seekers were treated at the reception center. He stated that it was an insult to the reputation of the North's tradition of hospitality. This distinction between the people in the North and the central government in Oslo also came up frequently in the conversations we had with people in Kirkenes, as we will discuss later.

The humanitarian actions (donating food and clothes) that Merete, Eirik, and the other volunteers started out with are based on the idea of a common humanity and dignity and on the moral responsibility to help those who are suffering, whoever they are. Such humanitarian action nevertheless often constructs a hierarchical relation between the one who helps and the helpless victim, keeping them distinct and distant. The one who feels responsible and compassionate has already identified the other as being in need of care, and this may allow her to feel distinct and even better. The politics of compassion, therefore, are not contrary to or outside of the politics of inequality.

This paradox of humanitarianism often contrasts with rights-based solidarity, a practice that strives for a more equal relation between the two (Fassin, 2012, pp. 2–4; Ticktin, 2011). At one end of the continuum of politics of solidarity, there is a naïve humanitarianism (Squire, 2014) that perceives the Other as different and separate yet in a stereotypically positive way (Andersson, 2014; Horsti, 2013; Squire, 2014). In this process of making someone deserving of compassion, racialization intersects with other categories of gender, age, and class. A suitable victim who can be "saved" is often a woman who accepts Western values. In this dynamic, humanitarianism does not carry reciprocity but it is a gift, and the one who receives compassion is forever in debt to the one who gives (Mauss, 1923–1924; Neumann, 2013, p. 4). At the other end of the continuum of solidarity, the Other is perceived, fundamentally, as an equal human being, and the suffering and injustice that one meets are taken as a common fight against injustice. The actors involved are aware of the power dynamics and the privileges that one has and the Other lacks. There is no illusion of similarity, but the fight against injustice unites the different actors. This division between discourses on rights and humanitarianism manifests what Lilie Chouliaraki (2013, pp. 11–13) calls two forms of solidarity: revolution and salvation. The humanitarian solidarity of salvation is based on the morality of altruistic benevolence and compassion, whereas revolutionary responses to suffering take a more political form of solidarity that calls for attention to social justice and rights for all.

What we learn from the story of the activists of Kirkenes, however, is that humanitarianism is not always entirely apolitical, as many critics often claim, but that it is possible for a critical rights-based agency to develop from humanitarian action. The phase of engagement and friendship that followed the initial phase of basic humanitarian care not only shows a shift from one kind of moral response to another, but we also witness an entanglement of humanitarianism and solidarity. Further, the first engagements prepared the volunteers in Kirkenes for the more confrontational ways of demanding justice that we will examine in the next section.

## Breaking the Law to Do Justice

When the government (Conservatives and nationalist populist Progress Party), decided to deport those who had valid Russian visas back to Russia, the volunteers in Kirkenes took to more explicit political action and defiance of the state. Merete explains, "The Norwegian government deported 13 men on 19 January 2016 by bus. They just dropped them off in Murmansk ... in −38°C with nothing else than a sandwich. The ones we heard back from were either sleeping rough in the street or living in the hallway of a building, some had made it to Moscow. The government now planned to let another bus drop a new group of refugees including families with children off in Russia, and what would happen to them? They were stripping these people off their rights to have their asylum applications examined and wanted to drive them back to Russia, which had suddenly become a safe third country. We had to do something."

The asylum applications of those to be returned forcibly to Russia were hastily examined. After the negative decisions, Norway bussed those people who had valid Russian visas back to Russia.

The locals had heard rumors of when the second bus would leave for Russia. Several of those active in the Refugees Welcome to the Arctic had already arrived to the center and tried to prevent the returns. The local and national media were there, too, and a large police gathering, including support from other regions. Merete spontaneously took a family of asylum seekers from Syria into her car, in front of policemen and journalists. "A policeman stopped me. I said 'I am just taking this family for a cup of coffee in Kirkenes, are they under arrest?' The policeman answered yes. I demanded to see their arrest warrant. When he didn't show me one, I just acted on pure adrenaline, I didn't think but drove. I hadn't reached Kirkenes yet when I saw a human chain of policemen blocking the road. I didn't want to be a murderer, so I stopped the car. I cried. The mother was hysterical, 'No Russia!' she cried, 'No Russia!' The policeman told me I was banned from going back to the camp and that I should follow him to the police station, the family, too—they had a 1-year old! I was so angry! I yelled at him that he was a MF."

At the police station, Merete was told that she was under arrest: "He said, 'You have trespassed paragraph so-and-so of the foreign-law,' or something." Merete was submitted to a strip search, which she found just humiliating, demeaning as pointless: "I said to the police: 'Do you think I have a refugee up my bum?!' I was then taken to a cold cell. I have never been arrested before, but I know from the movies that you have the right to call a lawyer. I could hear one of my friends getting arrested, too. If you don't know her, she has a very strong voice and knows a lot of swear words. We were scared." The two women and Eirik, who also took asylum seekers into his car and drove them to Kirkenes, were prosecuted for "helping undocumented migrants in Norway." After the asylum seekers sought refuge at the local Lutheran church, people from Kirkenes came with food, clothes, and money, and a local supermarket sponsored food for them.

The national and international media attention, spurred by Merete, Eirik, and other volunteers' actions, the condemnation by human rights organizations, and finally the Russians' unwillingness to allow the people to return made the immediate forced returns impossible.

Three activists, including Merete and Eirik, were sentenced to pay a 5000 NOK fine (approximately 546 euros). While Merete and the other woman paid their fines thanks to donations from concerned citizens from Kirkenes and from all over Norway, Eirik refused to pay his and appealed his case. He told us that he did not want to pay because he had not done anything wrong. Judging his acts as criminal was not fair nor just. Eirik eventually won his case in July 2017.

Several scholars have shown how deportation can be stopped and legalizations obtained due to the activities of pro-immigration groups within civil society (Balibar, Chemillier-Gendreau, Costa-Lascoux, & Terray, 1999; Coutin, 2000; Lippert, 2004; Nyers, 2003), who "become border guards" and "gatekeepers of the nation-state" (Ticktin, 2011, pp. 24–25). As Susan B. Coutin stresses, the law should not be perceived as monolithic or entirely determinant, as it can be contested and negotiated. This leads to a processual understanding of the relationship between the law that creates illegality and illegal practices and the laws' implication in the redefinition of identities and in generating new forms of citizenship (Coutin, 2000, p. 23). This understanding is prevalent among the inhabitants of Kirkenes, as it is in many other communities who have experienced various kinds of class-based legal and economical vulnerabilities, often due to their geographical distance from the power centers of the capital.

## MEMORIES FROM THE MARGINS

What turned the two locals, Merete, a nurse, and Eirik, an iron miner, who had recently been laid off due to the closing of the mine, into human rights activists? And when they were both sentenced to pay a fine for preventing the forced return of asylum seekers, what made Eirik decide to meet the state in court for not paying the fine?

The identity in Kirkenes is open to multiple identifications. We already mentioned "the traditional hospitality of the North," which both the mayor and the locals of Kirkenes often stressed. Sometimes, this narrative identity of hospitality and strong community spirit, *dugnadsånd*, is explained by a rough climate where survival depends on helping one another. However, this sense of helping the neighbor is not necessarily unconditional. In this case, it is particularly interesting to examine how these narratives of the Northern identity translate into arguments for welcoming responses to refugees. Oftentimes, these same arguments of community spirit are used in anti-immigration actions. Therefore, we explore further how this Northern hospitality is constructed. What are the memories and shared notions behind this hospitality that made such movement of solidarity possible?

First of all, Kirkenes needs to be understood in the framework of borderland. All inhabitants of Kirkenes are aware that the tracing of the border was somewhat accidental, that Kirkenes might as well have ended up in Russia or Finland and that this tracing came from "above." We were often reminded that many of the indigenous Sami who inhabited the area upheld a seminomadic lifestyle and that locals have friendly daily exchanges across the border. Intermarriages, friendships, and business relations are common and visits frequent for those who hold a multiple-entry borderland visa, whether they have Norwegian, Finnish, or Russian citizenship. While the end of the Cold War increased cross-border connections, perceptions of the neighboring Russian citizens had been positive even before. There were cultural contacts when the Soviet border was closed and the elderly locals in Kirkenes recalled Russians as allies in the partisan battles against the Germans in the war 1939–1945 (Viken, Granås, & Nyseth, 2008, p. 27). The sense of borderlessness or open borders goes back much further. The European idea of nation-state borders reached the North relatively late, in the early 1900s. In addition to these memories and sense of the region's history, people have other family memories of more or less voluntary movement in the region, due to wars and nation-state boundary-making.

The people in Kirkenes experienced displacement and disposition during World War II. Merete explains that her response might be inspired by her grandmother who experienced the destruction of Kirkenes during World War II when the Germans and Russians fought in the area and German troops ended up burning everything as they withdrew. Both she and Eirik tell us how, during the fighting, 3000 locals hid in the tunnels of the local mine for three months with their cows and other animals, with the snow providing them clean drinking water. Eleven children were born in the tunnels. They said that everyone in Kirkenes knows this story, and part of the narrative is that the villagers were saved only because they took care of one another.

The winter of 2015–2016 was not the first time Kirkenes has welcomed refugees. The locals still remember the stories from 1939–1940 when the Finns arrived to seek protection during the Winter War against the Soviet Union. Moreover, the same sports hall where the cycling refugees were housed had already been used to house refugees from Kosovo in the late 1990s. "We have a long history of protecting people," Eirik and Merete explain.

Eirik, as all the other miners, lost his job when the mine went bankrupt in 2015. He was a member of the worker's union, which had been a fundamental part of the community since the mine was opened in 1906. Throughout the turmoil with the mine, the workers stood together, as they had done for a century. In the 1980s and 1990s, the workers struggled against the closing of the mine. As Eirik walked Carolina through the section concerning the mine at the local Varanger museum, he explained the rough working conditions, the tragic accidents that could occur in the mines, and the fear they stirred among the miners. He paused, and Carolina asked, "Do you miss it?" Eirik's face lit up in a mild smile, "Every single day!" Eirik had been part of the workers' solidarity movement for years, and now, thinking back in time, he believes that that experience contributed to his response to the refugees. "I couldn't see other people's rights being violated, I couldn't, and I had to show my solidarity," Eirik says.

In addition to the struggles to keep the mining going, there are numerous other historical examples of local defiance to state planning (Scott, 1998) in Kirkenes, as historian Marianne Neerland Soleim at Kirkenes' Barentsinstitutet has written about. Many locals told us of such examples of the ways in which official history making can take away the heroism of some or rehabilitate others, as in the case of Sami people who guided refugees in the wilderness over the border during World War II and who have been treated both as heroes and as traitors to the nation. Another example of struggles over hegemonic politics was the management of Russian prisoners of war and, later, their graves. While the POWs were presented by state authorities as dangerous, local Norwegians who lived near the prisoner camps had great sympathy for them. When the Norwegian state decided to move to centralize POW graves during the Cold War, many locals refused to undertake the task, out of criticism of the state's rewriting of history (Soleim, 2015, 2016).

Such examples of state defiance that had taken place in their parents' or grandparents' lifetime had been transmitted through family stories much more than in official school programs. The notion that what the school and national television tell us is not always in accordance with the history we know from our elders may also explain why the people of Kirkenes hold a certain suspicion toward the mainstream narratives. Eirik Nilsen told us how he'd always heard on national television that Muslims were bad people but how his skepticism toward Muslims disappeared very quickly when he met the first Muslim asylum seekers personally.

Criticism and defiance of state regulations are commonplace in the region, and not only in regard to the refugees but also when discussions turn to the amount of fishing of king crab or tax-free goods that one can take from the Russian side to the Norwegian one. We heard many stories of small-scale illegalities, of trafficked trunks and glove compartments that made it possible to bring over an extra liter of alcohol or a cartridge of cigarettes, which border or police authorities often know about but do not enforce. The idea that Oslo or Brussels has supported laws that the people thought were arbitrary and absurd and the notion that it is legitimate to circumvent them with micro-arrangements may also explain the reaction caused when the locals in Kirkenes saw injustice and irresponsible public expenditure toward asylum seekers.

A contemporary example of the people in the North criticizing the central government includes responses to the building of the 200 meter (660 ft) and 4 million Norwegian kroner "grensegjerde"—a border fence built by the Norwegian state on the border between Norway and Russia in 2016 (Johnson, 2016). First of all, the Russians control the border on their side and already have an old fence in place. Second, the new Norwegian fence was built 1 cm too close to Russian territory, according to international law, and the Norwegian state had to spend additional money to move it, which only added absurdity to an already-senseless and costly project. The passing of refugees in the zone had already stopped. The fence was only symbolic and could easily be circumvented, as most border fences can. The locals saw the fence as a waste of tax money decided by a government that makes wrong decisions, either out of a lack of knowledge or deliberately, to instrumentalize refugees as a dangerous group, which politicians pretend to protect them from. In other words, xenophobia from "above" (Cette France-là, 2012) disregards the experiences of a local community. The "grensegjerde" became a topic of ridicule in Kirkenes: people equaled it to the US President Donald Trump's dreams of a wall at the US-Mexico border.

Many inhabitants of the border region further believe that the 5542 persons who crossed the border had been too perfect an opportunity for the Russian regime to threaten Norway and other European countries that had put sanctions in place due to Russia's military intervention in Ukraine. As in the cases of Mediterranean diplomacy, such as readmission agreements (Migreurop, 2009, 2017), exiles were once more pawns in geostrategical considerations, which neither the exiles themselves nor the local population of the border region had any take on.

Norwegian-ness in Kirkenes is thus, in many ways, a distinct kind of identity, a position from which the center and the capital can and must be challenged. As we exchanged in Norwegian and Danish with people in Kirkenes, the fact that neither of us belong to the capitals of our countries of citizenship, not Copenhagen nor Helsinki, was a distinct asset. This awareness of a local, regional identity that opposes the "capital" and the governing elites may, then, partly explain the defiance of the law and the center and that local allegiances extended to the refugees. These identifications among the locals in Kirkenes reflect the historical continuities at the Norwegian-Russian border: self-understanding of the region as a "dynamic frontier" or "wild North" and the desire for open borders. These desires and imaginaries have been in constant conflict with the concerns of nation-state logic and the international power blocks (Niemi, 2009; Schimanski, 2015).

The stories of Eirik and Merete show how attentiveness to the suffering of strangers can be prompted by past experiences of one's own or that of others by stories that have become collectively shared memories. In Kirkenes, the response to the cycling asylum seekers extended from humanitarianism toward human rights, a solidarity that became increasingly politically challenging. For Eirik and Merete, these were not two different moralities but entangled into one. Also, they refused any sort of categorization that opposed foreigners to Norwegians in their merit. Eirik explains: "We got so much shit from people who disagreed with us for helping refugees and not Norwegians. For instance, we collected reflectors so that the refugees would be visible when walking in the dark, and people said that we ought to give them to Norwegian children instead. We got so much of that "Norwegians first.""

As both national and international media started reporting on the strange case of bicycling refugees in the Arctic, the humanitarian work taking place in the border region became more and more known. Merete was interviewed by Norwegian and foreign national media, a visibility that quickly made her vulnerable to hatemongers. She received calls, texts, and emails from strangers, both anonymous and ones who did not even care to hide their identities. Merete stresses that no local in Kirkenes ever attacked her directly. The hate mail was anonymous or came from outside of Kirkenes. Some Norwegians called Merete a "traitor" to the national community, "a disgrace to your country." The messages entangled misogyny and nationalism in a way that shocked Merete deeply, and it was the first time that she experienced such bullying and hate. Eirik even received a letter with a death threat at his personal address, which had been posted from Southern Norway.

Merete's and Eirik's experience of being unjustly treated by hatemongers and police officers positioned them at the margins of mainstream Norwegian society. Nevertheless, in that position, they felt privileged. From the people that mattered to them, they received prizes and praise, encouragement, and support. Furthermore, as Eirik explains, the tradition of worker's solidarity extended to solidarity with asylum seekers and to an anti-racist stance. These Northern identities and histories of solidarities transformed into an ability to bear witness to injustice being done to others, whom they saw as guests or possibly as fellow citizens in an international community of citizens who, sometimes, are separated by populist politics and who suffer from the arbitrary decisions of central governments.

As Merete and Eirik look back on the experiences they had a little over a year earlier, they realize that the events changed them. Merete says, she has two lives, the one before refugees and the one with them. Merete and Eirik are very invested in the friendships they have created with asylum seekers who are now refugees while staying involved in refugee activism more broadly. Eirik has volunteered in the infamous Idomeni refugee camp in Greece several times. Because staying abroad means that he loses the monthly benefits that his status as a former miner provides, he must live on his savings when he is in Greece, but he would be there most of the year if he could.

News from the world's war zones have suddenly become personal, while phone calls from unknown people who accuse them of betraying their country no longer hurt as much as they did in the beginning. Their emotional landscape has changed. "Every time I pass by the Airport and the place where the police stopped me and forced a Syrian family out of my car, I remember and I get the chills," Merete recalls.

## Conclusion: Aftermath

Refugees Welcome networks across Europe have responded to the arrival of refugees mainly by humanitarian actions. Though humanitarianism is often depicted as and criticized for being an entirely depoliticized action toward populations that are given clothing, food, shelter, medical care, and other strictly basic help, this is often more true in theory than in practice. Though many ordinary citizens with no previous history of politicized civil society engagements joined the Refugees Welcome movement and did strictly humanitarian work, such as cheering in train stations and bringing home-baked pastries or children's toys, as in the case of the Venligboerne in Denmark, many quickly got a sense of some of the injustices of the asylum system and went from more humanitarian action to more politicized action. Humanitarian and politicized pro-migrant activisms, we argue, are less opposites or strictly two poles on a specter, and more entangled forms of engagement.

In Kirkenes, the local activists not only offered humanitarian assistance but also voiced their solidarity with the refugees and their criticism of the asylum industry as well as the unjust treatment of asylum seekers. These speech acts took the movement toward a more politicized position, which started in the form of a protest with torches and signs. However, when the forced returns began, the locals in the Refugees Welcome to the Arctic movement raised their voice and put themselves on the line. To be heard in public and in the spheres of politics, Eirik Nielsen went even further and chose to confront the state in court, through legal action.

Second, through humanitarian actions, activists are often made aware of the differences between the law, legal action, and their own sense of what a just asylum system should be. Before encountering asylum seekers, Merete and Eirik, for instance, had not been so aware of international human rights law, asylum law, and the rights of noncitizens. Through humanitarian action many become conscious that their state and legal system does not respect the country's own laws nor the international treaties signed by the government. Some get involved in actions that are in the gray zone of the law.

Such experiences can profoundly alter the traditional trust in the authorities that has characterized majority populations of the Nordic region, who are otherwise known to show high levels of belief in the goodness and of the fairness of the state. For example, in the Eurobarometer opinion survey, citizens of Finland and Sweden rank among the highest in trust to national parliament and government in Europe. The confrontation and suspicion of the central government in the Northern part of the Nordic countries that we discussed earlier need to be understood in this context. Distrust in state institutions and politicians has of course been prominent in extreme right-wing and left-wing discourses for quite some time, but experiences of an unjust asylum system and illegal actions from state authorities themselves spur anti-political and anti-system rhetoric at the center, on the liberal left and the moral pro-migrant right. This is an aspect that has been much less explored, and the case of Kirkenes and the axes of Northern identity and engagement with asylum seekers point to the need to further examine the complexities of the relations between the state, noncitizens, and citizens from the margins.

The solidarity shown by a community of 3500 who welcomed 5542 asylum seekers questions certain assumptions and stereotypes concerning the values and ideologies of white working class (males) from economically and culturally disenfranchised regions of the North. Further, as enchanted as we were by the actions taken by the people and municipality of Kirkenes, their example is not unique. All over Europe, locals, who are often living precariously, have helped migrants and asylum seekers, whether upon arrival in Southern Spain, Italy, Greece, or at border crossings in la Vallée du Roya on the Italian-French border or in Calais at the French-British border. These regions, just as the neighborhoods in which exiles gather in Paris, are also those where locals are among the most marginalized and precarious; and it may be the awareness that history favors powerful elites that drives them not to vote for populist parties but to welcome other precarious populations. The experience of the locals in Kirkenes resonated with the stories which we have both heard from locals in other border zones, such as Lampedusa and Calais.

These regions where European borders are policed and enforced are often considered as the periphery when seen from the urban and political centers. From an economic perspective, they are, indeed, often places that are characterized by low income or high levels of unemployment whether they have a subsistence economy from fishing, agriculture, mining, sometimes tourism, or (post-)industrialization. Places such as the Greek islands, Lampedusa, and Calais are considered borderlands like Kirkenes in the public imaginaries, though they have often traditionally been places of passage, the sea being more of a waterway than a border. In these places, locals have responded in similar ways as in Kirkenes (Gerbier-Aublanc, 2017; Puggioni, 2015). In some instances, humanitarian response by locals has attracted media attention, and both Lampedusani and the people of Lesbos have been nominated for the Nobel Peace Prize. Recently also, scholars have paid attention to the networks of solidarity and confrontation that emerge in response to arriving refugees and the security and humanitarian industry that follows. Raffaela Puggioni (2015), for instance, examines how the locals in Lampedusa refused to be complicit in the detention industry that has grown on the island. Through such acts of dissent, people who are expected to respond negatively to the arrival of others, more often than not, develop politics of equality. Puggioni argues that by aligning with the migrants, the Lampedusani positioned themselves in disagreement with the central government in Rome and the European Union. While the elite response to the arrival of asylum seekers across the Mediterranean was militarization, security measures, and cooperation agreements with third countries, the Lampedusani advocated for an alternative that treated migrants more humanely. Many locals protest and speak against securitization and militarization of the island (Tucci, 2017) and in doing so have cultivated a discourse and practices of attentiveness to the migrants as human beings who have social lives. As in Kirkenes, humanitarian assistance entangles with solidarity and politicized action against the European border regime and against xenophobia, which is perceived to be generated by politicians from the political centers who care little about the experiences of locals in the margins.

As in other groups in society who experience cuts in welfare and unemployment benefits, or the financial and cultural marginalization of their regions, the notion that the law is no longer just is becoming more and more mainstream. This notion often goes hand in hand with skepticism toward economic globalization and the idea of an "elite" of politicians and citizens who vote for them, who are privileged and care little about those who are not, whether they are nationals or foreigners.

## REFERENCES

Andersson, R. (2014). *Illegality INC: Clandestine Migration and the Business of Bordering Europe.* Oakland: University of California Press.

Balibar, É., Chemillier-Gendreau, M., Costa-Lascoux, J., & Terray, E. (1999). *Sans-papiers: l'archaïsme fatal.* Éditions La Découverte et Syros.

Boe, C. S. (in press). *The Undeported: The Making of a Floating Population of Exiles in France and Europe, Series: Challenging Migration Studies.* Lanham, MD: Rowman and Littlefield.

Boe, C. S., & Mainsah, H. N. (2017). Traces and Places: Making Borders Visible in Paris' 18th Arrondissement. Retrieved from https://www.law.ox.ac.uk/research-subject-groups/centre-criminology/centreborder-criminologies/blog/2017/06/traces-and-places

Cette France-là. (2012). *Xénophobie d'en haut. Le choix d'une droite éhontée.* Paris: La Découverte.

Chouliaraki, L. (2013). *The Ironic Spectator: Solidarity in the Age of Post-Humanitarianism.* London: Polity Press.

Coutin, S. B. (2000). *Legalizing Moves.* Michigan: University of Michigan Press.

Fassin, D. (2012). *Humanitarian Reason: A Moral History of the Present.* Los Angeles: University of California Press.

Gerbier-Aublanc, M. (2017). L'umanitaire instrumentalisé à Calais. *Plein droit, 1*(112), 32–35.

Gullvik, I. K., & Mortensen, R. (2016). Ett år etter milliardkonkursen er Sydaranger Gruve i gang igjen. *NRK.* Retrieved from https://www.nrk.no/finnmark/xl/ett-ar-etter-milliardkonkursen-er-sydvaranger-gruve-i-gang-igjen-1.13226536

Horsti, K. (2013). De-ethnicized Victims: Mediatized Advocacy for Asylum Seekers. *Journalism: Theory, Practice & Criticism, 14*(1), 78–95.

Horsti, K., & Neumann, K. (2017). Memorialising Mass Deaths at the Border: Two Cases from Canberra (Australia) and Lampedusa (Italy). *Ethnic and Racial Studies,* Online first.

Johnson, H. (2016, October 7). Norwegians Laugh at the New Fence on Russian Border. *BBC News.* Retrieved from http://www.bbc.com/news/world-europe-37577547

Lippert, R. (2004, November–December). Sanctuary Practices, Rationalities, and Sovereignties Alternatives: Global, Local, Political. *Governing Society Today, 29*(5), 535–555.

Mauss, M. (1923–1924). Essai sur le don. Forme et raison de l'échange dans les sociétés primitives. *l'Année Sociologique, seconde série.*

Migreurop. (2009). *Atlas des migrants en Europe. Géographie critique des politiques migratoires.* Paris: Armand Collin.

Migreurop. (2017). *Atlas des migrants en Europe. Géographie critique des politiques migratoires.* Paris: Armand Collin.

Neumann, K. (2013, July 22). Attentiveness and Indifference. *Inside Story.* Retrieved from http://insidestory.org.au/attentiveness-and-indifference

Niemi, E. (2009). Grenseland og periferi: Møtested for stat, nasjon og etnisitet. In E. Niemi & C. Smith-Simonsen (Eds.), *Det hjemlige og det globale: Festskrift til Randi Rønning Balsvik* (pp. 431–455). Oslo: Akademisk Publisering.

Nyers, P. (2003, December). Abject Cosmopolitanism: The Politics of Protection in the Anti-Deportation Movement. *Third World Quarterly, 24*(6), 1069–1093.

Pian, A. (2009). *Aux nouvelles frontières de l'Europe. L'aventure incertaine des Sénégalais au Maroc.* Paris: La Dispute.

Puggioni, R. (2015). Border Politics, Right to Life and Acts of Dissensus: Voices from the Lampedusa Borderland. *Third World Quarterly, 36*(6), 1145–1159.

Schimanski, J. (2015). Border Aesthetics and Cultural Distancing in the Norwegian-Russian Borderscape. *Geopolitics, 20*(1), 35–55.

Scott, J. C. (1998). *Seeing Like a State. How Certain Schemes to Improve the Human Condition Have Failed.* New Haven: Yale University Press.

Soleim, M. N. (2015, April). *War Graves and Collective Memory, Vol. 4,* 101–108.

Soleim, M. N. (2016). "Soviet Prisoners of War in Norway 1941–45—Destiny, Treatment and Forgotten Memories." *Modern History of Russia* no. 1, 22–32.

Squire, V. (2014). Desert 'Trash': Posthumanism, Border Struggles, and Humanitarian Politics. *Political Geography, 39*, 11–21.

Ticktin, M. (2011). *Casualties of Care: Immigration and the Politics of Humanitarianism in France*. Berkeley: University of California Press.

Tucci, I. (2017). In Response to Migration Policies and to the Militarization of Territories: Activism in the Community of Lampedusa. In M. Ojala-Fulwood (Ed.), *Migration and Multi-Ethnic Communities: Mobile People from the Late Middle-Ages to the Present*. Oldenbourg: De Gruyter.

Viken, A., Granås, B., & Nyseth, T. (2008). Kirkenes: An Industrial Site Reinvented as a Border Town. *Acta Borealia, 25*(1), 22.

# PART III

# Examining Anti-Racism

# CHAPTER 9

# Do Antiracist Efforts and Diversity Programs Make a Difference? Assessing the Case of Norway

*Christian Stokke*

## INTRODUCTION

In European academic debates about multiculturalism and antiracism, Norway is marginal. However, the country's extreme right and populist right have attracted international attention because of Anders Behring Breivik's terror attack on 22 July 2011, the populist Progress Party's strong public support, and its participation in government from 2013. The party's hardline immigration minister Sylvi Listhaug (2015–2018) has also garnered attention (see Faiola, 2016; Palazzo, 2016). While anti-immigrant and anti-Muslim attitudes, largely resulting from negative media coverage and populist rhetoric, remained stable through the last decade (ECRI, 2015; IMDI, 2014), Norway is developing into a multicultural society (Stokke, 2012) increasingly accommodating minorities according to the Banting-Kymlicka Multicultural Policy Index. While fear of Muslims is

C. Stokke (✉)
Department of Culture, Religion and Social Studies, University of Southeast Norway, Drammen, Norway
e-mail: Christian.Stokke@usn.no

© The Author(s) 2019                                                    205
P. Hervik (ed.), *Racialization, Racism, and Anti-Racism in the Nordic Countries*, Approaches to Social Inequality and Difference, https://doi.org/10.1007/978-3-319-74630-2_9

widespread, media and government have recognized Islamophobic hate speech as a problem. Over time, the Progress Party has lost ground, from record highs of 30% in opinion polls and 22.9% in national elections in 2009, down to 16.3% in 2013 national elections and 9.5% in 2015 local elections.

While the Progress Party strives to exploit the refugee crisis to make immigration policy the strictest in Europe and deport "illegal" immigrants, integration policy (Meld.St. 6, 2012–2013) follows Council of Europe (2008) recommendations. It explicitly values difference and disagreement and recognizes minorities' rights to cultural and religious identities and practices, within a framework of universal human rights, no longer equated with Norwegian values. On the Migrant Integration Policy Index (Huddleston, Bilgili, Joki, & Vankova, 2015), Norway ranks high, comparable to Canada. Norway scores high on minority employment and political participation, but restrictions on family reunification and dual citizenship pull down scores. Like Britain, Norway thus combines strict immigration policy with partial multiculturalism.

Minorities are visibly present in most sectors of society, with Norwegian-born descendants of 1960s' Pakistani labor migrants taking the lead. Minority participation in the public sphere has increased strongly (Bangstad, 2013; Eide, 2011; Stokke, 2012), shifting public debate from whites worrying about minorities (Hage, 1998) to multicultural negotiations (Modood, 2007). Public debate is no longer a battle between politically correct and populist rhetoric but also a place of discursive struggles between racism and antiracism including minority voices (Stokke, 2012). While often confrontational, there are dialogical tendencies allowing people to get to know each other.

## OBJECTIVES

This chapter assesses if antiracist efforts and diversity policies have made a difference in Norway in the last decade. From a critical multiculturalist and antiracist perspective, I focus on anti-Muslim racism in the mediated public sphere, Norwegian Muslims' antiracist activism, its impact on public debate and public opinion, and state responses in law, policy, and education. I attempt to give a nuanced account based on two case studies, the cartoon affair and the hijab debates, intended to highlight antiracist voices and positive developments while criticizing policy shortcomings and acknowledging persistent racism. I also consider recent developments in the 2015 European refugee crisis and conclude with discussing how school teachers approach racism and how antiracist education can develop as part of multicultural education.

## Norwegian Literature on Multiculturalism and Racism

In Norway, the academic literature on multiculturalism and (anti)racism closely relates to political debate, where three prominent anthropologists with distinct positions acted as public intellectuals in the 1990s and early 2000s. Two liberal positions, one nationalist (Wikan, 1995, 2002) and one cosmopolitan (Eriksen, 2005; Eriksen & Tretvoll, 2006), have competed for hegemony, challenged by a critical position (Gullestad, 2002, 2006). In Scandinavia, Norway positions itself between Denmark, where nationalist discourse dominates (Myong & Danbolt, 2018; Vertelyte & Hervik, 2018), and Sweden, where critical multiculturalism is stronger (Haavisto, 2018). Norwegian integration policy approximates Kymlicka's (2002) liberal theory of multiculturalism (Borchgrevink & Brochmann, 2003, pp. 72, 90–92), giving extensive rights to the indigenous Sami people but expecting immigrants to integrate into the national culture and remaining skeptical of conservative religious groups restricting the individual freedom of their members (Kymlicka, 2002; Modood, 2007).

The nationalist approach represented by Wikan (1995, 2002) aligns itself with the "critique of multiculturalism" as in Okin's (1999) concern with minority cultures' internal restrictions on its individual members, women in particular, and proposes assimilation into national values confused with universal human rights values (Gressgård & Jacobsen, 2003). Other researchers following the nationalist paradigm (Borchgrevink, 2002; Brochmann & Hagelund, 2012; Brox, 1991, 2005) problematize immigrants in relation to the welfare state. A common denominator in this research is that it sees immigrants as a problem, a challenge to the assumed "national values" of gender equality and the welfare state, assuming a conflict between the others' culture and Norwegian/Western values. The nationalist approach has set the agenda for public debate as well as policy: In recent years, Brochmann has led several government commissions on integration.

Defense of multicultural society mainly comes in the form of promoting "diversity" from a liberal cosmopolitan perspective represented by Eriksen (2005; Eriksen & Tretvoll, 2006), resembling the interculturalist position (Barrett, 2013) promoted by the Council of Europe (2008). While sometimes presented as an alternative to multiculturalism, it partly overlaps with multiculturalism, and its attempt to find a dialogical "third way" between universalism and cultural relativism/particularism resonates with Parekh's (2000) philosophy of intercultural dialogue. This approach is liberal in the individualist sense, but not "color-blind" (Bonilla-Silva, 2010; Törngren, 2018), as it recognizes cultural differences and promotes open-minded intercultural understanding, not necessarily resulting in consensus. The cosmopolitan perspective has some political influence, especially under the 2005–2013 social democratic government with its dialogical approach to the Mohammed cartoon affair. While it recognizes the importance of fighting discrimination and emphasizes listening to minority voices, this perspective pays insufficient attention to structures of domination, in contrast to critical and postcolonial perspectives, which explicitly challenge power relations. Nevertheless, intercultural dialogue opens up a space where critical minority perspectives can be heard (Stokke & Lybæk, 2016).

The critical approach, represented by Gullestad (2002, 2006), takes minority voices as a starting point and engages with postcolonial perspectives and critical race theory. It resembles Modood's (2005, 2006, 2007) critical multiculturalism, which starts from the insights and sensibilities of minorities experiencing and mobilizing against various forms of racism. Gullestad (2006) critically analyzes the Norwegian ideology of "imagined sameness" and the conformist idea that differences are essentially bad and that equality presupposes sameness—an ideology that supports dominant color-blind liberalism ("treat everyone the same regardless of difference") and makes recognition of positive difference hard for Norwegians. While the two versions of liberalism discussed above compete for hegemony, critical approaches have grown stronger in recent years in connection with critical minority persons'—Norwegian Muslims in particular—increasing access and visibility in the public sphere since about 2005. Younger researchers following in the critical paradigm include Gressgård and Jacobsen (2003), Jacobsen (2011), Bangstad (2013, 2016) and myself (Stokke, 2012; Stokke & Lybæk, 2016), and engage to a larger extent Anglophone multicultural and critical race theory.

Critical research in pedagogy and teacher education draws on Freire's critical pedagogy and Banks' (2004) multicultural education (Stenshorne & Stokke, 2015; Svendsen, 2014; Westrheim, 2011) and antiracist education (Børhaug, 2009). In the field of education, critical multiculturalism

(Harlap & Riese, 2014; May & Sleeter, 2010) is explicitly opposed to liberal and color-blind perspectives that everyone should be treated the same and advocates that minority perspectives need to be heard and accommodated in the curriculum, in the classroom, in decision-making processes, and in parent-teacher relations. This necessarily implies addressing racism as lived experience and fighting its structural, discursive, and interpersonal manifestations. The social democratic government's diversity policy (Meld.St. 6, 2012–2013) recognized that diversity be appreciated in education and seeks to increase teachers' multicultural competence, opening a space for teacher educators to introduce Anglophone multicultural and antiracist education theory.

## THEORETICAL PERSPECTIVES

Like most contributions to this book, this chapter positions itself within the critical paradigm outlined above. Antiracist research (Okolie, 2005) is a critical approach with a normative agenda to reveal and delegitimize racism in hegemonic discourses and support counter-discourses, by giving voice to antiracist resistance and politically conscious minority persons (van Dijk, 1993, p. 19). Racism is a dominant discourse culturally inherited from colonialism, which individuals learn and unlearn through socialization. Structural racism refers to power relations where majority dominates minority, legitimized by racist discourse. Racism consists of a division between "us" and "them", ascription of negative characteristics to the other, and power to translate "race thinking" into discriminatory action (Hervik, 2004). This covers more than the narrow liberal definition of racism as racist ideology, individual intentions and acts of discrimination (Midtbøen, Orupabo, & Røthing, 2014, pp. 35–36).

To contribute to antiracist struggle, research should be empirically grounded and give a nuanced account, acknowledging positive developments while remaining critical. Antiracist theory takes account of both power and resistance in real-world discursive struggles, accounting for individual and collective actions, in addition to power structures. Said's *Orientalism* (1994), a key reference for understanding Islamophobia, combines Foucault's notion of discourse with Gramsci's concept of resistance but largely renders alternative voices invisible. While individuals do reproduce dominant discourses more than we are aware of, voices of resistance always exist and antiracist research intends to let these be heard. Taking an educational approach to antiracism, I believe that highlighting minorities' own voices, analyses, and activism will do more to change negative perceptions among the majority, than a critical normative attitude alone can achieve.

## Case Study 1: The Cartoon Affair

In January 2006, Norway was drawn into the Danish and international cartoon affair when a small weekly magazine republished *Jyllands-Posten*'s 12 cartoons of Prophet Muhammad. The Norwegian cartoon affair was an international relations event first, before becoming domestic: Attempting to avoid escalation of Muslim anger, which climaxed with attacks on Norwegian embassies in Iran and Syria, Foreign Minister Gahr Støre initiated dialogue with Muslim countries and later with Norwegian Muslims. While Denmark's Fogh Rasmussen refused to meet Muslims, Norway's government arranged a reconciliation where the cartoon publisher, editor Vebjørn Selbekk, shook hands with Islamic Council leader Mohammed Hamdan, who called off—or so he thought—further Muslim protests. The government recognized the Islamic Council as "dialogue" partner and gave it regular funding in return for silencing Norwegian Muslims' voices of protest—an example of cooptation (see Stokke, 2012, pp. 73–87).

Kristin Halvorsen, then-finance minister and Socialist Party leader, spoke at a reconciliation rally afterward, illustrating the government's narrow perspective:

> Norwegians are used to be seen as peaceful and welcome .... Now we are threatened ... 100 persons threw stones at the Norwegian embassy .... If a small number of people try to harass Muslims in Norway, we must remember that 4.5 million people do not wish to do that .... (Dagbladet, 11 February 2006b)

She framed the issue as a foreign problem, outside of Norway, while revealing white privilege: "We are used to be seen as peaceful and welcome" (Dagbladet, 11 February 2006). How many Muslims could say the same, post-9/11? She construes Norwegians as well-intentioned ("do not wish to do that"), denies widespread anti-Muslim racism in Norway ("if a small number of people tries to harass Muslims)", labels Muslims opposed to the cartoons as extremists, and silences legitimate and peaceful Muslim protest.

In a climate of public fear of violence from Islamist and right-wing extremists, Norwegian Muslims did not let themselves be silenced. Without organizational backing, a group of volunteers gathered 1500 people for a peaceful protest the next day, carrying posters showing a variety of slogans (see Aftenposten, 12 February 2006; Dagbladet, 11 February 2006; 12 February 2006c; Dagsavisen, 12 February 2006; VG, 11 February 2006a; 12 February 2006b), including:

> Mutual respect, please.
> Peace and respect for our values.
> Respect our faith, then you respect us.
> Shame on you, media, for making hate speech.
> Politicians and media, this is the result of your irresponsibility.
> What we witness now is the result of misused freedom of expression.
> Your freedom of expression ends when you step on my feet.
> The caricatures are lying, free speech is to say the truth.
> We condemn the lies about the prophet.
> Media, stop terrorizing us and our lives.
> Stop the hate speech. Muslims demand protection against hate speech and bullying.
> Do you want a sweet life—Stop making it sour for others.
> Building a good society takes time, tearing it down takes seconds.
> Media, mouthpiece of lies.
> Freedom to practice our religion.
> When truth comes, lies disappear.
> Islam is the truth.

While the last slogan is in religious language, and some protesters called for reviving anti-blasphemy laws, no slogans rejected Western values or invoked a culture clash. No calls for violence or terror threats, as in certain other anti-cartoon protests. Muslims, of course, do not speak with one voice, but this message was clear: peace and mutual respect, appeals to the media to stop hate speech and stigmatizing Muslims. Protesters criticized media, not the Norwegian nation, and not just for the cartoons but general negative coverage of Muslims in media and public debate. It was mostly an ethical appeal for respect, truthfulness, and responsibility more than a call for legally banning hate speech (Thorsen, 2018). Thus, it was a Muslim antiracist mobilization against anti-Muslim racism in the media: antiracism with a religious dimension, as Modood (2005, pp. 104–106) discusses in the British context.

## Case Study 2: The Hijab Debates

Since the 1990s, white feminists operating on a "white savior" logic (Abu-Lughod, 2002; Razack, 2008) had dominated Norwegian public debates about Muslim women—echoing Spivak: "white men [here: women!] saving brown women from brown men". The loudest was Hege Storhaug from the *Human Rights Service*, described by the Norwegian Antiracist Center as a "cornerstone in the domestic hate industry" (Dagbladet, 26 March 2010b). Her think tank/women's help organization seeks to liberate young Muslim women from human rights violations imposed by their families and communities, for example, female genital mutilation, forced marriages, and restrictions on freedom, including the hijab. More recently, her attacks have turned more and more toward the Islamic religion itself. In 2007, she published the book *Veiled. Unveiled.* (Storhaug, 2007) with the double meaning of "Covered up. Uncovered" claiming the hijab is a symbol of Islamism and essentially oppressive, regardless of hijab wearers' own perceptions. With the Progress Party, which guarantees public funding for her organization, Storhaug called for banning hijabs in elementary schools, following French law. In 2009–2010, Muslim feminism had a public breakthrough after the government turned down a Muslim police students' request to allow hijab for uniformed police. Many Norwegian Muslim women wrote op-ed articles, gave interviews, and joined the Women's Day parade with a "hijab brigade". They called themselves Muslim feminists and justified women's rights with reference to Islamic religious scripture (Mir-Hosseini, 2006). Like Black and postcolonial feminism, Muslim feminism is an intersectional struggle fighting both traditional minority patriarchy and majority racism, including paternalistic white feminism.

Ilham Hassan, Somalian student leader at the University of Oslo, hijab wearer, and brigade organizer, asserted in an interview:

> We ourselves have to define the meaning of feminism …. The right to decide over one's own body is also about being able to decide what to wear … the right to wear hijab ….
>
> Hijab is not oppressive as long as it is chosen, as it is for most women …. There is no coercion in religion … the Qur'an gives rights to women … In Norway … Muslim women's struggle is about discrimination … hijab-wearing girls cannot get the education and job they want …. Hijab is allowed in … low status jobs. But when talking about a profession that symbolizes power, it becomes a problem. (Klassekampen, 7 March 2009)

She speaks the language of feminist struggle while referring to religious scripture—a key characteristic of Muslim feminism. Muslim women want to decide for themselves how to define feminism and how to analyze the oppression Muslim women are facing, without white feminist instructions.

Bushra Ishaq, Muslim Student Society leader, of Pakistani ancestry and not wearing hijab, appeared as an op-ed writer in major newspapers in 2009–2010:

> In contemporary debate, a perception is cultivated that Muslims constitute a problem simply by their existence, and are static carriers of certain characteristics that imply social problems—a sort of racism that stigmatizes and judges Muslim children before they are born.
>
> Following my faith as practicing Muslim, I am supposed to strive for peace and ... abstain from activities that ... increase ... conflict .... My purpose ... to introduce the values of dialogue into the debate arena—listen to my opponents with an open mind, respect and neighborly love. (Dagbladet, 11 May 2010c)

> The government's conclusion to say no to hijab is a demand for assimilation, not integration, where one has to change one's religious practice in order to pursue a career. (Dagsavisen, 4 May 2009)

> Feminist values can be justified by Islamic theology ... [but] the Muslim adaptation of feminism will differ from the Western one. (Dagbladet, 31 January 2009)

> When finding theological justifications for the right to pursue higher education and paid work, the battle against a strongly traditional parental generation has become easier. (Aftenposten, 5 September 2009)

She explicitly refers to racism and assimilation policies against Muslims. Like Ilham Hassan, she asserts Muslim women's right to define feminism grounded in theological justifications. She asserts a positive Muslim identity based on peace, dialogue, open-mindedness, respect, and neighborly love—the opposite of Orientalist images of Islam as violent, closed minded, and threatening. By speaking for themselves, and sharing experiences from a Muslim woman's position in Norway, they challenge images of passive and oppressed Muslim women. While white feminists' Orientalist descriptions of Muslim women invoke feelings of pity, assertive Muslim women's voices potentially lead to empathy and solidarity, recognizing difference as well as commonality. Despite these media interventions, Socialist Party leader, Kristin Halvorsen, then-education minister, comments on the proposal to ban hijab in schools in February 2010:

> Hijab for children is absolutely unwanted because it prevents children's development and opportunity to make independent choices .... We as a society must be clear that we don't want hijab in primary schools. (Dagbladet, 24 February 2010a)

Stopping short of supporting a legal ban, there is little tolerance for the hijab even from the most left-leaning party in parliament.

## Analysis

In Norway, policies and public debates on minorities are mostly discussed in terms of *integration*—an ambiguous concept with many interpretations. When using the term, politicians, media, and public opinion often mean cultural and social assimilation ("becoming Norwegian") followed by judgments that integration has failed. The Directorate of Integration and Diversity (IMDI) and Statistics Norway (SSB) define the term as language skills, employment, and political participation, and argue that integration is successful in Norway compared to other countries. Hage (1998) characterizes the expectation of cultural assimilation as a "white fantasy" and argues that real integration in local communities, the latter sense, takes place all the time independent of white people's worries about failed integration.

In multicultural theory, integration is a mutual process of accommodation and adjustment, whose outcome can take more assimilationist and multicultural directions. As Kymlicka says, minorities seek to negotiate the terms of integration. Modood's critical multiculturalism (2007, pp. 39–50) theorizes this negotiation process, where minorities mobilize politically in social movements and the state accommodates some of their demands. He emphasizes that antiracist resistance by each minority group is the primary means of mutual integration. There is increasing recognition that Islamophobia and anti-Muslim attitudes are forms of new racism, parallel to anti-Semitism's racialization of Jews. People who "look Muslim", irrespective of individual religiosity and political beliefs, are ascribed negative characteristics and seen as essentially suspect and potential threats. Current images of Islam draw on colonial stereotypes, when Orientalism (Said, 1994) misrepresented the Islamic world as the West's negative mirror image. Ignoring Muslims' own voices and complex empirical reality, "clash of civilizations" thinking recycles these abstract generalizations of an unchanging, homogeneous, violent, and oppressive religion (Bangstad, 2016; Mamdani, 2004). Orientalism constructs Muslims as enemies, who must be feared and controlled—Islamophobia refers to this "irrational fear" of Islam. The Mohammed cartoons and Western obsession with hijabs reproduce Orientalist images of essentially violent Muslim men, and oppressed and passive veiled women (Yegenoglu, 1998).

As in the Black American struggle, Muslim minorities also mobilize to turn a stigmatized difference ascribed to them into a positive identity they are proud of. Because anti-Muslim racism stigmatizes their religion, which is personally important to most self-identified Muslims, a common response is to promote a positive image of Islam as peaceful, liberating, and egalitarian. Doing this, they follow other multicultural movements like black pride and gay pride. Thus, Muslim antiracism inevitably has a religious dimension, not least because Muslims draw moral and spiritual strength from their religion (Modood, 2005, pp. 104–106). Progressive Norwegian Muslim activists have interpreted street protests and involvement in public debate as part of the greater jihad, that is, the social and personal effort or struggle for justice (Jacobsen, 2011, p. 188), to rectify negative interpretations of Islam promoted by Islamophobics and Islamists alike.

In the process of multicultural mobilization, a minority claims the right to speak for itself, to define itself in positive terms, and the power to do their own analysis of oppression, redefining racism and modifying antiracist and feminist theory. This discursive and epistemological struggle challenges Eurocentrism, that is, Western claims to monopolize interpretation of the universal, and insists on formulating alternative versions of the universal. Minority assertiveness also criticizes white antiracists who believe they have the correct answers, as when white antiracists told Muslims to "fight racism, not Rushdie" in Britain in 1989. In critical race theory, white attempts to tell minorities how to lead their struggle are theorized as an illegitimate "white privilege". Antiracist analysis starts instead with the perspectives of politically conscious minority persons (van Dijk, 1993, p. 18). For antiracist activism to make a difference, minority voices need to be heard, to influence law and policy, and change dominant attitudes and perceptions.

## MULTICULTURAL ACCOMMODATION IN LAW, POLICY, AND PUBLIC DEBATE

Antiracist social movements' pressure to democratize the state is a key element of multiculturalism from below, but so are the state responses that accommodate minorities in law and policy, as well as what Habermas (2005) calls the mutual learning processes in the public sphere. Following Modood (2006, pp. 40–41), public debate "allows for the changing of certain attitudes, stereotypes, stigmatizations, media images and national symbols", and from minority protest, dominant groups may learn what offends minorities and develop empathy (Haavisto, 2018). Let us look at the Norwegian case.

### Law Proposals

In December 2008, the government attempted to ban attacks on religion and allow police hijab but withdrew both proposals after public pressure and internal disagreement (see Stokke, 2012, pp. 108–110, 182–184). Referring to the cartoon affair, the Ministry of Justice proposed to extend the hate speech act to include "qualified attacks on religion" (specified as ridicule or insult; criticism of religion would be protected by free speech) to replace the blasphemy act. After massive protest by media editors and public intellectuals, the government withdrew the proposal in February 2009. Simultaneously, the ministry announced that police uniform regulations would change to accommodate religious headdress. This also caused public protest, and the ministry reversed the decision claiming that a police hijab would undermine public trust in police neutrality. The Progress Party then had 30% support in opinion polls, and the labor-led coalition refused to accommodate Muslims out of fear of losing votes.

### Media and Public Opinion

Subsequently, Muslim women gained increased access to media. In 2010, the Norwegian Freedom of Expression Foundation (Fritt Ord) gave the Free Speech Prize to Bushra Ishaq (they also gave a Free Speech Tribute to Flemming Rose and Vebjørn Selbekk at the cartoons' tenth anniversary in 2015). Coverage of Muslims has become more diversified (Eide, 2011), with more critical minority voices in 2010 than 2006. Media is a prime source of information about minorities for many Norwegians, and these developments open an opportunity for the public to acquire a more nuanced image of Muslims. To an extent, the mediated public sphere can provide a dialogue arena allowing the majority to learn from minority perspectives and develop empathy with their requests for accommodation. Surveys (IMDI, 2014) show that public attitudes toward Muslims have not changed significantly: Still 40% consider Muslim values incompatible with Norwegian values and ask for assimilation. However, media editors, journalists, women's activists, the Norwegian Church, policymakers, and some politicians have heard the Muslim voices. Most mainstream media practice "responsible free speech" and do not publish cartoons of the prophet. A protest against the Islamophobic film *Innocence of Muslims*, organized by the Islamic Council in 2012, gathered 5000 people, and the bishop and mayor of Oslo spoke to support Muslims. Simultaneously, 150 Muslim extremists held their own protest, but the liberal mainstream now knew that they did not represent Norwegian Muslims. Similarly, Storhaug's white savior agenda and negative portrayal of Muslims are still present and perhaps more extreme than before (Bangstad, 2016), but her lobbying has less influence on the liberal mainstream; debates about women's rights now show a greater awareness of postcolonial feminism.

### Policy

Integration policy (Meld. St. 6, 2012–2013) now explicitly values diversity, indicating that policymakers are listening. It argues that everyone living in Norway should be able to identify as Norwegian and be able to feel part of the Norwegian community regardless of religion, dress codes, and ancestry. It emphasizes shared values based on universal human rights, which are not particularly Norwegian but have room for a diversity of interpretations, priorities, and ways of life; and it rejects the idea of a value conflict between minorities and ethnic Norwegians. It argues that disagreement and conflict are necessary in a living democracy and that everyone has the right to criticize policies, work for legal changes, and influence decision-making. To solve political disagreement, it promotes public dialogue—understood as listening, learning, and transformation as well as deep disagreement, argumentation, and quarreling. This may appear as self-evident platitudes, but compared to previous policy and a strong Norwegian ideology of egalitarianism and conformism (Gullestad, 2002), it represents a new approach. Minority voice and protest can lead to awareness, empathy, and change if the state and majority are dialogue oriented.

Compared to the Danish government's confrontational denial of racism (Vertelyte & Hervik, 2017) during the cartoon affair, the official Norwegian approach is clearly more dialogue-oriented.

## Assessing the Impact: What Difference Does Antiracism Make?

Accommodation of social movements has been central to social democracy, especially in Norway and Sweden, ever since the class compromise brought formerly revolutionary labor movements into government. "State feminism" refers to a Nordic model of political inclusion where the women's movement mobilizes and makes demands, which are accommodated by the state and political elites (Skjeie, 2013). However, social movement agendas are only partially incorporated in state policy, often giving the movement little real influence and impact (Roald, 2013). Beatrice Halsaa (2013) argues that Norwegian women's organizations were not incorporated in decision-making when gender equality policy was developed in the 1970s; they were selectively consulted but not equal partners in dialogue. Similarly, Kymlicka argues that multiculturalism is in the interest of the state, which partially accommodates minority demands to ensure minority loyalty and legitimize nation-building. While his liberal-nationalist perspective sees this as a success, from a critical perspective from below, these compromises entail both progress and shortcomings. Ålund and Schierup (1991) speak about cooptation, containment, and depoliticization of social movements in the case of Swedish multiculturalism and antiracism, which were implemented at the rhetorical level of political correctness, while social movement organizations were depoliticized through public funding, and minorities remain marginalized and excluded from decision-making. Unlike Sweden or Canada, Britain has no official multicultural policy but rather a pragmatic accommodation of minority demands (Modood, 2007). Since the 1980s, neoliberals and later neoconservatives, like Thatcher in the UK, and various right-wing populist parties across Europe have fought to reverse democratic advances won by social movements: attacking workers' rights and multiculturalism, welfare cuts, restricting immigration, and increasing securitization, surveillance, and policing of political activism under the guise of anti-terror measures (Omdal, 2015). Still more social democratic than Britain, Norway also joins this trend toward neoliberal governmentality (Djuve, 2011).

While social movement demands express the collective interests of a group, liberal state accommodation tends to recognize only individual rights and reduce antiracism and feminism to equal opportunity and non-discrimination, failing to change structural power relations. Liberal diversity policies can be similarly criticized: The tentative European consensus expressed in the Council of Europe's (2008) "White Paper on Intercultural Dialogue" is more of a cosmopolitan attitude than a multicultural policy for group recognition. But like multiculturalism, it focuses on reshaping national identity to recognize (mostly individual) diversity, constructing new national identities around human rights as shared values, and is supposed to be wide enough to accommodate all ethnic, cultural, and religious groups.

Norwegian intellectuals, newspaper editors, and policy- and lawmakers strongly believe in public debate as democratic deliberation in Habermas' sense. The dominant view is to maximize free speech and counter hate speech with arguments rather than exclusion, which means public debate makes room for both Islamophobia and antiracism, while hate speech laws are rarely enforced. The UN Committee on the Elimination of Racial Discrimination (CERD) is concerned about Islamophobia in Norwegian debate and questions the acceptance of hate speech and the funding of the Human Rights Service (United Nations Human Rights, 2015). Following Modood (2007, p. 57), multicultural respect goes beyond legislation against hate speech and relies on ethical "sensitivity and responsibility to refrain from what is legal but unacceptable". Like the Rushdie affair in Britain in 1989–1990 that led to multicultural negotiations and intercultural dialogue and over time facilitated mutual understanding between Muslims and majority and the emergence of multiculturalism, the cartoon affair appeared to have played a similar role in Norway. The balance sheet for multiculturalism is mixed: Law proposals to accommodate Muslims were withdrawn due to public pressure, while policy has changed toward multiculturalism. The impact on public opinion is unclear: Anti-Muslim attitudes remain widespread, but some people are learning a more nuanced perspective. Public opinion remains divided.

It is risky to build state policy toward marginalized groups on volatile public debate when large parts of the majority are rather conformist and susceptible to nationalist rhetoric. A weakness of Habermas' model of democratic deliberation lies in its individualist assumptions; it understands the public sphere as consisting of presumably rational, "free and equal" citizens, insufficiently recognizing group-based inequalities. The model I suggest, drawing on Modood's critical multiculturalism, sees the public sphere as an arena for discursive struggles: It is polarized, not between majority and minority but between dialogue-minded and accommodating liberals on one hand and hardline confrontational populists on the other. These two ideological positions are constantly struggling for hegemony, while both are being challenged by more critical, antiracist voices. Whichever becomes more influential at a given point depends, among other things, on the public availability of populist, liberal and critical voices in the media.

## RECENT DEVELOPMENTS: THE REFUGEE CRISIS

According to researcher Helge Lurås (NRK, 22 November 2015), hospitality and empathy characterized Norwegian public opinion during the 2015 refugee crisis when growing numbers of Syrian refugees arrived in Europe. In November 2015, increasing refugee arrivals also to Norway, combined with renewed public fear after the terror attacks in Paris, turned the tide and provided the governing Progress Party with an opportunity and public legitimacy to propose stricter border control and a new asylum and immigration policy, claimed to be the strictest in Europe. In subsequent months, refugee arrivals to Norway almost came to a full stop due to Europe's internal border controls, and the feeling of crisis and panic partly subsided. Now, the proposed new regulations were widely criticized, especially the restrictions on family reunification, and the increased use of temporary residence permits was criticized for violating human rights as well as preventing integration. While the coalitions' parliamentary support parties, Christian Democrats and Liberals, voiced objections, the Labour Party mostly supported these restrictions. When the new hardline immigration minister, Sylvi Listhaug, presented a slightly revised law proposal to parliament in April 2016 (VG, 5 April 2016), she defended the restrictions and argued that current asylum arrivals to Norway were "artificially low". The government also presented a new white paper on the integration of asylum seekers (Meld.St. 30, 2015–2016). It does not explicitly contradict the previous white paper's emphasis on inclusion and diversity; rather "refugees" now replace "Muslims" as the main problem (Kristensen, 2018). Overall, Norway continues to combine strict immigration policy with a diversity-friendly policy for permanent residents but intends to make acquiring citizenship more difficult. Restrictions on family reunification and citizenship will negatively affect Norway's score on the multicultural policy index.

Critical voices of asylum seekers reached the public also during the crisis. In the autumn 2015, asylum seekers protested against poor conditions in Norwegian asylum centers, specifically insufficient food and dirty conditions as well as lack of internet access to keep in contact with families. Progress Party politicians saw the discontented asylum seekers as ungrateful (Dagbladet, 8 November 2015), but media also documented the bad conditions in several asylum centers run by private, for-profit companies. A significant example of refugee voices in the media, the Norwegian-produced documentary *The Crossing* (2015), directed by George Kurian and shown on national TV across Europe, told the stories of Syrian refugees themselves. Based on a group of well-educated Syrians' own footage, the documentary shows them smuggled by boat from Egypt to Italy. The movie's groundbreaking significance lies in allowing the audience to identify and empathize with the view of the refugees, realizing that they are "just like us" when preparing for the trip but then gradually lose hope and become deeply disillusioned, isolated, and passive in Northern European asylum centers. This film is suitable for antiracist education: Listening to refugees' own voices allows us to identify and empathize with "the others" and an experience-based counterpoint to the populist rhetoric constructing them as threats to the welfare state and as potential terrorists.

## ANTIRACIST EDUCATION

The Council of Europe (2008) emphasizes schools as key arena for living together in a multicultural society, and its concepts of intercultural dialogue and competence (Barrett, 2013) open a space for developing antiracist education beyond liberal ideas of diversity (Børhaug, 2009, p. 238). Diversity policy (Meld.St. 6, 2012–2013) argues that all schoolchildren and parents should feel included, respected, and recognized, and that cultural and religious diversity be appreciated as resources. Increasing teachers' multicultural competence—to include minority cultures, knowledge, and experiences in dialogical teaching practice—has become official priority. Norwegian researchers and teacher educators (Harlap & Riese, 2014; Stenshorne & Stokke, 2015; Westrheim, 2011) look to American critical multicultural education (Banks, 2004) for inspiration.

In education, critical multiculturalism (May & Sleeter, 2010) combines Freire's critical pedagogy, critical race theory, and antiracism, and goes beyond liberal multiculturalism's superficial focus on celebrating cultural diversity. Antiracists criticize liberal approaches, like mainstream multicultural education and diversity programs, for assuming that a cosmopolitan society emerges simply by changing individual prejudice and learning about cultural diversity, without changing structural power relations where majority dominates minority. However, structural change starts with individual consciousness-raising—not just acquiring knowledge but also becoming aware of and "unlearning" white privilege and transforming attitudes and behavior. For privileged persons, this implies entering a genuine dialogue with minority perspectives, learning to see oneself through the eyes of others (Gullestad, 2002).

Norwegian textbooks define racism narrowly as a historical phenomenon with little relevance today, but teachers often compensate with alternative learning materials that minority students can identify with, and students appreciate discussing current affairs like the hijab debates (Midtbøen et al., 2014; Svendsen, 2014). This practice reflects multicultural education's aim to include and validate minority students' experiences and perspectives. Racism remains a difficult topic for many teachers. When using the textbook definition of racism, they dismiss minority students' experiences (Midtbøen et al., 2014; Svendsen, 2014). When they take for granted ideologies of color blindness (Bonilla-Silva, 2010) and "imagined sameness" (Gullestad, 2006), they fail to recognize minority students' perspectives. Norwegian education policy tends to have a universalist/Eurocentric emphasis on inclusion, shared values, and sameness—as in France—at the expense of recognizing difference (Børhaug, 2009). Teachers and many students perceive schools as color-blind societies without racism, but minority students do experience forms of marginalization that fit to a broader concept of racism (Midtbøen et al., 2014, p. 72). While teachers tend to focus on possible problems of minority youth like weak Norwegian language skills, most minority youth are Norwegian-born, native Norwegian speakers with mixed identities (Frøyland & Gjerustad, 2012, pp. 33–60). Minority youth and parents tend to have higher ambitions and work harder in school than whites, and while minority women are more likely to pursue higher education, on average, minorities get lower grades. In high school, they experience less supportive teachers and more bullying and have higher dropout rates.

Minority youth identify as foreigners more often than as Norwegians and well-integrated third-generation Norwegian Pakistanis feel least Norwegian (Frøyland & Gjerustad, 2012, pp. 33–60). In Oslo, where minority population ranges from 10% in wealthy western suburbs to 50% in eastern working-class areas, 40% of youth live in multicultural communities:

Most minority youth have white friends, but even in the east, many whites have only white friends. Few minority youth report discrimination and often play down such incidents, but many say they are "perceived as foreigners". Importantly, half of minority youth in this survey say they have experienced racism *as they themselves define it,* and Muslim youth say that negative media coverage is the predominant form of racism. Research (Vestel & Bakken, 2015) indicates that clash of civilizations thinking is less widespread among Oslo youth than among Norwegians in general.

While many teachers use alternative learning materials to include and involve minority students, in line with critical and multicultural education ideals, there is a wide "perception gap" between teachers' color-blind perspective and minority students' experiences. Many teachers lack an analytical framework that connects students' experiences of everyday racism with contemporary anti-Muslim discourses in media debates and with historical forms of racism. Antiracist research provides such a framework seeking to bridge the gap between majority and minority perspectives on racism. O'Brien (2003) argues that learning about minority perspectives and developing empathy require stepping across the gap and acknowledging the extent of contemporary racism. Genuine empathy—as part of "mutual understanding"—takes more than a token black friend who shares the dominant white perspective. White people's failure to validate minority experiences may explain why many minority youth prefer to socialize with other minorities.

## Conclusion

Norwegian diversity policy increasingly accommodates minorities, and multicultural education has become a priority. To some extent, teachers practice dialogical pedagogy, allowing minority students to speak for themselves, and include alternative knowledge to which they can relate. Racism remains a difficult topic to teach, indicating a need to learn from antiracist research and education and go beyond commonalities, inclusion, and equality to acknowledge difference—not least between differently situated experiences of privilege and racism. Like in North America, color-blind ideology dominates in Norway: Well-intentioned whites believe that differential treatment equals negative discrimination. The cartoons and hijab debates are instructive: Norwegian Muslims want recognition as *both equal and different*—they share the values of free speech and gender equality but want to have their say when these are defined, interpreted, and negotiated. They point out that Eurocentric attempts to monopolize interpretation of universal human rights and values are oppressive and hypocritical. Accurately put by six Norwegian Muslim women in a Women's Day op-ed:

> When reducing feminism to taking off clothes, and integration to atheism, oppression hides behind a mask of liberation rhetoric. (Aftenposten, 8 March 2010)

## References

Abu-Lughod, L. (2002). Do Muslim Women Really Need Saving? *American Anthropologist, 104*(3), 783–790.

Aftenposten. (2006, February 12). *Rolig, men høylydt* [Calm, But Loud]. Oslo.

Aftenposten. (2009, September 5). *Muslimer i endring* [Muslims Are Changing] (op-ed by Bushra Ishaq). Oslo.

Aftenposten. (2010, March 8). *Vår feminisme* [Our Feminism] (op-ed by Ambreen Pervez, Iffit Qureshi, Nazia Parveen, Javaria Tanveer, Fazila Mahmood and Sophia Hussain). Oslo.

Ålund, A., & Schierup, C.-U. (1991). *Paradoxes of Multiculturalism.* Aldershot: Avebury.

Bangstad, S. (2013). Inclusion and Exclusion in the Mediated Public Sphere: The Case of Norway and Its Muslims. *Social Anthropology, 21*(3), 356–370.

Bangstad, S. (2016). Islamophobia in Norway: National Report 2015. In E. Bayraklı & F. Hafez (Eds.), *European Islamophobia Report 2015*, Istanbul, SETA. Retrieved from https://www.researchgate.net/publication/299337293_Norway

Banks, J. (2004). *Multicultural Education.* Hoboken, NJ: Wiley.

Barrett, M. (Ed.). (2013). *Interculturalism and Multiculturalism: Similarities and Differences.* Strasbourg: Council of Europe Publishing.

Bonilla-Silva, E. (2010). *Racism without Racists: Color-Blind Racism and the Persistence of Racial Inequality in the United States.* Lanham: Rowman & Littlefield Publishers.

Borchgrevink, T. (2002). Likestilling. Det flerkulturelle demokratiets hodepine. In G. Brochmann, T. Borchgrevink, & J. Rogstad (Eds.), *Sand i maskineriet. Makt og demokrati i det flerkulturelle Norge* (pp. 146–173). Oslo: Gyldendal Akademisk.

Borchgrevink, T., & Brochmann, G. (2003). Comparing Minority and Majority Rights: Multicultural Integration in a Power Perspective. *The Multicultural Challenge, Comparative Social Research, 22*, 69–99.

Børhaug, F. B. (2009). Hva er antirasistisk pedagogikk? *Prismet, 60*(3), 237–253.

Brochmann, G., & Hagelund, A. (2012). *Immigration Policy and the Scandinavian Welfare State 1945–2010*. London: Palgrave Macmillan.

Brox, O. (1991). *'Jeg er ikke rasist, men...'. Hvordan får vi våre meninger om innvandrere og innvandring?* Oslo: Gyldendal.

Brox, O. (2005). *Arbeidskraftimport. Velferdsstatens redning eller undergang?* Oslo: Pax.

Council of Europe. (2008). *White Paper on Intercultural Dialogue: Living Together as Equals in Dignity*. Retrieved from https://www.coe.int/t/dg4/intercultural/source/white%20paper_final_revised_en.pdf

Dagbladet. (2006a, February 11). (Online), *Skam dere media* [Shame on You, Media]. Oslo. Retrieved from http://www.dagbladet.no/nyheter/2006/02/11/457504.html

Dagbladet. (2006b, February 11). *Bare 300 for Fred* [Only 300 for Peace]. Oslo.

Dagbladet. (2006c, February 12). *-Vi har ikke kastet første andre eller tredje stein...* [-We Didn't Throw the First Second or Third Stone...]. Oslo.

Dagbladet. (2009, January 31). *Vestens enerett på feminismen* [Western Monopoly on Feminism] (op-ed by Bushra Ishaq). Oslo.

Dagbladet. (2010a, February 24). *Bort med barnehijaben* [Away with the Children's Hijab]. Oslo.

Dagbladet. (2010b, March 26). *Hatindustrien* [The Hate Industry] (op-ed by Rune Berglund Steen). Oslo.

Dagbladet. (2010c, May 11). *Populismens forsømmelse* [Neglected by Populism] (op-ed by Bushra Ishaq). Oslo.

Dagbladet. (2015, November 8). *Justisministeren reagerer på asyl-demonstrasjon* [Justice Minister Reacts to Asylum Demonstration]. Oslo. Retrieved from http://www.dagbladet.no/nyheter/justisministeren-reagerer-pa-asyl-demonstrasjon/60590396

Dagsavisen. (2006, February 12). *-Politikerne har presset imamene* [-Politicians Put Pressure on Imams]. Oslo.

Dagsavisen. (2009, May 4). *Rammene for religionsdebatt* [Framework for Religious Debate] (op-ed by Bushra Ishaq). Oslo.

Djuve, A. B. (2011). Introductory Programs for Immigrants. *Nordic Journal of Migration Research, 1*(3), 113–125.

ECRI. (2015). *Report on Norway (Fifth Monitoring Cycle)*. European Commission Against Racism and Intolerance.

Eide, E. (2011). Being Me, Being Us, Being Them. In E. Eide & K. Nikunen (Eds.), *Media in Motion*. Farnham: Ashgate.

Eriksen, T. H. (2005). *Engaging Anthropology: The Case of a Public Presence*. Oxford: Berg.

Eriksen, T. H., & Tretvoll, H. F. (2006). *Kosmopolitikk: En optimistisk politikk for det 21. århundre*. Cappelen Damm AS.

Faiola, A. (2016, May 19). Meet the Donald Trumps of Europe. *The Washington Post*. Retrieved from https://www.washingtonpost.com/news/worldviews/wp/2016/05/19/meet-the-donald-trumps-of-europe/

Frøyland, L. R., & Gjerustad, C. (2012). *Vennskap, utdanning og framtidsplaner*. Oslo: NOVA Rapport 5/2012.

Gressgård, R., & Jacobsen, C. (2003). Questions of Gender in a Multicultural Society. *Nordic Journal of Feminist and Gender Research, 11*(2), 69–77.

Gullestad, M. (2002). *Det norske sett med nye øyne*. Oslo: Universitetsforlaget.

Gullestad, M. (2006). *Plausible Prejudice*. Oslo: Aschehoug.

Haavisto, C. (2018). The Power of Being Heard: How Claims Against Racism Are Constructed, Spread and Listened to in a Hybrid Media Environment. In P. Hervik (Ed.), *Racialization, Racism, and Anti-Racism in the Nordic Countries*. Basingstoke: Palgrave Macmillan.

Habermas, J. (2005). *Religion in the Public Sphere*. Bergen: Holberg Prize Seminar.

Hage, G. (1998). *White Nation*. Annandale: Pluto Press.

Halsaa, B. (2013). Muligheter for mobilisering: stat og kvinnebevegelse. In B. Bråten & C. Thun (Eds.), *Krysningspunkter. Likestillingspolitikk i et flerkulturelt Norge* (pp. 51–84). Oslo: Akademika Forlag.

Harlap, Y., & Riese, H. (2014). Hva skjer når vi ser farge innen utdanning? In K. Westrheim & A. Tolo (Eds.), *Kompetanse for mangfold* (pp. 190–216). Bergen: Fagbokforlaget.

Hervik, P. (2004). Anthropological Perspectives on the New Racism in Europe. *Ethnos, 69*(2), 149–155.

Huddleston, T., Bilgili, Ö., Joki, A.-L., & Vankova, Z. (2015). *Migrant Integration Policy Index 2015*. Barcelona/Brussels: CIDOB and MPG.

IMDI. (2014). *Integreringsbarometeret 2013/2014*. Oslo: Integration and Diversity Directorate.

Jacobsen, C. (2011). *Islamic Traditions and Muslim Youth in Norway*. Leiden: Brill.

Klassekampen. (2009, March 7). *Bestemmer over egen kropp* [Decide Over One's Own Body]. Oslo.

Kristensen, H. M. (2018). In P. Hervik (Ed.), *Racialization, Racism, and Anti-Racism in the Nordic Countries*. Basingstoke: Palgrave Macmillan.

Kurian, G. (Dir). (2015). *The Crossing*. Gründer Film.

Kymlicka, W. (2002). *Contemporary Political Philosophy: An Introduction*. 2nd ed. Oxford University Press (ISBN 0-19-878274-8): Ch. 8: "Multiculturalism" (p. 50).

Mamdani, M. (2004). *Good Muslim, Bad Muslim*. Doubleday, NY: Three Leaves Press.

May, S., & Sleeter, C. (Eds.). (2010). *Critical Multiculturalism. Theory and Praxis*. New York: Routledge.

Meld.St. 6. (2012–2013). *En helhetlig integreringspolitikk*. Oslo: Ministry of Children, Equality and Social Inclusion.

Meld.St. 30. (2015–2016). *Fra mottak til arbeidsliv – en effektiv integreringspolitikk*. Oslo: Ministry of Justice and Public Security.

Midtbøen, A., J. Orupabo & Å. Røthing (2014): *Etniske og religiøse minoriteter i læremidler. Lærer- og elevperspektiver*. Oslo: Institutt for Samfunnsforskning. Rapport 2014: 11.

Mir-Hosseini, Z. (2006). Muslim Women's Quest for Equality. *Critical Inquiry, 32*, 629–645.

Modood, T. (2005). *Multicultural Politics*. Minneapolis, MN: University of Minnesota Press.

Modood, T. (2006). British Muslims and the Politics of Multiculturalism. In T. Modood, A. Triandafyllidou, & R. Zapata-Barrero (Eds.), *Multiculturalism, Muslims and Citizenship: A European Approach*. London: Routledge.

Modood, T. (2007). *Multiculturalism: A Civic Idea*. Cambridge: Polity Press.

Myong, L., & Danbolt, M. (2018). Racial Turns and Returns: Recalibrations of Racial Exceptionalism in Danish Public Debates on Racism. In P. Hervik (Ed.), *Racialization, Racism, and Anti-Racism in the Nordic Countries*. Basingstoke: Palgrave Macmillan.

NRK. (2015, November 22). Ytring. Retrieved from https://radio.nrk.no/serie/ytring/NMAG06001915/22-11-2015

O'Brien, E. (2003). The Political Is Personal. In A. W. Doane & E. Bonilla-Silva (Eds.), *White Out*. New York: Routledge.

Okin, S. M. (1999). Is Multiculturalism Bad for Women? In J. Cohen, M. Howard, & M. Nussbaum (Eds.), *Is Multiculturalism Bad for Women? Susan Moller Okin with Respondents* (pp. 9–24). Princeton, NJ: Princeton University Press.

Okolie, A. (2005). Toward an Antiracist Research Framework. In G. J. S. Dei & G. S. Johal (Eds.), *Antiracist Research Methodologies* (pp. 241–267). New York: Peter Lang.

Omdal, S. E. (2015). Vannkanoner mot gatens parlament. Hardere politimetoder svekker retten til protest. In S. Johannessen & R. Glomseth (Eds.), *Politiledelse* (Chap. 3). Oslo: Gyldendal Akademisk.

Palazzo, C. (2016, April 22). Norway Minister Ridiculed Online After Floating in the Mediterranean to See What It's Like to Be a Refugee. *The Telegraph*. Retrieved from http://www.telegraph.co.uk/news/2016/04/22/norway-minister-ridiculed-online-after-floating-in-the-mediterra/

Parekh, B. (2000). *Rethinking Multiculturalism*. Basingstoke: Macmillan.

Razack, S. (2008). *Casting Out*. Toronto: University of Toronto Press.

Roald, A. S. (2013). Majority Versus Minority: 'Governmentality' and Muslims in Sweden. *Religions (Open Access), 4*(1), 116–131.

Said, E. (1994). *Orientalism*. New York: Vintage Books, Random House.

Skjeie, H. (2013). Hva var statsfeminisme? In B. Bråten & C. Thun (Eds.), *Krysningspunkter. Likestillingspolitikk i et flerkulturelt Norge* (pp. 29–43). Oslo: Akademika Forlag.

Stenshorne, E., & Stokke, C. (2015). Utvikling av en mangfoldssensitiv klasseledelse. In S. Laugerud, M. E. Moskvil, & E. Maagerø (Eds.), *Flerkulturelt Verksted. Ulike tilnklasseledell kompetanse for mangfold* (pp. 226–239). Portal Akademisk.

Stokke, C. (2012). *A Multicultural Society in the Making* (PhD thesis). Trondheim, NTNU.

Stokke, C., & Lybæk, L. (2016). Combining Intercultural Dialogue and Critical Multiculturalism. *Ethnicities*. Published online ahead of print.

Storhaug, H. (2007). *Tilslørt. Avslørt. Et oppgjør med norsk naivisme* [Veiled. Unveiled. A Battle Against Norwegian Naivety]. Oslo: Kagge.

Svendsen, S. (2014). *Affecting Change* (PhD thesis). Trondheim: NTNU.

Thorsen, M. S. (2018). In P. Hervik (Ed.), *Racialization, Racism, and Anti-Racism in the Nordic Countries*. Basingstoke: Palgrave Macmillan.

Törngren, S. (2018). In P. Hervik (Ed.), *Racialization, Racism, and Anti-Racism in the Nordic Countries*. Basingstoke: Palgrave Macmillan.

United Nations Human Rights: Office of the High Commissioner. (2015). *Committee on the Elimination of Racial Discrimination Considers the Report of Norway*. Retrieved from http://www.ohchr.org/EN/NewsEvents/Pages/DisplayNews.aspx?NewsID=16330&LangID=E

van Dijk, T. (1993). *Elite Discourse and Racism*. Newbury Park, CA: Sage.

Vertelyte, M., & Hervik, P. (2018). Danish Sensitivity to 'Race': The Vices of Debating Racial Epithets in Danish Public Discourse. In P. Hervik (Ed.), *Racialization, Racism, and Anti-Racism in the Nordic Countries*. Basingstoke: Palgrave Macmillan.

Vestel, V., & Bakken, A. (2015). *Holdninger til ekstremisme. Resultater fra Ung i Oslo 2015*. Oslo: NOVA Report No. 4/16.

VG. (2006a, February 11). *-Respekter våre verdier* [-Respect Our Values]. Oslo. Retrieved from http://www.vg.no/nyheter/innenriks/muhammedtegningene/respekter-vaare-verdier/a/160336/

VG. (2006b, February 12). *Lederen for demonstrasjon stoppet bråk* [Protest Leader Prevented Trouble]. Oslo.

VG. (2016, April 5). *Oslo. Her er regjeringens asylinnstramminger.* [Here Are the Government's Asylum Restrictions] Retrieved from http://www.vg.no/nyheter/innenriks/flyktningkrisen-i-europa/her-er-regjeringens-asylinnstramminger/a/23652382/

Westrheim, K. (2011). Den flerkulturelle skolen – en ressurs og utfordring. In M. B. Postholm, E. Munthe, P. Haug, & R. J. Krumsvik (Eds.), *Elevmangfold i skolen*, 1–7 (s. 107–134). Kristiansand: Høyskoleforlaget.

Wikan, U. (1995). *Mot en ny norsk underklasse. Innvandrere, kultur og integrasjon*. Oslo: Gyldendal.

Wikan, U. (2002). *Generous Betrayal. Politics of Culture in the New Europe*. Chicago: University of Chicago Press.

Yegenoglu, M. (1998). *Colonial Fantasies*. Cambridge: Cambridge University Press.

# CHAPTER 10

# The Power of Being Heard: How Claims Against Racism Are Constructed, Spread, and Listened to in a Hybrid Media Environment

*Camilla Haavisto*

## INTRODUCTION

This chapter examines four mediated instances of intensified claims-making related to racism and racialization in Finland and Sweden. Two of these public debates centered around events that can be characterized as everyday acts of racialization in public space: nightlife harassment and ethnic profiling by the police. These testimonies caused uproars, but neither changed the dominant national narrative on racism nor shook the ingrained hierarchy of voices or the division of space within the media sphere. The other two public debates occurred after violent attacks conducted by neo-Nazis: in one attack, the victim was severely injured, the other was fatal. The first attack was the stabbing of Showan Shattak by a

C. Haavisto (✉)
Journalism and Communication, Swedish School of Social Science, University of Helsinki, Helsinki, Finland

Minority Studies, Åbo Akademi University, Turku, Finland

© The Author(s) 2019

P. Hervik (ed.), *Racialization, Racism, and Anti-Racism in the Nordic Countries*, Approaches to Social Inequality and Difference, https://doi.org/10.1007/978-3-319-74630-2_10

229

30-year-old neo-Nazi on Möllevångstorget in Malmö in 2014; the second was an aggravated assault that took place on the Helsinki Railway Square in 2016 and led to the death of Jimi Karttunen.

In Sweden, Shattak soon became a symbol for the resistance to the normalization of extreme right-wing ideologies. His face and name were used as devices in anti-racist rallies and in public space in the form of graffiti and banderols, and much of the mainstream debate centered on him as an individual. In Finland, the fatal attack on Jimi Karttunen was continuously referred to on anti-racist social media sites and in campaign meetings as evidence of failed policy and lawmaking, but Karttunen himself, a white youth with a dubious past, did not become a symbol for the anti-racist struggle in the same sense as Shattak. Despite their differences, these two events became loci of the partially interconnected anti-racist movements in Sweden and Finland and soon developed into so-called critical events (Das, 1995; Espeland & Rogstad, 2013; Sökefeld, 2006) containing strong transnational dimensions and allowing a variety of new voices and perspectives to challenge the ingrained national narratives on racism and racialization.

In the longer run, however, the political significance of the four public debates on race and racialization remains ambivalent due to a variety of simultaneous processes: the tendency of elite and civil commentators alike to understand racialization as an individual problem rather than a social and political problem; the tendency to contest experiences of racism, even in the context of "support talk", while relying on a paradigm of well-meaning colorblindness; and the tendency of elite politicians to engage publicly in racism scandals without a clear vision as to how to move forward on the level of policy and governance.

In this chapter, I will develop the points above in more detail by providing findings from an empirical analysis of mainstream newspapers, online discussions, and interviews, and by framing the discussion with the concepts of claims-making (Koopmans & Rucht, 2002; Koopmans et al., 2005) and political listening (Bassel, 2017; Dreher, 2009). My ambition is not to prove that these four events are examples of racism, but to evaluate how political claims, as understood by Koopmans et al. (2005), are constructed and circulated in a hybrid media sphere (Chadwick, 2013) when racism and racialization are discussed. I am interested in the meanings and consequences of these claims. In this chapter, I consider the claims of anti-racist activists within the broader frame of media and communication scholarship, identifying the demands of these claims-makers and of whom the demands are made and answering the question of whether their claims are listened to, and how.

## Two Forms of Nordic Exceptionalism: Finland and Sweden

The four events described above should not be seen as isolated events or individual tragedies with "lonely lunatics" as villains. Instead, they should be seen as evidence of the continuous and systematic infringement of individual rights and as events marked by the present understanding of history, contemporary political, ideological, and environmental developments in Europe, and the urban political culture in Helsinki and Malmö. Despite Finland and Sweden being neighboring countries, the differences in the abovementioned areas are significant. In addition to differing numbers of migrants and the dissimilar role of anti-racism in Finland's and Sweden's imagined national identities, there are also differences in the countries' historical relations to scientific racism.

For example, in nineteenth-century Sweden, when scientific racism was invested with political ideology and the theory of evolution and hence became deplorable with the purpose of reducing the rights of racialized groups, Finns were objects of racism, rather than supporters of scientific racist ideologies (Kemiläinen, 1993; Palmberg, 2009). In racial classifications, Finns were often thought to be related to the Mongolian "race" (Isaksson & Jokisalo, 1998). However, although the Finns themselves have been colonized by both Sweden and Russia and racialized by scientists, they have been far from innocent when the protection of national minorities is concerned. Discriminatory practices and outright racism toward Finland's so-called old minorities—the Sami, Roma, Tatar, and Jewish minorities—have flourished in historical times and today occur in both institutional and non-institutional settings (Isaksson, 1996; Nordberg, 2007). In contemporary postcolonial writing, a common understanding of Finland's relation to the outside world in general and the colonial project in particular is that Finland was indeed a case of exceptionalism, but also a case of complicity in colonialism (Vuorela, 2009).

Evidently, the different roles of Finland and Sweden in expansionist and colonialist projects and Finland's late history of migration and lower number of migrants in general and post-WWII migrants in particular[1] have influenced the development of two contemporary societies that, despite similarities in their social welfare policies, today differ from one another in terms of demographics, migration politics, and the role of anti-racism as a main signifier for national identity. At least so far, Finnish cities have been spared suburban riots or other significant "unarticulated" social justice movements with violent tendencies (see Dikeç, 2007 for the notion). And, although recent studies suggest that personal experiences of ethnic profiling in Finland does increase mistrust in the police (Keskinen et al., 2018, p. 48), there is not in Finland the kind of profound mistrust toward the police that exists in Swedish suburbs, which have become security hotspots subject to continuous police surveillance, identity raids, and stop-and-search raids (Peterson & Åkerström, 2008; Schierup, Ålund, & Kings, 2014 for Sweden; Kääriäinen & Niemi, 2014; Poliisibarometri, 2016 for Finland) (see Fig. 10.1).

With regard to anti-racist organizing, Finland and Sweden differ in the history of their movements, their strategies, and their vocabularies (for Sweden, see Jämte, 2013; Malmsten, 2009), for Finland, see Alemanji & Maji, 2016; Seikkula, 2017). One of the biggest differences is the "whiteness" of the field in Finland in comparison to Sweden, where members and activists represent a variety of backgrounds. There are also differences in the means chosen for the struggle. In Sweden, anarchists are more numerous and visible in anti-racist settings such as demonstrations, while in Finland, whose civil society mainly has been organized since the late nineteenth century into traditional NGOs, collectives, and networks (for Finland, Kuukkanen, 2017; Metsämäki & Nisula, 2006), members tend to put forward claims more or less in line with the public political culture (see Lentin, 2004, p. 2 for the notion), leaving little space for more radical anti-racist organizing. However, during the last few years, there has been more diversity within the anti-racist field in Finland than before (Keskinen's ongoing project Postethnic Activism in the Neoliberal Era, 2014–2019; Seikkula, 2017), and we have also seen that with the

---

[1] Prior to the 1990s, Finland was a country of emigration, with more than 700,000 emigrants heading abroad, mostly to Sweden, between 1945 and 1999 (Korkiasaari & Söderling, 2003, p. 3). Today, the difference between the two countries in the number of citizens with a foreign background is the following: at the end of 2016, more than 2.3 million people in Sweden—23.2% of Swedish citizens—were either born abroad or born in Sweden to parents born abroad (SCB, 2017), whereas in Finland, 6.5% of 358,000 citizens were born abroad (Statistics Finland, 2017). However, the sudden increase in asylum applications during 2015 (32,477 in Finland according to Migri (2017) and 162,877 in Sweden according to the Swedish Migration Agency (2017)) influenced both migration policy and public debates on ethnic relations, race, and racialization.

**Fig. 10.1** Poster on a street near Möllevångstorget in Malmö in spring 2014 reading: "A cop is a cop. We don't trust them"

growing presence of neo-Nazi groups and anti-immigrant street patrols, such as the Soldiers of Odin, the protesting crowds, with a variety of affiliations, have grown as well.

Further, the differences between the urban milieus of Malmö and Helsinki are significant. The Malmö region functions as a nexus for various types of transnational mobilities, is marked by a working-class past and a long and dense history of migration, and has a strong radical right-wing movement with a long record of brutal crimes (Wigerfelt & Wigerfelt, 2001)—but also a lively street politics scene maintained mainly by young people sympathetic to the left (Brink Pinto & Pries, 2013). Helsinki is less diverse in its demographic composition (Hiekkavuo, 2017) and lacks a tradition of protest culture, at least in comparison to other European cities (Luhtakallio, 2012). For example, in the Helsinki region, anti-racism cannot be said to constitute a significant and recognizable movement, in contrast to the Malmö region, where the movement, despite its inner factions, has a long history among both registered organizations and independent actors in the field (Brink Pinto & Pries, 2013, 2017; Malmsten, 2009 for the Malmö region).

In sum, Finland and Sweden form interesting but divergent cases of the history of racist thought in the Nordic countries and beyond. In terms of the history of biological racism, current demographic developments, and public political culture (Lentin, 2004, p. 2), there are some significant differences between the two urban mediated milieus that are of interest for this chapter. I refer here, in particular, to the numbers of refugees and migrants, the local histories of migration, and the ways in which street politics and the recent, but growing, claims of safe spaces for racialized people are generally related to. When compared to Sweden, Finland has a shorter history of migration, fewer migrants, and a stronger tradition of a political culture of consensus, and it is only recently that racialized youth in Finland have started to organize and pose questions concerning who has the right to put forward anti-racist claims in public and who does not.

## THE ROLE OF CRITICAL EVENTS IN CLAIMS-MAKING PRACTICES AND LISTENING STRATEGIES

In examining the claims put forward by the various actors who, in and through the media, testify about racist abuse or actively work against racism and racialization, the theoretical and methodological starting point for my study is political claims-making theory. In accordance with Ruud Koopmans et al. (2005), I see claims as strategic actions in the communicative space that consist of purposive and public articulations, such as political demands, calls to action, proposals, and criticisms, and that actually or potentially affect the interests or integrity of the claimant and other collective actors. A claim can be articulated in a declaration, a decision, a demonstration, in the mainstream media, in social media, and so on. In theory, claims can be put forward by or accompanied by violent actions, but in this study, my understanding of claims is limited to appeals made in verbal and textual articulations: mainstream media content, Twitter, Facebook pages (groups, the pages of public figures, and public material on private pages), discussion forums and blogs, and in a few complementary interviews with activists and journalists.

A crucial oversight in Koopmans et al.'s scheme on how claims are formed (2005) is whether claims are listened to and responded to and, further, who does the listening and in what manner. In today's hybrid media environment (Chadwick, 2013) where more people now have the opportunity to produce and stream content and give voice to claims, the aspect of listening becomes crucial. The theoretical idea of political listening has developed within different strands of scholarship—forensic science, the arts, gender studies, and studies on media and democracy—and the notion has come to mean somewhat different things, particularly concerning whether listening refers to auditory experiences in a literal or more symbolic sense. Whether one conceptualizes political listening in a framework of sound, technology and spatiality (Fischer, 2014; Abu Hamdan, 2015) or in a framework of social relations, structures and power hierarchies (Bassel, 2017; Dreher, 2009; Bickford, 1996), the main idea is consistent: we may be free to choose the way we speak and claim rights, but we are not free to choose the ways in which we are being heard.

Some scholars, such as Fischer (2014), argue that in Modern English *to listen* usually refers to an active act: not merely hearing, but hearing with intent. According to Fischer, while the verb *to hear* usually refers to automatic or passive sound perception, the verb *to listen* connotes intentional or purposeful use of the sense of hearing. It implies intensified concentration and an awareness of what one is listening to (Fischer, 2014, p. 11). Listening may not in an analytical sense be as fully intentional on the part of the listener as Fischer claims, although intentionality is certainly intertwined with politics. Since we cannot listen to everything we hear, we sometimes have to choose what to listen to, or someone else may choose for us. This selection process makes listening political, particularly when public and collective selection processes are concerned. However, listening as a choice and as a political act does not imply that a listener of an anti-racist claim, for example, would have to be sympathetic to the claim (Bickford, 1996, p. 11). Instead, my understanding of political listening acknowledges the centrality of conflict and inequality in politics and communicative interaction. Hence, when listening occurs, the listener does not have to feel friendship, empathy, or shared interest, but need only pay attention to what is said and how it is said, despite possible skepticism or distrust toward the claims-maker. (For more on the agonistic premises of political listening, see e.g., Maasilta & Haavisto, 2014.)

In today's hybrid media environment, where consumers are producers and social media is intertwined with mainstream media, it is difficult to predict which claims will be listened to by media users, journalists, and political decision-makers and which will be neglected. Stories about racism and racialization that are produced and circulated by unconventional and marginal media platforms sometimes serve as a trigger for extensive mainstream media coverage that can lead to politically challenging agency, but there is no guarantee that this will happen. In this chapter, I argue that two of the four aforementioned mediated events that lead to intensified debate on racism and racialization can, despite certain limitations, be approached as "critical events". The concept of critical event is not just the outcome of a particular historic situation, but also the consequence of collective action framing, as Espeland and Rogstad (2013, p. 128) state. In other words, whether an event becomes critical depends not only on the magnitude, topicality, or policy-changing potentiality of the event as such, but also on how "sticky" claims become and how well they are listened to. Sara Ahmed (2014, p. 11) has used stickiness to describe how objects that are shared and circulate socially can become "saturated with affect" as sites of personal and social tension. As items "go viral", they are stuck together by affect, and the stickiness can be measured by how often people reply to comments, share, or like content on social media or mainstream journalism sites (Lindgren, 2017; Paasonen, 2015).

In order to understand more profoundly the critical potential and "stickiness" of individualized and collective experiences of racism and racialization, I will examine how claims against racism are constructed, circulated, and listened to in a hybrid media sphere in four intensified moments of claims-making. An understanding of these processes will shed light on the premises and challenges of public debate in the context of hybridization (Chadwick, 2013), the crises of journalism (Alexander, Butler Breese, & Luengo, 2016), and the "end of multiculturalism" (Titley & Lentin, 2011). Who gets to define what racism is and to put forward opinions and experiences of racialization in Nordic societies, and who listens to these claims?

In order to answer this, I present an analysis of two mediated scandals of "everyday" racism in Finland (nightlife harassment and ethnic profiling) and two cases in which intensified debate on Nazism, racism, and anti-racism occurred in the aftermath of severe racist violent attacks, one in Helsinki and one in Malmö. The cases of nightlife harassment and ethnic profiling were brought to public awareness by reality TV personality Alexandra Alexis and rap musician James Nikander who posted their testimonies of racism on their Facebook pages whereafter they went viral.

## MATERIAL AND METHODS

The material consists of a wide range of Facebook pages, blogs, discussion forums, online comments on web-based news sites, and mainstream news media and magazines in Finland and Sweden. In order to better understand a controversy uncovered in the preliminary findings, I also interviewed key claims-makers in the Malmö case: two activists from the activist network *Skåne mot rasism* (Skåne against racism)—a network for non-parliamentary anti-racist groups in the region established in 2008—and two journalists from the newspaper *Sydsvenskan*.

The search for data was a three-step process. First, with the help of a research assistant, I manually collected everything we could find on the web that had been written about the four cases. We stopped collecting when the material no longer provided new insight into how the cases were discussed. To contrast this first stage with big data analytics, I call this method the "hand net fishing technique". Using Google,[2] I searched for anything written on "Alexandra Alexis AND racism OR Teatteri" (name of nightlife establishment), "James Nikander AND mother OR ethnic profiling OR handcuffing", "Showan Shattak AND assault OR Möllan OR Möllevångstorget", and "Jimi Karttunen AND Helsinki Railway Square OR nazi*".

The purpose of this Google-aided search technique was to obtain an overview of how the events were discussed in general, and on the basis of this stage, I managed to distinguish a certain anatomy of the first two mediated events of everyday racism in public and semi-public space (see Appendix). I was also able to relate the overall publicity of the events to aspects of listening and to select central pieces of data for the second stage, a more detailed analysis of claims-making.

In the second stage, I used a more targeted "fish-hook technique" to select certain texts and discussion threads for in-depth examination. Especially in cases involving news agency bulletins that spread to various media, resulting in identical or very similar stories, this is a crucial stage for organizing the data. It is important to underline that many comments, texts, and threads containing features of organized hate speech were not selected for a more detailed analysis in the second stage, which influences the findings and conclusions of my study. This choice is partially due to my aspiration to move beyond a dominant focus of "extremist site" in order to contribute to the scholarly endevour of *unsettling the idea that extremists sites, and thus extremist groups, form the exceptional local of racism in contemporary Europe* (Titley, 2014, p. 51). Having said this, one shall acknowledge that there is a large number of overtly racist comments with features of extremist ideology and organized hate speech. Many of the comments are very similar to one another and contain claims that center around two issues: that borders should have been closed a long time ago and the sooner they close, the better, and that people with experiences of migration or who work against racism or support humanitarian border

---

[2] Using Google for research purposes can be problematic, since algorithms steer the prioritization of content, therefore possibly listing different sites for different researchers. I used three different IP addresses in order to improve my chances of compiling as varied a data set as possible.

policies are less worthy than others, naïve, or deserve unjust or bad treat-ment. In my study, I do not wish to echo outright racist comments or to promote the distribution of videos produced by members of far-right movements. Instead, the material for the second stage was selected in order to examine the more implicit, complex, and perhaps unexpected ways in which "ordinary" media users, journalists, bloggers, and decision-makers relate to claims against racism.

In the third stage of data collection, I manually searched four newspa-pers—*Helsingin Sanomat* and *Iltalehti* for the periods 20–30 May, 10–20 July, and 17–26 September 2016, and *Sydsvenska Dagbladet* and *Dagens Nyheter* for the period 9–19 March 2014—to ensure that no crucial texts and articles were missing.

I am aware that some news articles and discussion threads might still have gone unnoticed, since not all newspapers publish all their articles online and because of algorithmic challenges. Another weakness of this kind of broad research technique at the first stage of the data gathering is its genre-blindness. When referring broadly to online discussion threads and forums, as I do, one must be aware of the fact that these forums may differ from one another—they may follow different moderation and sub-scription policies and may serve completely different purposes. Some of these forums are targeted toward people with certain types of interests or professional backgrounds, while other wide-ranging forums host a broad range of topics. These forums are, however, united by the unique charac-teristics of online communication, namely, the ability of participants to transcend time and space while maintaining anonymity. This characteristic has democratizing potential, but it may also turn against itself. When allowing people to form and express frank opinions without (in most cases) having to be afraid of the consequences, there will always be "trolls" who post racist, extraneous, or off-topic messages[3] (Paasonen, 2015).

In addition to gathering material from social media and mainstream newspapers, and the interviews, and analyzing the texts through close reading (DuBois, 2003), I also observed and documented several street

---

[3] An example of this is a thread on the website *MV-lehti*, in which commenters start a discus-sion of the Alexis case but soon shift to a discussion of the role of the Swedish language in Finland—another topic popular on certain so-called immigrant-critical forums, such as *MV-lehti* and HOMMA (Pöyhtäri, Haara, & Raittila, 2013; Saukkonen, 2011) on online hate speech involving hate against the Swedish language minority in Finland. I have chosen not to provide direct links to racist forums, but the thread that I am referring to is titled "Hillitön causti ravin-tola Teatterin 'rasistisesta' tapauksesta", started by "Rasmus" on 21.05.2016 at 04:26.

events organized during spring 2014 in Malmö and autumn 2016 in Helsinki, focusing particularly on the claims presented in slogans, symbols, and speeches. It is worth to underline that I do not aim to compare the public debates on racism and racialization in the two countries or urban milieus. Instead, I seek commonalities between the claims against racism put forward by the victims of racist abuse, their relatives, or anti-racist activists, and I seek to understand listening processes that occurred during these two intensified moments of claims-making.

## Two Cases of "Everyday" Racism: Contesting Testimonies of Racism

On 19 May 2016, Alexandra Alexis, a Finnish-American reality TV personality and singer, was verbally and physically molested by two middle-aged white women at a VIP party at one of the classier nightclubs in Helsinki. According to Alexis, the pejoratives used by the abusers were exceptionally harsh and referred clearly to phenotypical features and biological dimensions of racial inferiority (e.g., "murjaani", which is an old word for "someone with a dark skin"). Humiliated by the abuse of the other guests and the staff of the nightclub, Alexis was asked to leave the party, while the white molesters were allowed to stay. The next day, Alexis wrote a lengthy status update on her Facebook page, made it public, and included a picture of her two molesters, asking people in her network to help identify the two women. Alexis' post got 1437 shares, 1700 reactions, and 197 comments (Alexis, 2017).[4] Soon after, Finland's major national newspaper (*Helsingin Sanomat*, 2016a, 20 May) wrote about the case, and the story went viral (see Appendix for a more detailed description of the anatomy of the mediated scandal).

Six weeks later, on 10 July, another celebrity, musician James Nikander (stage name Musta Barbaari, "The Black Barbarian"), wrote a lengthy status update on his personal Facebook page describing how his mother and sister were victims of ethnic profiling (which is illegal in Finland according to an act to amend to the Aliens Act 301/2004, §129 a and 129 b, amendment 193/2015) in a stop-and-search raid in central Helsinki and forced to the ground with force. The case of Nikander's mother quickly went viral; the original post got 15,000 emoticon reactions, was shared over 2000 times, and was commented on 1000 times[5] (Nikander, 2016). The national news

---

[4] These reactions, comments, and shares are as of 7 December 2016.
[5] These reactions, comments, and shares are as of 7 December 2016.

agency STT and all the major newspapers in Finland reported on the case; journalists wrote follow-ups and editorials, and the case was the subject of a current affairs television program at the national broadcasting company (A-studio, 11 July 2016) (see Appendix for the anatomy of the scandal).

These two stories may not seem as exceptional as the two other events—the death of Jimi Karttunen in Helsinki and the stabbing of Showan Shattak in Malmö—which evoked protest demonstrations with thousands of participants and came to function as symbolic cases of merciless Nazi violence. The two testimonies on racism on the streets and in the public places of Helsinki are, however, analytically interesting, because they highlight some common tendencies in how claims opposing racism are discussed and responded to in social and mainstream media.

The data revealed a handful of differing but related reactions to these two cases that influenced the framing of news stories. First, we discovered an "anti-racism as mere rhetoric" reaction, in which racism is condemned, but at the same time, discriminatory behavior is legitimated in some way. In most cases, the behavior is legitimized discursively through references to security, a lack of reliable (often meaning white) witnesses, or by speculations as to the unintended nature of the racist behavior. This discourse is similar to the idea of "I'm not a racist, but…". In cases where anti-racism appears to be mere rhetoric, we can see a close association with various representatives of the authorities and the nightclub. This discourse is also associated with civil commentators who mitigate the racist experiences presented in personal testimonies. These mitigation strategies, used mainly by white people to deny racialized experiences of discrimination, are numerous and may take the form of disbelieving the one who has witnessed or experienced racism, referring to the case as an exception to the norm, and speculating that the claimant has a hidden or desperate agenda, such as seeking media visibility to advance one's career, as seen in the thread below.

**Commenter 1** We don't know what happened until we've ALSO heard what the other party has to say. The R-card[6] [i.e., accusing someone of being racist.] is so easy and tempting to use, particularly if you are a person who likes to be in the spotlight anyways.
Like · Reply · 16 · 22 May at 02:21

(*continued*)

[6] "Playing the race card", an expression used in the thread, refers to social situations in which a non-white person falsely accuses another person of being racist in order to gain per-

(continued)

**Commenter 2** There is no "R-card" here. If this happened, it literally is a textbook definition example of racism. If it didn't happen, then nothing happened, and that would be a different issue. But there is absolutely no "alternative opinion" way to interpret comments like that.
Like · Reply · 29 · 22 May at 09:13

**Commenter 3** Never heard about R-card 😄
Like · Reply · 22 May at 22:34

**Commenter 4** R-card has an incredibly bad bonus plan.
Like · Reply · 10 · 23 May at 14:30

**Commenter 5** So, you are saying that the story is a lie?
Like · Reply · 3 · 23 May at 17:58
[One irrelevant comment in the thread removed.]

**Commenter 1** Indeed, one should always apply rational thinking before being absorbed in the pleasures of a web scandal. In a democratic state, we must also listen to the "accused" person, and we aren't even talking about legal charges here yet. It may be that the "prosecutor" and her loyal fans soon will be charged of defamation. So be patient with the R-card, despite the temptation to use it.
Like · Reply · 2 · 25 May at 00:48
(Public thread on Alexandra Alexis' Facebook-profile 2016, May 25)[7]

sonal advantage. This study shows that on social media, to say that someone has used the race card tends to cause discursive jamming, because it often leads to a situation characterized by short arguments ("yes, she/he did", "no, she/he did not"). Moments of reflection may occur ("maybe she did, maybe she did not" and "well, there is no way to tell"), but when new people join the discussion, the yes-no game resumes.

[7] The post and the thread are public, but for this publication, profile pictures have been removed, names anonymized, and the posts by Commenter 1 have been translated from Finnish to English.

The most common logic in these cases of mitigation from non-official claims-makers is drawing on "well-meaning colorblindness". Commenters may claim that nightclub quarrels occur all the time and that there will always be a few drunken lunatics on the streets and a few rotten eggs in the police force, but that mostly, native Finns are "nice" and that Finland would be a much nicer for everyone if the victim-claimants would not engage in the "public lynching" of their molesters. Interestingly, the lonely lunatic logic and the discourse emphasizing niceness even to racists are used to mitigate racist experiences by commenters who self-identify as non-white and "white natives" alike.

The use of the niceness discourse and well-meaning colorblindness to mitigate racist experiences is not detached from "support talk", which flourishes online and was particularly evident in the Alexis case. Gendered support, therapeutic expression, and an excessive use of icons representing love and strength are sometimes combined with an encouragement to act ("Report them to the police!"), but most often are not. However, the online consolers of the claimant are acting spontaneously and position themselves as consumers. Many commenters wrote that they had visited the website of the nightclub and given the place bad reviews.

Many of the mechanisms through which Alexis's claim against racism was questioned and mitigated came into play in the case of the stop-and-search of James Nikander's mother and sister, as well. However, partially due to the fact that one party in this case is the police, the discourse reached a more general and critical level than in the Alexis case, which circled around the accused racists and their presumed backgrounds and identities. The Nikander case was dealt with extensively in the mainstream media and on online forums, and on the one hand, the debate was more polarized than the Alexis case. On the other hand, it was also more targeted toward relevant social problems, that is, whether the police and other authorities are implementing the law prohibiting ethnic profiling (Aliens Act 301/2004). Nikander has also been more actively involved in anti-racist campaigning than Alexis. Nikander and what he represents (rap and hip-hop culture, an idol for young people, an anti-racist symbol) seemed to provoke those who are "critical of immigration" more than Alexis, who was less well-known to the broader audience.

The "social critic" discourse and claims against ethnic profiling in the Nikander case have not reached anywhere near the intensity that Swedish debates on the REVA project did (Rättsäkerhet och effektivt verkställighetsarbete, "Legal Certainty and Effective Enforcement"). However, in a Finnish context, the debate was fierce, partially triggered by a Facebook update by MP Leena Meri (the Finns), in which she states that "those who are not happy in Finland can just return to their countries of origin" (*Iltalehti*, 12 July 2016a). James Nikander and his sister were born in Finland, and due to the inaccuracy and populist character of the update, the MP was ridiculed in the mainstream media. However, the commentary follows a logic similar to that of the Swedish prime minister on the Husby riots on 21 May 2013 when he talked about "angry young men who need to overcome cultural barriers"—casting young Swedes as strangers (Schierup, Ålund, & Kings, 2014, p. 6). The commentary also follows the same logic as hundreds of comments on the Nikander case in various online forums and highlights a common belief among many Finnish citizens: that the right to be treated respectfully and as a full member of society depends on the tone of your skin.

**Commenter 1** [who according to his profile picture is white and male] I've been asked to prove my identity on the street and I did. They were looking for a suspect. So why is it so weird that they need to examine [people] when they've let in anybody in huge numbers. I think it's perfectly sound that they check people who look like foreigners, that's not racism or discrimination. [...]
Like · Reply · 11 · 10 July at 20:03

**Commenter 2** "who look like foreigners" "that is not racism" okay then
Like · Reply · 6 · 10 July at 20:33
[16 comments marked by inappropriate language and racism removed]

**Commenter 20** You people who whine about racism. Don't you have better things to do than find racism in ordinary events. Find real problems to cry about.
(Public thread on James Nikander's Facebook-profile, 2016, July 10)[8]

---

[8] This thread appears in response to the original post on James Nikander's Facebook profile. The post and the thread are public, but for this publication, profile pictures have been removed, names anonymized, and all quotes have been translated from Finnish to English.

Despite the potential of the "social critic" discourse to influence legislation and policy, the effect on decision-making was low in the case of Nikander's handcuffed mother. A representative of the government's non-discrimination ombudsman got the opportunity to speak up against ethnic profiling (Yle, 2016a, July 11), and there were several television programs discussing ethnic profiling, but little pressure was put on the police despite obvious holes in their arguments, which were built on "mere anti-racist rhetoric".

One difficulty in mediated and public pressuring of the police (and other authorities) is their right or duty to not comment on individual cases under investigation. In using this right or duty as a shield and avoiding commenting on racist events in concrete terms, spokesmen for the police and other authorities easily shift from discussing the issue on a general level to instead addressing it only vaguely. Besides, as Sigurd Allern and Ester Pollack (2014) argue in their analysis of public debate in Norway on a police action in which a student of African origin lost his life, news coverage on the police and investigations into police conduct are event-driven. In the case of Finland, the news coverage on police operations also appears to be non-critical when issues of racialization and migration are concerned. When trying to produce viable excuses for why innocent bystanders of color sometimes suffer for the sake of security, the police is allowed, without challenge by journalists, to form an argument that police budget cuts somehow explain accidental ethnic profiling, as seen in the quotation from a news article below. As shown by previous studies, the police tend to point out how few resources the Finnish Police have in comparison to other European countries when trying to legitimize dubious actions of its officers (Haavisto, 2011, p. 96).

> *Three years ago, the European Commission against Racism and Intolerance determined that the Finnish Aliens Act allows ethnic profiling. [National Police Commissioner] Kolehmainen does not want to speculate how frequent this kind of conduct is in Finland. The police commissioner says that it is illegal and it isn't done.*
>
> *KOLEHMAINEN also commented on the threat of terrorism in Finland.*
>
> *"We shouldn't allow ourselves to become hysterical. Instead, we must keep our feet on the ground and stay calm. At the same time, we must understand that [terrorism] can happen here as well. The likelihood of Finland being the target for a terror attack is not significant, but it is possible. So we have to stay alert in these matters".*
>
> *According to Kolehmainen, the Police struggles with limited resources. Although the capacity to act is high at the moment, adequate preparedness can not be ensured for long-term operations taking place in multiple locations.* (*Helsingin Sanomat*, 12 July 2016b, free translation, caps in the original)

The claims against racism put forward by James Nikander in his original post and later in journalistic interviews were listened to much more attentively than the claims put forward by Alexis. In Helsinki, there is no systematic follow up of how bars and nightclubs treat ethnic minorities, as there is in Oslo, for example,[9] so one possibility for action-oriented claims-making could have been the need for policy change. However, no such discourses took place. In other words, although Alexis's testimony was visible in the media, no spaces opened up for discourses that could lead to policy change in particular or collective action or intervention in general (other than giving bad ratings to the establishment online). When there are several hundred NGO-driven projects actively working against racism in Finland, it is noteworthy that not one organization saw a window of opportunity here. In contrast, in the Nikander case, socially relevant aspects came up and space was created for public administrators to come together in and through the media to discuss whether the recently added amendment on ethnic profiling was being implemented or not. However, as time passed and the legal aspects of the arrest became more complicated (see the anatomy of the event in the Appendix), the supporters of Nikander's claim went silent.[10] Despite growing criticism, particularly on anti-immigration forums, Nikander continued to support the viewpoint of his family members in the mainstream media (e.g., in the talk show *Enbuske, Veitola & Salminen*, 9 September 2016), hence keeping the spotlight on the recent amendment to the Aliens Act and thereby indirectly contributing to the pressure on authorities to comply with the amendment in their daily operations.

## TWO CRITICAL EVENTS: OPENING UP SPACES FOR STREET POLITICS BUT RESTRICTING THE RIGHT TO WITNESS

The anti-racist claims circulating in the hybrid media environment in the Malmö region during spring 2014 were formed during a "red alert" month marked by crises, high alertness, and even severe post-traumatic

[9] This is an initiative of Gunnhild Haugen and overseen by the Norwegian authority Næringsetaten. Three warnings to a bar or nightclub result in the temporary suspension of the establishment's liquor license, which effectively means it must shut down until further notice (LDO, 2011). Haugen was interviewed in English by the magazine *Vice* on 18 February 2016.

[10] According to Yle (2017, 1 September), Nikander's mother was finally prosecuted for resisting an officer and his sister for insubordination.

stress, as interviews with the two main anti-racist claims-making activists indicate. On the night of 8 March 2014, after a peaceful feminist demonstration, Showan Shattak, an anti-racist activist and football supporter, was stabbed by a Nazi near Möllevångstorget, a popular square in Malmö.[11] Besides the severely injured Shattak, a handful of other people, both Nazis and people with connections to leftist or feminist groups, were also injured. As a protest to the nightly neo-Nazi presence in an urban space with a multicultural identity and working-class past, and as a protest against the violence of 8 March, two anti-fascist demonstrations were organized on 9 and 16 March 2014. According to estimates, the second demonstration gathered around 10,000 people (Kämpa Malmö, 2014; *Sydsvenskan*, 2014, 16 March). While Shattak himself was in a coma and fighting for his life, demonstrations against Nazi organizing and violence were organized in several cities in Sweden, as well as at the Narinkkatori square in Helsinki on 15 March 2014.

While Sweden seems recently to have returned to 1990s' levels of far-right racist violence when a trade unionist was assassinated, refugee centres were firebombed and many people of migrant origin were murdered (Fekete, 2014, p. 1) including several life-threating attacks since 2013, in Finland, the attack on Jimi Karttunen in September 2016 was the first fatal Nazi assault since WWII (Andersson, Brunila, & Koivulaakso, 2013 and YLE, 2015, 13 September, for far-right organizing in Finland in general. Karttunen was walking past a group of demonstrating Nazis in the middle of the day at the Helsinki Railway Square, possibly insulting the neo-Nazis verbally and spitting on the ground whereafter he was assaulted by Jesse Torniainen, an active member of SVL, the Finnish Resistance Movement, with a remarkable criminal record (Turun Sanomat, 20 September 2016) (In 2016 the organisation changed its name to PVL, the Nordic Resistance Movement). Immediately after the attack (a jump kick making the victim hit his head on the ground), SVL activists bragged about the assault on Twitter and in YouTube videos, as shown by the anti-racist collective Varisverkosto on their webpage. A week later, Karttunen died of head injuries but the court said it was unable to determine whether

---

[11] Prosecutors initially requested that the suspects be charged with attempted murder but, instead, the court of appeal convicted a 31-year-old neo-Nazi for aggravated assault to three years in prison and awarded approximately 40,000 euros in compensation to Shattak. The court of appeal changed the verdict of the district court in October 2016, by setting free Andreas Karlsson,a well-known neo-Nazi,who had been sentenced to three years in prison. The Supreme Court decided not to take up the case (Sydsvenskan, 4 October 2017).

his death was a direct result of the assault.[12] The connection of Karttunen's death to the Nazi demonstration was initially revealed by his father through a Facebook post on 17 September 2016. The event was reported widely in the days that followed in both Finnish and international media. A demonstration was organized on 19 September, followed by another mass demonstration on 24 September 2016, with about 15,000 participants, which, in a Finnish context, is a remarkable number of people coming together for a joint cause.

The two tragic events have certain features in common, but also contextual differences. While Shattak was already a public figure, known locally as a football supporter and anti-racist activist, Karttunen's name was unknown to the public before the Nazi assault. As noted earlier, the debate in Sweden around far-right organizing and, in particular, the claimed failure of the police to take the organizing seriously has been fiercer than in Finland. Therefore, in Sweden, the debate on the Shattak case formed a continuation of the ongoing public debates on media bias, the government's standpoint on extremism, police passivity and culpability in discrimination and neglecting to investigate racist violence, projects and events such as REVA, the racist events in Kärrtorp in 2013, and the unauthorized Roma register maintained by the police. The debate involved established collective actors, such as the Researchgruppen network of freelance journalists, activists, journalists, and political elites with various standpoints on violence, democracy, and anti-racism. The debate took place in a variety of forums, such as the mainstream media, social media (e.g., under Twitter hashtags), public space (stickers, posters, graffiti), and in face-to-face discussions between politicians, journalists, scholars, and activists (e.g., a debate organized at the cultural center Inkonst on 13 March 2014[13]) (Fig. 10.2).

In Finland, the debate around the Karttunen case involved fewer claims-makers and the discourses were not as multidimensional and sprawling as in Sweden. Instead, they mainly centered around two questions: whether political extremism is on the rise and whether there is need to criminalize

---

[12] The legal aspects of the case are still unsolved since the case has been taken to the Supreme Court. Prosecutors had initially requested that Torniainen be charged with aggravated involuntary manslaughter and to receive a 5.5 to six year prison term but the district court convicted Torniainen on a lesser charge of aggravated assault, but sharpened his sentence saying that the assault was racially motivated and handed him a two-year prison sentence (YLE, 2018, March 28). The victim, Karttunen, left the hospital earlier than recommended by the medical personnel and he used medication classified as drugs in Finland, which complicates the case.

[13] The event was titled "Bilden av. politisk extremism" ("Picturing Political Extremism"), and the invited debaters were Diana Mulinari, Heidi Avellan, Behrang Kianzad, Agneta Nordin, and Petter Larsson. The auditorium was filled to capacity.

**Fig. 10.2** "Kämpa Malmö—Antifascism är självförsvar" ("Stay strong, Malmö—Antifascism is self-defense"), the main slogan of the anti-racist rally in Malmö on 16 March 2014, evolved from the earlier slogan "Kämpa Showan" ("Stay strong, Showan")

certain organizations representing far-right ideologies. The latter question divided the main claims-makers across political lines. A citizens' initiative promoting a legislative amendment restricting the assembly of racist groups was initiated within days,[14] but some claimants also expressed concern for how hastily introduced legislative changes may not be what society needs in a post-crisis situation.

> *It's not only the laws or the politicians who make them that are the problem, but rather the common air that we breathe. Today, if not earlier, it has become very stuffy and thin. Let us say it in a loud voice: the Europe marked by peaceful societies is dead, there is no neutral ground to stand on, no auditorium for the neutral observer, no option to safely observe political events without forming an opinion on them. In order to break the silence, new laws or police*

[14] The initiative has been named Huominen ilman pelkoa—järjestäytynyt rasismi rikoslakiin 2016 (A future without fear—add organized racism to the criminal law 2016).

*intervention alone are not enough. Instead we all have to act together—to call the game off—not just today, but every day.* (Section of activist Mikael Brunila's speech that circulated widely on anti-racist Facebook groups in the days after the *Peli poikki* (Enough is enough) demonstration in Helsinki on 24 September 2016.)

The debate in the mainstream media first focused on providing a clearer picture of the Helsinki attack. The main claims-makers at this stage were representatives of the police, who without much pushback from journalists were allowed to make valid-sounding excuses for why they had not supervised the neo-Nazi demonstration despite the fact that a picture depicting a police car nearby at the precise time of the event was circulated widely (Yle, 2016b, September 16). Soon after, in the second stage of reporting, politicians from various parties appeared in the mainstream media (*Helsingin Sanomat*, 2016c, September 18). They also commented on the events through their own Facebook and Twitter accounts. Generally speaking, violence was condemned in their comments, but a discourse on extremism flourished in which activities by the far right and far left were lumped together. Politicians of the Finns party made some provocative claims about the government's migration policy and the assault, but when pressured by journalists to elaborate on the causality between the two issues, one of the MPs, Ritva Elomaa, was unable to explain herself (*Iltalehti*, 2016b, September 19).

While journalistic effort was put into ridiculing comments such as Elomaa's, a comment by MEP Jussi Halla-aho (the Finns) was allowed to stand without much scrutiny. Halla-aho downplayed the significance of the tragic event and told YLE that "The event is used in order to shift attention away from the security threat posed by asylum seekers and immigrants /.../" (Yle, 2016c, September 22). As journalist Jens Finnäs has shown in a non-scholarly but convincing explorative data graphic (*Dataist*, 2011), Halla-aho is a significant thought leader within the anti-immigrant blogosphere (also see Horsti, 2015; Keskinen, 2013; Pyrhönen, 2015). Therefore, it comes as no surprise that in the aftermath of the event, Halla-aho's view on the case and his unwillingness to condemn brutal violence from the far right is echoed in various forums frequented by supporters of the Finns party, among others.[15]

[15] It is difficult, if not impossible, to study Google's algorithms, but even six months after the tragic event, the top ten sites suggested by a Google search on "Jimi Karttunen" link to far-right webpages and unreliable "news media" in which various versions of Halla-aho's reasoning, given above, are put forward. Strikingly, when the name of the prime minister, "Juha Sipilä", and the name of the main Finnish newspaper, *Helsingin Sanomat*, are added to the Google search field, seven out of ten hits still lead to far-right sites such as Vastarinta.com.

At the third stage of reporting, more analytical views on the events were presented. On the one hand, they often concerned growing political extremism in general and related the present to historical events that took place in Finland in the 1920s and 1930s. On the other hand, particularly in the aftermath of the demonstrations on 19 and 24 September, activists and representatives of human rights NGOs were also allowed to make claims (*Helsingin Sanomat*, 2016d, September 24). The main claim of the activists at this time was aimed at getting the political elite, particularly Prime Minister Juha Sipilä, to more actively and clearly take a stance against hate crimes in general and racist violence in particular. A fiercer pressuring of decision-makers to take a stance against racism occurred on Twitter, and politicians were encouraged to at least use the word *racism* instead of euphemisms when talking about the event (e.g., Honkasalo, 2016) (Fig. 10.3).

These activist claims put forward by anti-racist activists in Helsinki in autumn 2016 echo the ones put forward in the case of the attack on Shattak in Malmö in spring 2014. Within an "Elites, you are not doing enough" master paradigm, the criticism of anti-racists targeted the police,

**Fig. 10.3**  The *Peli poikki* demonstration in Helsinki on 24 September 2016. The speaker's podium was under the red canopy on the left, where an entire symphony orchestra also squeezed in to play the Finlandia hymn. The choice of hymn and the use of the Finnish flag indicate an attempt to "take back" nationalistic symbols from the far right and to ascribe to them different meanings

the governing parties, and the media. Claims critical of the media were presented in the form of letters to the editor, Facebook updates, comments on the Facebook pages of various media, and phone calls and e-mails to journalists demanding the correction of "biased" media representations that did not clearly state whether it was anti-fascists and feminists or Nazis that started the violence on Möllevångstorget (interviews with Journalist 1 and Journalist 2).

In interviews, Activists 1 and 2 claim that the media in southern Sweden has neglected their claims for years and that their right to "witness" racist violence has been restricted. The activists claim that the reasons for their restricted right to witness are the divergence of the political views of most mainstream journalists and anti-racist activists and the unwillingness of allegedly white middle-class journalists to accept that Sweden, despite its self-image as an anti-racist haven, has serious social and political problems. In addition, journalists are afraid for their well-being and their lives and are afraid of "pissing off right-wing people by telling the truth" (Activist 1). The journalists, on the other hand, argue that the claims of radical anti-racists are listened to and taken seriously in the newsrooms. Journalists say that the reason the concrete claims of anti-racists are not always voiced in the media is because it is increasingly difficult to get in touch with activists and to persuade them to give interviews.

> *This is my personal interpretation: As journalists we do not accept their truth right away. That makes the anti-racist activists so furious that they refuse to continue cooperating with us.* (Journalist 1)

The problematic relationship between journalists and anti-racist activists in the Malmö area that has led to a power struggle over voice, withdrawn voice, visibility, and listening strategies must not be seen as a temporary or isolated issue. First, the actions of the mainstream media, which anti-racist actors see as a crucial part of the establishment, had been previously criticized by activists after similar events elsewhere (e.g., after the reporting on the events in Kärrtorp). Second, the tone of journalistic writing, such as the use of the word *squabble* instead of *attack*, was as a major provocation to activists.

> *So, if you look at our media strategy, it's not about getting as much visibility as possible. Instead, it's about getting through with issues that we believe in. So of course our slogan is controversial, because the media gives the interpretative prerogative to right-of-center Liberals [borgerliga liberaler], and this is why it*

*is controversial to point at conflicts in society that make antifascism self-defense .... In one of our first meetings we said that we want a slogan that we can stand behind, not something like "this is a day against stupid people" but something political—what we believe in—and we want to push that forward. Then if a more liberal or mainstream Social Democrat says that she or he can't march behind that slogan then we just say, "okay, that's bad but maybe you just have to organize your own demonstration then, because this is ours". Then it's in the media's interest to make it appear as something more than a non-political bal-lyhoo .... Either they want to make it into a non-political ballyhoo or then they want to make it into an event where masked activists ruined the demonstra-tion. There was not one daily that re-printed our slogan ["Antifascism is self-defense"] ... I think this kind of thing [i.e., that ten thousand people marched behind that slogan] just doesn't fit into their conceptual world ... For them, anti-racism is humanism, non-violence and stuff like that, you know.* (Activist 2 representing Skåne mot rasism)

## CONCLUDING REMARKS: CRITICAL EVENTS BECOME THE NEW LOCI OF MOVEMENTS—BUT ONLY FOR A WHILE

In recent years, a number of campaigns against racism have emerged online and on the streets in the Nordic countries in support of victims of racist abuse and to demand that the political elite not disregard racism in nightclubs and ethnic profiling in their own operations and address the intensified neo-Nazi organizing taking place across national borders. The four mediated debates analyzed in this chapter illustrate how various dis-cursive power struggles are played out in a number of mediated arenas—online, offline, and in between. These power struggles are related to the ideological and demographic changes taking place in the Nordic coun-tries; they are debates on how to govern societies undergoing these changes. They are also related to the role of cultural capital in the forma-tion of voice: not everyone has the qualifications required to put forward testimonies of racism and racialization in the media sphere and to be heard through all the noise that marks it.

In this chapter, I have shown how moments of intensified anti-racist claims-making sometimes lead to the transformation of a personal tragedy into a public issue and other times do not. The nightclub quarrel with rac-ist overtones remained on a personal level and did not transform into a public issue, while the three other cases, to varying degrees, were more easily dealt with as political issues highlighting contemporary social prob-lems. The legal twists in the case of alleged ethnic profiling in Helsinki and journalists' disinterest in looking into similar cases, which may have helped make a stronger case to present to politicians and the police, contributed to the story's slow retreat from the spotlights.

On the other hand, the two cases involving severe neo-Nazi violence prompted the emergence of social movements that mobilized through social media. Thanks in part to these movements and the mass·demonstrations they managed to put together in a short time, two potentially critical events emerged—with both events reported on both within and beyond national borders.[16] Due to ongoing legal processes, published books (Rasmussen & Shattak, 2016) and other cultural productions (e.g., a play based on the Shattak case, which was planned but later canceled according to *Sydsvenskan* 2016, October 20) and due to the fact that the two resultant anti-racist movements continue to construct and distribute claims against racism, the visible role of these two events within the anti-racist civic field has remained intact. It is worth underlining that these two new players in the area of anti-racism strengthened their roles after having organized mass protests. It is an important political and symbolic signal to the far right, the political elite, and the media alike that demonstrations against racism attract large numbers of people—and not just anarchist youths, but also families and center-liberal citizens who are utterly tired of neo-Nazi presence and symbols in their own neighborhoods.

There was more than one factor that made these events potentially critical. The mainstream media showed great interest in the cases, the cases were returned to in mediated debates when associated issues were reported on months and even years later, and after initial silence and activist pressure, elite politicians in both countries publicly condemned the violence and said that they would examine whether there is need for policy change.

However, the true potential of these two critical events to influence policy is more ambiguous due to the fact that during the process of becoming critical events, listening processes were marked by truth contestations and restrictions of the right to witness and testify. This was also the case with the two more everyday cases of racist abuse.

As such, it is not a surprise that not all critical events that become new loci of discourse effect a change in policy, practice, or structure. Consider such examples as police brutality against Blacks in the USA, the Dakota Access Pipeline protest, or previous series of ruthless racist crimes in the Nordic

---

[16] For example, Al Jazeera 2016, September 24.

countries. Nick Couldry (2010, p. 101) has even argued that this is a common problem of contemporary neo-liberalism: we are offered a proliferation of opportunities to speak up about important issues both as individuals and as part of claims-making collectives, but all too often this voice does not matter or does not have an influence on policy and power hierarchies.

In my view, the low to moderate odds of critical events maintaining their "criticalness" over time and their alleged powerlessness to actually change policy underline the political nature of the act of listening. Listening is an active choice (Abu Hamdan, 2015), and the act of listening should come about as an open process despite potential underlying conflicts or suspicion (Dreher, 2009). Hence, listening should not be a simple act of hearing—an act on the basis of which decision-makers can form responses intended merely to mitigate potential political scandals or placate large crowds who they believe are inclined to violence.[17] Besides, it is not only the loud claims-making of high-alert periods that politicians must listen and react to, but also claims that are made when the collective feeling of urgency has faded. It is during the calm periods that NGOs, autonomous groups, and networks should remind decision-makers of their claims, and it is during these periods, when there is no immediate need to respond for the mere sake of responding, that political elites should really engage in listening practices. They may soon notice that the deepest expertise in questions of Nazism, racism, race, and racialization lies somewhere other than on the office desks of their public servants. In Finland, this became all too clear when, in response to the Karttunen case, the political elite said that they will "investigate" the need for more state intervention against neo-Nazi organizing.[18] Only a few months later, on 6 December, Independence Day, neo-Nazis marched in central Helsinki while simultaneously bragging on social media that the alleged killer, temporarily freed from custody, was marching along. This case demonstrates that although critical events such as public racism scandals produce spaces for new voices, when it comes to making elites accountable for double standards in policy

[17] I am here referring, in particular, to the Twitter storm "Where is Reinfeldt", protesting against the Swedish prime minister's initial silence on the Nazi violence in Malmö (Fekete, 2014, p. 5).

[18] One policy change was implemented in the aftermath of the event, but the change does not relate to the organizing of right-wing organizations but rather to the procedures of the Government Situation Centre that produces real-time reports and situation pictures to the PM. PM Sipilä was abroad during the assault and got the information only on the following day, which woke concern about slowness in the crisis information system (HE 261/2016 vp, ESS, 24 September 2016).

and governance, critical journalism and civic engagement groups have failed. The reasons to this failure are not weak media and lobbying tactics but rather an ideological climate that neither acknowledges nor encourages political listening in general and the listening to vulnerable social groups with experiences of racism in particular.

## Appendix

### *A Manually Assembled Description of the Becoming Viral of the Original Post by Alexandra Alexis*

Alexandra Alexis posts the original post in the evening of 20 May 2016, https://www.facebook.com/alexandraalexis/posts/10154240514753724, right after discussion starts on the RASMUS pages which is lively group maintained by a national network against racism, https://www.facebook.com/groups/114311111913455/permalink/1158480620829827/, soon after the nightlife establishment publishes their view on what had happened (https://www.facebook.com/ravintolateatteri/posts/483684211824677) where after the main newspaper *Helsingin Sanomat* reports on the case (http://www.hs.fi/kaupunki/art-2000002902329.html). In the interview conducted by *Helsingin Sanomat*, the representative of the nightlife establishment manages to turn the attention to the choice Alexandra Alexis has made in publishing a camera picture of her abusers, which come to influence the tone of the debate thereafter. The *Metro* newspaper publishes a story on the event, http://www.metro.fi/uutiset/a1387817846478, another thread starts in the RASMUS group, and the tone of the discussion is more condemning of Alexandra Alexis than the previous one. One day later, on 21 May, discussion escalates on the major forum for so-called immigrant critics and supporters of the Finns party, the HOMMA-forum, and on the discussion forum for *MV-lehti* where commentators follow attentively the discussion on the RASMUS page on Facebook. On the same day, both Alexandra Alexis and the nightlife establishment post new posts on their own platforms. *Iltalehti*, another major paper publishes an article on the scandal (http://www.iltalehti.fi/uutiset/2016052121599602_uu.shtml) which makes the tone of the debate on *MV-lehti* even worse. Alexis and her fans are accused for forming a lynch mob against the accused racist abusers whose identity stays more or less dissolved throughout the entire scandal. Two days later on 23 May, Koko

Hubara, one of the most influential racialized bloggers in Finland, writes a more reflexive blog on the case (http://www.lily.fi/blogit/ruskeat-tytot/case-teatterista-mista-myos-kyse).

### *A Manually Assembled Description of the Becoming Viral of the Original Post by James Nikander*

On 10 July 2016, James Nikander publishes the original post on his Facebook page, https://www.facebook.com/mustabarbaariofficial/posts/700302376788030; *Iltalehti* makes two news articles of the case the same night, http://m.iltalehti.fi/uutiset/2016071021882940_uu.shtml, http://m.iltalehti.fi/uutiset/2016071021883605_uu.shtml; on the following day, the YLE writes two stories on the case with one update, which is a separate story, http://yle.fi/uutiset/3-9017554, http://yle.fi/uutiset/3-9018028; *Aamulehti* writes a story, http://www.aamulehti.fi/kotimaa/nain-poliisi-kommentoi-mustan-barbaarin-aidin-ja-siskon-tapausta-23780774/; and *A-studio* deals with the case on 11 July 2016. Simultaneously, at the main immigrant-critical forums, HOMMA and *MV-lehti*, Nikander is accused for being biased, for lying, and for only seeking publicity to boost his career. The span of the James Nikander event is much longer than the Alexandra Alexis event, which partially is due to an extensive portrait article done by the monthly supplement to *Helsingin Sanomat, Kuukausiliite*, in http://www.hs.fi/kuukausiliite/art-2000002914036.html about a month later. The public prosecutor announces in September that they will not raise charges against the Police officers accused by Nikander and his family to have adapted ethnic profiling when handcuffing Nikander's mother. James Nikander appears on a live television show giving support to his family members' version of the story, http://www.mtv.fi/uutiset/kotimaa/artikkeli/musta-barbaari-pysyn-aitini-ja-siskoni-kertomuksen-takana-totuuden-on-tultava-esiin/6066970. After the data collection period, in December 2016, the prosecutor announces that Nikander's mother and sister will be pressed charges for assaulting a public servant trying to do his job. The Finnish news agency takes up the new twist in the story, which spreads to a variety of mainstream news media, for example, http://yle.fi/uutiset/3-9328457, http://www.mtv.fi/uutiset/rikos/artikkeli/mustan-barbaarin-perheeseen-liittyvasta-jupakasta-syyteharkinta/6194574?mtv_ref=twb_uutiset_uusimmat, and also the main so-called immigrant-critical platforms. There was a third twist to the mediated event when, after one and a half years, in August 2017, Nikander's sister and mother were charged for resistance to cooperate with law enforcement officials and insubordination against the police. The police were cleared of all wrongdoings in the case. (www.migranttales.net/must-barbaaris-mother-sister-charged-police-ethnic-profiling-case/).

## References

Abu Hamdan, L. (2015, April 24). The Politics of Listening [Video file]. *Continent, (4)4*, 2015, pp. 28–29. Keynote presentation held at conference What Now? 2015: The Politics of Listening at the New School in New York City. Retrieved from https://vimeo.com/129018344

Ahmed, S. (2014). *The Cultural Politics of Emotions.* New York: Routledge.

Al Jazeera (2016, September 24). *Finland: Tens of Thousands March in Anti-Racism Rallies* [News Article]. Retrieved from http://www.aljazeera.com/news/2016/09/finland-tens-thousands-march-anti-racism-rallies-160924132128863.html

Alemanji, A. A., & Mafi, B. (2016). Antiracism Education? A Study of an Antiracism Workshop in Finland. *Scandinavian Journal of Educational Research, 62*(2), 186–199.

Alexander, J. C., Butler Breese, E., & Luengo, M. (Eds.). (2016). *The Crisis of Journalism Reconsidered: Democratic Culture, Professional Codes, Digital Future.* Cambridge: Cambridge University Press.

Alexis, A. (2017, May 19). *[Facebook Status Update].* Retrieved from https://www.facebook.com/alexandraalexis?fref=nf

Aliens Act 301/2004, §129 a and 129 b, Amendment 193/2015.

Allern, S., & Pollack, E. (2014). Criticism of the Police in the News: Discourses and Frames in the News Media's Coverage of the Norwegian Bureau for the Investigation of Police Affairs. *Nordicom Review, 35*(1), 33–50.

Andersson, L., Brunila, M., & Koivulaakso, D. (2013). *Äärioikeisto Suomessa – Vastarintamiehiä ja metapolitiikkaa.* Helsinki: Into.

Bassel, L. (2017). *The Politics of Listening: Possibilities and Challenges for Democratic Life.* London: Palgrave Macmillan.

Bickford, S. (1996). *The Dissonance of Democracy. Listening, Conflict and Citizenship.* Ithaca: Cornell University Press.

Brink Pinto, A., & Pries, J. (2013). *Trettionde November: kampen om Lund 1985–2008.* Lund: Pluribus kf.

Brink Pinto, A., & Pries, J. (2017). Rethinking Transformative Events to Understand the Making of New Contentious Performances: The "Autonomous Left" and the Anti-Fascist Blockade in Lund 1991. In M. Wennerhag, C. Fröhlich, & G. Piotrowski (Eds.), *Radical Left Movements in Europe* (pp. 156–172). London: Routledge.

Chadwick, A. (2013). *The Hybrid Media System: Politics and Power.* London: Oxford University Press.

Couldry, N. (2010). *Why Voice Matters: Culture and Politics After Neoliberalism.* London: Sage.

Das, V. (1995). *Critical Events: An Anthropological Perspective on Contemporary India.* New Delhi: Oxford University Press.

Dataist. (2011, July 31). *The Finnish 'Immigration Critics' Blog Network* [Blog Text]. Retrieved from https://dataist.wordpress.com/2011/07/31/the-finnish-immigration-critics-blog-network/

Dikeç, M. (2007). *Badlands of the Republic, Space, Politics and Urban Policy.* Oxford: Blackwell.

Dreher, T. (2009). Listening across Difference: Media and Multiculturalism Beyond the Politics of Voice. *Continuum, 23*(4), 445–458.

DuBois, A. (2003). Introduction. In F. Lentricchia & A. DuBois (Eds.), *Close Reading: The Reader* (pp. 1–40). Durham, NC: Duke University Press.

*Enbuske, Veitola & Salminen.* (2016, September 9). [Audiovisual File]. Retrieved from https://www.mtv.fi/uutiset/kotimaa/artikkeli/musta-barbaari-pysyn-aitini-ja-siskoni-kertomuksen-takana-totuuden-on-tultava-esiin/6066970#gs.t5EaG2U

Espeland, C., & Rogstad, J. (2013). Antiracism and Social Movements in Norway. The Importance of Critical Events. *Journal of Ethnic and Migration Studies, 39*(1), 125–142.

ESS. (2016, September 24). *Pääministeri Sipilä: Tilannekeskuksen ohjeistusta muutettiin äärijärjestöistä nousseen kohun takia.* Retrieved from http://www.ess.fi/uutiset/kotimaa/art2304786

Fekete, L. (2014). Sweden's Counter-Extremism Model and the Stigmatisation of Anti-Racism. *Briefing no. 9*, September 2014. Retrieved from http://www.irr.org.uk/wp-content/uploads/2014/09/ERP-Briefing-No-9-Sweden.pdf

Fischer, B. (2014). On the Notion and Politics of Listening. In B. Fischer (Ed.), *[Hlysnan] The Notion and Politics of Listening* (pp. 9–19). Luxembourg: Casino Luxembourg – Forum d'art contemporain asbl.

Haavisto, C. (2011). *Conditionally One of 'Us': A Study of Media, Minorities, and Positioning Practices*, Skrifter 30, Swedish School of Social Sciences, University of Helsinki.

HE 261/2016 vp. (2016). *Hallituksen esitys eduskunnalle laiksi valtioneuvoston tilannekeskuksesta.* Retrieved from https://www.eduskunta.fi/FI/vaski/KasittelytiedotValtiopaivaasia/Sivut/HE_261+2016.aspx

Helsingin Sanomat. (2016a, May 20). *"He kutsuivat meitä halvoiksi ja murjaaneiksi" – tarina tappelusta Ravintola Teatterissa leviää Facebookissa* [Newspaper Article]. Retrieved from http://www.hs.fi/kaupunki/art-2000002902329.html

Helsingin Sanomat. (2016b, July 12). *Poliisiylijohtaja Seppo kolehmainen: 'Väärä etninen profilointi on ehdottomasti kielletty'* [Newspaper Article]. Retrieved from http://www.hs.fi/kotimaa/art-2000002910569.html

Helsingin Sanomat. (2016c, September 18). *Sisäministeri Risikko Asema-aukion pahoinpitelystä: Äärijärjestöjen toiminnan laillisuus arvioidaan uudelleen* [Newspaper Article]. Retrieved from http://www.hs.fi/kotimaa/art-2000002921415.html

Helsingin Sanomat. (2016d, September 24). *Rasisminvastaiseen mielenosoitukseen tuli 15 000 ihmistä, vastamielenosoituksiin joitain kymmeniä – HSTV tallensi tunnelmia* [Newspaper Article]. Retrieved from http://www.hs.fi/kaupunki/art-2000002922384.html

Hiekkavuo, A. (2017). Population with foreign background in Helsinki 2016. Statistics 2017:2, City of Helsinki, Urban Facts. Retrieved from https://www.hel.fi/hel2/tietokeskus/julkaisut/pdf/17_01_16_Tilastoja_2_Hiekkavuo.pdf

Honkasalo, V. (2016, September 24). *Miksi sanaa rasismi on niin vaikea sanoa?* [Twitter]. Retrieved from https://twitter.com/veronikahonka/status/779737058734706693

Horsti, K. (2015). Techno-Cultural Opportunities: Anti-Immigration Movement in the Finnish Media Environment. *Patterns of Prejudice, 49*(4), 343–366.

Huominen ilman pelkoa. (2016). *A Campaign Site for the Citizens' Initiative to Make the Criminal Law Harsher Against Racist Organising, Assembly and Racist Abuse.* Retrieved from http://www.rasismirikoslakiin.fi/

Iltalehti. (2016a, July 12). *Kansanedustaja selittää kohukomenttiaan Musta Barbaarin perheen tapauksesta: 'Vitsailua'.* Retrieved from http://www.iltalehti.fi/uutiset/2016071221895215_uu.shtml

Iltalehti. (2016b, September 9). *Kike Elomaa hyssyttelylausunnostaan: "Ei pidä lukea kuin piru raamattua"* [Newspaper Article]. Retrieved from http://www.iltalehti.fi/uutiset/2016091922339967_uu.shtml

Isaksson, P. (1996). Kun koko kyläkunta piiloutui: Saamelaiset Yrjö Kajavan antropologisessa ohjelmassa. In J. Jokisalo (Ed.), *Rasismi tieteessä ja politiikassa – aate – ja oppihistoriallisia esseitä.* Helsinki: Oy Edita.

Isaksson, P., & Jokisalo, J. (1998). *Kallonmittaajia ja Skinejä; Rasismin aatehistoria.* Helsinki: Like.

Jämte, J. (2013). *Antirasismens många ansikten.* PhD thesis, Statsvetenskapliga institutionen, Umeå Universitet. Retrieved from http://www.diva-portal.org/smash/get/diva2:660975/FULLTEXT02.pdf

Kääriäinen, J., & Niemi, J. (2014). Distrust of the Police in a Nordic Welfare State: Victimization, Discrimination, and Trust in the Police by Russian and Somali Minorities in Helsinki. *Journal of Ethnicity in Criminal Justice, 12*(1), 4–24.

Kämpa Malmö – antifascism är självförsvar. (2014, September). *Vilken Mäktig dag!* [Facebook Post]. Retrieved from https://www.facebook.com/events/250586945123741/?active_tab=discussion

Kemiläinen, A. (1993). *Suomalaiset, outo pohjolan kansa. Rotuteoriat ja kansallinen identiteetti.* Historiallisia Tutkimuksia 177, SHS, Helsinki.

Keskinen, S. (2013). Antifeminism and White Identity Politics: Political Antagonisms in Radical Right-Wing Populist and Anti-Immigration Rhetoric in Finland. *Nordic Journal of Migration Research, 3*(4), 225–232.

Keskinen, S. (2018). The Stopped – Ethnic Profiling in Finland. 1/2018 SSKH Notat, Swedish School of Social Science, University of Helsinki.

Koopmans, R., & Rucht, D. (2002). Protest Event Analysis. In B. Klandermans & S. Staggenborg (Eds.), *Methods of Social Movement Research* (pp. 231–259). Minneapolis, MN: University of Minnesota Press.

Koopmans, R., et al. (2005). *Contested Citizenship: Immigration and Cultural Diversity in Europe*. Minneapolis, MN: University of Minnesota Press.

Korkiasaari, J., & Söderling, I. (2003). *Finnish Emigration and Immigration after World War II Turku*. Finland: Siirtolaisuusinstituutti. Retrieved from http://www.migrationinstitute.fi/files/pdf/artikkelit/finnish_emigration_and_immigration_after_world_war_ii.pdf

Kuukkanen, M. (2017). Diffusion of Radical Repertoires Across Europe. The Arrival of Insurrectionary Anarchism to Finland. In M. Wennerhag, C. Fröhlich, & G. Piotrowski (Eds.), *Radical Left Movements in Europe* (pp. 193–210). London: Routledge.

LDO. (2011). *Sammen mot utelivsdiskriminering*. Broshyr by Likestillings- og diskrimineringsombudet.

Lentin, A. (2004). *Racism and Anti-Racism in Europe*. London: Pluto Press.

Lindgren, S. (2017). *Digital Media and Society*. London: Sage.

Luhtakallio, E. (2012). *Practicing Democracy. Local Activism and Politics in France and Finland*. Basingstoke: Palgrave Macmillan.

Maasilta, M., & Haavisto, C. (2014). Listening to Distant Sufferers: The Kony 2012 Campaign in Uganda and the International Media. *Forum for Development Studies, 41*(3), 455–476.

Malmsten, J. (2009). Antirasism med symboliska inslag – tecken i tiden? *Norsk tidsskrift for migrasjonsforskning, 10*(2), 25–43 Retrieved from http://tapir.pdc.no/pdf/NTMF/2009/2009-02-3.pdf

Metsämäki, M., & Nisula, P. (2006). *Aktivistit: Suomalaisten kansalaisliikkeiden tarina*. Helsinki: Kleio.

Migri. (2017). *Statistics, Applications 2015*. Retrieved from http://statistics.migri.fi/#applications?start=540&end=551

MTV. (2017, December 30). *Syyttäjä vie Helsingin Asema-aukion pahoinpitelyjutun hoviin* [News Article]. Retrieved from https://www.mtv.fi/uutiset/rikos/artikkeli/syyttaja-vie-helsingin-asema-aukion-pahoinpitelyjutun-hoviin/6246044#gs.Te=a424

Nikander, J. (2016, July 10). *[Facebook Status Update]*. Retrieved from https://www.facebook.com/mustabarbaariofficial/posts/700302376788030

Nordberg, C. (2007). *Boundaries of Citizenship: The Case of the Roma and the Finnish Nation-State*. PhD thesis, SSKH Skrifter 23.

Paasonen, S. (2015). A midsummer's bonfire: Affective Intensities of Online Debate. In K. Hillis, S. Paasonen, & M. Petit (Eds.), *Network Affect* (pp. 27–42). Cambridge, MA: The MIT Press.

Palmberg, M. (2009). The Nordic Colonial Mind. In S. Keskinen (Ed.), *Complying with Colonialism: Gender, Race and Ethnicity in the Nordic Region* (pp. 35–50). Farnham: Ashgate.

Peterson, A., & Åkerström, M. (Eds.). (2008). *Den sorterande ordningsmakten: Studier av etnicitet och polisiär kontroll.* Lund: Bokbox.

Poliisibarometri. (2016). Poliisibarometri – Kansalaisten käsitykset poliisin toiminnasta ja sisäisen turvallisuuden tilasta. *Sisäministeriön julkaisu 27/2016.* Retrieved from http://julkaisut.valtioneuvosto.fi/bitstream/handle/10024/75567/Poliisibarometri_2016_Valto.pdf?sequence=1. English abstract on pp. 10–12.

Pöyhtäri, R., Haara, P., & Raittila, P. (2013). *Vihapuhe sananvapautta kaventamassa.* Tampere: Tampere University Press.

Pyrhönen, N. (2015). *The True Colors of Finnish Welfare Nationalism: Consolidation of Neo-Populist Advocacy as a Resonant Collective Identity Through Mobilization of Exclusionary Narratives of Blue-and-White Solidarity.* PhD thesis, University of Helsinki, Swedish School of Social Sciences and CEREN. Retrieved from http://urn.fi/URN:ISBN:978-952-10-8837-7

Rasmussen, A., & Shattak, S. (2016). *Ingen jävla hjälte.* Kira Förlag.

Saukkonen, P. (2011). *Mikä suomenruotsalaisissa ärsyttää? Varför irriterar finlandssvenskar?* Helsinki: Finlands svenska tankesmedja Magma. Retrieved from http://magma.fi/images/stories/reports/ms1101_mikasu_s.pdf

SCB. (2017). *Befolkningsstatistik i sammandrag 1960–2016.* Retrieved from http://www.scb.se/hitta-statistik/statistik-efter-amne/befolkning/befolkningens-sammansattning/befolkningsstatistik/pong/tabell-och-diagram/helarsstatistik--riket/befolkningsstatistik-i-sammandrag/

Schierup, C. U., Ålund, A., & Kings, L. (2014). Reading the Stockholm Riots – A Moment of Social Justice. *Race and Class, 55*(3), 1–21.

Seikkula, M. (2017). Adapting to Post-Racialism? Definitions of Racism in Non-Governmental Organization Advocacy that Mainstreams Anti-racism. *European Journal of Cultural Studies* (First published online 2017, August 11).

Sökefeld, M. (2006). Mobilizing in Transnational Space: A Social Movement Approach to the Formation of Diaspora. *Global Networks, 6*(3), 265–284.

Statistics Finland. (2017). *Ulkomailla syntyneet, Väestö syntymämaan mukaan 1990–2016.* Retrieved from http://www.stat.fi/tup/maahanmuutto/maahanmuuttajat-vaestossa/ulkomailla-syntyneet.html

Swedish Migration Agency. (2017). *Statistics for 2015.* Retrieved from https://www.migrationsverket.se/English/About-the-Migration-Agency/Facts-and-statistics-/Statistics/2015.html

Sydsvenskan. (2014, March 16). *Tusentals demonstrerade mot rasism.* Retrieved from https://www.sydsvenskan.se/2014-03-16/tusentals-demonstrerade-mot-nazism

Sydsvenskan. (2016, October 20). *Föreställningen 'Kämpa Malmö' ställs in.* Retrieved from https://www.sydsvenskan.se/2016-10-20/forestallningen-kampa-malmo-stalls-in

Sydsvenskan. (2017, October 14).Tre års fängelse för attacken på Showan Shattak – hovrättens dom står fast. [News Article]. Retrieved from https://www.sydsvenskan.se/2017-10-04/tre-ars-fangelse-for-attacken-pa-showan-shattak-hovrattens-dom-star-fast

Titley, G. (2014). No Apologies for Cross-Posting: European Trans-media Space and the Digital Circuitries of Racism. *Crossings: Journal of Migration & Culture, 5*(1), 41–55.

Titley, G., & Lentin, A. (2011). *The Crises of Multiculturalism: Racism in a Neoliberal Age.* London: Zed Books.

Turun Sanomat. (2016, September 20). Kääntöveitsellä selkään ja 13 muuta rikosta – Näistä Jesse Torniainen on aiemmin tuomittu. [Newspaper Article]. Retrieved from http://www.ts.fi/uutiset/kotimaa/2785855/Kaantoveitsella+selkaan+ja+13+muuta+rikosta++Naista+Jesse+Torniainen+on+aiemmin+tuo mittu

Vuorela, U. (2009). Colonial Complicity: The 'Post-Colonial' in a Nordic Context. In S. Keskinen et al. (Eds.), *Complying with Colonialism: Gender, Race and Ethnicity in the Nordic Region* (pp. 19–33). Aldershot: Ashgate.

Wigerfelt, B., & Wigerfelt, A. (2001). *Rasismens yttringar: exemplet Klippan.* Lund: Studentlitteratur.

YLE. (2015, August 15). Högerextremismen har fått växa ifred. [News Article]. Retrievedfromhttps://svenska.yle.fi/artikel/2015/08/13/hogerextremismen-har-fatt-vaxa-i-fred

Yle. (2016a, July 11). *Viranomainen: Summitaisen ulkomaalaisvalvonnan aika on ohi – poliisin keinot vanhentuneita* [News Article]. Retrieved from https://yle.fi/uutiset/3-9018723

Yle. (2016b, September 16). *Sisäministeriö: Suurin osa Suomen ääriliikehdinnästä äärioikeiston käsialaa* [News Article]. Retrieved from https://yle.fi/uuti-set/3-9097375

Yle. (2016c, September 22). *Halla-aho: Perussuomalaisten äärioikeistosidonnaisuuksien selvittäminen mahdotonta lakia rikkomatta* [News Article]. Retrieved from https://yle.fi/uutiset/3-9184736

Yle. (2017, September 1). *Mustan Barbaarin äitiä ja siskoa vastaan on nostettu syytteet* [News Article]. Retrieved from https://yle.fi/uutiset/3-9751269

YLE. (2018, March 28). Neo-Nazi Aggravated Assault Convict Requests Supreme Court Appeal. [News Article]. Retrieved from https://yle.fi/uutiset/osasto/news/neo-nazi_aggravated_assault_convict_requests_supreme_court_appeal_hearing/10137432

CHAPTER 11

# (Re)Framing Racialization: Djurs Sommerland as a Battleground of (Anti-)Racism

*Kjetil Rødje and Tess Sophie Skadegård Thorsen*

*Take an exciting Jungle Safari and help Chico the Ape by freeing his
friends from the dangerous poachers. Or act like Tarzan and show off
your muscles on the exciting Tarzanbaner. Finish with a spin on
Hottentot Karrusellen, before ending up in a family stew in the
dangerous Kannibal Gryder. (Djurs Sommerland, 2017)*

Taking a spin with Hottentots and ending up in a black pot as stew for
cannibals are just some of the attractions Djurs Sommerland can offer to
its more than 700,000 annual visitors. A popular family theme park in

K. Rødje (✉)
Department of Media and Communication, University of Oslo, Oslo, Norway
e-mail: kjetil.rodje@media.uio.no

T. S. S. Thorsen
Department of Culture and Global Studies, Aalborg University,
Aalborg, Denmark
e-mail: thorsen@cgs.aau.dk

© The Author(s) 2019
P. Hervik (ed.), *Racialization, Racism, and Anti-Racism in the
Nordic Countries*, Approaches to Social Inequality and Difference,
https://doi.org/10.1007/978-3-319-74630-2_11

Denmark since 1981, Djurs has been steadily expanding, most notably with the introduction of Afrikaland in 1993. Today, the park offers eight themed areas, including Piratland, Bondegårdsland, Mexicoland, Vikingeland, Westernland, Vandland, and Sommerland.

Afrikaland stirred controversy in the summer of 2015 following a comment made to the park's Facebook profile by activist Jin Vilsgaard. When we interviewed Vilsgaard for this article, she explained that she had been following the open Facebook group Everyday Racism Project DK, where the theme park was discussed as racist. "I don't remember exactly what initiated it, but I then chose to make it known that this is racist on DSs [Djurs Sommerland's] fb-page [Facebook). It created a pretty big counter-reaction, but also a good few that supported my message. I was very engaged in the debate, which as I remember it [took place] over a weekend, before DS moderated it, they first entered the debate, but after about a day, they deleted my post along with the discussion" (J. Vilsgaard, personal communication, August 3, 2017, trans).

Vilsgaard did not remember her exact wording of the critique and did not document all of it before it was erased. She did, however, remember that she wished to problematize not only Afrikaland but Mexicoland and Westernland (where the rides thematize "Cowboys and Indians") as well. Nonetheless, the question of the park reconsidering its reproduction of negative racial stereotypes, which in particular were associated with Hottentot Karusellen (The Hottentot Ride) and Kannibal Gryderne (Cannibal Stew Pots) both in Afrikaland, quickly became the main focus. The Cannibal Stew Pots feature large rotating stewpots, which circulate quickly around a caricatured facemask. The Hottentot Ride is a fast-paced ride centered around a caricatured Hottentot figure with entirely black skin, big white lips, bone in hair, large earrings, shield, spear, and over-sized feet and head. In 2018 the figure was eventually replaced with a group of gorillas and the attraction was renamed Abekatten (The Monkey).

As shown in our illustration of the course of events (Fig. 11.1), an online petition was started by Everyday Racism Project about the same time that the debate set out, encouraging the director of Djurs Sommerland to "heavily reconsider its themed area 'Afrikaland', due to its extremely outdated and racist caricatures of African tribes and stereotypes" (Skriveunder.net, 2015a).

An intense debate followed, both on the Facebook site (where Djurs Sommerland eventually closed down the discussion due to the inappropriate language and tone the post commentary featured) and across other media. Vilsgaard explains: "The debate was picked up thereafter by multiple media

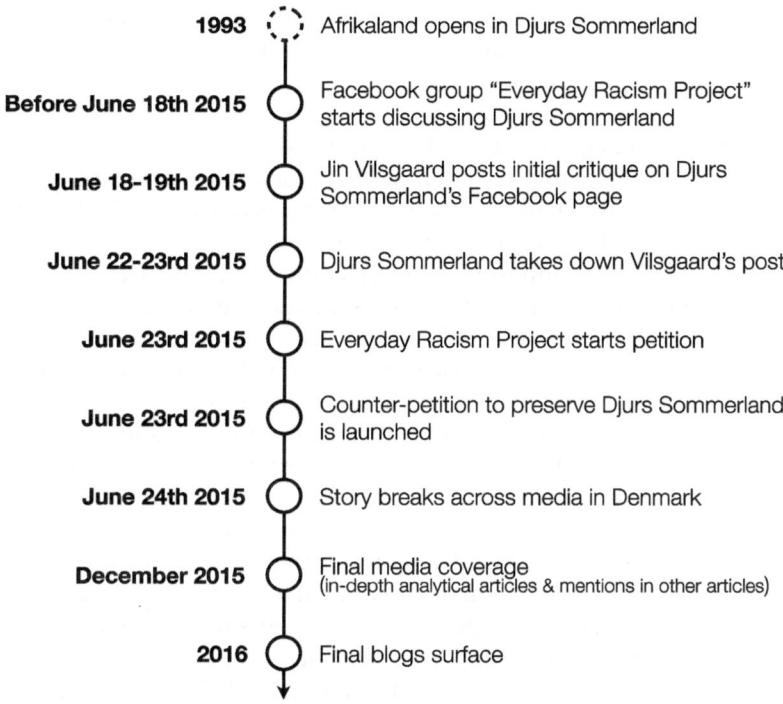

| 1993 | Afrikaland opens in Djurs Sommerland |
| Before June 18th 2015 | Facebook group "Everyday Racism Project" starts discussing Djurs Sommerland |
| June 18-19th 2015 | Jin Vilsgaard posts initial critique on Djurs Sommerland's Facebook page |
| June 22-23rd 2015 | Djurs Sommerland takes down Vilsgaard's post |
| June 23rd 2015 | Everyday Racism Project starts petition |
| June 23rd 2015 | Counter-petition to preserve Djurs Sommerland is launched |
| June 24th 2015 | Story breaks across media in Denmark |
| December 2015 | Final media coverage (in-depth analytical articles & mentions in other articles) |
| 2016 | Final blogs surface |

**Fig. 11.1** This timeline illustrates the course of events before, during, and after the debate about Djurs Sommerland took place

and fora, where I said no to commenting, I only debated on fb[Facebook]. In part I didn't feel comfortable/safe being in the media, in part the racism debate tears on my resources because I get so upset/personally engaged, in part because the debate centered on PADs [People of African Descent], which I don't represent [Vilsgaard self-identifies as of south-east asian descent] and AEC [African Empowerment Centre] and Josef [Josef W. Nielsen, theatre director and then head of AEC] were willing to take a lot of the media" (J. Vilsgaard, personal communication, August 3, 2017, trans). In our interview with Josef W. Nielsen, former head of the African Empowerment Centre, he explained that by the time he entered the conversation, it was too late to "have dialogue over coffee", which he would have preferred. Nielsen described the debate as a "shitstorm" by the time he began engaging. Between June 24 and 26, 2015, the story quickly developed into a nationwide discussion with articles describing the case across more than 30 media channels (web-news, articles, radio, etc.). It even reached the news in Norway, Sweden, the Netherlands, Ireland, France, South Africa, and India. Coverage of the story continued until December 2015 and on blogs into 2016.

Having examined more than 45 articles (identified over the course of two years through continuous broad-scale and media-specific searches based on key words "Djurs Sommerland", various wordings of "Hottentot-Karrusel", "Cannibal Stewpots", and the names of the activists in question and supported by continuous conversations and interviews with Jin Vilsgaard and Josef Nielsen.), blog posts, online debates, and news pieces, in this case, some patterns begin to emerge. Thirty-five of our selected entries are news coverage in newspapers (on- and offline). In addition, a radio program, six blog posts, and three debate sites have been analyzed. In our review, we found that several postings and commentary articles argued that the park indeed contributed toward promoting and reproducing racial stereotypes, while the overwhelming majority of the responses rejected this view. A counter-campaign was launched, with a petition in support of Djurs Sommerland and the attractions, collecting approximately ten times as many signatures as the first petition. In total, close to 2000 people have signed the petition asking Djurs to reconsider its attraction, while the petition in support of the theme park has collected nearly 20,000 signatures (Skriveunder.net, July 22, 2015b). The counter-campaign supports Djurs "as it is" and is targeted against "someone who has launched a petition, against Djurs Sommerland, in order to make them close down Hottentot Karusellen and Kannibal Gryderne. This because they think that these [attractions] are racist and that our children are exposed to involuntary racism by visiting the park. This is a petition against theirs. Sign and show that you support Djurs Sommerland, just as it is. Including Afrikaland, Westernland, and all the other beautiful and fun attractions". While the petition asking Djurs Sommerland to reconsider was clearly marked with Everyday Racism Project Denmark as the sender, the counter-petition did not mark who was behind it. In a later update, thanking for the massive support the petition gained, the petition was positioned by its authors as "an important tool in the fight against political correctness, which eventually has become predominant, in far too many places" (Skriveunder.net, July 22, 2015b).

The central point of controversy is thus established as whether or not Djurs Sommerland represents a case of racism. The first petition, developed along with Vilsgaard's critique, argued that the "caricatures" and "stereotypes" in Afrikaland are "outdated" and "racist", while the counter-petition stated that "someone [...] think[s] that these [attractions] are racist [...]". The counter-petition furthermore mobilized the term political correctness, to label those voices that are accusing Djurs Sommerland of racism. As we will outline in this chapter, this sets a pattern for the media discourse on this controversy, where the relevance of the term *racism* is a center of discussion and where the voices that defend Djurs Sommerland position themselves as fighting a larger trend toward political correctness.

In this chapter, we look into this turn in the debate. In particular, we focus on the role of participants in the online/media discourse who self-identify as anti-racists while positioning themselves as a voice of reason against what is perceived as groundless accusations about racism.

As we point out, "politically correct" claims about racism are here rhetorically framed as an elitist perspective far removed from the lives and everyday concerns of regular Danes, thus bringing into question the validity of the critique of racism while positioning those raising these concerns as being mistaken and overly sensitive.

We have chosen to zoom in on arguments associated with the majority positions in the Danish discourse, which claim an explicitly anti-racist stance while at the same time rejecting the accusations against the theme park, what is sometimes referred to in radicalization theory as the "gray zone", which is discussed in Chap. 8 of this book by Karina Horsti and Carolina Sanchez Boe. We could have elaborated on the examples that take a more direct political stance either in favor of or against the rides in question; for instance, we could have analyzed the very aggressive debate posts on blogs, Facebook sites, or the wording of the petitions, but we wanted to look at what happens in the "middle ground", or in the spaces occupied by opinions that would read as within the norm, nonabrasive, or even neutral. Our cases are the *Århus Stiftstidende*, a local newspaper in one of Denmark's largest cities, editorial from June 27, 2015, penned by editor in chief Jan Schouby, and an op-ed article in *Jyllands-Posten*, a national newspaper with a relatively right-leaning political stance, from June 30, 2015, by social democrat politician Camilla Schwalbe as well as examples from the seemingly "neutral" reporting of the case through news media including *TV2 Nyheder, Politiken*, and *Avisen.dk*.

## RACIALIZATION AND RACISM IN DJURS SOMMERLAND

As we will show in the following sections, our selected articles reject a direct link between the Djurs Sommerland case and race and racism. Nonetheless, we approach this case, and the ensuing debate, as a matter of racialization. In academic discourse, *racialization* is used as a concept that describes "the processes by which ideas about race are constructed, come to be regarded as meaningful, and are acted upon" (Murji & Solomos, 2005, p. 1). With this wide definition as a starting point, we proceed to pinpoint how racialization is at play here on multiple levels.

In our data, the terminology of race and racism was introduced to the case when the Everyday Racism Project Denmark started writing about Djurs Sommerland on Facebook and then became a point of controversy in the debate about racism that began following Vilsgaard's introduction of the term in her posting on Djurs' Facebook page. This critique was born out of the Everyday Racism Project Denmark, thereby inferring Philomena Essed's (1991) concept Everyday Racism, taken from a Dutch context.

In the early stages of the controversy, Vilsgaard and Nielsen abstained from relying heavily on terminology about race and racism, although they both use the term racism, both in their online comments and in our interviews with them. As Nielsen explained: "Afrikaland is problematic because it features stereotypical, demeaning and stigmatizing representation of blacks as Hottentots and cannibals. I didn't have that wording ready at the time [of the media and interviews], which unfortunately muddled the debate and shifted the argumentation to "saying no" rather than racism" (J. Vilsgaard, personal communication, August 3, 2017, trans).

With the anthropological concepts of the emic and etic, one could argue that within the Djurs Sommerland debate (from the debate beginning on Djurs Sommerland's Facebook page and in the following discussions across media), the terms *race* and *racism* come into use when Vilsgaard introduces her critique. However, there are diverging emic understandings of the meaning of racism. These diverging meanings allow for a discussion in the media of whether or not this is even a question of race. The focus thereby shifts from the question of the alleged racist nature of the Djurs Sommerland attractions toward a discourse about how these allegations about racism pose a threat to Danish values and traditions. From an etic perspective, or even a theoretical one, we will argue that this case was about race before the term race was even introduced in the data.

At an empirical level, we suggest that Djurs Sommerland has itself performed a movement of racialization, by inscribing its rides and attractions with racial markers and stereotypes. In their visual representations and linguistic descriptions, the theme park here thematizes "Africa" through figures of Hottentots and cannibals. As such, the park reproduces and mimics racial stereotypes and colonial history. In this respect, the theme park is already racialized, prior to the outbreak of these media controversies, regardless of both intent and awareness. While on an emic level, the initial development of Afrikaland and its rides might not have been considered to have any racial meaning, from an etic one, where the historical and geographical backdrop to these developments is taken into account, the racial meaning is hard to overlook.

However, racialization only becomes a topic with regard to Djurs Sommerland when the debate erupts when the racial stereotypes, which previously had not been subjected to public scrutiny, are moved to the forefront. This establishes a discursive terrain where the theme park's use of racial markers becomes a matter of controversy. The discussion follows a line of conflict where the central question is whether these presentations can be perceived as operating in a manner that reinforces racist oppression. This discursive process becomes a further matter of racialization, whereby notions of race and racial representations are made into controversial discussion topics. As such, another, discursive, process of racialization is sparked, which furthermore feeds back into the already established empirical racialization of the theme park. The park can, as such, be argued to both already having *been* racialized and, at the same time, has *become* racialized as these controversies are sparked.

The concept of racialization underscores how constructions and enactments of racial categories reinforce and further effectuate these very categories, which explicitly and/or implicitly target and shape the everyday experiences of racialized subjects across global and local scales. Simultaneously, racialization co-constructs and co-enacts the same categories. The strength of the term racialization, rather than racism or merely race, is thus that it allows us to focus on these processes of construction, deconstruction, and reconstruction of race categories, as well as the effects of these processes. Our conceptualization of racialization therefore signifies an examination of the processes by which race and racial categories are constructed, contested, and upheld in the debates about Djurs Sommerland.

In other words, we examine how ideas about race are reflected and reproduced in the discourses surrounding the case while emphasizing that these discourses have implications for lived experiences. A key part of our argument is that *racialization* is not a remote or extreme practice but a matter of processes that take place throughout society and discourses on multiple levels and in more or less visible ways. In other words, racialization is both what happens in the park and also, and maybe even to a higher degree, what happens in the discursive controversies about the park. As argued by Murji and Solomos, and most other racialization theorists, racist ideologies and race categories are upheld, reproduced, or strengthened by the processes theorized as racialization, regardless of the intent or severity of these processes. Much in line with Bonilla-Silva's work on color-blind racism and racism without racists (2006), we consider racialization processes to be built into seemingly neutral and naturalized arguments and understandings. Hence, our subject matter is an analysis of postings representing a Danish "majority" position, where the theme park is perceived as devoid of any bias along racial terms. These postings thus deny the legitimacy both of the claims made about the Djurs Sommerland attractions being racist and of the potentially negative experiences of racialized subjects when encountering these attractions.

## Racism and "Real" Racism

I actually think that, out of respect for the shadowy (dark) history, one should make room for the caricatured and satirical. It is a way to handle it. This is where the admission of the mistakes of the past can also be understood (/contained). (Schwalbe, 2015)

In positioning the rides and their racial caricature as a tool for negotiating the past ("shadowy history" and "mistakes of the past"), Schwalbe links colonial history to today's colonial memorabilia while negating that the Djurs Sommerland attractions support this racism of the past. The rides are "a way to handle it", not a potential source of painful racist objectification. As such, in arguing that the rides serve to educate us about our past, questions of race and racism are also linked to the past. In Schwalbe's view, the stereotypes and caricatures are thus considered memories of past meanings are inferred through the artifacts. In this logic, the artifacts cannot be racist, because they are not interpreted as a reproduction of historical racism but as a critical commentary to it. Nonetheless, viewing it only as such requires that racism be seen as something finite, containable, and, most importantly, something of the past, something historical. As such, the argument for the rides becomes an easy parallel to Danbolt's concept of *retro racism* (2017), where melancholic memories serve to comfort us, even if we are distanced from the severity or gravity of the hate and pain associated with these memories, or even an explicit effort to celebrate colonial memorabilia as a tool for education and reflection. The legitimization of the rides through their link to history thus re-centers white agency as reflective upon the said history (Ahmed, 2004).

Schouby said: "Without doubt, racism is disgusting, humiliating, and antihuman. And it should be spoken out against, wherever we happen to encounter this. The problem with this case [the alleged racist nature of the Djurs Sommerland attractions] is just that it has nothing whatsoever to do with racism". And Schouby went on to say, "The fight against racism is far too important to be led astray by a case as insignificant as this". Schwalbe said, "In my opinion, we should end such elitist discussions that distract from the real and important problems of everyday racism and intolerance", and "Imagine if the Danes would be as concerned with putting a stop to the fundamental injustice of society, as they are with making Djurs Sommerland close down 'The Hottentot Ride'". Both of these quotes deny the claims about racism and make a distinction between this case and "real racism". The two writers paint racism as something negative, problematic, and real—and as something far removed from the case of Djurs Sommerland. Both commentators argue that the accusations made about Djurs Sommerland are counterproductive in the fight against "real" racism. While none of them provide any clear definition or example of what "really" constitutes racism or where such "real" racism is to be found, they both suggest that "real" racism is a matter of intent: "The amusement park is for everyone, and does of course not have the intent of offending anyone" (Schouby, 2015). Schwalbe says: "And sometimes we should perhaps make an attempt at putting ourselves in the position of the other. Is there any malicious intent?" (2015).

This focus on the intention of an expression excludes a focus on the reception of these expressions. This is made evident in Schwalbe's call to put oneself in the position of others. By "others", she refers here to those making the contested expressions, while no attempt is made to put oneself in the position of those objecting. In extension of this, her argument positions the debate within the domain of the majority opinion. The "other" whose perspective the reader is invited to share is positioned as a non-racist representative of Danish majority culture—while this invitation does not include the potentially offended minority position (Delgado & Stefancic, 2012; Pincus, 1996); here, the standard definition of minority/majority position (Downing & Husband, 2005) is used, which is based on access to power, political stance, and societal gains rather than respective sizes of the groups, although in this particular case the minority position also represents a minority in respective numbers of people represented and publications in which they are represented. By framing racism as a question of intent, Schwalbe shifts focus toward overt expressions of racial hatred and away from structural patterns of racial exclusion and discrimination.

Taking an explicitly anti-racist stance, Schouby and Schwalbe position themselves, and Djurs Sommerland, outside of the realm of racializing processes, racist ideologies, and racism itself. Under the guise of polite acknowledgment and informed education, their arguments indicate that experienced racism and processes of racialization are not real, since more serious or clear-cut cases can obviously be found. Framing their support of the theme park in anti-racist terms intuitively serves to deny the possibility that the attractions could somehow be understood and experienced as racist. This furthermore deems the topic of racism as irrelevant to a rational discourse about this phenomenon. In other words these arguments illustrate efforts to *deracialize* the debate by making the claim that critics of Djurs Sommerland unnecessarily introduce race into a phenomenon which is "really" to be perceived as nonracial and definitely non-racist.

## "Neutral" Reporting

The pattern of denial identified in the previous section repeats itself in the seemingly neutral reporting across newspapers on the Djurs Sommerland case. Out of the 45+ blogs, articles, and news pieces on Djurs Sommerland, 15 are (more or less directly) pro-carousel or more or less directly deny the case as an example of racism. Most of these are blog sites or articles in openly right-wing national newspapers or local newspapers. Only two articles are decidedly anti-carousel and clearly state the case as one of racialization and/or racism. The additional articles are national and foreign reportings of which the 16 national reportings take a seemingly neutral or non-opinion position in their reporting. Nonetheless, these "neutral" reportings invite further analysis when aiming to examine the broader framing of the Djurs Sommerland debate.

Here, we define "neutral" reporting as not taking a direct stance or having an easily identifiable opinion on the matter and as having been authored by journalists, not op-ed writers. These articles report the news in a chronological matter-of-fact way and were examined particularly because they assume positions of reporting rather than opinion.

In the Danish national newspaper *Politiken* on June 25, a news article titled "The Politically Correct have become more visible" reports on the case through the use of multiple sources, including, in addition to Josef W. Nielsen, "Scientist Rikke Andreassen" who explains that this case is not necessarily evidence that we are more "conscious of being politically correct" but rather that organization through social media has made this consciousness more visible (Kristiansen, 2015). In the same article, the journalist, Cecilie Lund Kristiansen, states: "This is far from the first time that a rebellion organizes around something that has otherwise worked perfectly well for many years .... Last year pieces of licorice with motifs of masks with Asian and African faces were removed from the Skipper Mix candy bags from Haribo following debate on social media in Sweden. The candy was accused of being based on racist caricatures of ethnic groups, and Haribo made the decision to remove the masks from the bags" (Kristiansen, 2015).

While Kristiansen, the political reporter in *Politiken*, does quote a representative from Djurs Sommerland, who raises the exact point that Afrikaland has existed for so long that the sudden critique on Facebook is not enough for them to consider changing the names of the rides in question; what is worth noting here is that Kristiansen internalizes and reproduces the rhetorical logic at play rather than questioning the premise—why the fact that something has existed for long legitimizes its continued existence.

In a seemingly neutral manner, Kristiansen's reporting reiterates and reproduces one party's opinion in this conflict. By acknowledging that Djurs Sommerland, like many other cases, has "otherwise worked perfectly well for many years", the journalist makes space for the reader to question why the critique occurs now. As such, the reporter goes along with questioning the premise of the critique while not fully questioning the premise of the critiqued. The article's less-than-neutral neutrality becomes increasingly clear, when the sub-headline reads that The Politically Correct have become more visible, since this is hardly the statement Rikke Andreassen actually made.

Additional articles, for instance, *TV2 Nyheder*'s "Djurs Sommerland accused of racism: is this crossing the line?" (Moestruup, 2015), *Ude og Hjemme*'s "Is Afrikaland Racist?" (Mortensen, 2015), and *Avisen.dk*'s "Racism in Djurs Sommerland? More than 1000 sign petition in protest" (Bondesen, 2015), questioned, both in titles and in subtext, whether or not this was actually racism and framed it as people "being offended".

The very questioning of whether or not this is racist, or whether or not it is wrong, perpetuates the same contestation and challenge of the lived experience of the implicated parties (Jin Vilsgaard, Josef W. Nielsen, and the nearly 2000 people who signed the petition) that the more critical and directly pro-carousel articles and debates illustrate. Rather than asking "what happened?" or "what can be done?", the mainstream reporting of the Djurs Sommerland case consistently asked "is it real?" and "is it racist?", thereby reframing the focus onto the claim of racism rather than the actual racism. It is interesting that so many of the articles reporting this story ask their readers to question what racism is, or whether or not this is racism, while few, if any, question what the artifact in question symbolizes and why it has meaning to us. This counts on both "sides" of the fence— neither the Everyday Racism Denmark petitioners and activists nor the petitioners in favor of preserving Djurs Sommerland "as is" seem to be asked about the meaning and importance of the actual artifacts in question—the actual mask and pots in the cannibal stewpots and the Hottentot at the center of the carousel. Instead, the artifacts that spurred on the debate to begin with slide into the horizon and soon become opaque symbols for other much more pressing matters, however hard to grasp. As such, the question of whether or not this is racist is an effective means of rhetorical distraction.

## Political Correctness

Schwalbe makes a point to mention her "black friends" who find Djurs Sommerland inoffensive, while it is notable that she does not incorporate the perspective of those who actually object to the racial stereotyping (2015). Rather, Schwalbe uses the reactions of her friends to support the claim that this is an elitist discussion hindering the struggle against "real" racism. She further links elitism to the term "political correctness" that features prominently in both Schwalbe and Schouby's articles. For example, Schouby states: "Political correctness has quite simply taken over, and this to an extreme degree. If we are not careful, we will end up like Sweden, where the attempt at providing 100% equality and at not offending any-one whatsoever, has created a completely hysterical society. A society where freedom of speech is put under pressure and where common sense has long since vanished" (2015). Schwalbe states: "In my opinion, we ought to be careful that we do not, by striving towards political correct-ness, create divisions in the society—where some topics are not addressed". Both of these quotes associate political correctness with a restriction of freedom of speech, as part of an intervention from above (outside of the majority Danish culture) that limits the range of possible and acceptable expressions. The implicit assumption is that the majority culture is under attack, threatened by those (politically correct elitists) that take offense where none is intended. Furthermore, this assumption shifts the discursive terrain toward a question of social standing, whereby those making the accusations about racism are framed as part of a powerful elite.

This pejorative use of the term *political correctness* follows a pattern established in the US, where "politically correct liberal elites" in the "cul-ture wars" of the late 1980s and early 1990s were a target of conservative and right-wing attacks (Berman, 1992; Bloom, 1988; D'Souza, 1991; Kimball, 1990). The concept has since become a staple of American politi-cal and social discourse. In fact, in a national telephone survey undertaken by the Fairleigh Dickinson University in October 2015, a substantial majority of Americans, across the political spectrum, sees political correct-ness as a major problem in their society. 68% of those polled agreed to the statement "A big problem this country has is being politically correct", while 27% answered that they disagreed (Public Mind Poll, 2015). Furthermore, the concept has traversed political and geographical bound-aries and, today, can be found as a prevalent derogatory trope in Danish discourse on racism as well as a number of other topics.

In this widened scope, "political correctness inculcates a sense of obli-gation or conformity in areas which should be (or are) matters of choice" (Hughes, 2010, p. 4). Hence, political correctness can be seen as restrict-ing practices and inhibiting freedom of speech. In his analysis of the con-cept, Stanley Fish identifies its rhetorical strength to define the premises upon which a topic is to be understood and discussed (1994). Political correctness, Fish claims, "is a wonderfully concise indictment that says that a group of unscrupulous persons is trying to impose its views on our campus populations rather than upholding views that reflect the biases of no views because they are common to everyone. It is these commonly shared views, we are told, that are really correct, while the views of feminists, multiculturalists, Afrocentrists, and the like are merely politically correct, correct only from the perspective of those who espouse them" (Fish, 1994, p. 8).

The term is commonly associated with identity politics, whereby particular social groups (such as women or racial/ethnic or sexual minorities) are perceived as being granted privileges unavailable, and in opposition, to the silent majority. Thus, a conflict is being perceived whereby political correctness is a weapon in the hands of liberal elites that furthers the interests of certain minorities to the detriment of the values and economic interests of common (white, male, heterosexual, traditional) people. The discourse on political correctness hence positions the cultural values and the economic interests of hardworking (lower-class) people as vulnerable and under threat by special interest groups.

The "anti-PC" rhetoric—the abbreviation *PC* is commonly found in cases where political correctness is used as a derogatory term (Hughes, 2010, pp. 68–69)—has two characteristics that are of key relevance also in the current Danish context: (a) political correctness is a construct that targets and politicizes aspects of everyday life and/or the "natural" or "given" order of society; (b) political correctness is a rhetorical and political tool in the hands of left-leaning or liberal (often academic and/or cultural) elites far removed from the lives and everyday concerns of regular (hardworking and honest) people (what Richard Nixon would label as the silent majority (Perlstein, 2008)). Thus, political correctness is, in this context, a political intervention from above that denaturalizes and undermines the concerns, interests, and traditions of regular people.

## REFRAMING ELITES

Schwalbe: "In my opinion, we should end such elitist discussions that distract from the real and important problems of everyday racism and intolerance" (2015). By inscribing elitism into the discussion, Schwalbe reframes the focus and shifts the power relations between the respective groups. She positions the voices criticizing the family attraction within a framework where they are characterized as elitist crusaders of political correctness. Rather than viewing them as responses to racism and discrimination, these voices are positioned as elites elevated above a "silent" majority that is framed as powerless.

This reframing replaces the exclusionary process typically associated with racializing practices (Murji & Solomos, 2005). The topic of discussion is no longer whether the attractions are racist and the potential negative effects of this. Within such a discussion about racism, the supporters of the theme park's attractions could be accused of upholding structures of racist discrimination, while the voices against the attractions could be heard as a reaction against racialized discrimination. Within this framework, the potential victims are those subjected to racism, and the potential perpetrators are those who support the structures of discrimination. However, this power relationship is dismantled when another axis of oppression is brought into the discussion, where the "silent majority" is positioned as subjugated by political correctness. The assumed "elite" status of the critical voices goes unproven, but it is also beside the point, because the effect is a shift in focus and a reversal of roles. Ironically, this repositioning defines the accusers as part of not only the elite but as part of an exclusionary national group: the Danes.

Schwalbe: "Imagine if *the Danes* [emphasis added] would be as concerned with putting a stop to the fundamental injustice of society, as they are with making Djurs Sommerland close down 'The Hottentot Ride'" (2015). Schwalbe argues that the politically correct elitist Danes are misguided in focusing on problems that cannot be considered "fundamental injustices". Furthermore, her positioning of the accusers as "the Danes" works to insinuate numerical superiority or at least superiority in power and to move the critical voices from margin to center.

Whereas Schwalbe's op-ed is a general rejection of such politically correct elitists, Schouby directly targets Josef W. Nielsen. Schouby repeatedly suggests that Nielsen's arguments are an emotional (and implicitly nonrational) reaction: "Josef W. Nielsen felt offended by the amusement attraction and its name"; "Josef W. Nielsen's offended attitudes"; "Instead of acting offended, Josef W. Nielsen and his organization ought to focus their energy on the cases where racism really shows its ugly face" (2015). Nielsen's reaction is dismissed here as a mere personal experience that does not address the "real" issues of racism. Again, the power to define what counts as real and relevant is ascribed to the majority positions. Furthermore, the majority position is situated as the voice of reason that stands robust against the emotional (and implicitly nonrational) claims made by Nielsen.

Despite positioning itself as the voice of reason, the extent to which the responses from Schwalbe and Schouby are emotionally charged and seemingly fueled by a genuine (if somewhat overbearing) offense taken against the claims made by Nielsen and others is remarkable. Furthermore, their rhetorical tone directly appeals to the emotional responses of their readers, stressing the ridiculousness of the claims about racism and the potential danger of taking such claims seriously. Arguably, this emotional undercurrent is imperative to understanding the heated tone of this discourse and why so many Danes seemingly take offense to the claims about racism raised by Nielsen and others.

The term "political correctness" comprises a conceptual framework that naturalizes and normalizes what is being subjected to critique from the politically correct "others". As argued by Stanly Fish, the discursive strategy of political correctness "puts the other side on the defensive by assigning it a description it will feel obliged to refuse" (Fish, 1994, pp. 8–9). The introduction of the term political correctness shifts the frame within which a debate unfolds. When successful, the charges raised by the frame of political correctness stain the arguments on the one side as political and tainted by the bias of particular interests; while the other position, defending the status quo, comes to be seen as common sense and neutral. Hence, the debate is not between differing positions and political views but between the biased and the unbiased.

What makes this case particularly interesting in terms of discussions of elitism linked to political correctness, however, is that the critiques of Vilsgaard, Nielsen, Everyday Racism Project Denmark, and the activists implicated in the initial petition, are framed as elitist and politically correct by opinion pieces in both left-leaning and right-leaning media outlets. In one opinion piece, in the openly left-wing online media Modkraft (which has since closed down), the voices behind the accusations against Djurs Sommerland and behind the original petition are criticized for their academic manner: "Can one make a dent in the racism that soaks through our society by telling people off in cold academic terms?" (Hansen, 2015). This illustrates how the discussion of elitism quickly gained traction across the political spectrum, serving to reframe the "shitstorm" from the topic of the Djurs Sommerland attractions to the question of how racism can be addressed and from which positions.

Furthermore, the claims about a politically correct bias block any empathic response toward those who happen to react negatively toward the racialized aspects of the amusement park. Attempts at understanding the experiences of racialized subjects are hard to come by. The question of how a black family with children would experience Afrikaland is, for example, not raised, while frequent references can be found to the experiences of the majority population and how the claims about racism supposedly limit their ability to appreciate their own culture and traditions. This turning of tables makes those who make claims about racism into political correct killjoys, to use a term by Sara Ahmed. Killjoys are troublemakers, who question and bring out problematic aspects of the objects that provide others with happiness (Ahmed, 2010). A person that points out the racism inherent in an amusement park would, as such, be a killjoy par excellence.

## CONCLUSION

There is no neutral position to Afrikaland, and there is no "true" way to understand or experience Djurs Sommerland. The controversies we have studied here show a wide gap in how to conceptualize and make sense of the amusement park. This gap makes for hostile reactions and antipathies that reach further than the actual case of Djurs Sommerland. The nature of the attractions is pushed into the background and the discussion reframed as a matter about how cherished Danish traditions are under attack by political correctness.

While race, racism, and racialization do not really become meaningful to the parties involved in this case until Everyday Racism Project Denmark begin their discussion, which Jin Vilsgaard brings to the Djurs Sommerland Facebook page, one could argue that whether aware of it or not, Afrikaland has always been about race—thematized through the wording, symbolism, and caricatures of the park. Nonetheless, the very symbols and artifacts that initiated this debate end up playing a barely visible role in a debate, which became about everything surrounding them instead.

In our analysis of the discussion, we found that it follows a line of conflict where the central question is whether these presentations can be perceived as operating in accordance with oppressive and racist logics. However, this question becomes superfluous when one recognizes that the varying emic understandings of race, racism, and racialization among the many implicated parties of the case made it impossible for the conversation to move past a point of questioning its very premise.

## REFERENCES

Ahmed, S. (2004). Declarations of Whiteness: The Non-Performativity of Anti-Racism. *Borderlands e-journal, 3*(2). Retrieved from www.borderlands.net.au/vol3no2_2004/ahmed_declarations.htm

Ahmed, S. (2010). *The Promise of Happiness*. Durham: Duke University Press.

Berman, P. (Ed.). (1992). *Debating PC: The Controversy Over Political Correctness on College Campuses.* New York: Laurel Press.

Bloom, A. (1988). *The Closing of the American Mind: How Higher Education Has Failed Democracy and Impoverished the Souls of Today's Students.* London: Penguin.

Bondesen, L. (2015). Racisme i Djurs Sommerland? Over 1.000 skriver under på protest (trans). *Avisen.dk.* Retrieved from https://www.avisen.dk/racsime-i-djurs-sommerland-over-1000-skriver-under_331752.aspx

Bonilla-Silva, E. (2006). *Racism Without Racists: Color-Blind Racism and the Persistence of Racial Inequality in the United States.* Lanham, MD: Rowman & Littlefield Publishers.

D'Souza, D. (1991). *Illiberal Education: The Politics of Race and Sex on Campus.* New York: Random House.

Danbolt, M. (2017). Retro Racism: Colonial Ignorance and Racialized Affective Consumption in Danish Public Culture. *Nordic Journal of Migration Research, 7*(2). https://doi.org/10.1515/njmr-2017-0013

Delgado, R., & Stefancic, J. (2012). *Critical Race Theory: An Introduction.* New York: New York University Press.

Djurs Sommerland. (2017). Afrikaland: Safari fun and swinging vines for adventure lovers (trans). Retrieved from http://www.djurssommerland.dk/en/themed-areas/afrikaland/

Downing, J. D., & Husband, C. (2005). Representing race: Racisms, ethnicity and the media. Sage.

Essed, P. (1991). *Understanding Everyday Racism: An Interdisciplinary Theory* (Vol. 2). Newbury Park: Sage.

Fish, S. (1994). *There's No Such Thing as Free Speech, and It's a Good Thing, Too.* New York: Oxford University Press.

Hansen, D. (2015). Tanker om en hottentotkarrusel: Man skal vide, hvem man taler med (trans). *Modkraft.* Retrieved from http://modkraft.dk/artikel/tanker-om-en-hottentotkarrusel-man-skal-vide-hvem-man-taler-med

Hughes, G. (2010). *Political Correctness: A History of Semantics and Culture.* Malden, MA: Wiley-Blackwell.

Kimball, R. (1990). *Tenured Radicals.* New York: Harper and Row.

Kristiansen, C. L. (2015, June 25). Kritikere: Kannibaler og hottentotter i Djurs Sommerland er racistiske: Parkens 'Afrikaland' fastholder 100 år gamle opfattelser, mener forsker. *Politiken.* Retrieved from http://politiken.dk/indland/art5580971/Kritikere-Kannibaler-og-hottentotter-i-Djurs-Sommerland-er-racistiske

Moestruup, J. H. R. (2015, June 25). Djurs Sommerland Accused of Racism: Is This Crossing the Line? (trans). *TV2 Nyheders.* Retrieved from http://nyheder.tv2.dk/samfund/2015-06-25-djurs-sommerland-anklages-for-racisme-er-det-her-over-graensen

Mortensen, M. N. (2015). Er Afrikaland racistisk? (trans). *Ude og Hjemme.dk.* Retrieved from http://www.udeoghjemme.dk/familie/boern/er-afrikaland-racistisk

Murji, K., & Solomos, J. (2005). *Introduction: Racialization in Theory and Practice.* In K. Murji and J. Solomos (eds.), (pp. 1–27). Oxford: Oxford University Press.

Perlstein, R. (2008). *Nixonland: The Rise of a President and the Fracturing of America.* New York: Scribner.

Pincus, F. L. (1996). Discrimination Comes in Many Forms: Individual, Institutional, and Structural. *American Behavioral Scientist, 40*(2), 186–194.

Public Mind Poll. (2015). *Trump Taints America's Views on Political Correctness: Poll Suggests Perceptions of Political Correctness Are Trumped by Trump.* Fairleigh Dickinson University. Retrieved from http://view2.fdu.edu/public-mind/2015/151030/

Schouby, J. (2015). Leder: Kampen mod racisme er for vigtig til sagen om Djurs Sommerland (trans). *Århus Stiftstidende.* Retrieved from http://stiften.dk/aarhus/Leder-Kampen-mod-racisme-er-for-vigtig-til-sagen-om-Djurs-Sommerland/artikel/259869

Schwalbe, C. (2015). Hverken Skipper Mix, Negerboller eller hottentot-karussellen er racisme (trans). *Jyllands Posten* (Blog). Retrieved from http://jyllands-posten.dk/debat/blogs/camillaschwalbe/ECE7839594/Hverken-Skipper-mix-negerboller-eller-Hottentot-karrusellen-er-racisme/

Skriveunder.net. (2015a). Djurs Sommerland: Stop reproduktion af racistiske stereotyper! (trans). Retrieved from https://www.skrivunder.net/djurs_sommer-land_afskaf_jeres_racistiske_hottentotkarussel

Skriveunder.net. (2015b, July 22). *Vi støtter Djurs Sommerland som det er.* Retrieved from https://www.skrivunder.net/vi_stotter_djurs_sommerland_som_det_er

# CHAPTER 12

# Whiteness and Racialization

## Nasar Meer

In a typically perceptive discussion of the trajectories of scholarship in whiteness studies, Garner (2017: 1585) recently argued that 'the sword Damocles hanging over the scholar of whiteness is the question of how to wrestle its meanings into connection with other social relationships … and remaining true to the first wave origin: *make white supremacy visible*' (original emphases). The profound breadth and depth of the present collection, examining racialization, racism, and anti-racism in the Nordic countries, is an excellent showcase of how both established and emerging scholars are leading the charge in Nordic cases.

It is also worth noting how racialization inter alia whiteness is a relatively recent area of scholarship, even though many of the questions it addresses are inherently intertwined in being elementary issues of race. Perhaps peculiarly, whiteness sits at an intersection between historical privilege and identity, something that has a contemporary dynamic but which is not universally shared in (or can be distant to) how many white people experience their identities. As Frankenberg (2001: 76) puts it: 'whiteness as a site of privilege is not absolute but rather cross-cut by a range of other

N. Meer (✉)
University of Edinburgh, Edinburgh, UK
e-mail: Nasar.Meer@ed.ac.uk

© The Author(s) 2019
P. Hervik (ed.), *Racialization, Racism, and Anti-Racism in the Nordic Countries*, Approaches to Social Inequality and Difference,
https://doi.org/10.1007/978-3-319-74630-2_12

axes of relative advantage and subordination; these do not erase or render irrelevant race privilege, but rather inflect or modify it'.

In thinking about whiteness, there is often a tension between its study from (1) contexts marked by historical segregation (e.g. the US and South Africa), (2) where whiteness has either functioned (at least formally) as a repository of white-majority conceptions of the given identity of societies (Hage, 1998; Hewitt, 2005) or (3) ordered social relations in occupied colonial states. What each reading shares in common is that while whiteness was once 'seen as both invisible and normative, as being a state of "racelessness"' (Rhodes, 2013: 52), this is no longer the case. Yet what this means and how it falls, as this collection shows, is not best studied through a postcolonial category or at least requires racialization scholarship to forge the analytical path.

This does not mean marginalizing the capacity of postcolonial scholarship to enrich this exercise, including the ways in which the history of whiteness also serves as 'a geography' of the West (Bonnett, 2008: 18), in precisely the kind of ways postcolonial scholars attest. But it does mean grasping the ways in which 'the history of whiteness is one of transitions and changes' (ibid.). This is especially pertinent to the story of how the Irish in the UK or the Italians in the US became white; perhaps more complicated is the story of Jewish minorities, as Jacobson (2009: 306) argues:

> 'Are Jews white?' asks Sander Gilman. […] Given the shades of meaning attaching to various racial classifications, given the nuances involved as whiteness slips off toward Semitic or Hebrew and back again toward Caucasian, the question is not *are* they white, nor even how white are they, but how they been both white and Other.

In his account Bonnett (2008) excavates an 'ethno-cultural repertoire' of whiteness and how this is given particular content by writers who anxiously debated the 'decline' of white dominance (ibid., 23). Among others, Bonnett (2008) identifies Benjamin Kidd's *Social Evolution* (1894) and *Principles of Western Civilisation* (1902), each of which prefigures the current theories of *Eurabia* and European decline (Meer, 2012). Of course, Kidd was writing at a time when the British Empire reigned over nearly a quarter of planet's landmass (and nearly 500 million people) and other European powers exploited the people and territories they had taken. Nonetheless, pointing to the thesis of Charles Pearson in particular, Bonnett (2008: 18) describes some recurring features in this perception of decline:

Pearson's principle explanation of why white expansion was at an end and white supremacy in retreat rests on demographics (notably Chinese and African fertility), geographical determinism (the unsuitability of the 'wet tropics' for white settlement) and the deleterious consequences of urbanisation on human 'character'. Moreover, and crucially the economic ascendancy of those who Inge, following Pearson, was later to term 'the cheaper races' (Inge, 1922, 27), meant the white 'will be driven from every neutral market and forced to confine himself within his own'. (Pearson, 1894: 137)

There is much here which spans several presumed features of culture and civilization (intertwined in biology and environment) but which is principally underwritten by the ways in which whiteness served as a form of substantive rationality that fashioned geopolitics in its own image. Empire and colonialism are thus understood as natural states of international relations and indicative of human progress.

Among writers of the day, challenges to this hegemony (and related geopolitical formations) must have raised some profound existential concerns. Such concerns were certainly prompted by the Japanese naval annihilation of the Russian fleet in 1904, where 'for the first time since the Middle Ages, a non-European country had vanquished a European power in a major war' (Mishra, 2012: 1). What is especially interesting is that this violent disruption occurred just at the moment the transaction (a notion we will return to) between whiteness and the West had been taking place but in a manner 'in which the mass of white people are treated with suspicion' (Bonnett, 2008: 20).

This seeming paradox is explained by an internal racial hierarchy that drew upon notions of both race and class and informed what would later become familiar tropes of social Darwinism and eugenicist thinking. This tension 'of asserting both white solidarity and class elitism was resolved, in part, by asserting that the 'best stock' of the working class had long since climbed upwards' (ibid., 21) and which continued to feed into parallel debates about culture and political economy (McDermott, 2006). The especially relevant implications of the genealogy for our discussion are that '[w]hilst "Westerner" can and does sometimes operate as a substitute term for "white", it also operates within new landscapes of power and discrimination that have new and often fragile relationships with the increasingly widely repudiated language of race' (Bonnett, 2008: 18).

In a competing reading, meanwhile, Virdee (2014) has charted the ways in which whiteness during the same period became democratized, not least through the expansion of social democratic politics on which pivots a historical seesaw of inclusion and exclusion. It is a dramatic and compelling account in so far as '[e]ach time the boundary of the nation was extended to encompass ever more members of the working class, it was accompanied and legitimized through the further racialization of nationalism that prevented another more recently arrived group from being included' (Virdee, 2014: 5). In his account race and whiteness were 'constitutive in the making, unmaking and remaking of the working class in England across two centuries' (Virdee, 2014: 5–6). As such, and especially in the organization of social and political life, 'there were historical moments when the working class suppressed such expressions of racism, and on occasion, actively rejected it' (ibid.). Such is the nature of racialization: a juddering movement of the rejection of one group and the incorporation of another (or later indeed the same group) and which can be quite consistent with intellectual and popular logics of racializing.

## WHITENESS OR WHITE PEOPLE?

The distinction between whiteness and white individuals has been usefully elaborated in well-known arguments by Bonnett (1997) and Leonardo (2002), respectively. For the latter, 'whilst whiteness represents a racial discourse, the category of white people represents a socially constructed identity usually based on skin colour' (Leonardo, 2002: 31). Bonnett (1997: 189) meanwhile highlights both the distinction and relationship between white people and whiteness further. Indeed, Gillborn (2005) draws on Bonnett's argument that it is not necessarily the case that white people as individuals inevitably reinforce whiteness any more than heterosexuals are necessarily homophobic or men are necessarily sexist. However, the likelihood is that most homophobic individuals are heterosexual, and most sexist discrimination occurs against women. This point is simply that white people are not necessarily always consciously acting in the interests of reinforcing whiteness. What is also suggested here is that individuals do not have to be 'white people' to actively reinforce and act in the interests of whiteness (Ladson-Billings, 1998) as also shown in the Danish debate book that works to deny racism in Denmark (Myong & Danbolt, this volume).

Building on the distinction between white people and whiteness, Preston and Chadderton (2012: 92) move to think about this in terms of white positionality but register that this is also informed by intersectionalities across social class, gender, sexuality, and ability/disability. Thus, 'temporary ambiguities' may occur where white people are positioned on the margins of whiteness. If this is so, the critical focus on whiteness in CRT is not an assault on white people but on the socially constructed and constantly reinforced power of white identifications and interests (Gillborn, 2005: 488). Furthermore, Preston and Chadderton (2012: 92) condense extensive inquiry into the distinction between whiteness and white people through arguing that the many and various ways in which the white working classes, white immigrants, and white women have been positioned on the fringes of white respectability are key examples where these groups are given a liminal position within whiteness (see also Nayak, 2011). For Winant (1997: 76) two features of contemporary whiteness nonetheless remain and which turn on questions of supremacy and privilege:

> [M]onolithic white supremacy is over, yet in a more concealed way, white power and privilege live on .... Whites are no longer the official "ruling race" yet they still enjoy many of the privileges from the time when they were.

In thinking about these, we need to focus on two slightly different frames. By supremacy what is meant is dominance, explicitly as coercion but also implicitly through kinds of prevailing consensus among white-majority society, what Dyre (1988: 44) once termed as 'seeming not to be anything in particular'. This is less visible than the ways in which once racially segregated societies continue to operate racial zones even while there is no formal policy to support it. Obvious examples are post-apartheid South Africa and post-segregation southern states in the US, where racial categories are keenly related to the exercise of power. Yet there are also less obvious examples found in every liberal-democratic European Union state, manifested in the reluctance of visible minorities to move or live outside of urban centers that are often considered much safer than nonurban conurbations (Neal, 2009). This is a different kind of white dominance to that of explicitly 'white nationalist' movements such as the Ku Klux Klan in the US, though of course far right-wing parties in Europe often form part of the political mainstream and may also be in governing coalitions.

White supremacy might be easier to name than the ways in which whiteness serves as what Twine and Gallagher (2008: 8) describe as a 'public and psychological wage' and what others have termed a 'knapsack' (McIntosh, 1988) or 'possessive investment' (Lipsitz, 1998). Each of these refers to a kind of capital and is illustrated in what Duster (2001: 114–15) elaborates as 'deeply embedded in the routine structures of economic and political life. From ordinary service at Denny's restaurants, to far greater access to bank loans to simple *police-event-free* driving—all these things have come unreflectively with the territory of being white'. Other examples are amusement parks (Rødje & Thorsen, this volume), mixed marriages (Törngren, this volume), and control of 'what we may or may not' as in racial epithets and cartoons (Vertelyté & Hervik, this volume). Whiteness here is a type of habitus and the norm against which others are judged, in which 'culture and ideology constantly re-cloak whiteness as a normative identity' (ibid., 12) or what is also called 'habitual whiteness' (Nielsen, this volume). Scholars and intellectuals have not stood outside these conventions, however, for

> Throughout much of the twentieth-century mainstream, white social scientists did not focus on the institutions that created, reproduced and normalized white supremacy. The focus that guided whites in the academy primarily concerned itself with the pathology of racist individuals rather than the structural forces that produced racist social systems. (Twine & Gallagher, 2008: 10)

One of the sociological implications of this is that there is a documented tendency among 'ethnically ambiguous' minorities to seek the material and symbolic rewards of whiteness by positioning themselves as white in such things as applications for education employment and other trainings (Warren & Twine, 1997). This is evident, argue Twine and Gallagher (2008: 14), in how 'whiteness is continuing to expand in the United States, and that it continues to incorporate ethnics of multiracial, Asian, Mexican and other Latinos of non-European heritage'.

It is not clear to me how these tendencies are sufficiently explained through a postcolonial category unless it is anchored in an approach that *begins* with an account of racial processes. This includes a wide front of messy sociological realities. For example, much of the discussion of whiteness has attributed a conscious or unwitting white dominance in a way that under-recognizes how '[t]he economic and psychological wages of whiteness may be more meagre (and thus more precious) the lower down the social hierarchy the white subject is located' (Garner, 2006: 262). In opening up these readings from a European perspective, Nayak's (2003a, 2003b) research has utilized ethnographic methods in postindustrial settings in order to explore how whiteness intersects with class and masculinities, and so is negotiated in ways that take on 'multiple and contingent' meanings (Nayak, 2003a: 319). This is especially evident in terms of how 'young people inhabit white ethnicities to different degrees and with varying consequences' (ibid.) not least because 'whiteness is not simply constituted in relation to blackness, but is also fashioned *through and against other versions of whiteness*' (ibid., 320, emphasis added).[1] Another example is the Kempele rape case, where racialization not merely intersects with sexism and gendering but is inseparable from them (Saresma, this volume).

## The Racialization of Muslims

What this emphasizes is that whiteness needs to be understood as more than supremacy, privilege, and capital; it needs to be understood as a sociological identity than can be intersectional and negotiated, and so is curated and sustained by much more than imperial legacies. This is only part of the story, for what we also need to grasp is how it can be mobilized to cultivate new racialization processes, the case of Islamophobia being the most obvious. For example, the Pew European attitude surveys report worryingly high levels of representative samples of Hungarians (72%), Italians (69%), Poles (66%), Greeks (65%), Spaniards (50%), Swedes (35%), Dutch (35%), Germans (29%), French (29%), and Britons (28%) reporting 'unfavorable' views of Muslims (Pew Global Attitudes Projects, 2016). In the last British Attitudes Survey, for example, Voas and Ling (2010) report that one fifth of the total population responds negatively only to Muslims and that relatively few people feel unfavorable toward any other religious or ethnic group on its own. Mahitab Ezz El Din provides an excellent example of how this negativity works through simple, asymmetric, Orientalizing binaries (this volume), while Christian Stokke shows how Muslim feminists in Norway seek to counter the images and negativity (this volume), and Camilla Haavisto dismantles the contradictions within anti-racism activism in a hybrid media environment (this volume). Across Europe meanwhile, Zick, Kupper, and Hövermann (2011) conclude:

> [I]t is conspicuous that Europeans are largely united in their rejection of Muslims and Islam. The significantly most widespread anti-Muslim attitudes are found in Germany, Hungary, Italy and Poland, closely followed by

[1] Nayak illustrates this by describing three different subcultures of working-class young boys.

France, Great Britain and the Netherlands. The extent of anti-Muslim atti-
tudes is least in Portugal. In absolute terms, however, the eight countries
[Britain, France, Netherlands, Germany, Italy, Poland, Portugal and
Hungary] differ little in their levels of prejudice towards Muslims.

The visibility of Muslims, in terms of sometimes distinctive dress and
appearance, is frequently the means through which this Islamophobic feeling is turned into Islamophobic behavior (Meer, Dwyer, & Modood,
2010). A good European-wide illustration may be found in the summary
report on Islamophobia published by the European Monitoring Centre
on Racism and Xenophobia shortly after 9/11. As Allen and Nielsen
(2002: 16) show, this identified a rise in the number of 'physical and verbal threats being made, particularly to those visually identifiable as
Muslims, especially towards women wearing the hijab'. What is of particular note is that despite variations in the number and correlation of physical
and verbal threats directed at Muslim populations among the individual
nation-states, one overarching feature that emerged among the 15 EU
countries was the tendency for *Muslim women* to be attacked because of
how the *hijab* signifies an Islamic identity (ibid., 35). (For a Nordic hijab
debate analysis, see Stokke, this volume.)

This is precisely how sociologists have explained that racism can in practice become mixed up with a host of different kinds of '-isms' and frequently
overlap in 'sharing a common content or generalised object which allows
them to be joined together or interrelated, to be expressed in ways in which
elements of one are incorporated in the other' (Miles, 1989: 87). It is a find-
ing that raises problems for people who want to distinguish between antipathy toward Muslims and antipathy toward those appearing to follow Islam.
What is common to such findings is that these are *overlapping* and *interact-
ing*—rather than remaining distinct—something that can be illustrated further in the attitude polling of non-Muslim Britons one year after 9/11, in
which reference to religious doctrine, practitioners of a religion, and violent
extremism is intertwined. For example, Field (2007: 455) reports that:

> There could be little doubt that 9/11 had taken some toll. Views of Islam
> since 9/11 were more negative for 47%, and of Britain's Muslims for 35%
> (almost three times the first post-9/11 figure). [....] Dislike for Islam was
> expressed by 36%, three in four of whom were fearful of what it might do in
> the next few years. One quarter rejected the suggestion that Islam was mainly
> a peaceful religion, with terrorists comprising only a tiny minority....

If these examples and the preceding discussion begin to make manifest a number of confusions contained within contemporary references to racial and religious antipathy toward Muslims and Islam, then—as debates concerning racism and other religious minorities, not least with respect to anti-Semitism, betray—this is not uniquely problematical in the conceptualization of anti-Muslim sentiment.

But it is also related to a second issue of 'scale' that goes beyond frequency per se and relates directly to the US political anthropologist Matti Bunzl's (2005) observation that we have progressed from the 'Jewish question' that haunted the continent throughout the eighteenth, nineteenth, and twentieth centuries. This cyclically facilitated episodes of persecution and genocide. In contrast, there is overwhelming evidence today that being Jewish and being European are not deemed mutually exclusive. Of course, and as we have already noted, this does not mean that European societies are free from anti-Semitism—far from it. The point instead is that while it is sociologically documented that Jewish have historically been accused of 'interfering' with the alleged 'purity' of nation-states, from the vantage point of a supranational Europe, Jewish minorities are deemed less of a 'threat' (but not entirely unthreatening), that is, that they have moved on from being the perpetual 'historical outsiders'; as Bunzl notes:

> Consider Europe's realities against the backdrop of antisemitism's political project. That project sought to secure the purity of the ethnic nation-state, a venture that has become obsolete in the supranational context of the European Union. There, Jews no longer figure as the principal Other but as the veritable embodiment of the post national order.

Whether or not Bunzl is too optimistic is a matter of debate, but the problematic he identifies raises a significant question for the fate of Muslims in Europe too. For according to Valéry Giscard d'Estaing (former president of France and head of the Convention on the Future of Europe which drafted the Lisbon Treaty), the status of Muslims is rightly more uncertain because they have 'a different culture, a different approach, a different way of life' (quoted in Bunzle, 2005: 32). Pertinent here is the late Pim Fortuyn's insistence on the need to defend European 'Judeo-Christian humanistic culture' and the ways in which he characterized Judaism as 'a creative and constructive element in society' (ibid., 38). Or as his most natural heir Geert Wilders has it, as long as Europe is unwilling to defend 'the ideas of Rome, Athens, and Jerusalem', it will 'lose everything: our cultural identity, our democracy, our rule of law, our liberties, our freedom'. Hence Jean-Marie Le Pen previously characterized himself as the defender of European Jewry, arguing that 'the Jews understand who is truly responsible for antisemitism' (ibid., 32). Such sentiments may be contrasted with the same European political parties' attitudes toward Muslims.

It is in this context that the charter of *Cities Against Islamization* has risen to warn that the 'fast demographic increase of the Islamic population in the West threatens to result in an Islamic majority in Western European cities in a few decades'.[2] This is the language of 'Eurabia', and it associates the Muslim presence with a number of detriments to European culture and social harmony. Sometimes sourced to the interventions of the controversial polemicist Bat Ye'or (2001, 2005), the notion of 'Eurabia' describes a numerical and cultural domination of Europe by Muslims and Islam. It is a reading that has not gone undisputed on the grounds that they both radically overestimate base figures and then extrapolate implausible levels of population growth. The demography panic has nonetheless achieved a degree of traction that bears the chilling hallmarks of recent European history. This is why, as this book demands, we *must* talk about race, culture, and belonging—about racialization—for these issues are not limited to hostility to a religion alone but are instead tied up with pressing issues of community identity, stereotyping, socioeconomic location, and political conflict among other dynamics.

## REFERENCES

Allen, C., & Nielsen, J. S. (2002). *Summary Report on Islamophobia in the EU15 after 11 September 2001*. Vienna: European Monitoring Centre for Racism and Xenophobia.

Bonnett, A. (1997). Geography, 'Race' and Whiteness: Invisible Traditions and Current Challenges. In P. Werbner & T. Modood (Eds.), *Debating Cultural Hybridity: Multi-Cultural Identities and the Politics of Anti-Racism*. London: Zed Press.

Bonnett, A. (2008). Whiteness and the West. In C. Dwyer & C. Bressey (Eds.), *New Geographies of Race and Racism*. Aldershot: Ashgate.

Bunzl, M. (2005). Between Anti-Semitism and Islamophobia: Some Thoughts on the New Europe. *American Ethnologist, 32*(4), 499–508.

[2] http://www.citiesagainstislamisation.com

Duster, T. (2001). The 'Morphing' of Properties of Whiteness. In B. B. Rasmussen, E. Klinenberg, I. Nexica, & M. Wray (Eds.), *The Making and Unmaking of Whiteness* (pp. 113–137). Durham: Duke University Press.

Dyre, R. (1988). White. *Screen, 29*(4), 44–65.

Field, C. D. (2007). Islamophobia in Contemporary Britain: The Evidence of the Opinion Polls, 1988–2006. *Islam and Christian–Muslim Relations, 18*(4), 447–477.

Frankenberg, R. (2001). The Mirage of an Unmarked Whiteness. In B. Rasmussen et al. (Eds.), *The Making and Unmaking of Whiteness* (pp. 72–96). Durham & London: Duke University Press.

Garner, S. (2006). The Uses of Whiteness: What Sociologists Working on Europe Can Draw from US Work on Whiteness. *Sociology, 40*(2), 257–275.

Garner, S. (2017). Surfing the Third Wave of Whiteness Studies: Reflections on Twine and Gallagher. *Ethnic and Racial Studies, 40*(9), 1582–1597.

Gillborn, D. (2005). Education Policy as an Act of White Supremacy: Whiteness, Critical Race Theory and Education Reform. *Journal of Education Policy, 20*(4), 485–505.

Hage, G. (1998). *White Nation: Fantasies of White Supremacy in a Multicultural society*. Annandale: Pluto Press.

Hewitt, R. (2005). *White Backlash and the Politics of Multiculturalism*. Cambridge: Cambridge University Press.

Jacobson, M. F. (2009). Looking Jewish, Seeing Jews. In L. Back & J. Solomos (Eds.), *Theories of Race and Racism* (pp. 238–256). New York: Routledge.

Kidd, B. (1894). *Social Evolution*. London: Macmillan.

Kidd, B. (1902). *Principles of Western Civilization*. London: Macmillan.

Ladson-Billings, G. (1998). Just What Is Critical Race Theory and What's It Doing in a Nice Field Like Education? *Qualitative Studies in Education, 11*(1), 7–24.

Leonardo, Z. (2002). The Souls of White Folk: Critical Pedagogy, Whiteness Studies, and Globalization Discourse. *Race Ethnicity and Education, 5*(1), 29–50.

Lipsitz, G. (1998). *The Possessive Investment in Whiteness: How White People Profit from Identity Politics*. Philadelphia: Temple University Press.

McDermott, M. (2006). *Working-Class White: The Making and Unmaking of Race Relations*. Berkeley: University of California Press.

McIntosh, P. (1988). *White Privilege and Male Privilege: A Personal Account of Coming to See Correspondences Through Work in Women's Studies*. Working Paper #189, Wellesley College Center for Research on Women, Wellesley, MA.

Meer, N. (2012). Misrecognising Muslim Consciousness in Europe. *Ethnicities, 12*(2), 178–197.

Meer, N., Dwyer, C., & Modood, T. (2010). Embodying Nationhood? Conceptions of British National Identity, Citizenship and Gender in the 'Veil Affair'. *The Sociological Review, 58*(1), 84–111.

Miles, R. (1989). *Racism*. London: Routledge.

Mishra, P. (2012). *From the Ruins of Empire*. London: Allen Lane.

Nayak, A. (2003a). 'Ivory Lives': Economic Restructuring and the Making of Whiteness in a Post-Industrial Youth Community. *European Journal of Cultural Studies, 6*(3), 305–325.

Nayak, A. (2003b). Last of the 'Real Geordies'? White Masculinities and the Subcultural Response to Deindustrialisation. *Environment and Planning D: Society and Space, 21*(1), 7–25.

Nayak, A. (2011). Geography, Race and Emotions: Social and Cultural Intersections. *Social and Cultural Geography, 12*(6), 548–562.

Neal, S. (2009). *Rural Identities: Ethnicity and Community in the English Countryside*. Farnham: Ashgate.

Pearson, C. (1894). *National Life and Character: A Forecast*. London: Macmillan.

Pew. (2016). *Europeans Fear Wave of Refugees Will Mean More Terrorism, Fewer Jobs*. Pew Global Attitudes. Retrieved from http://www.pewglobal. org/2016/07/11/europeans-fear-wave-of-refugees-will-mean-more-terrorism-fewer-jobs/ga_2016-07-11_national_identity-00-01/

Preston, J., & Chadderton, C. (2012). Rediscovering 'Race Traitor': Towards a Critical Race Theory Informed Public Pedagogy. *Race, Ethnicity and Education, 15*(1), 85–100.

Rhodes, J. (2013). Remaking Whiteness in the "Postracial" UK. In N. Kapoor, V. S. Kalra, & J. Rhodes (Eds.), *The State of Race*. Basingstoke: Palgrave.

Twine, F., & Gallagher, C. (2008). The Future of Whiteness: A Map of the 'Third Wave'. *Ethnic and Racial Studies, 31*(1), 4–24.

Virdee, S. (2014). *With Racism, Class and the Racialized Outsider*. Basingstoke: Palgrave.

Voas, D., & Ling, R. (2010). Religion in Britain and the United States. In A. Park et al. (Eds.), *British Social Attitudes: The 26th Report* (pp. 65–86). London: SAGE.

Warren, J., & Twine, F. W. (1997). White Americans, the New Minority? Non-Blacks and the Ever-Expanding Boundaries of Whiteness. *Journal of Black Studies, 28*(2), 200–218.

Winant, H. (1997, September–October). Behind Blue Eyes: Contemporary White Racial Politics. *New Left Review, 225*, 73–88. Retrieved from https://newleftreview.org/I/225/howard-winant-behind-blue-eyes-whiteness-and-contemporary-us-racial-politics

Ye'or, B. (2001). *Islam and Dhimmitude: Where Civilizations Collide*. Madison, NJ, Fairleigh: Dickinson University Press.

Ye'or, B. (2005). *Eurabia: The Euro-Arab Axis*. Madison, NJ, Fairleigh: Dickinson University Press.

Zick, A., Kupper, B., & Hövermann, A. (2011). *Intolerance, Prejudice and Discrimination*. Berlin: Forum Berlin, pp. 62–63. Retrieved from http://library.fes.de/pdf-files/do/07908-20110311.pdf

# Index[1]

## A

Abstract liberalism, 144–146, 148, 150, 152

Activism, 16, 24, 30, 174, 186, 196, 197, 206, 210, 215, 218, 290

Activists, 6, 20, 24, 26, 27, 164, 166, 168, 171, 176, 187–191, 197, 215, 217, 230, 232, 234, 236, 239, 246, 247, 249–251, 253, 264, 266, 274

Affect, 25, 69, 71, 79, 85, 113, 117, 119, 120, 122, 123, 140, 151, 155, 185, 220, 234, 236

Afghan, 184

African Empowerment Centre (AEC), 265

Ahmed, Sara, 66, 68, 69, 78, 83, 85, 112, 115–117, 119, 122–127, 129, 236, 271, 279

Anderson, Carol, 20, 25

Andreassen, Rikke, 15, 16, 24, 43, 48–50, 48n9, 53, 113, 114, 130, 172, 173, 273

Anthropologists, 14, 16, 17, 207, 291

Anti-anti-racism, 24, 42, 44

Anti-intellectualism, 4, 14, 176

Anti-Muslim racism, 11, 206, 210, 211, 215

Anti-racism, 3, 5, 11, 12, 19, 23–26, 30, 44, 56, 116, 138, 174, 183–199, 205, 206, 209, 211, 215, 218, 219, 221, 231–233, 236, 240, 247, 253, 283, 290

Anti-racist, 7, 16, 23–27, 29, 30, 40, 44, 46–48, 51–53, 55–57, 142, 196, 230, 232, 234–236, 239, 242, 245–253, 267, 272

Anti-racist campaigning, 242

Anti-racist education, 207–209, 221–223

Anti-racist racism, 40

Anti-racist researchers, 41, 41n3, 50, 51, 54, 57

Anti-racist totalitarianism, 55

*Are Danes Racists?*, 40–44, 42n4, 46, 48n9, 50, 51, 53–56, 53n16

[1]Note: Page numbers followed by 'n' refer to notes.

© The Author(s) 2019

P. Hervik (ed.), *Racialization, Racism, and Anti-Racism in the Nordic Countries*, Approaches to Social Inequality and Difference, https://doi.org/10.1007/978-3-319-74630-2